Systemic Semiotics

Bloomsbury Advances in Semiotics

Series Editor: Paul Bouissac

Bloomsbury Advances in Semiotics publishes original works applying semiotic approaches to linguistics and non-verbal productions, social institutions and discourses, embodied cognition and communication, and the new virtual realities of the digital age. It covers topics such as socio-semiotics, evolutionary semiotics, game theory, cultural and literary studies, human-computer interactions, and the challenging new dimensions of human networking afforded by social websites.

Titles published in the series:

The Semiotics of Architecture in Video Games, Gabriele Aroni
Semiotics of the Christian Imagination, Domenico Pietropaolo
Computational Semiotics, Jean-Guy Meunier
Cognitive Semiotics, Per Aage Brandt
The Semiotics of Caesar Augustus, Elina Pyy
The Social Semiotics of Tattoos, Chris William Martin
The Semiotics of X, Jamin Pelkey
The Semiotics of Light and Shadows, Piotr Sadowski
Music as Multimodal Discourse, Lyndon C. S. Way and Simon McKerrell
Peirce's Twenty-Eight Classes of Signs and the Philosophy of Representation, Tony Jappy
The Semiotics of Emoji, Marcel Danesi
Semiotics and Pragmatics of Stage Improvisation, Domenico Pietropaolo
Critical Semiotics, Gary Genosko

Systemic Semiotics

A Deductive Study of Communication and Meaning

Piotr Sadowski

BLOOMSBURY ACADEMIC
LONDON • NEW YORK • OXFORD • NEW DELHI • SYDNEY

BLOOMSBURY ACADEMIC
Bloomsbury Publishing Plc
50 Bedford Square, London, WC1B 3DP, UK
1385 Broadway, New York, NY 10018, USA
29 Earlsfort Terrace, Dublin 2, Ireland

BLOOMSBURY, BLOOMSBURY ACADEMIC and the Diana logo are
trademarks of Bloomsbury Publishing Plc

First published in Great Britain 2022
Paperback edition published 2024

Copyright © Piotr Sadowski, 2022

Piotr Sadowski has asserted his right under the Copyright,
Designs and Patents Act, 1988, to be identified as Author of this work.

For legal purposes the Acknowledgments on p. xii constitute an
extension of this copyright page.

Cover image © Brain light / Alamy Stock Photo

All rights reserved. No part of this publication may be reproduced or
transmitted in any form or by any means, electronic or mechanical,
including photocopying, recording, or any information storage or
retrieval system, without prior permission in writing from the publishers.

Bloomsbury Publishing Plc does not have any control over, or responsibility for,
any third-party websites referred to or in this book. All internet addresses given
in this book were correct at the time of going to press. The author and publisher
regret any inconvenience caused if addresses have changed or sites have
ceased to exist, but can accept no responsibility for any such changes.

A catalogue record for this book is available from the British Library.

A catalog record for this book is available from the Library of Congress.

ISBN: HB: 978-1-3502-4066-7
PB: 978-1-3502-4070-4
ePDF: 978-1-3502-4067-4
eBook: 978-1-3502-4068-1

Series: Bloomsbury Advances in Semiotics

Typeset by Integra Software Services Pvt. Ltd.

To find out more about our authors and books visit www.bloomsbury.com
and sign up for our newsletters.

For Ewa, Bartek, Adam, and Isabela

Contents

List of Figures   viii
Acknowledgments   xii

Introduction   1

Part I   Theory

1   Interaction as Communication   9
2   Types of Communication   35
3   Information and Levels of Meaning   55
4   Between Indexicality and Iconicity   75
5   The (Mostly) Symbolic Signs of Verbal Language   107

Part II   Applications

6   Oscar Wilde and Dynamism of Character   135
7   The Esthetics of Light in Early Cinema   151
8   Photography and the Limitations of Indexicality in Michelangelo Antonioni's *Blowup* (1966)   171
9   The Iconicity of the Pictorial Frame   183
10   The Iconic Magic of Cinema in Woody Allen's *The Purple Rose of Cairo* (1985)   199

Postscript   209

Notes   215
Bibliography   238
Index   254

Figures

1.1	Internal and external causes of the system's behavior	12
1.2	*The Beeches*, oil painting by Asher Brown Durand, 1845 (courtesy of the Metropolitan Museum of Art, New York)	27
1.3	Making repulsiveness cute (photo by Maaillustrations, courtesy of Freeimages)	28
1.4	Phoenix Park, Dublin (photo by author)	30
2.1	Interactions between systems	35
2.2	Cartoon by George Du Maurier, *Punch*, December 9, 1878 (courtesy of Wikimedia Commons)	39
2.3	A cast human shadow (photo by author)	41
2.4	A "roundabout" road sign (photo by author)	50
4.1	Emoji toys (courtesy of British Library/Open Culture)	76
4.2	Disney cartoon (courtesy of British Library/Open Culture)	78
4.3	Osage Indians, lithograph by Louis Leopold Boilly, 1761–1845 (courtesy of Smithsonian American Art Museum)	81
4.4	Modern tattoo (courtesy of British Library/Open Culture)	82
4.5	"Venus" of Willendorf (Naturhistorisches Museum, Vienna, courtesy of Wellcome Collection, attribution 4.0 International CC BY 4.0)	84
4.6	The cobble from Makapansgat cave, Africa (courtesy of Smithsonian American Art Museum)	87
4.7	"Venus" of Berekhat Ram, Israel (courtesy of Wikimedia Commons)	88
4.8	Horses' heads painted in Chauvet cave, France (courtesy of British Library/Open Culture)	89
4.9	*Der einsame Baum* (The Solitary Tree), 1822, oil painting by Caspar David Friedrich (reproduced with the permission of bpkbildagentur/Staatliche Museen zu Berlin)	91
4.10	The burning of an effigy, India (photo by Tushar Dayal, courtesy of Courtesy of British Library/Open Culture)	94
4.11	*Pygmalion and Galatea*, oil painting by Jean-Léon Gérôme, *c*. 1890 (courtesy of the Metropolitan Museum of Art, New York)	95
4.12	*The Corinthian Maid*, oil painting by Joseph Wright, 1785 (courtesy of the National Gallery of Art, Washington)	96

4.13	The Holy Cross Cemetery, Yeadon, Pennsylvania (courtesy of British Library/Open Culture)	97
4.14	Imprint of a hand in Chauvet cave, France (courtesy of British Library/Open Culture)	99
4.15	*Piazza San Marco*, oil painting by Canaletto, late 1720s (courtesy of the Metropolitan Museum of Art, New York)	100
4.16	*Madonna and Child with Saints Francis and Jerome*, oil painting by Francesco Francia, 1500–10 (courtesy of the Metropolitan Museum of Art, New York)	103
5.1	Robert Fludd's *Utriusque cosmi… Historia*, Oppenheim and Frankfort, 1617–19 (courtesy of Wikimedia Commons)	116
5.2	*Erasmus of Rotterdam*, engraving by Albrecht Dürer, 1526 (courtesy of the Metropolitan Museum of Art, New York)	120
5.3	A limestone tablet, Mesopotamia, late fourth millennium BCE, Louvre Museum (courtesy of Wikimedia Commons)	121
5.4	Cuneiform writing on a clay tablet, Mesopotamia, 1500–539 BCE, British Museum (courtesy of Wikimedia Commons)	122
5.5	The Dongba script, China, about 1,000 years old (courtesy of British Library/Open Culture)	123
5.6	The Rosetta Stone, 196 BCE, British Museum, photo by Hans Hillewaert (courtesy of Wikipedia Commons)	124
5.7	*Study in a Wood*, oil painting by Daniel Huntington, 1861 (courtesy of the Metropolitan Museum of Art, New York)	129
6.1	Oscar Wilde, photo by Napoleon Sarony, New York, 1882 (courtesy of the Metropolitan Museum of Art, New York)	136
6.2	The dynamic spectrum of character	138
6.3	*Hamlet* directed by Kenneth Branagh © Castle Rock Entertainment 1996. All rights reserved	148
7.1	Photograph by Joseph Nicéphore Niépce, 1826 (courtesy of British Library/Open Culture)	152
7.2	*A Goldsmith in His Shop*, oil painting by Petrus Christus, 1449 (courtesy of the Metropolitan Museum of Art, New York)	155
7.3	*The Penitent Magdalen*, oil painting by Georges de La Tour, *c.* 1640 (courtesy of the Metropolitan Museum of Art, New York)	156
7.4	The "Black Maria" studio film © Edison Manufacturing Co. 1894. All rights reserved	158
7.5	*Sortie d'usine* directed by Lumière brothers ©1895	158
7.6	*Bataille de boules de neige* directed by Lumière brothers ©1896	159

7.7	*Rescued by Rover* directed by Lewin Fitzhamon © Hepworth Company, 1905. All rights reserved	161
7.8	*Histoire d'un crime* directed by Ferdinand Zecca © Pathé Frères company, 1901. All rights reserved	162
7.9	Human shadow etched in stone, Hiroshima, August 6, 1945 (courtesy of British Library/Open Culture)	163
7.10	*M* directed by Fritz Lang © Nero-Film AG 1931. All rights reserved	164
7.11	*Nosferatu—A Symphonie of Horrors* directed by F. M. Murnau © Jofa-Atelier Berlin-Johannisthal 1922. All rights reserved	165
7.12	*Warning Shadows* directed by Arthur Robison © Pan-Film 1923. All rights reserved	166
7.13	*Warning Shadows* directed by Arthur Robison © Pan-Film 1923. All rights reserved	167
7.14	*Warning Shadows* directed by Arthur Robison © Pan-Film 1923. All rights reserved	168
8.1	*Blowup* directed by Michelangelo Antonioni © Premier Productions 1966. All rights reserved	175
8.2	*Blowup* directed by Michelangelo Antonioni © Premier Productions 1966. All rights reserved	177
8.3	*Blowup* directed by Michelangelo Antonioni © Premier Productions 1966. All rights reserved	180
9.1	*Draughtsman Making a Perspective Drawing of a Reclining Woman*, engraving by Albrecht Dürer, *Underwysung der Messung*, Nuremberg, 1538 (courtesy of the Metropolitan Museum of Art, New York)	185
9.2	*Playtime* directed by Jacques Tati © Specta Films 1967. All rights reserved	186
9.3	*Dancer Onstage*, drawing by Edgar Degas, *c.* 1877 (courtesy of the Metropolitan Museum of Art, New York)	189
9.4	Bord Gáis Energy Theatre, Dublin (photo by author)	191
9.5	*The Cabinet of Dr. Caligari* directed by Robert Wiene © Decla-Bioscop AG 1920. All rights reserved	192
9.6	Vertical smartphone video as seen on TV screen (photo simulation by author)	193
9.7	*Two Women at a Window*, oil painting by Bartolomé Esteban Murillo, 1655/60 (courtesy of the National Gallery of Art, Washington)	195
9.8	*Citizen Kane* directed by Orson Welles © RKO Radio Pictures 1941. All rights reserved	196

9.9	*Butch Cassidy and the Sundance Kid* directed by George Roy Hill © Campanile Productions 1969. All rights reserved	197
9.10	*The Grand Budapest Hotel* directed by Wes Anderson © Fox Searchlight Pictures 2014. All rights reserved	198
10.1	*Sherlock Jr.* directed by Buster Keaton © Buster Keaton Productions 1924. All rights reserved	202
10.2	*The Purple Rose of Cairo* directed by Woody Allen © Orion Pictures 1985. All rights reserved	203
10.3	*The Purple Rose of Cairo* directed by Woody Allen © Orion Pictures 1985. All rights reserved	205

Acknowledgments

I want to thank Professor Paul Bouissac, renowned scholar and editor of Bloomsbury Advances in Semiotics series, for his vision and confidence in my project on systemic semiotics. Together with the Bloomsbury publisher Andrew Wardell, Paul has helped me develop the original idea into a logically structured and clear book format. My thanks are also due to Bloomsbury editors Morwenna Scott, Becky Holland, Elizabeth Holmes, Laura Gallon, and Viswasirasini Govindarajan for smoothly guiding the manuscript to production.

My debt of gratitude extends to Olga Fischer, Professor Emerita at the University of Amsterdam, for inspiring and encouraging my interests in iconicity in linguistic and visual communication.

The book is dedicated to my family: Ewa, Bartek, Adam, and Isabela—the main people in this world who make me happy.

Every effort has been made to trace copyright holders and to obtain their permission for the use of copyright material. The publisher apologizes for any errors or omissions in the above list and would be grateful if notified of any corrections that should be incorporated in future reprints or editions of this book.

The third-party copyrighted material displayed in the pages of this book is done so on the basis of "fair dealing for the purposes of criticism and review" or "fair use for the purposes of teaching, criticism, scholarship or research" only in accordance with international copyright laws and is not intended to infringe upon the ownership rights of the original owners.

Introduction

All living organisms, from bacteria to humans, exchange information with their environments to enhance their existence by finding food, mating opportunities, and protecting themselves against predators. Crickets rub legs or wing cases together to send their characteristic chirping sounds to potential mates, ants communicate by exchanging chemical signals, while bats use echolocation to find their way in dark caves without crashing into walls. Humans, with their comparatively advanced cognitive faculties, additionally develop abstract worldviews to make sense of their lives through artifacts of art, religion, philosophy, and science. No living organism can afford to ignore environmental stimuli likely to jeopardize its existence or to enhance its opportunities to survive, procreate, and flourish. If exchanging information with the environment, natural and social, is what we understand as communication, interpreting that information is the domain of semiotics, a study of the meaning of communication.

Creative Deduction

Among humans, the ultimate Darwinian imperatives of survival and procreation also underlie the generation of culture, with its storytelling, art, value systems, and intellectual inquiry[1]—a "semiosis" that is mind-bogglingly complex and ultimately beyond grasp and comprehension, certainly not by any single mind. Which raises some important methodological questions: how to devise a coherent and comprehensible semiotic approach to account for this complexity? How to infer general principles of meaning-formation from an infinite number of instances of animal and human communication? And how much empirical evidence is needed to justify an inductive generalization?

Alternatively, we can start from top-down, in a deductive way, by establishing general premises and transforming them into more specific formulations regarding the exchange and interpretation of information among living systems. Rather than trying to look for regularities in an enormous and confused body of observations, a deductive semiotic model can be more manageable, even if its necessary reductionism should ultimately fall short of accounting for all the complexities of life. But this is how explanatory models work; they are not mirrors of the real world, but merely its simplified descriptive analogues—what the philosopher Karl Popper calls the "verisimilitude" of a theoretical model, its correspondence to what it is devised to explain.[2] In semiotic terms, an explanatory model functions as an iconic sign: it is a theoretical analog of a fragment of empirical reality under investigation. The phenomenal world may appear too complex and ultimately beyond description, but the explanatory models, whether theological, philosophic, or scientific, are by comparison simpler and therefore more comprehensible. A useful, or at least elegant theory is one that explains more with less, using the smallest possible number of principles to account for a maximum number of phenomena—what the biologist Edward O. Wilson calls "the completest presentation of facts with the least possible expenditure of thought."[3]

It is clear, however, that just as an inductive accumulation of data on its own will not yield a strong theoretical model through generalization, so equally no deductive theory exists without some expectations as to the nature of the underlying empirical world.[4] This reciprocal relationship between theorizing and data gathering is not just a concern of scientists. Karl Popper sees it as part of human nature: there is no such thing as impartial and unbiased observation, because all perception is predicated upon expectations based on human innate dispositions and propensities to react. In a transactional, dynamic relationship between the world and the mind, argues Popper, observation is always preceded by expectations, which give rise to hypotheses and theories about what we observe.[5] For the neuroscientist Karl Friston too the observing brain makes constant active predictions about the outside world, based on expectations derived from both experience and genetic memory.[6] There is no such thing therefore as pure induction or pure deduction, although philosophers of science have always regarded deductive inferences rather than inductive generalizations as a more reliable way of getting a sense of what the world is "really like."[7] Deduction relies basically on formulating axiomatic constructions to consider all possibilities in the behavior of theoretical systems, and then applying this construction to a particular empirical situation. While the usefulness of a theory is ultimately measured by its power to explain empirical data, the data alone cannot dictate the shape of a theory. Theories are created speculatively rather than induced from observations and experiments, no matter how numerous, consistent, and systematic.

Systemic Semiotics: Basic Premises

The basic premises as the building blocks of a deductive theory of communication and meaning are presented below in descending order, from general to more specific:

1. Both the world as an object of inquiry and the human inquirer exist in the physical and biological sense. For all its immaterial and ethereal nature, intellectual speculation is the product of a material brain, a biological organ designed by evolution to process information entering the brain from the outside world and generated by the brain itself. The brain's power to produce meaning is enabled by neural circuits and cognitive modules designed to solve problems faced by our ancestors during their evolutionary history.[8]

2. The innate structures of the brain determine and constrain the content and meaning of communication. Semiosis is not about everything and anything, because the generation of meaning is guided by universal human needs and related cognitive modules.[9] The main semiotic domains include procreation and sexuality, nutrition, physical protection, socialization, exploration of the natural environment, esthetic sense, and the search for the purpose and meaning of life.
3. The main system of communication evolved by humans to negotiate their social environment and explain the world is the verbal language.[10] The natural world pre-dates the emergence of the human species with its cognitive and linguistic faculties, which means that most bio-physical facts are essentially non-linguistic phenomena, although we need of course a language if we wish to talk about them.
4. Scientific inquiry, including systemic semiotics presented in this book, consists in devising verifiable but ultimately falsifiable models of the world. These models are primarily mental and linguistic constructs, but because they are verifiable, they correspond in an ever-increasing degree to the actual properties of the world as it is, including such categories as space, time, substance, and causality. Scientific models are not arbitrary impositions of the internal workings of the mind or the structures of language, because the brain, the sensory organs, and language are themselves evolutionary products of the world, which they were designed to represent in a limited but accurate measure.[11]
5. The world is intelligibly structured rather than chaotic, and as such is open to rational inquiry. The main building block of the world's structure is a *system*, defined as a set of interrelated elements. A system is an abstraction for any empirical entity such as an object, a living organism, or an artifact. The systems comprising the world interact with one another by exchanging information and energy. Some systems, such as living organisms, have the capacity to maintain internal equilibrium in respect of the processed information and energy—these are referred to as self-regulating, or *autonomous*.[12] The behavior of autonomous systems can be described as purposeful and goal-oriented.
6. Interaction understood as exchange of information and energy is equivalent to *communication*. Given the possible spatial and temporal relationships between interacting systems, we can talk about the following types of communication:
   — *contiguous* communication, in which systems interact directly within the same space and time, while remaining within each other's natural sensory or physical range;
   — *indexical* communication, in which systems interact indirectly by means of a physical trace (index) left by one system in the environment;
   — *iconic* communication, in which systems interact indirectly by means of a sign (icon) whose properties bear a perceptual resemblance to another system;
   — *symbolic* communication, in which systems interact indirectly by means of a sign (symbol) whose properties are perceptually unrelated to the system implied by the symbol.[13]

7. *Information* will be defined as any physical change caused by a system in the environment. Perceived information produces internal reactions, or *meaning*, in communicating systems. There are two basic types of meaning: a system's reaction to information, which will be referred to as *parainformation*; and a system's reaction to its own parainformation, which will be referred to as *metainformation*.[14] Parainformation and metainformation are what are otherwise called denotation and connotation, or explicit and implicit meaning respectively.

Systems and Their Definitions

Definitions of the key concepts in systemic semiotics introduced in the above premises are themselves part of language as a system of communication. Assuming that language is based on correspondence between linguistic signs and non-linguistic reality (Premise 3), definitions have two dimensions: linguistic and referential. Scientific definitions are expressions of language treated first of all referentially, as a tool to describe and explain the world by providing verbal equivalents of empirical objects and phenomena. In everyday life too there seems to be little problem in attaching linguistic labels to systems that can be perceived and examined: the material objects such as minerals, plants, tools, animals, and people. Physical objects have identifiable properties, which can also be given linguistic labels, making the problem of relationship between language and empirical reality relatively unproblematic.

Things are less straightforward when language is used to describe intangible systems such as concepts or emotional states—things that are physically elusive but are nonetheless subjectively felt to be real. Words for emotions, esthetic qualities, moral values, and abstract concepts of philosophy and science belong to this category. Verbal language must have evolved primarily as a referential system of communication, to enhance cooperation over important domains of life such as survival, search for food, courtship, and social cohesion. For prehistoric speakers it probably paid in survival terms to assume that words have meanings matching material objects and physical states in the outside world, as well as emotions and intentions on which cooperation and social stability depended. The default disposition would be therefore to assume the referential function of language—in other words, its truthfulness. The flip side of this disposition is, however, gullibility and self-deception, easily exploited by liars, con men, and charlatans.[15] Petty opportunistic deceptions apart, whole systems of thought can be built by exploiting people's intuitive assumption that words mean things.[16] All it takes is to invent new words or alter the existing ones to create an impression of objective reality behind them. If the word "physics," for example, refers to the empirically verifiable domain of matter and energy, simply adding the prefix "meta-" miraculously creates a "metaphysical" domain of abstract thought of dubious extra-linguistic validity. The entry on "metaphysics" is among the longest in *The Oxford Companion to Philosophy*, where it is also described as a "'high-falutin' part of philosophy."[17] This is not to say that abstract concepts never have any external referents, but that the indeterminate nature of these referents, combined with the cognitive bias in favor of essentially referential function of language, may account for the persistence and strange attraction of awe-inspiring but often empty vocabulary.

Much of modern humanistic discourse seems to have inherited this penchant for "metaphysical" language. For example, post-structuralist thought, to which much of semiotic theory is indebted, borrowed from Ferdinand Saussure the notion of language as a system of self-referential, immanent relationships and differences, with the implication that all concepts and truth-claims are at bottom just linguistic constructs (sense without reference).[18] Denied its referential function, language is accordingly treated mainly as a tool to communicate about itself. Abstract concepts are explained not in terms of their possible external referents, but in terms of other abstract concepts. For example, in Thomas A. Sebeok's *Contributions to the Doctrine of Signs* (1976), semiotic vocabulary is treated more as part of linguistic semantics than as a tool to study communication and meaning in the real world. Sebeok's book includes an extensive discussion of the meanings of the term "semiotics" and its cognates in different languages,[19] as if the question was not how and why empirical systems communicate but something like "what are the received meanings of the word 'semiotics' in different languages?" Discussing the meaning of words was what Karl Popper advised to avoid "like the plague," as he recommended instead that philosophers should formulate propositions that are truthful in the sense of corresponding with facts.[20] The philosopher Bryan Magee echoes Popper by stating that "the only thing that discussion of the meanings of words extends our understanding of is the meanings of words: it does nothing, or next to nothing, to extend our understanding of non-linguistic reality." The preoccupation with the meanings of words is for Magee a "disastrous error" of twentieth-century philosophy, one that has led to interminable word-spinning, logic chopping, and scholasticism.[21] Ultimately, what matters is not what linguistic label we choose but what empirical reality is denoted by the label. And the reality behind "semiotics" remains, as always, communication and meaning, that is, the practice of living systems to exchange, interpret, and react to information.

Another problem with definitions is that they are often made in an arbitrary, ex-cathedra manner, which makes them sound more like intellectual decrees than logical inferences from an observation or theory. To use a classic example, here is C. S. Peirce's definition of a sign, that fundamental concept of semiotics:

> A sign, or *representamen*, is something which stands to somebody for something in some respect or capacity. It addresses somebody, that is, creates in the mind of that person an equivalent sign, or perhaps a more developed sign. That sign which it creates I call the *interpretant* of the first sign. The sign stands for something, its *object*. It stands for that object, not in all respects, but in reference to a sort of idea, which I have sometimes called the *ground* of the representamen. "Idea" is here to be understood in a sort of Platonic sense, very similar in everyday talk... *etc*.[22]

Peirce's convoluted definition seems spun from thin air, with no evidence or logical proof to back it. How does the philosopher know that a sign is what his definition says it is? He may well be right, but there is nothing in his description to support its assertive, authoritative, if impressionistic tone. Without empirical evidence or inferential logic that would explain how the definition has been arrived at, the reader is simply presented with an argument from authority to be accepted on faith.

Similar arbitrary definitions are routine in semiotic literature. For example, the *Dictionary of Semiotics* (2000), edited by Bronwen Martin and Felizitas Ringham, consists entirely of ex-cathedra "explanations" of semiotic terms, mostly inspired by the Paris school of semiotics as represented by Algirdas J. Greimas. Asked about the development of his semiotic theory in 1985, Greimas is reported to have said: "My theoretical genius, if I can so call it, was a form of 'bricolage.' I took a little Levi-Strauss and added some Propp." Greimas's other inspirations included Dumézil, Saussure, and Hjemslev.[23] But an eclectic "bricolage" of ideas borrowed from different authors and somehow stitched together is the opposite of a coherent method, and it hardly denotes a "theoretical genius" or makes the resulting theory "scientific," which is what Martin and Ringham call Greimas' contribution to semiotics. An eclectic approach is more like taking pieces from different jigsaw puzzles and somehow forcing them together; the resulting picture, however, is inevitably disjointed and chaotic. Equally cavalier are the entries in Martin and Ringham's *Dictionary*: it is not clear what logic or evidence justifies their authoritative tone. Despite the insistence of some semioticians on the scientific nature of their theories, their vocabulary is often dictated more by the idiosyncrasies of intellectual temperament than by explicitly stated assumptions and methods.

Specialized terminology and stipulated definitions are of course part and parcel of any theoretical inquiry, including the systemic semiotics presented in this book. The main semiotic terms introduced in premises 1–7 will be further discussed in the theoretical chapters of Part I, in which deductive inferences will lead to more formulations about how communication and meaning formation have evolved and what their functions are. The purpose is to ensure that all definitions be logically traceable back to the premises, and that any conclusions be also consistent with them. Part II in turn contains applications of systemic semiotics to the study of topics relating mainly to visual culture, including film, photography, and pictorial arts.

Part I

Theory

1

Interaction as Communication

If systems consist of interrelated elements (premise 5), they are organized wholes rather than loose sets.[1] A scrapyard, a casual group of pedestrians, a random sequence of words form loose sets, whereas a jumbo jet, an orchestra, a grammatical sentence, or a living organism are organized systems. Adding or subtracting an element from a set affects it only quantitatively, but it does not change the properties of the set as a whole. A new word added to a random series of words only makes the series longer, but it does not alter its structure or meaning because there is none to begin with. On the other hand, removing an organ from a body or changing a word in a sentence affects the overall structure of these systems in a qualitative sense: the body's health will be compromised, and the sentence will have a different meaning. Other examples of systems include social groupings, such as families and organizations, and purposeful appliances, such as cars and computers. Integrated systems thus defined refer to any sphere of empirical reality traditionally labeled as physical, biological, social, technological, cultural, and psychological.[2]

Empirical systems never exist in total isolation because they are immersed in their environment, which in turn consists of other systems. No living organism would exist without the inputs and outputs of energies, substances, and information, without air or water, food, sensory stimuli, and disposal of its wastes. In premise 6, exchanges of information and energy between interacting systems are referred to as *communication*.[3] Information means registering or causing changes in the environment, while energy is what systems need to sustain their internal processes and motivate their behavior. As systems communicate, their structures also change. For instance, friendship or a romantic relationship generates in both partners emotional and cognitive experiences that would never happen to either partner on their own. Similarly, a conversation, in which people adjust what they say at each turn to what they have just heard from their interlocutors, results in a greater knowledge for all involved than the knowledge that each of the interlocutors possessed at the start of the conversation. Sustained verbal and psychological interactions based on feedback exchanges of information and energy (here: emotions) constitute dynamic wholes with properties irreducible to those of the individual persons involved in the interaction.

Autonomous Systems

As also stated in premise 5, some empirical systems are self-regulating, or autonomous. Such systems, represented by all replicating organisms, are able to maintain internal equilibrium with regard to the information and energy exchanged with the environment.[4] This is accomplished by means of a built-in homeostatic mechanism based on negative feedback, which controls the levels of inputs and outputs to ensure the system's *functional equilibrium*—an optimal state achieved by removing or minimizing disturbances of that equilibrium. Negative feedback basically means that a strong stimulus is countered by the system's weak response, while a weak stimulus is amplified by the system. Excessive inputs (relative to the system's needs) reduce the system's activity, while weak inputs of needed information and energy make the system spring into action. On a hot day (excess of energy) warm-blooded creatures are less mobile to reduce heat-generating physical exertion, perspire more to lose heat, lie in the shade, and drink more water. On the other hand, a hungry organism (deficiency of energy) becomes more resourceful in finding food to restore the necessary nutritional balance. Examples of excessive informational inputs include loud noise, over-intensive social contact, dazzling light, work overload, mental stress—any stimulus considered as "too much" and therefore intolerable. On the other hand, deficiencies of information include imposed silence, solitude, darkness, boredom, and monotony, likewise considered intolerable and prompting actions such as increased socialization, travel, search for new sensations, study, watching films on Netflix, surfing the internet, whatever the case may be, to restore the upset informational equilibrium. Disturbances of functional equilibrium are what we call *needs*, as discussed in greater detail below.

Functional equilibrium is a matter not only of comfort but of survival. All plants, animals, and humans live in a potentially hostile environment, and they must guard themselves against inputs that can cause damage to their delicately balanced structures. Excessive quantities, even of needed energies and stimuli, can be perilous, and organisms must be able to reduce or avoid deviations from the required levels of interaction with the environment. Of course, what is tolerable or intolerable, needed or unnecessary, varies from species to species, from individual to individual: what is "too much" for one person may not be enough for someone else. In all cases, however, the fundamental principle of deviation-reducing negative feedback defines the purposeful behavior of living organisms, which regulate their interactions with the environment to increase their chances of survival and optimize their existence by satisfying their manifold needs.[5]

Self-regulation is precisely what it says it is: to be truly autonomous a system must be able to act in its own interest. This is probably the main difference between humans and computers. The latter can process information faster than humans, have more retentive memory, retrieve information quicker and fully accurately, but they are (as yet) not autonomous. Computer hardware and software are designed and controlled by humans, the ultimate decision makers in charge. Alternative scenarios are the stuff of science fiction, as in Stanley Kubrick's film *2001: A Space Odyssey* (1968), in which a space mission is compromised by the supercomputer Hal, apparently equipped with its own homeostat, whose view on the purpose of the mission turns out to be different from that of the human crew. Whatever the future of Artificial Intelligence and the robotization of life, even if it were technically possible to grant computers full self-control, it would be perfect folly to do so. Ordinary computers malfunction and cause enough problems as it is, so the last thing humanity needs is to create machines with a built-in possibility of willful dissent and rebellion.

Self-regulating reactions to contiguous situations are also a short-term equivalent of what biological sciences call (long-term) *adaptation*. The latter describes features in the organization of living systems formed over millions of years of evolution through interactions between the ever-changing environment and generations of organisms. Biological adaptations include morphological, physiological, and behavioral features—practically everything that constitutes bodies and minds—resulting from natural selection acting upon heritable genetic variation, the most adaptive variants being those that enhance the likelihood of survival and reproduction.[6] Unlike the satisfaction of needs during an organism's lifetime, biological adaptations work through inter-generational interactions between organisms and the environment, whereby the best-adapted organisms pass on their genes to their offspring. Exchanges of information and energy are thus ever present across the natural world, on both the phylogenetic (species focused) and ontogenetic (individual) levels. From the point of view of evolutionary adaptation therefore, what humans communicate about in their social life and culture is ultimately defined and constrained by their genetic endowments, current sociocultural circumstances, human psychology and individual needs. Homeostatic self-regulation of autonomous systems thus makes systemic semiotics consistent with evolutionary semiotics, biosemiotics, and cognitive semiotics. The difference between systemic semiotics and these exciting neo-Darwinian approaches is more in method than substance. In fact, as demonstrated below, the theoretical premise of the autonomous system, its interactions with the environment, and self-regulation have Darwinian evolution through natural selection built into them as an implication.

Internal and External Causes of Behavior

As autonomous systems communicate, they transform received information and energy into reactions. This transformation is possible due to processes occurring inside the system, that is, due to the system's individual *reactivity*. In humans reactivity includes bodily functions and personality developed during lifelong interactions between a person's genome and the sociocultural environment. The uniqueness and complexity of the combined effects of biological and cultural programs is what produces an equally unique and complex personality, with its individual identity, needs, and dispositions. Neither of the two generators of behavior, genetic and cultural, nor their combined effect causes behavior deterministically[7]—they are both too complex, with too much left to chance, which means that human behavior is always to some extent unpredictable and often surprising, as any observation of life will probably confirm.

How a system of given reactivity reacts to stimuli is represented in the schema (Figure 1.1), in which reactivity (r) transforms stimuli (S) into reactions (R). Reactivity can be defined as a ratio of reaction to stimulus, which means that the stronger the

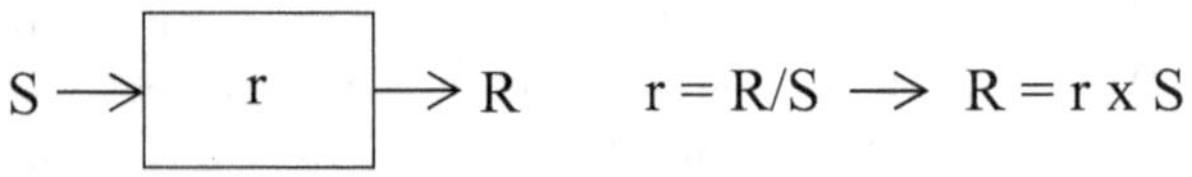

$$S \rightarrow \boxed{r} \rightarrow R \qquad r = R/S \rightarrow R = r \times S$$

Figure 1.1 Internal and external causes of the system's behavior.

system's reactivity, the stronger its reactions. A simple transformation of this formula gives us an equation for the reaction of the system as $R = r \times S$, which has important implications for the behavior of living systems.[8] The equation effectively says that a system's reactions result from the *combined* effects of two causes: internal reactivity and external stimulus. Behavior depends neither on external influence alone nor solely on a system's internal properties, because reaction is a product, not a sum, of reactivity and stimulus (if either r or S equals zero, then R also equals zero). Consequently, a system understood as an active transformer rather than a passive transmitter of stimuli will always be to some extent independent from external pressures and influences. This is probably the most important thing about autonomous systems: they possess properties that cannot be changed by the environment. One of these properties is dynamism of character, which determines motivation of behavior, discussed in Chapter 6 in relation to Oscar Wilde's artistic personality.

In natural sciences the interactive formula for the reaction of the system is implied in the concept of the *phenotype*, defined as the observable characteristics of an individual, which are always a result of the genetic blueprint meshing with the environment in which an organism develops.[9] Every living organism as a phenotype is a product of internal and external causes, genome and environment, and it will not exist in the absence of either. A seed deprived of fertile soil, water, and sunlight will not develop into a plant, just as the sun, water, and soil alone will not spontaneously breed organic life, as was once believed.[10] The conclusive proof that internal genetic programing, not just socialization, affects the formation of personality is provided by research on monozygotic twins raised together and apart. If our personalities were solely a product of environment, as is often believed, one would expect them to differ widely in people brought up separately, no matter how genetically related. But research has shown that there is comparatively little difference between monozygotic twins brought up apart and those brought up together. What is more, identical twins brought up together can sometimes differ more widely than identical twins brought up apart, probably due to sibling rivalry.[11] To insist on one cause of behavior, internal or external, is therefore like shooting oneself in one foot: the argument becomes lame and incomplete.

The Nature-versus-Nurture Debate, Again

In view of the inseparable connection between internal and external causes of behavior, it is quite astonishing for how long the philosophic and scientific debates have regarded the two causes as separate and autonomous, in turn prioritizing one and downplaying or ignoring the other. This "either/or" fallacy is probably best illustrated by the notorious nature-versus-nurture debate.

Among the most influential nurturist theories are the early modern empiricist philosophy of John Locke, Marxism with its socioeconomic determinants of behavior, behaviorist psychology, cultural materialism, postmodern gender studies, and other "social construct" theories based on the dogma of the mind as a blank slate at birth.[12] On the other hand, the views stressing the decisive influence of internal, ultimately biological determinants of behavior include the premodern essentialist theories of unchanging human nature, all racist pseudo-science and right-wing ideologies, and the Romantic idealization of individual "genius" unaffected by the base conditions of life.

Once we accept that living systems react under a combined influence of their internal reactivity and external influence, any exclusive insistence on either "nature" or "nurture" is not only limiting but simply false. The fact that the nature-versus-nurture controversy has lasted for so long without a possibility of reconciling the entrenched positions probably shows that the very formulation of the problem was based on a fundamental misunderstanding.[13] As is now widely accepted, behavior is never a question of innate versus acquired, but is always both, although biologists are still working out the mechanism through which genes effect behavior and cultural learning.[14] The combined effect of genes and environment amounts essentially to a co-evolution whereby, according to the psychologists John Tooby and Leda Cosmides, ultimately and counterintuitively even "'the environment' is just as much the product of evolution as are the genes."[15] Far from being a passive pawn of either heredity or environment, each individual picks and chooses from a range of stimuli and events of life largely on the basis of their predispositions and preferences, creating a unique set of experiences.[16] In other words, by acting on their innate inclinations people gravitate toward congenial situations in life and help create their own living space. For the psychologist Thomas J. Bouchard Jr., the theory of evolution "views humans as dynamic creative organisms for whom the opportunity to learn and to experience new environments amplifies the effects of the genotype on the phenotype."[17] For the biologist John Cartwright too it is a truism worth repeating that environmental factors need something to act upon. Without the environment, genes would have nothing to do; without genes, the environment could have no influence.[18]

While neither the blank slate nor the nativist view of the mind alone explains how humans think and act, an integrated systemic approach that combines the internal and external causes of behavior (Figure 1.1) is probably nearer the truth. The linguist Jean Aitchison, for example, uses the behavior of honeybees to illustrate how innate dispositions interact with learning in the animal kingdom. Bees are not born with an encyclopedia of flower types in their brains, yet they unerringly fly to flowers rather than to hats or bus stop signs. In doing so they are naturally guided by scent above all, but also by color and shape. They instinctively fly to flowers because of a combination of factors that they naturally notice and prioritize, but they also have to learn details of particular plants in their environment.[19] Similarly, nature provides humans with a framework by focusing attention in certain directions, with experience and learning filling in the details. In human sexual behavior, to use a spectacular example, the innate drive of obvious evolutionary importance motivates the need to learn complex rituals of courtship that are as universal as they are culture-specific. For the astronomer John D. Barrow, "no mind was ever a *tabula rasa*. We enter the world with minds that possess an innate ability to learn. What we learn; how we learn; what we notice; and what we know but never learnt—these things bear witness to our past in subtle ways."[20] The literary scholar Joseph Carroll likewise emphasizes the importance of the innate psychological structures in human thinking and creativity, including that expressed in fictional narratives, arguing that creativity is not as untrammeled as it seems because it is constrained by those very structures.[21]

Cognitive sciences apart, the environmentalist position makes no evolutionary sense and does not even stand logical scrutiny. All living systems exist in competitive environments, in which survival and a chance to reproduce often depend on quick and correct assessments of situations involving danger to life, vital search for food, and mating opportunities. This means that systems equipped from birth with ready-made responses to certain standard existential situations stand a better chance of survival than systems deprived of such innate instructions. In a cut-throat environment in which our ancestors have evolved, having to learn correct responses the hard way, by trial and error, was not always an option. An organism unable to react appropriately in time may not be given a second chance and could be eliminated by natural selection, like an unlucky sapper defusing mines, the first time it makes a vital mistake. The blank slate or the social construct theory thus requires a highly improbable separation between the (biological) body and the (cultural) mind. It is like saying that the brain, the most complex organ in the human body, has in some magical and inexplicable way escaped the pressures of the evolutionary process of which it is a result. Without the genetically transmitted knowledge, not only would our species never manage to survive, but it would simply never have appeared on this planet in the first place.

The decision on what position one takes in the nature/nurture controversy is also crucial for semiotics. The blank slate view of the mind, which prioritizes language, society, and culture as generators of meaning, and downplays the importance of individual autonomy in the meaning-creating process, removes any constraints on what cultural communication can be about. But meaning as generated in individual minds and shared in society is not about everything and anything, because human thinking and behavior are guided by cognitive structures designed by evolution to deal with a range of specific, adaptive, mainly social problems.[22] Whatever humans, or other animals for that matter, communicate about is focused on what is ultimately necessary to them, what helps them satisfy their vital needs, navigate social life to their advantage, make sense of the world, and ultimately survive.

Needs as Homeostatic Disturbances

A temporary disturbance of the system's functional equilibrium caused either by a deficiency or by excess of certain types of information and energy will be called a *need*.[23] For Richard Dawkins, living organisms are equipped with a measuring device, which gauges the discrepancies between the current state of things and the "desired" state. As this discrepancy grows, the device makes the organism work harder to reduce the gap between the existing state and the desired state.[24] Examples of needs thus understood are of course legion, depending on the generic nature of the system and its environment. What all needs have in common, however, is the underlying principle of homeostatic disturbance, which motivates behavior toward reducing deviations from the desired state of functional equilibrium.

What prompts the system to restore this state is an internal reaction, which we can call by a familiar term *emotion*. The linguist Derek Bickerton captures the motivating function of emotions by calling them "bridges between representation and response."[25] Henry Plotkin too is emphatic about the adaptive function of emotions: they are like "postcards from our genes telling us, in a direct and non-symbolic manner, about life and death."[26] In short, emotions energize behavior. From a homeostatic point of view it is possible to talk about two main types of emotion: *negative* emotions, caused by a disturbance of the system's functional equilibrium, and *positive* emotions, caused by a restoration of the system's functional equilibrium. In both cases emotion is an internal, genetically programmed reaction which causes the system to avoid dangerous stimuli through negative emotions and to seek agreeable stimuli through positive emotions.

In case the basic division of emotions into negative and positive appear too general, the psychologist Paul Ekman has established a larger but still limited and probably exhaustive number of seven basic emotions as displayed universally by the human face. They include, on the negative side, sadness, anger, fear, disgust, contempt, and surprise, while the positive side is covered by a blanket emotion of happiness, understood as a general sense of relief, satisfaction, and fulfillment.[27] As also argued by Joseph Carroll, the seven universal emotions identified by Ekman are essential components in the tonal and generic structures of literary narratives, whereby sadness underlies tragedy and the elegiac genre; happiness dominates the conclusions of comic plots; surprise is provoked by suspense; while anger, contempt, and disgust are expressed in satire.[28] Emotions are primarily triggered by informational stimuli, but they also have their characteristic "energic" and physiological manifestations, found in such intuitive linguistic expressions as "getting hot under the collar" when agitated or nervous, having "cold feet" when indifferent or uninterested, "freezing with fear," meeting with "cold/lukewarm reception," having "the hots" for someone, experiencing the "fire" of desire, and so on. Physiological reactions combined with facial expressions, bodily postures, and emotive vocalizations are part of human contiguous indexical communication discussed in Chapter 4.

Individual examples of needs may be legion, but it is still possible to deduce a limited and possibly exhaustive number of their functional types. Let us begin by dividing the needs into those involving primarily the excess or deficiency of energy, and those involving primarily the excess or deficiency of information. "Primarily" means that emotions and mental computations are interconnected rather than separated within the system. Consequently, the needs involving more energy than information will be called *dynamic*, and the needs involving more information than energy will be called *cognitive*. On this dynamic-cognitive scale it is possible to distinguish more specific functional types of needs (see the sections below), as determined by environmental challenges typically encountered by living systems.

As also mentioned in premise 2 in the Introduction, the satisfaction of needs is supported by evolved computational devices in the brain, or cognitive modules, which guide the need-related behavior. At birth these modules already contain a substantial amount of knowledge about the world, which is common to all members of our species as the foundation of the universal human nature.[29] The ultimate number of cognitive modules is at present impossible to ascertain, as it would require a hypothetical reverse-engineering of all recurrent types of challenges faced by our ancestors during their evolutionary history. While the full cognitive architecture of the human mind is yet to be mapped out by psychologists, it is possible to identify at least some of the key experiential domains and the corresponding modules. These include the psycho-physiological structure of personality, sexual identity, family roles, social relations, responses to nonhuman physical and biological environments, as well as the specifically human meta-cognitive behaviors expressed in art, literature, religion, philosophy, and science.[30]

The Procreative Need

The inescapable law of entropy, or disorder, makes sure that all living systems in time slow down processing information and energy and eventually die, even if they do not die prematurely due to disease, starvation, violence, or fatal accidents.[31] From a homeostatic point of view, termination of life constitutes of course a final and irreversible disturbance of the system's functional equilibrium. Since no living system can (as yet) live forever, the only available way to ensure continuous existence (of sorts) is to produce one's own near-copy. This is accomplished by a universal process of biological reproduction (sexual in most species) involving the mixing of parental genetic material to create if not an identical then at least a genetically related organism.[32] The need to extend one's individual existence will be called *procreative*. It is accordingly the most dynamic of needs, motivated by powerful instincts and emotions, and least subject to volitional control.

The cognitive components of the procreative need include what psychologists identify as the sexually differentiated mate-choice module, responsible for the interpretation of cues and signals of sexual display in prospective partners as indexes of their genetic fitness. Universally, most human males are attracted to certain physical correlates of female nubility, such as those indicating onset of menstruation, while most females cross-culturally appear to be attracted to men who exhibit signs of high status.[33] The sex-related differences in the mate-choice module spring from widely differing investments in terms of time, energy, and resources that men and women have to make toward the raising of their biological offspring. It requires more energy to produce an egg cell than to produce sperm, and while the man's biological involvement is limited to a few minutes of sex and a spoonful of semen, the woman's biological investment continues for nine months of pregnancy and two to four years of lactation and nursing.[34] The differences in biological investment lead to other secondary sexual characteristics in body structure, physiology, and behavior. The comparatively small biological investment of the male means that he has more time and energy to compete for the female, which has led to larger on-average body size, strength, pugnacity, play fighting and genuine aggression, sexual salesmanship and self-advertising, as well as to tendencies toward promiscuity and polygamy. On the other hand, the larger biological investment of the human female has developed innate resistance to courtship, fastidiousness in choosing males, smaller body-size and, on average, less pugnacious temperament. With males competing and females choosing, the pugnacity and sexual assertiveness of the former contrasts with the more conciliatory and gentler disposition of the latter (again on average).[35]

Consequently, the mate-choice module in men will be geared toward mostly visual cues and signals produced by women suggesting youth, good health, and extension fertility—cues that cross-culturally define female sexual attractiveness and beauty. In the words of the psychologist Nancy Etcoff, "beauty is one of the ways life perpetuates itself, and love of beauty is deeply rooted in our biology."[36] Cues of physical attractiveness in women include in most cultures such anatomical features as average body size (neither too big nor too small, neither too slim nor too fat); the hour-glass body shape (waist-to-hip ratio of 0.67–0.80); smooth, moist, tight, and unblemished skin; firm breasts; small-jawed, light-boned face; large, clear eyes; white, intact teeth; full, red lips; thick and shiny scalp hair as an index of current good health and as a record of health in the years before; behavioral traits such as sprightly and graceful gait, alacrity, and coyness; high (but not shrill) voice; cleanliness; good reputation (related to sexual behavior, or rather lack of it, prior to courtship) to confirm that the displayed sexual cues and signals are honest, that is, that they do not conceal physical blemishes, symptoms of infection, sexual promiscuity, or previous pregnancy.[37]

These natural traits can be culturally enhanced (or faked) by makeup, hair dressing, personal adornments such as jewelry and clothing, and plastic surgery. (Semiotically, these cultural enhancements are intentional signs while phenotypic traits are unintentional cues.) According to Etcoff, the perception of bodily beauty, especially female, is a universal biological adaptation which provokes pleasure, rivets attention, and impels actions that ultimately ensure the survival of our genes. Etcoff argues that our extreme sensitivity to bodily beauty is hard-wired rather than learned; that is, it is governed by circuits in the brain shaped by natural selection rather than being picked up by observing how men behave toward women in particular culture.[38] At the same time, since most of human behavior is bio-cultural, canons of bodily beauty are calibrated by a local culture. For example, historically African American males considered as sexy and desirable African American women with fat and fleshy bodies. But research has shown that in a college environment African American male students often find slimmer females more attractive under the influence of dominant culture.[39]

By contrast, the mate-choice module in women will be geared toward men's "unfeminine" visual cues. Thus, on average and subject again to cultural variation, men considered handsome are recognized by a strong chin, prominent forehead and brows, low voice, broad shoulders, more than average height and symmetrical body without deformities or handicaps. Men also tend to remain attractive longer than women, because men's fertility does not decline as quickly with age. While scalp hair in men appears to possess neutral sexual appeal, facial hair (a complete turn-off in women) is considered attractive as a way of enhancing the visual aspect of aggressive displays. Beards, moustaches, sideburns, and goatees accentuate the size of the lower face, emphasizing its maturity and masculinity. Facial hair is common among males of other mammalian species (lions of course), in which the hair growth around the face makes the individual appear larger and more awesome.[40] Because aggressiveness, physical strength, and other hallmarks of typical masculine behavior work against female reproductive fitness and interest, such external features as facial hair have been selected out in women, in whom the evolutionary pressure has produced copious scalp hair instead as a cue of good health and fertility.[41]

Nancy Etcoff also postulates the existence of a related cognitive module based on auditory cues and signals, which helps to gauge sexual attractiveness by one's voice. The adult male voice is lower and louder than that of the average woman, because men's vocal cords are longer and larynx larger, while women tend to have softer, breathier voices, and their intonation range is broader. Men's voices considered attractive are low, slow, and smooth, whereas to sound attractive women sometimes exaggerate the pitch and breathiness of their voices (the British Prime Minister Margaret Thatcher took voice lessons to lower her pitch after she was told that her voice sounded shrill, that is, too feminine).[42]

If the above evolutionary profiles of femininity and masculinity appear too stereotypical and old-fashioned, the corrective "on average" implies a statistical distribution of sex-related traits in the form of two overlapping curves. This means, for example, that despite the difference in average body size in favor of men, there will always be a small number of men shorter than most women, some women will display more pugnacious and aggressive temperament than most men, some men will be gentler and more conciliatory than most women, and so on. There are tomboys, tomgirls, and viragos; most men are men, but some, like Leopold Bloom from James Joyce's *Ulysses*, are "womanly men."[43] While biological sex can be treated as a zero-one category, psychological genders and their cultural expressions reveal a statistically distributed spectrum of differences and commonalities.[44]

The Nutritional Need

The nutritional need refers to regular intakes of energy captured in foodstuffs obtained from the environment to support the system's metabolic and physiological processes. Related to digestion is the respiratory system, which provides oxygen to the cells and removes carbon dioxide, as well as sleep, which rebuilds proteins in the body, restores the central nervous system, and boosts the immunity.[45] The related cognitive components of the nutritional need include the ability to recognize edible things in the environment, the skills and social practice of producing and processing food, and the related culinary culture.

Humans are essentially omnivorous, with a potentially long list of animals and plant stuffs to choose from as food. However, many animal and vegetable species, or parts of animals and plants, are either inedible or toxic. Because absorbing organic substances for their energy is just as important for survival as avoiding toxic substances, one would expect a corresponding food-selection module to identify food stuffs both for their nutritional value and for their potentially dangerous, toxic qualities. Due to the chemical nature of nutrition, the food-selection module will depend primarily on gustatory and olfactory stimuli as cues of nutritional value. Accordingly, tastes and smells associated with food stuffs will provoke either positive or negative emotions (pleasure or disgust) to trigger the corresponding reactions of acceptance or rejection.

Thus as a general rule the sweet taste of milk, fruits, and juices obtained from high-calorie, sugary plants, as well as the taste of high-protein meat, eggs, and fish, again because of their highly nutritious value, will motivate actions toward obtaining them and trigger positive, pleasant emotions during ingestion. On the other hand, bitter or sour tastes, often associated with toxins, and foul smell of putrefying, that is, infectious substances will automatically provoke distaste and disgust, and will motivate avoidance or rejection by spitting and vomiting. As the psychologists Paul Rozin and A. Fallon have demonstrated, disgust is a universal human emotion, associated with a fear of incorporating a toxic or infectious substance. Equally universally, the offending organic substances tend to include decaying, that is, pathogenic, animals and plants, as well as animal body products such as mucus, pus, and, of course, urine and feces. By comparison, inorganic or non-nutritive stuff like sand, stones, wood, cloth, bark, and so on are simply avoided without feelings of disgust or distaste.[46]

An interesting thing about disgust is that while the emotion itself is universal, there exist wide cross-cultural differences in attributing disgust to certain otherwise tasteful and nutritious animals and plants. For example, most Westerners cannot stomach the thought, let alone the act, of eating insects, worms, toads, maggots, caterpillars, or grubs, despite the fact that these perfectly edible and nutritious little animals have been consumed by the majority of peoples throughout history.[47] The anthropologist Elizabeth Cashdan argues that the first two years of life are a sensitive period for learning about food, as this is when children acquire tastes for the food permitted by their social environment. After two years children's tastes become limited to the foods that they were given during the sensitive period, while all other perfectly edible foods become "distasteful" and "disgusting," in most cases for life.[48] The psychology of disgust is also part of the "semiotics of food,"[49] including ethnic cuisines and food taboos, where what people eat and with whom becomes a marker of ethnic and cultural difference and identity, which reinforce intra-group integration and inter-group segregation. Shylock's refusal to dine with Bassanio in *The Merchant of Venice* aptly captures the role of food taboos in separating the Jewish and Christian communities: "Yes, to smell pork, to eat of the habitation which your prophet the Nazarite conjured the devil into. I will buy with you, sell with you, talk with you, walk with you, and so following. But I will not eat with you, drink with you nor pray with you."[50] Nor are organic inedibles excluded from further symbolic connotations. In *Macbeth* the witches' brew, an evil inversion of a feast, replaces wholesome, nourishing foodstuffs with animal and vegetable toxic, inedible, cannibal or fantastic ingredients, including parts of toad, snake, newt, frog, bat, dog, adder, blind-worm, lizard, howlet, dragon, wolf, mummy, shark, tiger, baboon, goat, hemlock, and yew (4.1.26–30).

The Protective Need

To prevent the loss of the ability to interact with the environment to their advantage, autonomous systems must avoid or counteract dynamic inputs potentially dangerous to their bodily integrity. To avoid being injured or killed requires several innate cognitive modules responsible for intuitive physics and biology, which help humans safely negotiate their way among the inanimate, floral, and animal environments.[51]

From a very early age children understand that physical objects are subject to different sets of rules from those which govern mental concepts and living things. Concepts of solidity, gravity, movement, and inertia, for example, appear to be hard-wired into the children's minds, helping them to avoid making mistakes of using ideas appropriate to living things when handling inanimate, inert objects. According to the cognitive archaeologist Steven Mithen, intuitive knowledge of physics enabled our prehistoric forebears to develop instrumental skills and to rapidly draw on culturally transmitted knowledge about man-made objects, such as tools and weapons. Both our ancestors and modern hunter-gatherers are also compulsive and expert naturalists, able to interpret the tiniest clues in their environment as to their implications for the location and behavior of animals, both those dangerous to humans (such as large cats, insects, and reptiles) and those used as high-protein food.[52]

Fear and aggression and the associated reactions of fight-or-flight are the expected emotional components of the cognitive modules related to the protective need. As evolutionary theory predicts, the most common objects and features of the environment to provoke innate, spontaneous fear in us today are the same that scared our ancestors. Chimpanzees born in captivity scream in terror when they first see a snake, and people too dread snakes without ever having seen one.[53] Other common human fears and phobias include those of heights, storms, large carnivores, darkness, blood, strangers, confinement, deep water, social scrutiny and ostracism, emotional rejection, and so on, which also appear to be hard-wired in our brains because they refer to situations which put our evolutionary ancestors in danger. Evolutionary theory explains why even humans raised in modern cities are spontaneously scared of snakes, spiders, rats, and closed spaces rather than of knives, guns, fast driving, or electric outlets: the fear of the latter is not innate but must be either inferred from consciously imagined consequences or learned from unpleasant experiences related to these objects.[54]

The Social Need

Individual systems can also maximize their fitness by forming groups and benefiting from exchanges of knowledge and resources with other group members. Edward O. Wilson writes: "To form groups, drawing visceral comfort and pride from familiar fellowship, and to defend the group enthusiastically against rival groups—these are among the absolute universals of human nature and hence of culture."[55] The most common groupings involve biologically related individuals, as in the family, nuclear and distant, where the sharing of useful knowledge and resources benefits everyone's life interests in the short term and everyone's genes in the long term. Larger social systems involve ethnic communities, professional groups, organizations, nations, and ultimately, in an increasingly globalized and interconnected world, the entire humankind. Socialization is a universal phenomenon, caused primarily by the procreative need, which involves of necessity two parents, usually with the addition of the parents' kin who have a genetic stake in supporting the prospective offspring.

In positive-sum exchanges of information and resources within integrated groups everyone ends up with a net profit that is higher than if everyone acted on their own. A pack of hyenas can catch prey so much larger than a lone hyena can bring down, so it pays each selfish individual to hunt in a pack, even though this involves sharing food.[56] Fifty humans cooperating in an organization can accomplish far more than 500 individuals working in isolation.[57] The main benefit of cooperation can often be not just profit but simply survival. Emperor penguins endure an Antarctic winter, when temperatures plummet to minus 30 degrees Celsius (minus 22F) or below, by huddling in tightly packed groups to conserve body heat and shelter themselves in intense wind. In this way they all survive, whereas standing in isolation exposed to cold and wind they would all die.[58] Communication as an essentially social phenomenon is ultimately about sharing the often life-saving information and energy.

Social bonds are cemented by the warmth of positive emotions, whose intensity will be expected to be inversely proportional to the social (in practice genetic) distance: the closer the relationship, the stronger and more positive the emotion (loyalty, solidarity, friendliness, love). The weakest positive emotion (indifference) will be extended toward the most distant members of the group, while negative, aversive emotions (distrust, hostility) will by default apply to members of other groups, with their often-competing and antagonistic interests. Interactions with strangers, unless they are trading partners or co-citizens in modern states, tend to be a zero-sum game, in which for one side to win the other must lose. The cognitive components of the social need include character reading skills, recognition of kin-relations, and knowledge of group history as the basis of collective identity.

Within the group, the social need involves instinctive willingness to help others and to expect benefits in return. As the psychologist Denise D. Cummins explains, social living in our ancestral environment yielded a reduction in predator threat through improved cooperative detection and repulsion of enemies, improved foraging and hunting efficiency, improved defense of limited resources against intruders, and improved care of offspring through communal feeding and protection.[59] At the same time, the flip side of living cooperatively are the costs arising from increased competition within the group for food, mates, habitation sites, and other limited resources. John Tooby and Leda Cosmides argue in favor of a constellation of cognitive adaptations to social life, including a social map of the persons, relationships, motives, interactions, emotions, and intentions that made up the ancestral world.[60] For Steven Mithen, intuitive psychology is one of the four domains of human innate knowledge, the other including language, physics, and biology—all content-rich cognitive modules which would have helped our Paleolithic hunting-gathering ancestors and now underlie the emotions and instincts in our interpersonal relations.[61]

Intuitive psychology consists of several functionally interrelated modules, including what psychologists call *theory of mind*—the ability to "read" other people's personalities in order to guess their intentions and predict their behavior.[62] The biologist John Cartwright argues that the ability to mind-read and in consequence to deceive, what he calls Machiavellian intelligence, is already present in other primates, who can fake social signals to mislead and exploit others.[63] Machiavellian intelligence, Cartwright explains, was a major selective force in the growth of the hominid brain, which tripled in size in the last two million years, from 450 cm^3 to 1300 cm^3, very rapidly by evolutionary standards. According to this view, adaptive success depended on anticipating and manipulating the actions of others through an arms race between mind-reading and deception: large brains helped early humans to understand each other's minds, which led to deception, which in turn stimulated brain growth to detect and avoid deception, that is, to mind-read, and so the process ran on, causing an escalation of brain size.[64]

Theory of mind also includes so-called *orders of intentionality*, through which individuals psyche each other out in social interactions.[65] First-order intentionality is a prerequisite of self-awareness ("I know"), typical for humans and found among other primates. (By comparison, computers and most animals have zero-order intentionality: they know, but they do not know that they know.) Second-order intentionality involves both self-awareness and the realization that others have similar awareness about themselves ("I know that you know"). Second-order intentionality is responsible for tactical deceptions, a skill acquired by human children between three and four years of age, and found also among other primates. For example, vervet monkeys can use false alarm calls in the absence of a predator to distract other monkeys from aggressive intentions, or to remove potential competitors from a source of food.[66] Third-order intentionality in turn relates to one's realization that others may be aware of one's mental states ("I know that you know that I know")—a psychological disposition behind social role-playing, when one adjusts one's behavior to other people's expectations. Fourth-order intentionality ("I know that you know that I know about what you know") closes the interactive loop by acknowledging reciprocity in social role-playing. At fifth-order intentionality most people probably begin to forget who is thinking what about whom.

Third- and fourth-orders are commonly involved in the early stages of a relationship, when prospective partners still do not know each other's characters and suss each other out to infer what each thinks about the other, and how each person presents themselves to the other. In *Ulysses* James Joyce has his two characters, Leopold Bloom and Stephen Dedalus, silently try to figure each other out during their night-time conversation:

> What, reduced to their simplest reciprocal form, were Bloom's thoughts about Stephen's thoughts about Bloom and Bloom's thoughts about Stephen's thoughts about Bloom's thoughts about Stephen?
> He thought that he thought that he was a jew whereas he knew that he knew that he knew that he was not.[67]

In a short story by O. Henry one character is advising his friend on the subtle and delicate art of holding a woman's hand: "Don't let her know that you think she knows you have the least idea she is aware you are holding her hand."[68] From a writer's perspective, creating fictitious characters engaged in third- and fourth-order intentionality betokens a fifth-order intentionality, whereas assuming that the reader will accept the fictitious characters involved in such multi-layered interactions betrays a sixth-order intentionality in the writer, which is probably as far as any intelligent human being can go in social interactions. For the psychologist Richard Webster, the capacity to "read" other people's thoughts and feelings is not confined to novelists: it is probably one of the most biologically useful of all intellectual abilities which the human species has developed over the millennia of evolution.[69]

Other possible social modules include *kin-recognition*, which influences the way people mete out their support and acts of altruism toward genetic relatives. The module also explains the universal obsession with kinship and genealogical trees. The evolutionary logic of altruism directed at our kin is that relatives share genes to a greater extent than nonrelatives, and therefore by helping a relative an individual also promotes their own genes.[70] We find it easier to extend solidarity, sympathy, tolerance, and trust toward our relatives than toward strangers or even in-laws: to love one's biological kin comes naturally, whereas we have to learn to love our non-kin. As early tribal groups grew larger to become communities and societies, the kin-recognition module was expanded to encompass individuals outside the extended family. Today, in an age of global trade and communication, the spirit of non-antagonistic cooperation can potentially include individuals and groups from any culture and race.[71]

A related social module, but one tied to the negative emotions of distrust, fear, and often aggression, relates to what can be called the *enemy-recognition* module, directed at members of other groups with their often-competing interests. Animals as well as humans react aggressively to usurpations of essential resources by rivals, and violence typically erupts where territories are limited, when one's offspring are under threat, when food is scarce, and when potential mating partners are besieged by rivals. Across cultures, competition, fights, and homicide are predominantly a male affair, as they are in non-human animals.[72] According to the psychologists Martin Daly and Margo Wilson, our species-typical sex difference in violent aggression is one which we share with other mammals displaying a wide difference in the minimal parental investments of males and females. As discussed in the section about the procreative need, the sexual difference in parental investments makes the reproductive capacity of females a scarce commodity and explains why men are, on average, the violent sex, as is indeed testified by their larger and stronger bodies. Across cultures men kill men twenty to forty times more often than women kill women, and the lion's share of the killers are young men, between the ages of fifteen and thirty.[73] Related to the kin-recognition and enemy-recognition modules are the specialized *face-recognition* module and *body-language* module, discussed in Chapter 4 in the context of visual communication.

The Exploratory Need

In addition to benefiting from cooperation with social partners, humans also negotiate their way around the wider, non-social environment and its resources. It is typical for animals and humans, whose natural mobility is an evolutionary result of their exploratory behavior, to search the environment for thinly distributed foodstuffs, for mating opportunities and shelter, and to test one's responses in new situations, often by random curiosity, spontaneous experimentation, and playful behavior. Among humans, a spectacular if historically late example of exploratory behavior is science: a socially organized activity of collecting, storing, and utilizing knowledge of the world, acquired through data gathering, abstract theorizing, and laboratory experimentation. The underlying cognitive need will accordingly be called *exploratory*, supported by such emotions as curiosity and excitement of discovery.

All animals have evolved the sensory and neural apparatus to process environmental stimuli for what is relevant to their existence: what is dangerous, neutral, or safe, what is edible and what is not, how to find a congenial living habitat, how to recognize mating partners, allies, enemies, and so on. The brain, the most costly bodily organ in terms of energy needed to sustain its life, is basically a computational device designed to detect order and select patterns for response out of an enormous flux of information reaching it through the sensory channels. The human mind and by extension culture appear to have evolved to overcome the evolutionary fixed defenses of plants and animals, by applying cognitive modules to deal with various domains of the world, including solid objects, forces, paths, locations, manners, states, substances, hidden biochemical essences, and other people's beliefs and desires.[74] Language and artifacts such as art, rituals, and myths also help to sort out, comprehend, and assimilate otherwise intellectually diffuse and emotionally confused experience. Human pursuit of order can also become a goal in itself and a source of cognitive pleasure, as evidenced by the often-irresistible habit of estheticizing and philosophizing about things for no immediate adaptive reason.

The exploration of the environment in search of its life-supporting resources leads naturally to the accumulation of knowledge, both phylogenetic and ontogenetic. As Henry Plotkin reminds us, knowledge is a pervasive characteristic of all life, because all biological adaptations constitute forms of practical knowledge acquired by organisms during their phylogenetic development. The fleshly water-conserving cactus stem represents a form of knowledge about the scarcity of water in the cactus's environment, just as the elongated slender beak of the humming-bird is a manifestation of the knowledge of the structure of the flowers from which the bird draws nectar. Thus understood genetic knowledge is based on a complex set of relationships between genes and past selection pressures, between genetically guided developmental pathways and the conditions under which an organism develops. In plants and animals such knowledge is gained and stored wholly in the gene pool and expressed during individual development as a part of the hard wiring of the nervous system.[75]

Given the advantages of innate responses in the self-regulation of autonomous systems, there is no reason why humans should not possess a similar kind of phylogenetic knowledge about their ancestral environment, in addition to the individual and culture-specific knowledge accumulated during one's lifetime and stored in conscious memory. The psychologist Roger N. Shepard views human practical and scientific knowledge as being ultimately founded on our innate, evolutionary knowledge, described by him as "a deep, if implicit, wisdom about the world that is our genetic legacy from countless aeons of ancestral interactions with the world."[76] As noted earlier, for an individual to start in life without the benefit of innate knowledge would mean to have to acquire it from scratch, through trial and possibly fatal error. We are largely unaware of the implicit wisdom that underlies our ability to negotiate the world, because natural selection has made sure that our common phylogenetic experience serves us swiftly and automatically, at a largely unconscious level. An individual mind obviously possesses the capacity to register new stimuli and record new experiences, but ontogenetic learning is simply not enough to ensure survival and optimal existence.

Using as frame of reference certain persistent features and challenges of the natural environment in which humans have evolved, the principle of adaptive self-regulation can suggest several possible cognitive modules as innate experiential matrices. This reverse-engineering procedure has been used by the astronomer John D. Barrow in his analysis of the various features of the Earth's visible cosmic and natural environments and their role in shaping human innate psychological, esthetic, and even religious responses.[77] Accordingly, human farthest natural environment is the observable cosmos, including the sky with its stars and planets, as well as the sun and the moon as the largest heavenly bodies, whose movements determine the cyclical passage of time. The regularity and predictability of these movements, the correlation of astronomical cycles with the passage of the seasons and the biological rhythms in plants, animals, and humans would consequently be expected to inspire positive feelings of tranquility, safety, and awe. Unlike the earthly environment, the cosmos is (or was until the launching of the space program in the late twentieth century) inaccessible to direct human exploration and could only be contemplated passively, otherwise remaining beyond human penetration and control. The perception of the vastness of the cosmos, its position high above biological life, its enormity relative to the human scale, the blue color of daytime sky, the spectacle of countless tiny bright specks seen against the dark sky at night, and the geometric regularity of the heavenly movements would all be expected to induce a sense of jaw-dropping wonder, awe, and transcendence as the foundation of religious experience.

On the other hand, the experiences of sporadic astronomical disturbances such as solar and lunar eclipses, appearances of comets, rare cases of large asteroids crashing onto the Earth, and so on will be expected, because of their unpredictability, to induce the negative emotions of fear and panic, without, however, prompting any specific defensive reactions, precisely because of the total helplessness and fatalism in the face of random and uncontrollable forces. Due to the extremely long exposure of evolving humans to the remote but ever-visible cosmos, both positive and negative types of emotional responses to the astronomical phenomena should be expected to inform the earliest manifestations of culture, especially religion. According to John D. Barrow, during human evolution the cosmic environment has imprinted itself upon our unconscious minds and bodies, shaping our fascinations and influencing "the tenor of our philosophizing and feeling for the Universe."[78]

The main observable effects of the revolution of the largest and brightest heavenly body are the daily alternation between light and darkness, and the yearly succession of the seasons. Feelings of safety but also of alertness will be associated with daytime explorations of the natural environment, and with routine activities such as search for food during the warm seasons. On the other hand, darkness and the cold seasons will be accompanied by reduced activity, thermal discomfort, exposure to nocturnal predators, and so on, with the corresponding sense of insecurity and anxiety. Depending on their adaptive value the temporal features of the environment will inspire corresponding emotional and moral connotations: positive in relation to light and warmth, and negative in connection with darkness and cold, as illustrated by myths, fairy tales, the pastoral genre, romance, and nature poetry—art forms with the natural environment as the background and vehicle for emotional states and moral values.

Below the canopy of the sky, congenial atmospheric phenomena such as moderate and soothing winds, warm temperature, gentle and refreshing rain, clear blue sky granting good visibility and atmospheric calm (perfect holiday weather) will elicit tranquility, relaxation, and feeling of safety. On the other hand, strong winds and hurricanes, still air in hot climates, extremities of temperature, torrential rain, snow drifts, hail, dense fog reducing visibility, electric storms, droughts, and so on, as threats to safety and survival will be feared and if possible avoided. These ambivalent atmospheric phenomena will accordingly feature as attributes of nature deities: Zeus with his thunder bolt or metamorphosed into a fertilizing rain descending on the nymph Danäe. Human inborn sensitivity to atmospheric phenomena—crucial for the survival of our ancestors, exposed as they were to natural hazards most of the time—would explain our persistent preoccupation with the weather, not least in the clichés of daily conversation.

Below the atmospheric phenomena lies the natural terrain with its challenges and opportunities for survival and habitation. Feelings of safety and relaxation will accordingly be evoked by such natural features as level ground with undulations for good views and rapid orientation, grassy meadows, small and quiet rivers and lakes, groves offering shade and shelter. On the other hand, steep and rocky mountains, dry and barren deserts with no place to hide, thick jungles and deep forests with no cues for orientation and little chance of escape from lurking predators, fast-flowing and turbulent rivers, waterfalls, inaccessible swamps and marshes, glaciers and snowbound terrain, subterranean labyrinthine caves, occasional floods and bush fires, volcanic eruptions, landslides, and earthquakes—generally, natural features and phenomena hostile to human life and habitation, will be accompanied by fear, a sense of insecurity and vital threat, but also by fascination, curiosity, and awe. Positive emotions will also be evoked by green and lush vegetation promising abundant food and shelter, while lack of vegetation in the winter or in cold or hot climatic zones, as well as barren, lifeless landscapes will be dreaded and avoided as places of habitation. The life-supporting natural features will be reflected in myths of the earthly paradise and the pastoral genre, while the life-threatening features will inform the apocalyptic narratives, scary fairy tales, Gothic horror stories, and the Romantic sublime with its predilection for wild, bleak, and forbidding landscapes.

In his study of human environmental preferences, the psychologist Stephen Kaplan talks about "mystery" as a promise of more information and opportunities as one ventures deeper into the landscape. A sense of mystery in a view or painting is accordingly enhanced by such characteristics as screening in the foreground, a winding path, and deep perspective with a distant prospect. Equally inviting and stimulating are features that suggest more information while also partially obscuring it, such as a brightly lit area behind light foliage, or impenetrable vegetation with a hint of a gap where one could pass through (Figure 1.2). According to Kaplan, preference for mystery, often found in landscape painting and photography, is largely based on automatic, unconscious inferential processes that in the evolutionary past aided humans in finding optimal living environments offering safety and the promise of food and shelter.[79]

Figure 1.2 Landscape with elements of mystery: *The Beeches*, oil painting by Asher Brown Durand (1845). Courtesy of the Metropolitan Museum of Art, New York.

Apart from landscape and vegetation we seem to be instinctively interested in animal creatures great and small, and by extension in animal-like, man-made, self-propelled, laterally symmetrical moving objects such as planes, trains, and automobiles, both real and toy ones. Indeed, the most conspicuous external difference between vegetables and animals is the mobility of the latter, with our nervous system innately predisposed to pay instant attention to objects that move purposefully of their own accord. Plants are comparatively immobile because they draw their life-supporting energies from the evenly and abundantly distributed sources such as sun and soil, whereas animals have to search for their plant and animal food that is unevenly and scarcely distributed in space, and requires constant mobility simply to find it. The need to penetrate the environment in search of food has been, according to Henry Plotkin, the fundamental selection force in the evolution of the nervous system, both to coordinate motor activities of the body and to develop complex sense organs that allow for better-directed and energy-efficient movement. In this view movement, sensory perception, and the exploratory drive have been the main selection forces in the evolution of learning and intelligence, which is why animals have brains and plants do not.[80]

It comes as no surprise therefore that human infants attend intensely to motion and repetitive activities, preferring moving objects over static ones, and remaining very attentive to motion and noise combined, as in a bell ringing or a rattle shaking.[81] A natural predisposition to attend to animate motion more readily than to static objects would provide an evolutionary advantage when stalking a prey or monitoring the movement of a predator.[82] Given the animals' huge adaptive importance to humans (we eat them, they eat us), one would postulate a corresponding *animal-recognition module* in our phylogenetic memory. Accordingly, positive responses, combining curiosity and the instinctive movement toward the animal, will be directed at edible animal species, such as herbivores, other small animals, birds, and fish. Conversely, negative responses, mixing curiosity with the instinctive movement away from the animal, will be linked with potential predators, such as large cats and big fish. Small rodents, reptiles, and insects, largely indifferent as sources of food but often noxious or poisonous, will be instinctively avoided and repulsed. Predictably, the earliest art works on record, the Upper Paleolithic cave paintings and small sculpture, are largely dedicated to animals either preying on humans (large cats) or hunted by humans (deer, bison).[83] Zoomorphic representations also feature abundantly in myths, religious imagery, fairy tales, and not least in children's literature, fantasy films, and animated cartoons with their repulsive, slimy, insect/reptile-like, cold-blooded monsters on the one hand, and cute, cuddly, warm-blooded and endearing baby animals on the other hand (Figure 1.3).

Figure 1.3 Making repulsiveness cute: disproportionally large heads and eyes as well as smiles humanize and infantilize otherwise repulsive amphibians and reptiles. Photo by Maaillustrations, courtesy of Freeimages.

The Esthetic Need

The emotions elicited by the natural environment are prompted by sensory perceptions of the manifold features of objects such as shape, size, texture, color, sound, smell, and taste. Some things look or sound beautiful to us and make us smile with pleasure, while other things are perceived as ugly and make us wince with disgust. We find flowers and sunny days lovely because for millions of years these environmental features enhanced human life, and we find cold and rainy days depressing because for our ancestors they spelled the danger of hypothermia.[84] The emotions elicited by nature, often hard to verbalize, are known to everyone, including of course poets, painters, and musicians, whose role it is precisely to express in works of art the elusive and subtle emotions originally aroused by our ancestors' experience of their environment. For Oscar Wilde the sole function of art is to awaken "the exquisite sterile emotions" quite apart from the often-harsh and hurtful realities of life.[85] Ralph Waldo Emerson's rapturous appreciation of natural beauty captures a similar experience: "Such is the constitution of all things, or such the plastic power of the human eye, that the primary forms, as the sky, the mountain, the tree, the animal, give us a delight in and for themselves; a pleasure arising from outline, color, motion, and grouping."[86] The psychologist Ellen Dissanayake also argues in favor of the adaptive function of our fascination with the natural world, and of the emotional expression which can exist for its own sake, giving delight and satisfaction in and of itself. The artists' role therefore is to give shape and form to the amorphous and erratic sensations as intensifications of this innate proclivity.[87] Likewise for John D. Barrow the appreciation of the beauty of nature and works of art has its basis in latent instincts and unconscious responses to the natural environment, imprinted in the psyche and perpetuated by millions of years of human evolution.[88] For the anthropologist Donald E. Brown too our appreciation of "natural beauty" is based on an innate preference for settings that would have been optimal habitats for our foraging forebears.[89]

Thus we like lakes, rivers, cliffs, and savannah settings, that is, meadows and groves, in which food, water, and protection are in optimal combination. We innately prefer, seek out, and construct certain kinds of settings because we feel good in them, as evidenced by our fondness for parklands, recreation areas, landscape architecture, and painting. Many of the classically seductive landscape scenes combine hints of refuge and safety, uninterrupted panoramic views, and enticement to explore, tempered by verdant pastures and water. These features occur prominently in today's public parks and gardens, where they are calculated to aid relaxation and induce feelings of ease and well-being (Figure 1.4).[90] The geographer Jay Appleton likewise subscribes to the ultimately Darwinian "habitat theory" of environmental esthetics, in which our appreciation of certain types of landscape is directly related to the survival value they provided to our ancestors. What we call esthetic pleasure, argues Appleton, arises from perceiving and evaluating certain elements of our surroundings as conducive to survival, enabling us to hide and seek, to see without being seen, to find refuge and to explore, to assess degrees of danger and safety, and to feel nostalgic or apprehensive about landscape—real, painted, or photographed (see Chapter 9 on the semiotics of the pictorial frame).[91]

Figure 1.4 Natural landscape features of refuge and safety reproduced in public parks: Phoenix Park, Dublin.

The Teleological Need

Finally, it is possible to postulate another important cognitive need, at least among humans. Given the advanced cognitive faculties such as ontogenetic memory and consciousness (of which more in Chapter 3), the exploratory behavior can extend beyond the immediate adaptive responses of the kind described in the foregoing sections. The sustained observation of the regularities occurring in the cosmic, natural, and social domains, such as the cyclicity of the heavenly phenomena and the seasonal and generational rhythms of life, can lead to speculations regarding the causes and purposes of these regularities. A conscious mind, relatively free from the immediate existential concerns, can formulate questions about the origins and goals of things: of life, natural and social, individual and collective, and of the entire Universe. Such abstract speculation presupposes a conscious perception of time and a working memory extending beyond the immediate moment to embrace mentally both the remembered past and the imagined future—a cognitive faculty most probably available only to humans. A cognition detached from contiguous experience requires not only the ability to have ideas about things, but also to have ideas about ideas—a meta-cognitive faculty that enables humans to ask questions and formulate theories regarding the origin, purpose, and meaning of everything that surrounds them in their daily interactions with the world.

Despite the fact that the cognitive distance from the immediate pressures of life afforded by such speculation is not always conducive to the satisfaction of the more vital dynamic needs, it seems that the search for meaning in the world has been useful to our species in view of long-term adaptation. A species not constrained to its environmental niche but expanding throughout all ecosystems and even into the cosmos avails itself of more flexible cognitive faculties to adapt to almost any environment, not just to the one inherited by evolution. The historic success of "The Social Conquest of the Earth," as Edward O. Wilson calls it in the title of one of his books,[92] suggests that imagination and counterfactual speculation have been ultimately adaptive, and as such are part of human nature. Consequently, the cognitive need related to the search for the purpose and meaning of life will be called *teleological* (from Greek *telos*, goal). Historical expressions of the teleological need include individual introspection as well as such social phenomena as religion, philosophy, literature, art, and political ideology.

The teleological need assumes the form of a world-model, most typically of religious character, which describes the origin, history, and ultimate destiny of a people guided by human-like supernatural beings. The destiny is conceived of as an ideal future state, described as a more attractive version of the currently experienced life situation, and marked by an optimal satisfaction of all needs—a kind of perfect homeostasis variously described as salvation, paradise, heaven, nirvana, and so on. This imagined ideal state is saturated with positive emotions to motivate thoughts and actions leading toward its attainment, while deviations from the set goal are linked with negative emotions and punitive sanctions, such as moral censure, private guilt, ostracism, excommunication, exile, divine wrath, damnation, death penalty for apostasy, and so on. In teleological world-models the promised perfect homeostasis of the future is contrasted with the less-than-perfect current life, and is presented as a compensation for its discomforts, frustrations, and sufferings.

In encouraging reflection on the meaning of life's inevitable sorrows and frustrations teleological narratives also stimulate subjective mental experience, the "inner life" with its search for imaginative and moral order in the complex and emotionally rich circumstances of individual life, including one's place within the systems of familial and social relations. As argued by Joseph Carroll, for all their "otherworldliness" teleological world-models are indispensable for personal development in this life, for the coherent and meaningful ordering of ideas and feelings, and for the organization of shared experience that makes collective cultural life possible. With their irrepressibly restless inner lives, humans in all cultures use these world-models to provide them with ethical guidelines to mitigate instinctive behavior, to produce a sense of cognitive order, and to make sense of human needs and motives.[93]

Historically most persistent teleological world-model is the religious myth—the original matrix of all literary fiction. As the psychologist Merlin Donald observes, in preliterate societies, for both individuals and the group, the religious myth stands at the top of the cognitive pyramid: it not only regulates behavior and codifies collective knowledge but it also constrains perception and understanding of reality, and consolidates the group by channeling the thought skills of its adherents and uniting them around the shared repertoire of stories, rituals, and symbols.[94] The predisposition to religious beliefs is the most complex and powerful force in the human mind, and in all probability an ineradicable part of human nature.[95] It is one of the universals of social behavior, taking recognizable form in every society from hunter-gatherer bands to modern states. Edward O. Wilson views the cognitive processes behind religious beliefs, including concentration on personal and group identity, attention to charismatic leaders, and mythopoetics, in terms of genetic predispositions whose self-sufficient components were incorporated into the neural apparatus of the human brain by thousands of generations of evolution.[96] In other words, notwithstanding the fictitious character of its narratives, religion is the supreme manifestation of the teleological need and as such is a biological adaptation, an enabling mechanism for survival. Amid the disorienting chaos of everyday experience religion provides a transcendental if illusive sense of order and purpose in life, compatible on average with an individual person's self-interest, at the same time cementing the aspirations and sanctioning the actions of the group as a whole.

*

The seven distinguished types of needs: procreative, nutritional, protective, social, exploratory, esthetic, and teleological, extended on the scale from the most dynamic to the most cognitive, represent the totality of the motives behind animal and human behavior, and encompass all possible subject areas of communication in all cultures. In other words, human experience revolves around the problems caused by functional disturbances of one kind or another, as defined by certain standard situations likely to occur in life. While the types of needs remain the same everywhere as the ultimate motivators of behavior, their manifestations will of course vary from individual to individual, from culture to culture. Most people enjoy having children, although some are more inclined toward children-free life, or toward celibacy. Individual tastes in food and ethnic cuisines also differ within the range of what is edible and locally available, what a culinary culture recommends, and what religious food taboos permit. Levels of sociability likewise differ between individuals, and all societies have developed specific and complicated systems of kin relations, communal life, rites, customs, traditions, and power hierarchies to enhance group cohesion and identity. Curiosity about the social and non-human environments is variously satisfied depending on individual inclination and available educational opportunities. Equally individual is sensitivity to order and harmony found in music, visual arts, literature, and nature at large, as are the local practices of artistic creativity. Finally, all people want to see purpose and meaning in their lives, in the destiny of their near and dear, of their community, and of the world at large. These teleological yearnings are satisfied everywhere by personal reflection, organized religion, philosophical speculation, and political ideologies which set culture-specific long-term goals for their communities and prescribe practical means for their attainment.

The semiotic domains related to the seven needs are sustained by social circulation of information, in other words, by communication. A single communicative act, such as a casual verbal exchange, a literary description, a political speech, a work of art, an advertisement, a blog entry, or a media report can relate to one of the seven needs, or to any combination of them at the same time. For example, a person's physical attractiveness works on several semiotic levels: cues of biological fitness and fertility relate to the procreative need, which is why good looks are an asset in social life, and the beauty of the human body can be an important element of esthetic experience. The esthetic appreciation of the natural environment is directly linked to the recognition of its protective and nutritional qualities. Sociability too is in an obvious way bound up with cooperation required to maximize the satisfaction of the protective and nutritional needs, just as teleology provides additional reasons for integrating groups around common values and identities. In fact, any instance of communication involves any number of the types of needs as the ultimate causes of behavior. A semiotic analysis should thus consist in identifying both the underlying needs as part of the universal human nature, and their individual and locally specific expressions.

While innate motivations and their cultural manifestations determine the informational content and purpose—the "what" and "why"—of communication, we have yet to consider the "how"—the mechanics of social exchange of information. What physically happens between communicating systems, how information is transmitted from individual to individual, and how communication affects the behavior of the systems involved. Premises 5 and 6 about interacting systems are a convenient starting point to deduce possible types of communication, including direct and indirect communication; contiguous, indexical, iconic, and symbolic communication; as well as the functional components of the communication process, including sender, receiver, information, message, noise, cue, signal, sign, medium, and sensory modality.

2

Types of Communication

In a world of interacting autonomous systems of given reactivities (Figure 1.1), we are dealing, in the simplest case, with two systems, X and Y, as shown in Figure 2.1.

The schema describes a feedback loop rather than a one-way reaction of one system on another, as is sometimes presented in "transmission models" of communication,[1] because any interaction is always a reciprocal, give-and-take process. A typical turn-taking in a conversation is a good example, but so is a political speech or an artistic performance where the performer performs and the audience watches and listens. What may look like a one-way communication is in fact an implicitly reciprocal interaction, because to hold the audience's attention the performer must do what the audience expects. Even the performer's first reaction (a verbal greeting, a facial expression, a gesture, a bodily posture, and so on) is already a response to what the audience is likely to accept. A failure to strike the right tone from the start risks disappointing and "losing" the audience—a stand-up comedian's worst nightmare. Between systems joined by a feedback loop, any system's reaction is both its own output and the other system's input, and any interacting system is simultaneously a sender and a receiver.

As also emphasized earlier (Figure 1.1), any reaction depends simultaneously on two causes, external and internal, on the provided stimulus and the system's power to respond to it as defined by its reactivity (r_x and r_y in Figure 2.1). To start with, it depends on the system's reactivity whether a stimulus is accepted or rejected. Experimental, atonal music will fall on deaf ears with lovers of conventional harmonies, just as abstract painting will not go down well with advocates of realism in visual arts.

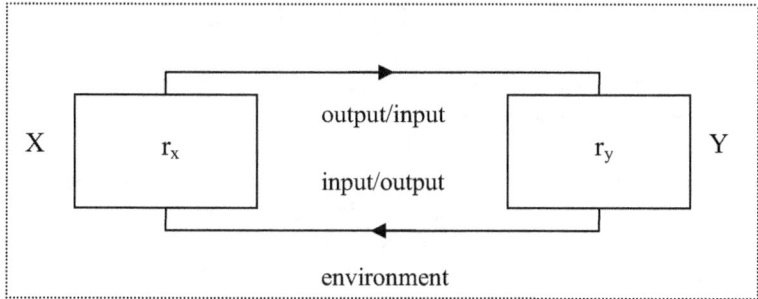

Figure 2.1 Interactions between systems.

The "input," or stimulus, and "output," or reaction, are in turn to be understood as differences in physical states, that is, information, registered or produced by the system in any of its five sensory modalities: visual, auditory, olfactory, gustatory, and tactile. Information is simply a perception of something that is different from something else. A difference between light and darkness is information, as is a difference between one person and another, between one facial expression and another, one speech sound and another, between two gestures, two different smells, and so on. Absence of a stimulus as compared to its presence is also information: the African elephant's alarm call is silence, what Thomas Sebeok calls a "zero stimulus."[2] Defining information in terms of difference and absence in the light of evolutionary theory is the subject of Terrence W. Deacon's illuminating essay.[3] Physical movement also automatically generates information, because a moving object constantly creates differences in the visual field by changing its position in relation to other objects. Mammalian vision appears to be geared toward moving objects rather than static ones, as movement is one of the key behavioral characteristics of the animals, the "quick," and it can be a matter of life and death to pay attention to what moving objects are doing in one's vicinity.[4]

Empirical systems never interact in a vacuum but in an environment, whose properties affect the accuracy of communicated information. A particular sensory modality in an obvious way depends on the right environmental conditions: vision is useless in the dark, and background voices in a public place can drown or distort a conversation. Accidental environmental effects that are not part of communication are referred to as *noise*, such as grain in traditional photographs or pixels in low-resolution digital images, crackling in a telephone line, or "snow" on a television screen.[5] Without interfering noise information is transmitted between systems accurately, in the sense that the difference between physical states in the sender corresponds with the difference in the physical states in the receiver. In daylight navy-blue trousers look navy-blue but in electric light they may look black. Frequent background acoustic interferences during conversation probably explain the need for linguistic redundancy, that is, the repetitiveness and predictability of casual speech (as in saying "hello" to a friend). Redundancy is a safeguard against instability in communication generated by noise: it is estimated that any English utterance is between two to four times longer than it should be for its information content.[6]

Contiguous Communication

An exchange of information between systems remaining within each other's natural sensory range and sharing the same space and time, as in locking horns, sitting together in a car, exchanging glances, talking face to face, grooming or shaking hands will be called direct, or *contiguous* communication. Contiguity is the most common form of communication, relying solely on unaided and unmediated sensory apparatus. For most non-human animals contiguity is the predominant form of communication, both within and across the species, as in mating and predation, respectively. Among humans, contiguous interactions exist both in and of themselves and as a precondition for indirect interactions involving displaced reference, as in indexical, iconic, and symbolic types of communication (of which below). Indexes, icons, and symbols must first be perceived as contiguous stimuli before they can be interpreted for their displaced meaning. A verbal account, spoken or written, must first be heard or read before it can provoke associations about distant persons, places, events, or somebody's abstract ideas. Indirect communication and displaced reference are thus predicated upon contiguous mediation.

As also discussed in Chapter 1, contiguous communication is what homeostatic self-regulation of living systems is primarily about. Plants react adaptively to light, humidity, and temperature that affect them directly, and animals too constantly assess direct inputs from their senses to adapt optimally to the contiguous here-and-now. Obvious and even banal to contemplate as contiguity is, it is fundamentally important in communication because it is *real*, and someone's life may literally depend on it. Indirect forms of communication relying on displaced reference are about *inferred* distant threats and opportunities, whereas contiguity is what confronts living systems face to face, with immediate existential consequences. For systems that do not process information internally, as is the case with inanimate objects, interactions with the environment rely solely on contiguous exchanges of physical states in the form of mechanical forces, radiation, and chemical reactions. For living systems in turn contiguity defines the necessary co-presence of communicators and their environment, before the exchanged information is even registered, processed, and interpreted.

Given the spatio-temporal relations between interacting systems, it is possible to distinguish three sub-categories of contiguous communication. The most common is the one described above, when interacting systems share the same time and space: what can be called *fully contiguous* communication. When interacting systems share the same space but not the simultaneity, we are dealing with *spatially contiguous* communication. This happens when an archaeologist finds an ancient piece of pottery, when a geologist scrutinizes a rock formed millions of years ago, or when we rummage through the contents of an old draw. Spatially contiguous communication, a domain of nostalgia and historical sciences, tantalizes the imagination by its combination of direct physical contact and elusiveness of past meaning. Spatially contiguous communication seems limited to humans, with their meta-cognitive powers of extended working memory, secondary mental representations, and the ability to imagine the past (see Chapter 3). The urge to transcend the present imaginatively underlies the "time machine" and "back-to-the-future" types of fiction, in which wide-eyed scientists, aided by eccentric gadgetry, transport themselves to a chosen location either in the past or the future. The same cognitive disposition explains what anthropologists call contagious magic[7]—a fetishist obsession with relics and memorabilia, in which an object is invested with special emotional or "mystical" significance because of its earlier direct contact with an important person: a child's lock of hair, a saint's bone, an old letter, and auctioneer's lots such as Jimmy Hendrix's guitar or Marilyn Monroe's crystal-emblazoned dress in which she sang "Happy Birthday, Mr. President."

Finally, when interacting systems share the same time but not the spatial proximity, we are dealing with *simultaneously contiguous* communication. Examples include talking over the phone or having a video meeting using telecommunication applications such as Skype or Zoom. Underlying these inventions is a universal social need to transcend the limitations of space and communicate directly with displaced persons, a disposition also found in the fantasy of teleportation, in which magicians "vanish" at will to reappear instantly at some other location. Spiritual mediums also claim to "summon" spirits of the dead from their otherworldly abodes to reconnect them with the living. For all we know, non-human animals do not speculate about locations other than the one in which they find themselves at the moment, nor can they consciously remember the past or imagine the future, and so they have no interest in engaging in communication with anything other than the immediate here-and-now.

Despite today's popularity of digital media, social and public, with their displaced reference, most of the time humans, like other animals, still satisfy their manifold needs by a communication default of fully contiguous interactions with their immediate environment. Notwithstanding the importance attached in media and cultural studies to telecommunication technologies such as television, the internet, radio, social media, as well as visual arts and traditional print culture, the bulk of human communication still occurs through direct, spontaneous, and unmediated social interactions. No matter how much time we spend daily switching through TV channels and surfing the net, we still enjoy a face-to-face chat and gossip with family and friends, and we love social gatherings in public spaces. One of the most important things that the forced isolation and social distancing during the Corona virus pandemic of 2020/21 have reminded us of is how vital to our mental well-being and social cohesion direct multi-sensory human contact is, and how frustrating imposed reduction of contiguity can be.

The innate need of fully contiguous communication explains why given the choice between watching a sports event on television in the comfort of one's living room, and taking the trouble and expense to join a tightly packed crowd in the stadium, many people still prefer the latter. Direct experience, with its tactile and olfactory sensations on top of the audio-visual ones, is fuller and more exciting, and certainly more real, than the mediated event, with its spatio-temporal displacement and the resulting partial sensory and cognitive alienation. Sensory-rich contiguity often beats the sensory deprivation of indirect communication. A soccer fan in the stadium watches the match from a distance and from one point of view only, while Sky Sports channels offer a multi-camera, dramatically edited spectacle, alternating between wide, medium, and close shots of otherwise unseen details, with replays in slow motion and freeze frames to prolong the visual excitement, accompanied by live commentaries from sports experts—all while sitting on one's sofa sipping beer. Still, for a fan in the stadium the contiguous event is more tangible and real than a displaced, mediated representation. It is like the difference between trekking the countryside breathing its air while feeling the earth under one's feet and contemplating landscape photographs or nature documentaries. This is also why Stephen Dedalus, the young artist from James Joyce's *Ulysses*, must convince himself of the "ineluctable modality of the visible," that is, of the undeniable solidity of what we see, to curb his tendency to over-intellectualize the world.[8] Much of life still revolves around live, contiguous experiences that appeal directly to the eye, ear, nose, and touch, whether in spontaneous social interactions or organized events such as fairs, festivals, political rallies, religious ceremonies, parades, theatrical performances, and concerts.

The evolutionary default of direct experience explains why even communication technologies continue to rely on contiguity. In 1947 the invention of the Polaroid camera created a sensation of producing photo prints within seconds of taking the picture, almost simultaneously with the photographed event.[9] For most of its history photography was basically a technology of recording visual experience to be contemplated a considerable time *after* the event—temporal displacement was an inherent property of the medium. But contiguity is now back, because the desire for it has never gone away. Today's smartphones not only display instantly images and videos but enable their users to share them remotely within seconds. Digital telecommunication devices both for personal use, such as the telephone or video call, and for public consumption, such as live television, offer simultaneous, "telepathic" communication in defiance of physical distance.

The historic popularity of television ("seeing at a distance") has everything to do with the desire to extend by technology the contiguous experience normally limited to natural spatio-temporal proximity. A cartoon in *Punch* from 1879 shows a mother and father watching on the wall of their English home a simultaneous tennis match in Ceylon in which their daughter was playing. The parents are also able to speak to her over the yet uninvented telephone (Figure 2.2). When television was first demonstrated to the public by John Logie Baird in London in 1926, its main thrill, despite poor picture quality and small screen compared with the cinema, was precisely the live transmission, which enabled viewers to witness events occurring far away at the time of broadcast.[10] Unlike cinema, a medium more suitable for fictional narratives

Figure 2.2 "Edison's Telephonoscope (Transmits Light as well as Sound)." Cartoon by George Du Maurier in *Punch* (1879).

or documenting spatio-temporally displaced events, television was from the start perceived first of all as a visual extension of live radio broadcasts, that is, showing images of real events at the time of their occurrence. Actuality and topicality thus became the defining features of early television, and to a large extent have remained so until today, as evidenced by the popularity of round-the-clock live TV news channels.

Indexical Communication

The media of simultaneous communication such as the telephone, radio, and television have thus enabled people to transcend the physical limitations of space when pooling knowledge from across wide distances. Technologically extended contiguity is not an evolutionary trait, but it nonetheless has obvious adaptive advantages as human groups scaled up and expanded territorially. To relay vital information in an emergency across longer distances can be a matter of life or death, as in calling an ambulance or the police, or when coordinating military or rescue operations with the help of the radar or satellite. Fundamental as full contiguity is as the default of human interactions, to be able to draw on instant support and expertise from beyond the immediate here-and-now confers an advantage, like the fact, pointed out in Chapter 1, that innate knowledge and behavioral predispositions are more adaptive than a mind that is blank at birth.

Which would mean that transcending not only the limitations of space but also of time when availing of collective knowledge would confer an even greater advantage. The knowledge contained in the genome already offers condensed phylogenetic experience accumulated over vast stretches of evolutionary time. On top of that, the ability to identify causes and effects in the world in real time should add flexibility to rigid and largely automatic innate responses. Accordingly, a physical change caused by a system in the environment will be called an *index* of that system. In C. S. Peirce's classic formulation an index "is a stimulus which refers to the Object that it denotes by virtue of being really affected by that Object," where the somewhat vague "really affected" corresponds to my stronger requirement that an index be *physically caused* by the object. Peirce also rightly points out that the origin of indexes depends "upon association by contiguity," whereby an index testifies to the objective existence of the object, whether it is perceived or not.[11] A crater in the ground caused by an exploded bomb is an index of that bomb, and loud music seeping through the ceiling is an index of a stereo system located in the apartment above. A footprint, handwriting, recorded voice, a photograph, and a video clip are indexes of persons represented by these records. In other words, as a physical extension or trace an index is a partial but truthful representation of an object, which is why forensic investigations rely more on objective indexical (material) evidence than on subjective verbal statements or accusations. Interacting with indexes means interacting indirectly with the objects that caused them, and so indexical communication, unlike fully contiguous communication, is already mediated and referential.

As with contiguous communication, it is possible to distinguish three sub-categories of indexical communication. When systems interact by means of an index while remaining within the same proximate time and space, we are dealing with *contiguously indexical* communication. The mercury in a barometer is an index of current atmospheric pressure which causes the mercury to expand or contract. During a face-to-face conversation we are technically communicating through voice as a contiguous index. This indexical mediation becomes apparent when the conversation takes place in the dark, and we are *inferring* someone's presence from the voice. In fact, contiguous communication in any sensory modality is always indirect and indexical, because it relies on internal representations of external objects communicated via a sensory system. Contiguously indexical communication is indeed often indistinguishable from fully contiguous communication, although it still makes practical sense to invoke indexicality when contiguous interaction does not provide full information of the situation, and the missing bits have to be inferred from clues. A smoke rising above the trees indicates a fire blazing underneath, and a shadow on the ground betrays the presence of a person hiding behind the corner of a house (Figure 2.3).

For evolutionary reasons contiguous indexes also provoke instinctive, goose bumpy sensations combined with anxious inferences about the identity and possible intentions of their proximate but hidden human or animal referents. We fearfully become aware of someone's presence in the dark by the sound of their breathing or the shuffling of the feet, and we are making a reasonable deduction that a cracking sound of a broken twig in the forest indicates an approaching large animal or a human. Probably the main difference between fully contiguous and indexically contiguous stimuli is that the latter tend to stimulate the imagination and emotions more than the former: in fully contiguous communication what we see is what we get, so there is little else left to the imagination, whereas a contiguous index is tantalizing because of its invisible but co-present source. Contiguous experience is self-referential and therefore easier to interpret than indexical communication, which relies on hidden or absent referents still to be inferred from traces. A visible figure of a human casting a shadow forms a perceptual whole in which the indexical shadow can be ignored, all attention being

Figure 2.3 A cast shadow as a contiguous index betraying a presence of an invisible person.

focused on the person as the main subject. We may not be missing a shadow of a person standing in front of us, but we are certainly missing a person if all we see is a human-like shadow emerging from behind a tree, a rock, or a house (Figure 2.3).

When communicating systems share the same time but not the spatial proximity, we are dealing with *simultaneous indexical* communication, which again is technically not unlike simultaneous contiguous communication. In a telephone conversation the voice is an index of a far-away caller, just as in a video call a moving image on the LCD screen provides a simultaneous visual index. When interacting systems share proximity but not the simultaneity, we are dealing with *spatially indexical* communication, probably the most important form of indexicality because it is most distinct from fully contiguous communication. Examples include footprints, seal impressions, death masks, photographs, voice recordings (whether on wax cylinders, vinyl records, magnetic tapes, compact disks, or computer audio files), handwriting, historical documents, documentary films, and so on. Unlike contiguous indexes, spatial indexes do not normally provoke anxious or panicky feelings, but rather relaxed curiosity due to the safe temporal distance between the index and its cause. It is the difference between watching a war documentary and experiencing war at first hand, or enjoying a nature film and confronting a large feline face to face in the African savannah. The experience of watching real animals safely from behind a barrier in nature parks or in the Zoo lies somewhere in between: more thrilling than contemplating spatial indexical images in nature films, and less exciting (thankfully) than the full contiguity of facing a large animal in the wild.

Indexicality and Sensory Modalities

The information obtained by sensory perception is inherently indexical, as stimuli are traces of physical features of the outside world.[12] Reliance on sensory modalities varies from species to species depending on the environmental niche, lifestyle, and genetic makeup. For example, most animals are poorer than humans at reading visual indexes: chimpanzees, intelligent as they are, are unable to notice, let alone interpret, spatial indexes such as animal tracks in the ground. Vervet monkeys observed in Kenya's Amboseli National Park were found unresponsive to a number of cues of ecologically relevant events: they ignored the presence of a dead antelope hanging in a tree (an unmistakable index of a recent leopard kill, and hence of leopard presence). They also ignored fresh python tracks in sandy soil, and would only react with panic when coming face to face with the snake itself.[13] Other animal species negotiate their space and social life by interpreting pheromonal (olfactory) cues as indexes of proximity of other animals and of their physiological and emotive states. Some fish use electrical signaling for orientation and in contiguous communication to identify species, sex, and age of a partner, and to gauge their motivational state such as presence or absence of aggression or willingness to mate.[14]

In humans, the traditional five senses—vision, audition, olfaction, taste, and touch—have attracted considerable interest from theologians of old and psychologists of today, who saw them (correctly) as the main channels through which humans relate, in a necessarily restricted way, to the outside world.[15] Interestingly, in medieval homiletic writing the order of the senses, those "five gates of the soul," was invariably "the eye, the eere, the nose, the tonge, and the hande," in recognition of the decreasing distance from which information about the external world can be gleaned by a sense.[16] The anthropologist Edward T. Hall has similarly divided the senses into two categories: the distance receptors (vision, hearing, smell) and the immediate receptors (taste and touch). There is also a general relationship between the evolutionary age of the receptor and the amount and quality of information it conveys to the central nervous system. Thus the tactile sense (the most proximate) is as old as life itself, while sight (the most distant sense) was the last and most specialized sense to be developed in humans: vision became more important with upright posture resulting from bipedalism achieved by early hominids, with its possibility of scanning the area from a height at a great distance.[17]

Vision

As the most efficient sense in humans, vision helps obtain crucial knowledge about the physical properties of objects in the environment, including shape and texture, brightness and color, size, distance, movement, and spatial distribution. The unaided eye registers an extraordinary amount of information within a hundred-meter radius and is still efficient for human interaction at a mile. The cosmic environment, at a practically unlimited distance from the Earth, is only accessible to the human mind through the eyes. Visual information also tends to be less ambiguous than for example auditory information: the optic nerve contains roughly eighteen times as many neurons as the cochlear (ear) nerve, so we assume that it transmits at least that much more information. Notwithstanding its relative efficiency, human vision offers a selective picture of the part of the world through a tiny segment of the electromagnetic spectrum.[18] The visible light covers the electromagnetic wavelengths ranging from 10^4m (10km, as in long radio waves) to less than 10^{-14}m (quadrillionth of a meter, as in gamma and cosmic rays). Within this range humans perceive light within the middle band of 400 to 700 nanometers (1 nanometer = 1 billionth of a meter).[19] Other animals live in a different visual world, oblivious to part of the human visible spectrum, but sensitive to some wavelength outside it. Below 400 nanometers, butterflies for example find flowers and sources of nectar by patterns of ultraviolet rays reflected off the petals. Where humans see a plain yellow or white blossom, butterflies see spots and concentric circles in light and dark.[20]

In addition to gathering information from a longer distance than any other sense, visual stimuli are highly variable as to shapes and colors, possessing also, as Thomas A. Sebeok notes, a high frequency of change: unlike smell for example, visual signals can be rapidly switched on and off, allowing for fine discrimination within a short time.[21] This is why the visual channel, with the ever-changing facial expressions, gestures, and bodily postures, rather than smells, touch, or even sounds, dominates in interpersonal communication. Writing too derives its communicative efficiency from its power to produce sequences of discrete visual differences at comparatively high frequency. Sight is thus the main modality of cultural transmission of information, also because visible natural objects and cultural artifacts are more durable than the volatile and ephemeral speech, allowing for continuity and standardization of knowledge communicated through tools, costume, sculpture, painting, architecture, writing, photography, film, and television.

A particularly important feature of visual perception is the ability to detect movement in the immediate surroundings. Most animals are mobile relative to plants and inanimate objects, and they move about in an environment containing other moving objects, both those to pursue as prey and those to run away from. For all animal species information about movement—its location, direction, and speed—is essential for survival. In the human eye the edge of the retina is sensitive only to movement, so that when the movement stops the object becomes invisible. The peripheral perception of movement functions as an early-warning system, crucial to detect potential predators or enemies sneaking up on us from behind and from the side. The perception of movement on the edge of the retina initiates a reflex which rotates the eye and the head to shift the moving object into central vision, neurally better equipped to identify and examine the object more closely.[22] Our innate alertness to moving objects has also been exploited in our highly technological age by mobile visual advertising, film, television, and computer games—always guaranteed to attract attention, quite independently of their dramatic or factual content, by the sheer amount of concentrated movement flashing across the screen.

Other types of visual stimuli likely to provoke spontaneous curiosity and alertness include daylight (a prerequisite for sight to work at all); the blue color of the sky with patches of clouds signaling congenial weather with a possibility of short, refreshing showers; fresh greenness of vegetation promising availability of food and shelter; the color pink (associated with healthy infant skin); round shapes safe to handle; unthreatening, medium-sized (relative to the human body) objects; and vertical and horizontal lines indicating gravitational balance. On the other hand, visual indexes provoking apprehension and withdrawal will include darkness (related to increased danger from nocturnal predators); deep grey color of the sky accompanying incessant rains; greenless, barren landscapes providing no food or possibility of shelter; dark green as the color of putrefying, infectious organic matter; the color red often signaling spilled blood and therefore danger; sharp edges likely to cause cuts when handled; very small or very large objects difficult or impossible to handle and control; and skewed lines indicating objects off balance, likely to fall and cause one injury.

Audition

Vision may be eighteen time more efficient in processing information than audition, but it works only during daytime. Hearing, on the other hand, is alert round the clock for acoustic indexes of objects and their position relative to us. It is also vital for social communication, and the use of sounds pervades the life of many birds and mammals as a way of signaling recognition and warning. Audition is also the second most efficient sense in humans, able to pick up stimuli from up to several hundred meters away, as well as such loud natural sounds as the thunder from a few kilometers away. Acoustic signals can also be culturally amplified: from tom-toms of tribal Africa to electronic high-volume amps and speakers at rock concerts. The human auditory range is 20 to 20,000 Hz (cycles of air compression per second). Above that range flying bats broadcast ultrasonic pulses into the night air and listen for echoes to locate moths. The function of echolocation, an adaptation to living in dark caves, is to provide the bat with information about prey type, distance, velocity, and spatial location—information that most species, including humans, gather by sight.[23]

For humans audition has another important practical advantage over visual communication: using vocal sounds frees hands and body to do other work while the person is talking. To get the news about the world while preparing food in the kitchen we tend to listen to the radio rather than watch TV. Nor is it necessary to maintain eye contact during conversation, which means that one can communicate just as well in the dark (important in our ancestral environment of equatorial Africa, where it is dark for twelve hours a day—elsewhere it is dark for six months in the year).[24] Hearing is therefore an important complementation to visual communication: the latter is also disadvantaged by the requirement of unobstructed spaces and clear air, whereas acoustic stimuli can travel round physical obstacles and can be heard in conditions of limited visibility such as fog or smoke.[25] Sounds are more reliable therefore as contiguous indexes of hidden or only partly visible objects. Acoustic stimuli also reveal a high frequency of change, similar to visual signals, and their transient character makes accurate timing possible, the property exploited in spoken language and music.

As with some categories of visual stimuli, we appear to be born with ready-made emotive responses to certain adaptively significant sounds, which later shape our auditory communication and social life. It was discovered for example that three minutes after birth infants instinctively move their eyes in the direction of sources of sounds, which suggests that there exists an innate co-ordination between auditory space and visual space. Infants can also distinguish between noise and tone. By four months the infant prefers harmonious sounds, sometimes reacting to out-of-tune notes with facial expression of disgust.[26] High-pitched, piercing sounds can likewise reach a physiologically determined pain threshold, as can loud noise produced at a rock concert, by the take-off of a jet plane, or a motorbike with its muffler removed (bless them). Low, roaring sounds, such as those produced by large, and therefore potentially dangerous animals, as well as loud thundering noises of the coming storm, earthquake, landslide, or avalanche will also provoke instinctive fear and panic.

Olfaction

Of the five human sensory channels two are referred to as chemical, namely smell and the related sense of taste, in contrast to vision, hearing, and touch, which are based on electromagnetic waves, air waves, and mechanical forces, respectively. Over 99 percent of all living species rely on chemical senses to find their way through their environment. In contrast, human beings, along with monkeys, apes, and birds, are among the rare life forms that are primarily audio-visual, and correspondingly weak in taste and smell.[27] The olfactory and gustatory senses use chemoreceptors, which bind internal neural stimuli with particular chemicals in the environment, especially those related to food substances. The sensations of taste and smell in association with food intake influence the flow of digestive juices and affect appetite. Furthermore, stimulation of taste and smell receptors induces pleasurable or objectionable sensations, and signals the presence of something to seek (a nutritionally useful, good-tasting food) or to avoid (a potentially toxic, foul-tasting substance). On the other hand, the odor preference, especially in relation to food, is determined by an organism's particular nutritious requirements. Thus for example the odor of carrion is repulsive to many animals, including humans, but is attractive to scavengers. In either case the chemical senses provide an adaptively important "quality control" for substances available for ingestion.[28]

In lower animals the sense of smell is also used in situations where vision is involved in humans: to find direction, to mark territory, to seek prey or to avoid predators, in sexual attraction to a mate, and of course to find food. Salmon famously use their highly developed olfactory sense (enhanced in water) to return across thousands of miles of ocean to the stream where they were spawned. The blind new-born kitten, barely able to crawl on its stomach, survives using smell alone, learning in less than one day to crawl short distances to the mother's belly with its preferred nipple.[29]

Once emitted, odors are likely to persist and can thus convey messages after the departure of its source from the site. Unlike acoustic stimuli, used mostly in contiguous communication, smells can therefore function as spatial indexes, similarly to visual traces. For example, reindeer, approaching a spot where one of their species has recently been frightened, will flee when they smell the scent excreted from the hoof glands of the frightened deer.[30] Humans too will infer the past presence of a person from a whiff of perfume (vide the Victorian "perfumed letter" indicating a female sender) or cigarette smoke left behind in the room, although for evolutionary reasons human sense of smell is not as acute as in other animals. Unable to register many of the olfactory indexes easily detected by other mammals, the strong visual sense and memory make humans comparatively better at reading spatial visual indexes such as footprints (or "a cigarette that bears a lipstick's traces" from Benny Goodman's song).

However limited its use compared with visual or auditory stimuli, smell too plays a role in human interactions conducted within the olfactory zone. Indeed, odor is one of the earliest and most basic methods of communication: it helps to differentiate individuals and to identify their emotional states by means of pheromones secreted by specialized glands and exchanged, in mammals mainly through sweat, among members of the same species. Pheromones have been identified as a sexual attractor among many insects and mammalian species. Humans too can identify sex and become sexually aroused using only the olfactory information in perspiration.[31] In a famous letter Napoleon Bonaparte once begged his Josephine not to bathe for two weeks before they met, so that he could enjoy all her natural aromas.[32] Studies also show that subjects could identify the gender of the wearers of undershirts worn by males and females for twenty-four hours, without washing or using any deodorants or perfume. It was also observed that subjects could discriminate males from females with over 80 percent accuracy by smelling the person's hand. Interestingly, women outperformed men in this task.[33]

Perfumes too contain pheromones derived from plants and male animals. Women generally have a much keener sensitivity to smell than men do, and, as Nancy Etcoff suggests, women use perfumes less as a way to lure men than to please themselves and put themselves in a calm state of mind.[34] Like other senses, the olfactory domain is not without its esthetic potential: the decadent French aristocrat des Esseintes from Joris-Karl Huysmans' novel *À Rebour* (1884) explores the world of perfumes to excite his jaded senses:

> For years now he had been an expert in the science of perfumes; he maintained that the sense of smell could procure pleasures equal to those obtained through sight or hearing, each of the senses being capable, by virtue of a natural aptitude supplemented by an erudite education, of perceiving new impressions, magnifying these tenfold, and co-ordinating them to compose the whole that constitutes a work of art. After all, he argued, it was no more abnormal to have an art that consisted of picking out odorous fluids than it was to have other arts based on a selection of sound waves or the impact of variously coloured rays on the retina of the eye.[35]

The importance of olfaction in interpersonal communication also varies from culture to culture. As Edward T. Hall has observed, Americans and North Europeans have historically had a less developed cultural use of the olfactory apparatus than the Mediterranean or Middle Easter people. It has been common in some Arab countries to consistently breathe on people during a conversation, and to infer a person's psychological disposition from the way they smell. According to Hall, in the Middle East to smell one's friend is both nice and desirable, and to deny a friend one's breath is to act ashamed. Far from eliminating or neutralizing personal odors people in Arab countries stay within each other's olfactory zone during conversation as a means of keeping tab on changes in emotions. On the other hand, in European and American countries, especially in urban, middle-class environments, people have reduced olfaction as a communication channel, either by neutralizing natural smell altogether or by replacing it with synthetic odors of perfumes, aftershave, and deodorants.[36]

Taste

The chemical senses of smell and taste have evolved primarily to serve the nutritional need. Smell is the distant receptor of food, while taste gives the food the ultimate seal of approval or disapproval (disgust at tainted or toxic substance) upon direct contact. Physiologists distinguish between four basic, or primary, tastes: sweet, sour, bitter, and salty, occurring in different combinations and intensities in different nutrients. Sweet taste, indicative of highly required sugar content, is usually found in substances of nutritional value. On the other hand, sour (acid) taste is often a warning of toxins and bacterial decomposition, while bitterness may signal the presence of noxious or toxic alkaloids such as strychnine, quinine, nicotine, or cocaine. Instinctive aversion to acidity and bitterness serves therefore as natural defenses against many plant and animal species, which repel predators by secreting irritating or toxic chemicals, such as the spray of a whip scorpion for example, which contains 84 percent of acetic acid.[37] Salt, on the other hand, plays a unique role in the regulation of bodily fluids, which means that a certain amount of salt in the blood is necessary for the healthy functioning of the organism. It is probable that gustatory sensitivity to salt also evolved as a warning against hypersalinity, that is, the ingestion of intolerably high, pernicious concentrations of salt. For these reasons many animals find sweet and moderately salty solutions appealing, and bitter and sour ones aversive. Human infants one to three days of age can discriminate a sucrose solution from plain water, showing a distinct preference for the former. New-born infants also show an unlearned aversion to bitter and sour substances, responding to each with a distinctive facial expression they will use for the rest of their lives.[38]

Touch

Finally the sense of touch, located on the skin, plays a paramount role in contiguous communication, by providing the organism with information about the nature of surfaces and objects that directly contact it. We perceive objects by touching and being touched, we feel warmth and coldness, and we experience pain. We also feel complex "blended" tactile sensations such as oiliness, stickiness, wetness, tickle, roughness, smoothness, itch, vibration, and so on. When handling or grasping an object we also recognize its three-dimensional shape, its solidity and weight. In short, the world of tactile, direct-contact sensations is rich and versatile, complementing in an important way the inputs from the main channels of distant sensations: vision, hearing, and smell. Edward T. Hall suggests that sculpture is best experienced when it is touched as well as viewed.[39] Also, just as sight is the most efficient spatial discriminator of things and events in the outside world, and audition the best discriminator of temporal relations, so the sense of touch, according to the psychologist Frank A. Geldard, stands midway between the two major senses in being endowed with the properties of both hearing and sight. Thus touch is better than vision at temporal discriminations, and better than audition at spatial discriminations, but it is also spatially inferior to vision and temporally inferior to audition. Tactile communication also works in the absence of both vision and hearing, in darkness and silence, and can therefore provide warnings of proximate threatening events outside the visual and auditory fields.[40]

Physiologically, cutaneous (tactile) information is registered by direct mechanical stimulation of the body's surface or by thermal stimulation from a radiant source. The skin sense differs from other senses in that its receptors are not restricted to a specialized, localized sensory structure, like the retina for vision or the cochlea for hearing. Instead, its sensory surface covers nearly the entire body, and it serves many purposes, especially the protective ones, besides mediating cutaneous sensations. Without the sense of touch we would lose pressure, thermal, and pain sensations, so crucial to the physical protection of the body. In fact, without the cutaneous sense we would not be able to move about at all, as constant feedback from touch is necessary for using limbs and muscles in all motor activities including walking, eating, and speaking.[41]

Apart from fulfilling a protective function, touch is an important channel of proximate social communication, conveying intimate psychological and emotional states that reflect the ever-changing dynamics in the structure and hierarchy of the group. All primates possess a highly developed system of tactile communication, involving grooming, preening, stroking, nudging, as well as aggressive, copulatory, and suckling behavior. Among humans many tactile expressions, found in reciprocal stroking, embracing, cuddling, and hand touching appear to be universal. In fact, close, intimate contacts with another body form a multi-sensory experience involving visual stimuli, the smell of the breath and perspiration, and tactile sensations of bodily heat, touch, and pressure—all the ingredients of such close social interactions as embracing, hugging, love-making, wrestling, comforting, and protecting.[42]

Iconic Communication

Indexicality is still tied to direct, animal-like, real-time physical interactions with the proximate environment. As pointed out above, indexical communication and contiguous communication are often one and the same thing, because perceptions in all sensory modalities are indexes of objects in the outside world. Both types of communication are mostly limited to the immediate space and time, and even spatial indexes are restricted to objects that leave behind physical traces, visual or olfactory. But as human groups grew larger and people had to keep up with more knowledge from across wider spatial and temporal domains, more effective indirect types of communication had to be invented. One way to transcend the limitations of indexicality is to free the stimulus from its physical dependence on the object. The stimulus can still be related to the object, but not necessarily through physical causality but, for example, through cognitive associations based on perceived similarity between stimulus and object. A stimulus which only subjectively resembles an object, but with which it has otherwise no objective causal relationship, will be called an *icon* of that object, and interacting by means of icons will be referred to as *iconic* communication. In other words, icons rely on mental *representations* of objects rather than on the objects' physical traces.

Iconicity can be regarded as the first step toward meta-cognition, that is, the ability to have associations about associations, of which more in Chapter 3. If indexical communication is still limited to inferences from perception, iconicity is more wide-ranging because it relies on the interpretations of perception based on similarity and comparisons with other perceptions. For example, a realistically painted portrait bears a resemblance, formed in the artist's and viewers' minds, to the sitter, despite not being caused by or physically connected to the sitter in any way. A road sign showing three curved arrows in a circle resembles but is not caused by a roundabout near it (Figure 2.4). In auditory modality, Antonio Vivaldi's Concerto No. 1 *La primavera* contains musical imitations of birdsong and a spring storm. The word "splash" conveys onomatopoeically the sound made by a heavy object hitting the surface of the water. Natural perfumes contain indexical traces of fragrant plants, while synthetic perfumes mimic the fragrant compounds found in flowers and other plants. Similarity, analogy, and imitation rather than physical causality are the essence of iconic thinking and communication.

Figure 2.4 Contiguous iconic communication: A "roundabout" road sign.

As with contiguous and indexical communication, it is possible to distinguish three sub-categories of iconic communication. When an icon shares the same spatio-temporal context as the thing it is referring to, we are dealing with *contiguous iconic* communication. Examples include a "roundabout" road sign placed at the roundabout itself (Figure 2.4), or when circling an index finger at one's temple is meant to imply that a person standing near us is confused or "crazy." When an icon shares the same time but not the spatial proximity with the thing it is referring to, we are dealing with *simultaneous iconic* communication, as in watching a live TV broadcast, in which the images on the screen resemble the actual event. Finally, when an icon is neither proximate nor simultaneous with the thing it is referring to, we are dealing with *displaced iconic* communication, probably the most important form of iconicity because most distinct from contiguous communication. History of figurative art is dealing mainly with iconic images of spatio-temporally displaced persons, objects, and places.

Because of their physical detachment from their referents, icons provoke less powerful emotions than indexes with their real, causal links with existentially important objects and events. Detached from direct experience, iconic communication tends to be more "cerebral" and meta-cognitive. Associating things through similarity leads to categorization, when non-identical objects are treated as equivalent on the basis of elements they have in common. Categorization can thus be generalized into a *concept*, in which otherwise different objects are mentally related through shared properties.[43] For example, the concept of a "book" combines different objects united by the recognition of common characteristics such as rectangular sheets of paper in a ream, covered with text and glued or sewn together along one side and bound in covers, of the size and weight that make them easy for people to lift, hold, and carry. A non-material concept of "friendship" denotes various psychological properties such as companionship, trust, reliability, willingness to help, and so on. Concepts thus understood are enabled by an innate tendency to relate like to like, in humans also enhanced by conscious reflection and learning. Other animals too instinctively associate objects by a sufficient degree of similarity. For instance, seagulls react to the eggs they lay following a generalized concept of an egg; if an egg is removed by an experimenter from the sea gull's nest and put nearby, the gull will retrieve it. It will also retrieve other round objects—pebbles or potatoes, if they are sufficiently close in shape and touch to the egg—but it will leave angular and soft shapes untouched.[44]

Genetically programmed iconicity plays a pivotal role in plant and animal mimicry and other forms of deception involving smell, taste, color, shape, sound, and behavior. Stick insects fool their predators by evolving body shapes that make them indistinguishable from the inedible twigs and branches that surround them. The angler fish attracts its prey by means of a lure in the form of a worm-like piece of flesh dangling at the end of a long "fishing rod" extended from the top of the head. The angler dances its bait in front of any little fish that comes near, lures it closer to its concealed mouth, then opens it and sucks the victim in. Similarly, human anglers exploit the little fishes' generalized concept of the "worm" by luring them to dummies of worms attached to the fishing line.[45] The co-evolutionary struggle between deceiver and deceived exploits the innate perceptual generalizations and the resulting vulnerabilities when an organism mistakes an imitation for the real thing. Harmless and edible species can also mimic a harmful and inedible species to avoid being eaten. For instance, some unusually brightly colored butterflies taste nasty, and birds learn to avoid them by their "warning" marks. Then other species of butterfly that do not taste nasty to birds have also evolved similar marks to "warn" potential predators.[46] Deceptive behavior apart, displaced iconicity and iconic properties of signals are ubiquitous in animal communication. For example, the chemical warning signals used by some ants have an iconic quality: the greater the danger the longer and stronger the dose of the pheromone released to the colony.[47] A famous example of visual displaced iconicity used by insects is the dance language of honeybees, which inform each other about the availability of food in their vicinity by correlating the number of turns and speed of their waggle dance with information about the food's location, direction, and distance from the hive.[48]

In animals the perception of resemblance between different objects and events is genetically determined and automatic, but its ubiquity in human behavior also suggests a strong innate motivation combined with learning and experience, which transform animal phenotypic mimicry and instinctive deception into conscious imitation. In human cultures imitation is one of the most basic ways of learning new things. It requires a human-type consciousness and memory which, by the way, the other apes appear to lack. The familiar verb "to ape," used to describe mindless copying, is in fact misleading, because apes are not really good at imitating behavior: humans are much better at aping than the apes. According to Steven Mithen even chimpanzees, our nearest animal cousins, cannot learn by imitation from one another, and prefer to do it the harder way, by trial and error.[49] Unable to imitate objects and actions, the apes are also incapable of producing pictorial representations, even with all the encouragement from psychologists.[50] Conscious imitation, in contrast to mimicry acquired through natural selection, appears limited to humans, for whom it is an important cognitive pre-linguistic adaptation and a prerequisite to culture understood as an acquisition of non-genetic knowledge and skills quickly and faithfully.[51] As will also be discussed in Chapters 4 and 5, human imitative thinking and behavior are a cognitive foundation of second-order representations of visual arts, metaphoric language, and storytelling.

Symbolic Communication

Just as associating objects and events through similarity offers a more efficient form of communication than one limited to physical traces of objects, so it is possible to imagine an even more detached form of indirect communication, in which a stimulus bears neither causal nor perceptual relation to its referent. In an indexical medium of photography, for example, a represented object has physically if inadvertently caused itself to be imprinted in the image, while in an iconic medium of painting an artist creates a visual analogy of an object. In both cases the properties of the object constrain the form of the sign, thus reducing the frequency of signal change and in consequence communicative efficiency, as less information is exchanged in an amount of time. A form of communication freed from these constraints, and therefore more efficient, would require signals that are related to objects only through arbitrary mental associations. As we know, human verbal language is the most spectacular example of such a system of communication, where a vocal signal has, as a rule, hardly any physical or formal relationship with what it refers to. An object's name is not an icon, still less is it a physical part of or a trace of the object. A photographed or painted rose does look like a rose, and the Eau Rose perfume offers an imitation of a rich rose scent, but "What's in a name? That which we call a rose/By any other word would smell as sweet."[52] On the one hand Shakespeare's Juliet objects to her lover's family name of Montague, hateful to her family of Capulet, but on the other hand she rationally points to an arbitrary nature of words and names, hoping that the negative stigma attached in her family to the Montagues will not affect her own feelings toward Romeo.

Communication based on arbitrary associations between stimuli and their referents is known as *symbolic*. The symbolic signs of language refer to things following a conventional, language-specific association between a vocal sound (or a written character) and its mental equivalent, as in Saussure's classic definition of the linguistic sign, which "exists only through the associating of the signifier [the form of the sign] with the signified [the concept the sign refers to]."[53] Earlier C. S. Peirce defined symbol as "a sign which refers to the Object that it denotes by virtue of a law, usually an association of general ideas, which operates to cause the Symbol to be interpreted as referring to that Object."[54] In Peirce's definition the "law" corresponds to social convention, a specifically human capacity to establish and socialize an arbitrary, perceptually unmotivated displaced mental connection between sign and its meaning. Thus understood arbitrariness became the cornerstone of structural linguistics with its insistence on the social and cultural origin of language as the source of its arbitrariness.[55]

A more contentious claim made by structural linguistics is that meaning, while generated neither by signs themselves nor even by the corresponding mental concepts, is solely a product of *relations* between signs, that is, of differences between signs forming a linguistic system.[56] This unfounded assertion implies that linguistic meaning has nothing to do with the speakers' evolved cognitive abilities or with the properties of the outside world, but is determined simply by the signs' opposition to other signs. What the critic Raymond Tallis calls structural linguistics' "denial of the pre-linguistic reality of the signified" is probably the most controversial aspect of the theory: the notion that linguistic meaning has no relation to the world "out there," or to human cognition and experience, much of which for evolutionary reasons predates language, but is purely relational.[57]

First of all, the predominance of arbitrariness in language does not imply exclusiveness. Language is not a closed semantic system, related neither to the extra-linguistic reality nor to the evolved human mind with its innate cognitive modules. Despite its influence in academia, the structuralist claim remains a non-sequitur: as the linguist Earl R. Anderson points out, the fact that all linguistic signs have arbitrary features does not mean that language does not contain nonarbitrary features. For Anderson linguistic structuralism was incomplete from the start because it ignored or downplayed the important and ever-present expressive dimension of language reflected in its indexical and iconic features, where meaning is affected and colored both by the speakers' physiological and emotive reactions and by a wide range of imitative associations on the levels of phonology, morphology, and syntax.[58] In fact, all media, language included, are polysemiotic, beginning with the default of contiguity and sensory indexicality, with the added dimensions of iconicity and symbolism, as further discussed in Chapter 5.

3

Information and Levels of Meaning

To recapitulate: premise 5 in the Introduction defines interactions between systems in terms of exchanges of information; the latter understood as differences between physical states. Chapter 2 describes how information is communicated between interacting systems, whether directly as in contiguous communication, or indirectly by means of indexes, icons, and symbols, each offering a different form of connection between the stimulus and its meaning: physical, imitative, and arbitrary, respectively. Transmission of information between systems is a physical prerequisite of communication, whose ultimate purpose is meaning, that is, effect produced by information on interacting systems. This again follows from another premise of systemic semiotics, namely, that a system's reaction (Figure 1.1), here the production of meaning, has always two causes: external, in the form of the informational input, and internal, based on the system's power to interpret that input. Chapter 1 describes in some detail the cognitive architecture involved in transforming environmental inputs into adaptive reactions.

Parainformation as Literal Meaning

A system's reaction results from internal associations provoked by received information. A change in the outside world has been noticed, and the system is analyzing what it can possibly mean. This internal association will be called *parainformation*, or direct, literal meaning of communicated information.[1] Parainformation can be either innate or acquired. The evolved modules relating to certain typical environmental and social stimuli are the source of innate parainformation, as in reacting with fear to darkness and large cats, with distrust to strangers, with pleasure to good food, or with excitement to a sexually attractive person. Examples of acquired parainformation include understanding one's native language or social custom. Thus to a speaker of English who reads this book the information it presents is *meaningful*. On the other hand, to a person without the right parainformation, as in being unfamiliar with a foreign language or with specialized vocabulary, a spoken utterance or text is *meaningless*.

For interacting systems to understand one another, they must possess corresponding parainformation. In contiguous communication for example, when two animals confront one another in the context of sexual or territorial rivalry, they are exchanging information in the form of cues and signals such as body size, movement, and posture, as well as behavioral traits such as bristling of the hair, bearing of the teeth, growling, and so on. Parainformation refers to correct interpretation of these displays: as threat or aggression, followed by appropriate behavior such as staying on guard, attack, or escape. Human contiguous interactions too consist largely of exchanging visual, auditory, tactile, gustatory, and olfactory cues and signals, of interpreting them using the right parainformation, and acting upon them.

The same co-presence of provided information and provoked parainformation applies to indirect forms of communication. As mentioned in Chapter 2, the failure of higher apes other than humans to notice and interpret visual indexes such as footprints has to do with the absence of specific innate parainformation in the former, and its presence in the latter. In humans the innate disposition is further developed through learning, as in hunting bands, where trackers acquire detailed expertise in identifying traces in the ground as indexes of the animals' species, sex, size, age, and physical condition. A person without the right kind of parainformation will either misinterpret the hoof print in the ground or will simply miss it altogether. Correct identification and interpretation of iconic representations also depend both on the innate ability to associate different objects through similarity, and on the cultural knowledge of specific details in the image and the represented object. For example, we know that Hans Holbein the Younger's portrait of King Henry VIII represents King Henry VIII, because of the close resemblance of the person in the portrait to other existing contemporary portraits of the king. On the other hand, today's art historians have insufficient parainformation, available to Holbein at the time, to identity the aristocratic ladies from the Elizabethan period represented in Holbein's other portraits. For symbolic communication to be meaningful, speakers must share the same ethnic language as well as specific linguistic registers related to the subject matter in question. In the first case a non-speaker of a language will perceive the foreign speech sounds simply as meaningless acoustic sensations, while in the second case a person, even when sharing the same ethnic language, will not have a clue about what a conversation or a written text is about.

Meaning as Interaction

If meaning is understood in terms of a system's reaction to information, its production must depend on the *combined* effects of that information and the sender's and the recipient's reactivity in the form of parainformation. In literature, for example, meaning neither depends solely on authors' intentions or readers' expectations, nor is it a property of the text itself: literary meaning results from an interaction between all systems involved. A text does not "contain" meaning or is "about" something until a human mind starts interacting with it. It also follows that there is no such thing as one meaning of a text, because while information (words on the page) remains the same, different autonomous systems, by virtue of their unique reactivities, will possess differing parainformation related to the same information.

Locating the source of meaning has been an important part of literary theory and criticism. Emphases on the three main elements of the literary process—author, text, and reader—have been tried in turn. Nineteenth-century critics for example saw the author's individual mind, sensibility, and circumstances of life as primarily responsible for literary meaning, while the text itself was seen as a window to the author's mind and personality. As a reaction to this author-oriented approach, the early twentieth-century New Criticism moved the emphasis onto the qualities of the text itself, now regarded as the autonomous source of meaning. The text's organic form, imagery, style, characterization, mood, patterns of metaphor, and diction became more important than possible authorial intentions. The author was ultimately pronounced dead in post-structural criticism, which moved the emphasis away from the text and onto the reader, whose own assumptions, as defined by the socio-cultural determinants of language, gender, class, race, or by Freudian unconscious, were now deemed responsible for the text's meaning. The dismissal of both authorial intention and the intrinsic qualities of the text has led to the assertion that there are as many legitimate readings of a text as there are readers or, as in deconstructive criticism, that there is no such thing as stable meaning because the text continuously defers meaning by generating an infinite chain of signifiers.[2] How can these divergent views on the source of literary meaning—the author's mind, the text, the reader's mind, language and society—be reconciled?

The interactive formula for the reaction of the system (Figure 1.1) would suggest that both the biographical criticism, the text-oriented New Criticism, and the reader-response approach are all partly right, with the correction that meaning resides neither in the text itself, nor alone in the writer's or reader's minds, but is created jointly by the writer's creativity and the reader's responsiveness interacting with the text. A holistic, interactive approach to the generation of literary meaning has been advocated for example by the phenomenological reception-theory. Wolfgang Iser speaks of literary meaning and the reading subject as "interacting operations that are both structured by the aspects of the text," in which the text works by "designating a network of response-inviting structures, which impel the reader to grasp the text." For Iser "reading is not a direct 'internalization,' because it is not a one-way process ... it is a dynamic *interaction* between text and reader," in which "every reading moment sends out stimuli into the memory, and what is recalled can activate the perspectives in such a way that they continually modify and so individualize one another."[3] The critic Ranulph Glanville likewise sees meaning as a cognitive category not inherent in but provoked by the text: "Meanings do not lie in words or other elements of representation but in the perceptions and cognitions each participant makes,"[4] a view echoed by David Porush:

> Reading itself is the source of meaning. The text ... is the trace of a set of codes, some of which are frozen there by the author, some of which are brought there by the reader ... The text may be an interplay of codes, but it is the reader who makes them play.[5]

The dependence of reading on two combined variables, words on the page and the reader's mind, also indicates that meaning that is relevant to the text cannot result from a "free play of the signifier," as postulated cavalierly by the deconstructive version of reader-response criticism inspired by Jacques Derrida. No matter how inventive a reader can be in "reading" her own preconceptions into a text, the conditions presented by the text itself always participate in the interrogation of meaning, by effectively limiting interpretation to what is relevant. Assuming that the reader respects the conditions of the text, the words on the page will always constrain the range of permissible meanings. For example, critics may quibble over the nature, heterosexual or homosexual, of love expressed in some of Shakespeare's sonnets (permissible meanings), but they are probably in agreement that these sonnets are about love and not about the possibility of life on Mars or the French cuisine (impermissible meanings).

Differing interpretations do of course exist as functions of differing parainformation in readers, which is what makes criticism interesting. Since complete agreement as to the meaning of literary works, films, plays, paintings, and other artifacts is neither possible nor desirable, let us acknowledge the differences in individual parainformation by identifying two types of meaning, one associated with the author and the other with the reader. Accordingly, the author's parainformation will be referred to as *meaning*, while the reader's parainformation will be called *significance*. The distinction is analogous to that made by E. D. Hirsch Jr, who speaks of meaning as a determinate and permanent aspect of the text, corresponding ultimately with the author's design, and of significance as a changeable, relative dimension of the text, defined in terms of critical response.[6] It is for a critic to decide which type of meaning she accepts as the more important, given her objectives and methodology. The problem ultimately boils down to weighing one's own response (significance) against the author's possible intention (meaning). This also means that the author can only be "dead" for a fully committed reader-response critic. The main advantage of the latter position is that one's own parainformation is for obvious reasons directly accessible while the author's is not. On the other hand, the exclusive preoccupation with one's subjective response, at the expense of the author's elusive because ultimately unknowable meaning, can lead to idiosyncratic, not always relevant or communicable responses, as evidenced by the often impenetrable rhetoric of deconstructive criticism.[7]

The fact that someone else's parainformation is always a matter of conjecture does not automatically imply that all meaning is inherently unstable, and that communication based on mutual understanding is therefore impossible. As the novelist Walker Percy once quipped, a "deconstructionist" is an academic who claims that the meaning of all communication is radically indeterminate but who leaves a message on his wife's answering machine requesting pepperoni pizza for dinner.[8] Besides, any claim about the indeterminacy of meaning is automatically self-refuting, undermined by the very fact of making such a claim. Notwithstanding the unduly pessimistic arguments about the instability of meaning, the very concept of communication implies at least a partial overlap of parainformation between interacting and usually cooperating systems, as otherwise the social fabric would simply disintegrate. But since full understanding and social harmony are clearly not always the case, let us identify the types of situations likely to occur between communicating systems.

When parainformation in sender and receiver is identical, we are talking about *understanding*. Even in common parlance "to communicate" does not just mean to exchange information but to agree on the meaning of that information. Speakers of the same language talking about a familiar topic understand one another, as in saying "pass me the salt, please," or "let's meet in Neary's pub tomorrow at 8." Most of social life consists of mutually intelligible communication. But autonomous systems are autonomous because they also possess parainformation unique to themselves, not shared with other systems, which can result in three types of miscommunication. In the first type the sender possesses parainformation but the receiver has no parainformation relating to the same information: this is called *incomprehension*. This happens when we hear a language that is foreign to us, or when we have no knowledge of a particular subject matter ("I don't know what you are talking about"). In the second type of miscommunication the sender does not possess any parainformation relating to the communicated information, but the receiver does: this is called *overinterpretation*. In a British 1964 comedy *Carry on Spying*, a sophisticated lady with a winking tic in one eye is in conversation with a gentleman who mistakes the involuntary reflex for an intentional signal, with obvious comic consequences. In the third type of miscommunication both sender and receiver possess parainformation relating to the same information, but it is in both cases different: this is called *misunderstanding*. For example, Bulgarians traditionally shake their heads from side to side when they mean "yes" and nod to mean "no." A single act of communication will be either a case of understanding, incomprehension, overinterpretation, or misunderstanding. Or we can reserve the term "communication" to situations of mutual understanding and the term "miscommunication" to cover the other three possibilities.

Communication and Deception

Autonomous systems typically exist in a world of limited resources, where survival depends not only on cooperation based on communication, but also on competition and rivalry often accompanied by hiding or misrepresenting information, especially in the struggle for such vital commodities as sex, food, and safety.[9] Opportunities for withholding and misrepresenting information in the competitive game of life are indeed broad, as our skills at lying and deceiving demonstrate. Deception is tempting also because producing meaningless information is often less costly, certainly in the short term, than communicating honest, meaningful information. Lying is cheap and easy, whereas providing truthful information requires both the effort of prior fact-checking, and attention to match statements with logic and available evidence. Also, no one wants to be cheated and taken advantage of, and so evolution must have put as much pressure on cheating skills and lying as on the ability to recognize cues of dishonesty in others.[10]

Deception is of course not the same as miscommunication, if by the latter we mean lack or incompatibility of parainformation between systems willing to understand one another. In deception at least one system does not intend to communicate, but instead hides the information or falsifies its meaning. For example, a sender may communicate meaningless information (without any parainformation attached to it) to provoke in the receiver some desired parainformation, as in making affirmative statements about non-existent events ("I saw it with my own eyes" when nothing happened), or in signaling absent emotions or states of mind: "Oh, I know that!" when one does not know, "With due respect" when it is obvious that respect is lacking, or "I love you" when one does not mean it. This kind of deception is already present as instinctive behavior in some animals, which can bristle their hair when they are aggressive to increase their apparent body size and scare the opponent. Some primates have also been observed to use alarm calls in the absence of a predator, to distract other primates from aggressive behavior or from a food source.[11] Presenting meaningless information as meaningful is what we call *fabrication* (lying, pretending, faking, conning).

When the sender possesses meaningful information but does not communicate it to the receiver, we are talking about *suppression* of information. Examples include animal camouflage (also used in human warfare), a deceptive tactic designed to make the sender blend with the surroundings to escape the attention of predators or enemies.[12] Failing to produce evidence, keeping silent, looking the other way, hiding, playing dead, pretending that nothing is happening, and so on are examples of suppression of information. It is also possible to distinguish a form of deception that combines suppression with fabrication, when the sender possesses meaningful information which he does not communicate to the receiver, but instead manipulates the receiver into accepting meaningless information. This type of deception will be called *substitution*, as in counterfeiting money, cheating during exam, forging works of art, plagiarizing, or accusing others of one's own misdemeanors. The cuckoo bird proverbially lays its eggs in the nests of other birds: here the suppressed information is the fact that the egg belongs to the cuckoo, and the fabricated information is the pretense that the egg belongs to the nesting bird. A vainglorious liar fabricates his non-existent achievements to suppress the fact that he has achieved nothing of note. A thief is often the one who shouts the loudest "catch the thief!" Deception presupposes the awareness of other people's mental states and exploits the self-deception arising from their wants and expectations; in other words, it uses the second order of intentionality as part of theory of mind (discussed in Chapter 1). Among non-human animals deceptive behavior does not necessarily presuppose advanced cognitive faculties, but is instead a result of trials and errors of natural selection, whereby an animal that has developed mimicry and camouflage has better chances of surviving and reproducing than an animal visible to potential predators.

Metainformation as Indirect Meaning

Parainformation as an internal reaction to perceived information is the communication default of all autonomous systems, from amoebas to humans. In non-human species differences in the complexity of the nervous systems appear to be largely quantitative, reflecting the species' adaptation to a particular environmental niche. A possible qualitative rival to communication based on parainformation would involve the ability to react not just to external stimuli but also to internal ones. Consequently, these second-order associations will be called *metainformation*. Metainformation in sender and receiver will be called *metameaning* and *metasignificance*, respectively, and the two forms of communication, one based on parainformation and the other on metainformation, will be referred to as *levels of meaning*.[13]

The fundamental difference between parainformation and metainformation is that while the former is prompted by external stimuli, the latter depends mainly on internal cognitive processes, even independently from perception and contiguous experience. Metainformation may either assume the form of extended thoughts and reflections about the outside world, via parainformation, or it can be generated "from within," as in internal monologue, daydreaming, being "lost in thought" and engaged in creative imagination, or in experiencing delusions. Dreaming during sleep is a classic example of spontaneous meta-cognitive activity of the brain in the absence of sensory inputs. As the psychologist Matthew Walker explains, during sleep the conscious brain is activated internally to create images within more or less coherent narratives, but in the absence of moment-by-moment sensory input it remains disconnected from external reality and creates fantasy instead.[14] Something similar happens during hallucinations, caused by sensory deprivation, chemical stimulation, brain dysfunction, or emotional trauma, when we "see" or "hear" things that are not there, that is, when internally generated sensations are subjectively transformed into perceptions.[15]

If parainformation is necessarily constrained by perception and therefore semantically limited, the meanings generated by metainformation are practically unlimited, as having thoughts about thoughts is recursive and combinatorial *ad infinitum*, forever flexible and creative. "Thinking about thinking" is how *The Oxford Companion to Philosophy* defines its subject matter.[16] Philosophy is a metainformational phenomenon, whereas empirical sciences are essentially a domain of parainformation. Or, if parainformation is the meaning of information, metameaning consists in reflection, commentary, speculation, belief, theorizing, and self-analyzing. Metainformation also underlies irony, humor, sarcasm, allusion, metaphor, deception, doubt, shame, guilt, hate, love, friendship, as well as reminiscing, long-term planning, having attitudes, agendas, values, biases, illusions, and prejudices. In a word, meta-cognition defines human mental life and its relative independence from the constraints of perception and the tyranny of facts. For individuals immersed in their imagination "nothing that actually occurs is of the smallest importance," as Oscar Wilde put it.[17] Parainformation and metainformation thus correspond to what Steven Pinker refers to as "the reality mindset" and "the mythology mindset," respectively.[18] Metainformation gives the human mind its literal "absent-mindedness," a detachment from the pressures of feet-firmly-on-the-ground contiguity. Non-human animals are forever enslaved to the here-and-now and cannot but react appropriately to the situation, whereas we have a choice to do right or wrong, to act heroically or dastardly, wisely or foolishly, to our benefit or against our interests. We can pretend if we choose to, unlike other animals, which never pretend because in the absence of meta-cognition they have no option but to run on automatic, innate responses. This is why animal behavior, with its blank unselfconsciousness, is so oddly fascinating to us, as captured by the novelist Hermann Hesse:

> Well, look at an animal, a cat, a dog, or a bird, or one of those beautiful great beasts in the Zoo, a puma or a giraffe. You can't help seeing that all of them are right. They're never in any embarrassment. They always know what to do and how to behave themselves. They don't want to impress you. No play-acting. They are as they are, like stones or flowers or stars in the sky.[19]

As far as we know, only humans can supplement the primary representations resulting from animal-like online experience with the secondary representations of interiorized, offline cognition.[20] The distinction between parainformation and metainformation is what is often referred to as literal, explicit meaning versus metaphorical, implicit meaning, or denotation versus connotation, respectively. It is metainformation that creates "hidden" meanings and double entendre, subtexts, and "points" we are making during a conversation or debate.

Human relations with the world consist therefore of three semiotic domains: (1) "information" as the empirical world available to sensory perception, (2) "parainformation" as a reaction to this world, and (3) "metainformation" as a reflection about our reaction to the world. Interestingly, these three domains, the first objective and the other two subjective, appear analogous to Karl Popper's theory of the "three worlds," in which World One refers to the objective world of material things, World Two to subjective mental states, and World Three consists of "the logical contents of books, libraries, computer memories, and suchlike," coded in permanent linguistic artifacts. In Popper's model the first two worlds are the domain of both animal and human experience, but the third world of theoretical systems such as science, philosophy, and myth is exclusively human. This world is largely autonomous, but it relates back to the second world, and even indirectly to the first world, because human knowledge of the empirical world is predicated upon the linguistically formulated third-world theories. For example, the human mind can see a physical object (World One, or information) in the literal, perceptual sense (World Two, or parainformation), but it can also "see" in an abstract sense of understanding an underlying law or principle (World Three, or metainformation).[21]

As with parainformation, metainformation can involve the following types of communication and miscommunication: (1) understanding, when an allusion, understatement, metaphor, or an abstract concept as intended by the sender is correctly interpreted by the receiver; (2) incomprehension, when metainformation is "lost" on the receiver unable to interpret an allusion or understatement due to insufficient social or cultural competence; (3) overinterpretation, when the receiver interprets a literal message metaphorically; and (4) misunderstanding, when sender and receiver have different meta-associations attached to the same message. For example, a work of art may provoke equally valid if different responses resulting from individual differences in knowledge, sensitivity, and life experience. Professional art history and criticism rely on reconstructing the metainformation relating to the original context: historical, cultural, and biographical, in which a work of art was produced, to reduce misunderstanding and incomprehension and to increase understanding in the above senses.

From Physical States to Signs

Let us sum up the systemic semiotic definitions introduced so far. Inanimate systems such as minerals inertly exchange *physical states* in the form of mechanical forces, chemical reactions, and radiation; autonomous systems such as plants and animals communicate purposefully by exchanging, interpreting, and reacting to information on the (first-order) level of parainformation; while humans avail additionally of (second-order) metacommunication. First-order communication can be of two kinds, depending on the involvement of *intentionality*. Intentionality presupposes active and goal-oriented behavior, which can be either innate, as in plants and animals, or both innate and volitional, as in humans. Intentional first-order communication uses active *signals*, whereas unintentional first-order communication relies on passive *cues* in the form of phenotypic features such as body shape, size, and color. Signals include manipulative behaviors such as barking, bristling up, shouting, assuming bodily postures, and conveying literal verbal messages. The greenness of leaves is accordingly a passive cue, a consequence of the color of chlorophyll, a chemical involved in photosynthesis, which just happens to be green. On the other hand, brightly colored flowers evolved by plants to attract pollinating insects are active signals. Also, phenotypic cues involve no immediate cost, whereas behavioral signals require additional physiological costs to produce. It is also possible to identify *symptoms*—a type of first-order communication that is unintentional, like cues, but active, like signals. Symptoms are automatic reactions motivated by an emotional or physiological state, such as sweating from overheating, trembling from fear, blushing from shame, getting goose pimples from cold, having fever from disease, or vomiting from an upset stomach.[22]

Human communication involves both first- and second-order levels of meaning, and can be of three kinds, depending on the involvement of intentionality: (1) unintentional first-order communication consisting of cues and symptoms, as reflected in bodily anatomy and physiological reactions, respectively; (2) intentional first-order communication expressed through signals, as in making eye contact, smiling, or hitting someone; and (3) second-order communication, which is by definition intentional, relying on *signs*, as in avoiding eye contact, smiling sarcastically, saying "hello," writing an email, dressing up for the occasion, or taking a photograph. In this understanding signs are used only in metacommunication, reserved in practice to humans.

Human behavior covers therefore the entire range of distinguished types of communication and levels of meaning. We constantly exchange physical states with the natural environment, through metabolism and by exploiting its resources. In social communication we inadvertently display bodily cues involving sexual dimorphism, skin color, age, and individual, especially facial, differences. We signal our intentions using body language, facial expressions, gestures, and denotative speech. We develop involuntary physiological symptoms such as perspiring, yawning, sneezing, or crying. And we produce meta-cognitive signs through bodily adornments such as makeup, jewelry, and clothes to emphasize our identity and status; through metaphor, irony, and humor in speech and playful behavior; and through literature, philosophy, music, and visual arts. A physiological cough is a symptom of respiratory tract infection, but a theatrical cough is a sign of concealed intent, to prevent someone's embarrassment for example.

Limiting the category of "signs" to inter-human meta-communication would preclude its application to natural phenomena, as in superstitiously attributing human-like agency to inorganic matter, natural forces, and animal behavior by, for example, overinterpreting a tsunami, an epidemic, or a plague of locust as "signs" of alleged supernatural intervention. But even if we do not attribute meta-cognitive, quasi-divine powers to mineral, vegetable, and animal kingdoms, we still interact reciprocally with them. Whether such interactions are "semiotic" or not would be a matter of terminology. Developments in biosemiotics and ecosemiotics have certainly extended the traditional concept of communication to non-human domains, both within and across kingdoms. For example, plants respond to water, nutrients, and temperature of their natural environment, but according to the biologist Olivier Van Aken plants also respond to the human touch and indirectly to human emotions.[23] As research continues, the nature of interactions between humans and the non-sentient organic and inorganic world may turn out to be more subtle than we today suppose, further expanding the domain of semiotics as a science of communication and meaning.

Metainformation and Memory

Contiguous animal interactions with the world require only constant alertness and instinctive responses to the here-and-now. On the other hand, human metainformation can be prompted in the absence of direct external stimuli. It requires, however, making an extra cognitive effort to create or recall an association between a currently perceived sign and its absent referent. Among the chief benefits of meta-cognition is transcending the limitations of contiguous experience to encompass both remembered and imagined events. Reliance on displaced reference in turn enhances memory by vastly expanding the range of topics of communication.

While contiguity-bound animal communication is limited to topics such as food, mating, bonding, safety, and sexual or territorial rivalry, meta-cognitive humans can communicate about an almost unlimited number of topics and events, present, past, and future, factual, hypothetical, and fictitious. The phylogenetic knowledge, evolved to deal with contiguous events through parainformation, has been complemented in humans by ontogenetic learning based to a large extent on metainformation. Unlike the limited animal learning acquired through conditioned reflexes, humans have an extraordinary capacity to learn a huge amount of new things during their lifetime, to store this knowledge in memory, and to share it via language and permanent artifacts of material culture, institutions, stories, ritual, and art. Ontogenetic knowledge is synonymous with memory, the ability to recall and hold in conscious attention the mental traces of past events and experiences. Memory also enhances the perception of the flow of time, including a sense of continuity of one's own existence—a psychological prerequisite for consciousness and individual identity.

Like everything in evolution, the interconnected cognitive faculties of ontogenetic learning, memory, and consciousness must have been built on earlier adaptations. Animals too have memory in the form of a genetically programmed capacity to store in the brain a limited range of new, species-specific behaviors. Squirrels, for example, can keep track of the many places in which they cache their nuts, and the male birds of some species can memorize their songs (up to two hundred in the case of the nightingale) to impress the females or intimidate other males.[24] Human memory, by contrast, is not specialized but open; it is what psychologists call "episodic" or "autobiographical" memory, employed mainly in the service of ever-expanding social life to keep track of who did what to whom, when, where, and why.[25] Autobiographical memory is continuous, carried over from one episode to the next, thus stimulating a cause-and-effect reasoning absent in other apes, whose memory is brief and situation-bound, prompting immediate and short-term responses. Unable to remember the past or anticipate the future, animals live in the eternal present, from one discrete episode to the next. This is probably why animal faces appear so blank and expressionless to us: they reflect no emotional effects of recent or more distant experiences, nor do they signal an expectation of things to come.[26] Human faces, on the other hand, can be read like a book: we can smile both at the current happy situation, at the pleasant memory of a past event, and while anticipating something nice to come.

The ability to hold in conscious attention events unfolding in time must have been acquired gradually, as the subjective "eternal now" was expanded to include more and more of the chronologically related events.[27] Steven Mithen suggests that the perception of time may have been correlated with some of the multi-stage, processual activities of early humans, such as the domestication of fire, the production of tools, and group hunting, which may have put evolutionary pressure on extending the scope of working memory.[28] Archaeological evidence suggests that the controlled use of fire dates to the *Homo erectus* populations of about 60,000 years ago, who passed the skill on to the Cro-Magnon people (about 40,000 years ago), from which modern humans evolved.[29] The intentional use of fire is one of human universals, with advantages including temperature control, illumination, protection from animals, and cooking.[30] Taming fire has also social benefits by providing a focus for family and friends to gather round to exchange gossip and cement bonds and alliances.[31] Cognitively, the processual nature of fire control, which includes choosing the site, finding and stocking up the fuel, igniting the fire and keeping it alive, requires planning, mental concentration, and expanded working memory. Any sustained, multi-stage activity encourages cause-and-effect thinking and continuity of thought processes focused on self and the immediate social environment, crucial for the development of individual consciousness. Similar cognitive benefits of focused, goal-oriented, memory-driven thinking can have arisen, argues Mithen, from habitual tool production by early humans, which required the ability to visualize in a lump of rock a still-unformed shape and to design it to fit the anticipated purpose.[32]

Ultimately, in contrast to the innate motivations of the phylogenetic part of the brain, the ontogenetic, conscious memory enabled humans to benefit from past experience to make plans about the immediate future. The resulting adaptive flexibility thus complemented the slow evolutionary adaptation by genetic mutation and differential survival, giving humans the advantage of culture—a quantum leap ahead of other animals. In the words of Edward O. Wilson:

> The elaboration of culture depends upon long-term memory, and in this capacity humans rank far above all animals. The vast quantity stored in our immensely enlarged forebrains makes us consummate storytellers. We summon dreams and recollections of experience from across a lifetime and use them to create scenarios, past and future. We live in our conscious mind with the consequence

of our actions, whether real or imagined. Placed out in alternative versions, our inner stories allow us to override immediate desires in favor of delayed pleasure. By long-range planning we defeat, for a while at least, the urging of our emotions.[33]

Rather than relying solely on inherited, limited, and rigid responses to the environment, humans can mold their destinies and create their own living environments in historical rather than evolutionary time, by making conscious decisions about the future based on remembered past. Thanks to memory, we can rehearse what we are going to do, consider alternative options, and evaluate likely outcomes, something that other primates, tied forever to contiguity, are unable to do.[34] The ability to navigate the full timeline of individual and group memory, to make imaginative connections between the past and the future through "remembered anticipations,"[35] is also the cognitive prerequisite of the specifically human teleological need described in Chapter 1. We are obsessively preoccupied with ends and goals, we consider the consequences of the decisions we make, we struggle in vain to comprehend the implications of our inevitable termination of life, and we create elaborate and obscure stories to satisfy our need to find purpose and meaning of our lives in the fabric of this universe.

Consciousness

A sense of the continuity of one's existence afforded by the perception of time and extended working memory is also a prerequisite for the mysterious entity called consciousness—the awareness of self or, in Robert L. Solso's definition, "a state of attentional wakefulness in which one is immediately aware of his subjective sensations."[36] Without our attention being sustained over time, we would have no way of knowing that we are experiencing anything. This is why Immanuel Kant insisted that time is the one indispensable form of inner sense, and that all experience must occur in that dimension.[37] For the philosopher Bryan Magee too our imagination and memory rely on the sustained lifelike representations before the mind of past sensory inputs.[38] Consciousness is also enabled by metainformation with its ability to have associations about associations, to become an observer not just of the outside world but also of one's own mental life. As Richard Dawkins puts it, consciousness can be understood as the brain's representation not only of the world but also of itself.[39] Equipped with evolutionary knowledge but without the sense of current passage of time, animals are capable of doing many clever things in the interest of survival, but as far as we know they are unaware that they can do these clever things. As the biologists Peter B. Medawar and Jean S. Medawar put it, "only human beings guide their behaviour by a knowledge of what happened before they were born and a preconception of what may happen after they are dead," because "only human beings find their way by a light that illuminates more than the patch of ground they stand on."[40]

It is the meta-cognitive brain focused on self-awareness that has liberated the human mind from the slavery to contiguity and has opened up a quasi-autonomous virtual inner world of imagination and of culture as its expression. By transcending the limitations of genetically programmed behavior, consciousness has conferred upon humans the advantages of cognitive fluidity and flexible planning within a socially defined teleological framework, and of carrying out these plans in the historic project of transforming, for better or worse, the natural environment.[41] The long-term planning based on meta-cognitive teleological narratives has historically transformed the given world into a created one, with agriculture, urbanization, commerce, technology, institutions, value systems, science, art, and everything else that makes us human.

Teleology versus Needs

The quintessentially human teleological need as expressed in individual introspection and collective narratives of religion, literature, philosophy, and political ideology, is directly predicated upon the meta-cognitive faculties, especially those relating to the perception of time. Teleological world-models are universal in human societies, where they define the historical or transcendental destiny of a group as well as the individual search for imaginative order and purposefulness of life. Teleology seems compulsive in humans, and if there is such a thing as human nature, the obsessive search for the underlying "metaphysical" meaning of everything may be among its defining characteristics.

In both individual and social life the teleological impulse is thus found to inform the totality of human experience as defined by the needs described in Chapter 1: procreative, nutritional, protective, social, exploratory, and esthetic. Often encouraged by group pressure, the teleological need compels many people to seek "transcendental" meanings in areas of life which, objectively speaking, may be simply a matter of biology. Originally evolved to serve the Darwinian imperatives of survival and propagation, the basic needs are often meta-cognitively overinterpreted for their supposed "spiritual" significance. For example, the pleasure of sex and the joys of parenthood can be either accepted literally as healthy expressions of natural instincts, or they become reinterpreted as a fulfillment of the divine injunction to "Be fruitful, and multiply" (Gen. 1:28). Other cultural contexts speak of the divine *hieros gamos* (the ancient Greek holy marriage), the wedding of Christ with Mother Ecclesia, the alchemical *coniunctio oppositorum*, the astrological conjunction of Mars and Venus, *animus* and *anima*, or the Taoist *yin* and *yang*.[42] Similarly with food, a biological necessity and a source of another physiological pleasure, but also a fruitful ground for metaphysics, including religious dietary laws with their mind-bending legalistic details of what is kosher or halal and what is not, with the parables of the vineyard and the Last Supper, the consumption of the mystical body of Christ, and so on. The protective need and the associated defensive/aggressive behavior, evolved to reduce the risk of injury and loss of life, become a battle between Good and Evil, a holy war, or a proletarian revolutionary struggle with the Enemies of the People. The social need, whose original function is to ensure mutual support within groups, is elevated to the doctrine of God's Chosen People, the elect as opposed to the damned, class prejudice, or the civilized world versus the barbarians. The instinct to explore the environment in search of life-supporting resources assumes a meta-cognitive expression in a hero's mythical journey to obtain the Golden Fleece or the Holy Grail, in the religious injunction to "seek, and ye shall find" (Mat. 7:7), or it is turned inward into a gnostic exploration of the Kingdom Within to seek enlightenment and divine truth. The emotional coloring we instinctively attach to various elements of the natural environment can also inspire an esthetic theory, an art movement, a meditative appreciation of beauty and the sublime in nature, and a personal lifestyle of esthetes such as Oscar Wilde or the decadent aristocrat from Joris-Karl Huysmans' novel À Rebours. Finally, the teleological need can "turn in on itself" as it were, inspiring superstitious obsessions with "hidden meanings," "mysteries," and supernatural "signs," as well as fatalistic beliefs in Divine Providence, Karma, eschatology, and divine judgments.

As earlier defined, needs are temporary disturbances in the systems' homeostatic equilibrium, which prompt emotionally charged reactions leading toward the restoration of a particular kind of homeostatic disturbance. All animal species live in a constant state of homeostatic imbalance of one kind or another, which they counter with a dose of healthy stress and alertness to the ever-changing world around them. Humans do that too, unless a particular teleology tells them to repress the needs in the name of some "ideal," as in ascetic self-denial, puritanical condemnation of pleasure, or martyrdom for a "cause." As the history of ideologies demonstrates, the teleological need is capable of radically modifying behavior in a way not found in the rest of the animal kingdom. Depending on a particular teleology and its value-system, needs can be either realistically accepted as part of the human condition or moralistically rejected and condemned as "evil," "sinful," "decadent," "animalistic," "degenerate," and so on. A positive and tolerant attitude toward human needs underlies a *humanistic*, or liberal, worldview, whereas a disapproving and intolerant attitude toward needs characterizes *fundamentalist*, or illiberal, worldviews.

Thus a fundamentalist attitude toward sexuality produces shame, guilt, self-loathing, celibacy, and the cult of chastity and virginity. A negation of the pleasure of food produces religious fasting. A denial of the protective need results in self-deprivation and self-mutilations, ascetic mortification of the body, religious martyrdom, and the cult of honorary suicide. Self-inflicted social deprivation leads to monasticism with its vows of solitude and silence. A denial of the exploratory need produces dogmatic condemnations of natural curiosity, persecution of freethinkers and heretics, and papal denunciations of "ungodly" science. Puritanical disapproval of art brands esthetic values as decadent and artists as immoral and degenerate. Finally, people holding different but equally dogmatic teleological views are condemned as infidels and traitors.

In a humanistic, liberal, and tolerant worldview, on the other hand, the aim of life is self-fulfillment and individual flourishing understood, ideally, as optimal satisfaction of all needs by all people. Socio-cultural systems organized around humanistic principles include the elites of the Greek polis of the ancient classical period, the progressive trends of the European Renaissance and the Enlightenment, and the liberal mainstream of modern democratic societies.[43] On the other hand, fundamentalist worldviews underlie all religious orthodoxies, twentieth-century communist and fascist totalitarianisms, and right-wing, conservative ideologies of today. If needs are part of human evolutionary endowment, it means that they cannot be erased and that any attempt to deny or culturally reprogram them leads only to self-deceptive and hypocritical contradictions. Humanistic worldviews are therefore more realistic and honest, and liberal societies generally make people happier than fundamentalist, repressive ones. This appears to be confirmed by spontaneous human migrations, whose direction tends to be away from repressive and toward liberal countries, rather than the other way round.

Ideology and Self-deception

As mentioned earlier, deception in the forms of fabrication, suppression, or substitution is often an advantageous strategy to outmaneuver competitors in a world of limited resources. But it is also possible, strange though it may seem at first, to imagine situations in which cognitively advanced systems such as humans can find it advantageous not only to deceive others but also to deceive themselves.[44] Self-deception is in fact part of human psychology, although it does look paradoxical: if having truthful representations of the world is beneficial in allowing for adaptive, life-saving reactions, why should false representations, potentially counter-productive and dangerous, be a viable strategy? In the animal kingdom any wrong assessment of impending danger has usually immediate fatal consequences, eliminating a careless organism from the genetic pool forever. Why should it be possible for humans to be careless and survive, even thrive, at the same time?

Among the seemingly "careless" aspects of human behavior are some of the worldviews and narratives produced by the teleological need, which often describe the world not as it is, but as it evidently is not. Tribal mythologies, epics of heroes and gods, Arthurian legends, Christian providential parables, and secular ideologies of national awakening, destiny, and glory are among the most prevalent counter-factual narratives designed to "explain" the meaning of collective and individual life. For thousands of years it was the fantastic stories of supernatural beings, miracles, and magic rather than historical and scientific accounts that provided explanations of how the world came about, and why it was the way it was. Claims that in our largely science-guided age are regarded as a matter of faith and folklore were absolute truths for most of history: gods and goddesses, spirits, demons, hobgoblins, nymphs, satyrs, unicorns, monsters, shape-shifting magicians, caps of invisibility, flying carpets, weightless angels, miracle healings, and mythical cosmologies with their paradises, purgatories, hells, apocalypses, last judgments, and life after death. As with deception, self-deception can assume three forms: fabrication, or delusion, as in accepting fiction as truth; suppression, or denial, as in repressing factual knowledge; and substitution, a combination of delusion and denial, as in refusing to accept the death of a loved one, believing that the person still lives somewhere, or in dismissing evidence that contradicts one's religious or political views.

Human meta-cognition appears therefore to be a mixed blessing. On the one hand, the extended working memory allows for long-term planning which has expanded human adaptation around the globe and created a new cultural environment to complement the natural one. Meta-cognition has also created literature, poetry, visual arts, music, philosophy, and science. On the other hand, these second-order representations often contradict the first-order perceptions inherited from our animal ancestors. Meta-cognition detached from empirical facts has created myths, religion, mysticism, astrology, occultism, scientology, and conspiracy theories. With the exception of science, which is only a few hundred years old and still not universally accepted, all other meta-cognitive domains on historical record are essentially non-referential, in the sense that they do not denote things that exist anyhow—the repertoire of "things" referred to by most meta-cognitive systems simply has no existence outside the systems themselves.[45]

A belief in non-empirical entities can, however, serve important social and cognitive functions: it can cement the group against external threats and provide answers, factually wrong but psychologically useful, to the pressing questions about the possible purpose and meaning of life. Also, some of the meta-cognitive domains found in human cultures past and present, such as law and science, are adaptive and utilitarian. Some, such as art, folklore, and mythical cosmologies, are probably indifferent to human well-being. But some may be deleterious, as when a group's metaphysical beliefs are challenged by unorthodoxy from within, or threatened by incompatible beliefs of another group. Ideological conflicts are the most bitter, leading in individual cases to serious existential crises and sometimes to suicide, and giving rise to violent conflicts between groups prepared to kill and be killed to defend ideas that have no objective validity anyway. When conflicting claims cannot be resolved by independent empirical evidence, as in science, compromise and mutual tolerance are often impossible, and any attempt to accommodate the other side is interpreted as the high crime of blasphemy and treason.

Religion is a classic case in point. The propensity for supernatural beliefs is both pervasive among humans and unique to our species, despite the apparent maladaptive character of religious concepts and ways of behavior. The particular details of religious beliefs and rituals vary from culture to culture, but no known society lacks some version of what Richard Dawkins describes as "the time-consuming, wealth-consuming, hostility-provoking rituals, the anti-factual, counter-productive fantasies of religion."[46] Archaeological evidence suggests that religion and ritual activities appeared relatively recently in human prehistory. The earliest intentional burials with grave goods were practiced by the Upper Paleolithic *Homo sapiens* between 60,000 and 30,000 years ago, and can be interpreted in terms of beliefs in the possibility of an afterlife. Steven Mithen explains the rise of religious thinking as a result of the collapse of the barriers that had existed between the multiple cognitive modules of the early mind, and the resulting cognitive fluidity, as manifested in the mixing in religious thinking of both intuitive, empirical, and counter-intuitive, unreal elements and knowledge about the world.[47] Pascal Boyer likewise interprets human propensity toward religion in terms of conceptual combinations of both real and fantastic elements that tap information from different cognitive modules. The fantastic elements are by definition unconstrained by reference, while the realistic elements give religious ideas a semblance of probability and hence of credibility. For example, the widespread notion that the minds of dead people linger after death in the form of immaterial "souls" combines the empirical recognition of individual mental activity of living people with an unempirical concept of the survival of the invisible mental essence after the demise of the material body. The attention-demanding quality of religious claims, which is so crucial for their acquisition and transmission, thus springs from the paradoxical fact that these claims at the same time confirm and violate many intuitive principles and expectations.[48] The spheres of reality referred to as "profane" and "sacred," found universally in religious thought, can also be seen as manifestations of first- and second-order cognition, respectively. The profane, or secular, is the realm of the waking mind and of adaptation to the material and biological conditions of life, including mundane workaday technology and alertness to the constantly changing environment. By contrast, the sacred is the realm of adaptation to the inner but socially shared meta-cognition, with its metaphysical anxieties and heatedly defended non-empirical notions, often associated with dreams, hallucinations, and "prophetic" visions.[49]

In principle, natural selection has favored notions that are empirically true over those that are false. The latter, by virtue of giving us a distorted picture of the world, can easily lead to disadvantageous or even lethal decisions and actions. Our primary system of perceptual representation is likewise designed to provide us with as accurate a model of the external world as possible, just as our capacity to think and solve problems is designed to give true rather than false answers. At the same time, having strong beliefs in fictitious entities can sometimes be of considerable benefit to an individual, in removing uncertainty in decision-making, in preventing worry about why the world is the way it is, and in providing one with a degree of confidence in one's actions in highly uncertain and unpredictable environments. The fact that religions have survived for millennia rather than been selected out is a proof that their potentially maladaptive fantasies are more than compensated by the benefits of certainty, however illusory, in decision-making, and of the cognitive fluidity gained from other more adaptive types of thinking. Pure rationality and respect for facts are not always in evidence in the history of our species: rather, the mystical, religious, mythical mindset seems to characterize human behavior everywhere and at every time.[50] It is as if there was indeed some adaptive advantage to such modes of thinking that offers benefits rationality cannot provide. As argued by John D. Barrow, one possibility is that rationality breeds caution (as in Hamlet's "Thus thought makes cowards of us all," 3.1.82), whereas irrationality, emotional fervor, and blind faith breed courage. In our ancestral world, where hostile conflicts were common and a matter of life or death, too much rationality might not be helpful. The fearless zealot who feels guided by supernatural powers is a difficult opponent to overcome, and the results achieved with such motivation can be, on balance, beneficial.[51]

For Steven Mithen in turn religious beliefs such as elaborate cosmologies and fantastic mythologies are adaptively neutral by-products of the cognitive fluidity that gave humans such unprecedented adaptive flexibility.[52] In a similar vein, Dan Sperber interprets the origin of religion in the light of a distinction between what he calls mental "dispositions" and "susceptibilities." The former have been positively selected in the process of biological evolution, while the latter are side-effects of the former. For example, our disposition to eat sweets gives way to susceptibility to over-consummate sugar. By the same token, acquiring empirical knowledge is an adaptive disposition, while religious beliefs develop as a result of susceptibility. In other words, religion with its capacity to imagine the world as it is not may have arisen not as a biologically advantageous adaptation, but as a side-effect of other cognitive representations that do correspond with the world as it is.[53]

For Richard Dawkins one of the cognitive adaptations that have accidentally produced religion is the natural credulity of children. Children arrive in the world equipped with the instinct to learn certain useful things, but without the specific knowledge needed in their environment, and they grow up surrounded by adults who have already acquired that knowledge. Learning important things by trial and error is often a bad idea because the errors are too costly: the first serious error may well be the last, as in playing with snakes, swimming in a crocodile infested river, or trusting strangers. It is easy to see why natural selection should penalize an experimental turn of mind and favor simple credulity in children, who are programmed to believe, without question, whatever the grown-ups tell them, which is generally beneficial. But the flip side of trusting obedience is slavish gullibility, a susceptibility to believe both true and false, as long as the source of such "wisdom" is the elders, usually parents. For Dawkins the persistence of credulity in adults stems from a hankering after the lost securities and comforts of childhood, but it is also clear that in the name of mental maturity and responsibility the child-like, automatic credulity should in time be replaced by the constructive scepticism of adult science. Religion can thus again be seen as a by-product of the misapplication of several otherwise adaptive cognitive modules, including the modules for constructing theories of other minds, for forming coalitions, discriminating in favor of in-group members and against strangers, and for assigning teleological purpose to things.[54]

The persistence of credulity into adulthood must also involve a degree of self-deception, a tendency to suppress both one's own doubts and the fact that the beliefs lack evidence to support them. The psychologists Randolph M. Nesse and Alan T. Lloyd argue that psychological repression may have evolved to facilitate self-deception, mainly for the purpose of effectively deceiving others. There must be strong selection to detect deception and this ought, in turn, to select for a degree of self-deception, rendering some facts and motives unconscious so as not to betray—by the subtle signs of self-knowledge—the deception being practised.[55] Cheating and self-deception are in fact two sides of the same psychological disposition, as also pointed out by Robert Trivers. Since it is useful to maintain a façade of morality and public beneficence, cheating must be disguised, not only to the potential dupes but to the deceiver himself, who becomes less and less conscious of the true nature of his motives and actions.[56] In other words, the most successful and convincing liars are those who do not realize that they are lying and who genuinely believe their own lies to be true—not the crafty and scheming conmen acting out their rehearsed part, but the "inspired" preachers lacking in self-doubt and remaining fully committed to their mission. The so-called "charisma" often attached to such individuals, with the accompanying ability to impose one's opinions and will on others, results ultimately from high self-deceptive certainty in one's own convictions, however irrational and false they may be.

For social beings such as humans the self-deception of blind faith may be a price to pay for the protection society provides, even at the cost of private doubts, as captured by Chico Marx in *Duck Sup* (1933): "Who are you going to believe: me or your own eyes?" In the clash between the social and the exploratory needs, the former—more dynamic and emotional—often wins over the latter, a "merely" cognitive and cerebral need. Put differently: the social need with its collective fictions is the domain of politics, while the exploratory need with its search for truth is the domain of common sense and science. Another reason why collective lies are often embraced and self-doubt is suppressed is that the meta-cognitive and teleological humans generally delight in fictions and illusions, both the harmless ones offered by art and the potentially harmful ones peddled by charlatans. Fictional scenarios give cognitive pleasure and are not necessarily experienced as deceitful or exploitative, as evidenced not just by Netflix junkies but also by a frightening number of people duped by conmen and political demagogues.[57] As Raymond Tallis puts it, "human beings like falsehoods. They have an appetite for accepting with some part of their minds what they know to be false with another."[58]

Another reason for persisting in false beliefs is the embarrassment and shame of having to admit that one has been fooled. As Carl Sagan puts it:

> One of the saddest lessons of history is this: if we've been bamboozled long enough, we tend to reject any evidence of the bamboozle. We're no longer interested in finding out the truth. The bamboozle has captured us. It's simply too painful to acknowledge, even to ourselves, that we've been taken. Once you give a charlatan power over you, you almost never get it back. So the old bamboozles tend to persist as the new ones rise.[59]

The fear of damage to self-esteem thus represses the disturbing knowledge or justified suspicion that, for example, the beloved leader is a psychopathic mass murderer of his own people, like Stalin or Mao Tse-tung. For their part, "charismatic" leaders constantly test their followers' loyalty by making them believe more and more bizarre and outrageous lies, because, as the historian Yuval Noah Harari puts it bluntly, "as a species, humans prefer power to truth."[60] Uncritical, self-deceptive surrender to groupthink under the pressure of equally self-deceptive, narcissistic leaders remains among the most emotionally potent and dangerous cognitive biases of otherwise decent and well-meaning people in the mainstream of the society.[61]

Because of its mixed reliance on both true and false notions, teleological thinking is thus responsible for what is most noble as well as most pathological in human behavior. On the one hand, teleological worldviews can remit the threat of existential emptiness and purposelessness with beautiful if illusory mythical and poetic accounts of the world. The psychologist Robert Trivers also presents evidence in favor of immunological benefits of self-deception, which would mean that people who cultivate illusions are, on average, healthier, happier, and live longer than skeptics and realists.[62] Notwithstanding possible health benefits, ideologies and groupthink trap people in a web of delusion and oppression, in which obsessive devotion to arbitrary beliefs limits individual freedom of thought, by imposing an illusory safety net that protects most people from the fear of purposelessness at the price of blind conformity to the group. The dark side of faith is that it often provides twisted justifications for needless, irrational conflicts, and for arbitrary destruction of lives. History is sadly written in the blood spilt not only by struggles over territory and natural resources, but also by clashes between irreconcilable ideological systems. One set of unverifiable beliefs does not tolerate other sets of equally unverifiable beliefs, and with both sides claiming possession of the absolute truth mutual understanding, tolerance, and cooperation are often impossible. Since the proof of faith cannot be found in hard and indisputable evidence that both sides can agree on, the only way to defend one's position is to accept it unquestioningly and to reject any other belief system with equally unquestioning and intolerant zeal. Tribal mentality based on dogmatic faith, religious or political, remains the most divisive force in human societies: no other badge of social identity, such as skin color, ethnic origin, language, territory, shared history, class or gender, antagonizes individuals and groups more than the incompatible and irreconcilable systems of self-deceptive beliefs and worldviews.

Ultimately, is there an objective meaning and purpose in life, individual or collective, which the teleological need expressed in religion, philosophy, and politics compels us to think there is? The answer offered by science is unequivocally negative. Evolutionary theory—the best biological explanation we have of how we arrived in this world—provides no reason to think that there is an objective purpose of human existence other than the dissemination of the genes that created us.[63] At the same time, it is within the limited freedom that humans have as meta-cognitive autonomous systems to use imagination and volition to defy the selfish gene, as in choosing celibacy or contraception, and doing many other things that we have not been evolved to do. While dogmatic ideologies offer illusions as an answer to the question of why we are here, only science—a meta-cognitive system programmatically rooted in empirical reality—tells us honestly and unsentimentally why things happen. As the psychologist David P. Barash puts it, things happen "because of thermodynamic, electromagnetic, or gravitational forces, selection pressure and so forth, including, in many cases, a hefty dose of chaos."[64] In the face of the cold and indifferent universe of impersonal physical forces that so terrified Blaise Pascal, humans have comforted themselves with infantile illusions that a cosmic, benevolent, human-like intelligence is looking over them, having first created the universe with each of us personally in mind. On the other hand, the mature choice is either to see life as ultimately meaningless or to recognize the responsibility to search for personalized meaning, not in any dogmatic sense but in molding one's life according to purposes of one's own choosing. An individual pursuit of happiness within a secular framework can work just as well, if not better, as faith in metaphysical doctrines and rituals.[65] Within the humanist worldview the well-tried ways to achieve meaningful contentment include happy family life, a circle of friends, a satisfying professional career, stimulating intellectual pursuits, artistic creativity, contact with nature, and all kinds of pleasure-giving hobbies and pastimes, including a glass of wine in the evening. In other words, while there is no objective preordained meaning to life, the teleologically inclined humans are free to invent goals of their own that can be more real than those supposedly imposed "from above" by superhuman intelligences. Religion may have evolved as a psychological adaptation to inner existential anxieties, ultimately focused on the fear of death, but human meta-cognition, unless hijacked by oppressive ideologies, is sufficiently creative to devise individual goals to fulfill the obsessive search for the ever-elusive because objectively non-existent meaning of things.

4

Between Indexicality and Iconicity

Among the sensory modalities described in Chapter 2 in the context of contiguous communication, vision occupies a central position in humans as the most efficacious sense in terms of the amount and diversity of information it picks up from the environment. Visual information provides us with crucial knowledge about the surrounding space with its physical objects and their properties, including shape, size, color, distance, and movement. Sight is adaptively the most powerful sense in humans, which makes blindness a serious, potentially life-threatening handicap. In social life, visual contiguous indexes in the form of bodily cues, symptoms, and signals offer crucial information about the intentions, emotions, and physiological states of communicating partners. For humans, visual communication includes both first-order, parainformational interpretations of external stimuli and second-order, metainformational representations held in memory and translated into permanent iconic signs of visual culture. Some of the most important cognitive modules designed to process first-order visual information relate to the social need, and include the *face recognition* module and the *body-language* module.

Let's Face It

Putting aside the anomalous jellyfish, clams, and the starfish, most animals have evolved faces—a front part of the body packed with forward-oriented sensing organs: eyes, nose, tongue, and ears, which serve a useful purpose in directing the rest of the body, perceiving important things in the world, and ingesting food. Most sea-based and all land-based creatures have faces that are archetypally similar: they consist of a forehead, two horizontally separated eyes, nose, mouth, and chin. Almost all animals, from birds, gorillas, penguins, vipers, kangaroos, even spiders, and of course humans adhere to the same formula for facial composition. None, for example, has a mouth over the eyes and nose, and none has only one eye in the back of its head. The uniformity of facial composition is the result of optimized survival. The eyes located high on the face at the front of the body occupy a commanding view of the world for sighting food, avoiding low-hanging branches and other obstacles, and directing locomotion. The nose is well designed by being turned downward to avoid becoming a rain gutter, and is also strategically positioned just above the mouth to serve as a last-ditch protection against eating stinking and therefore infectious food.

Not only is a face the first thing noticed about a person, but it also tells us more about an individual than any other part of the body. No wonder faces have become a popular theme of anthropologists, cognitive neuroscientists, and artists. Faces are an important part of visual culture: the majority of illustrations in standard art books are human portraits; faces dominate magazine covers, television, and cinema screen; and millions of people exchange daily portrait photographs through social media. Portrait-drawing courses are standard offerings in art schools, and some galleries specialize in portraits, like the National Portrait Gallery in London. Schematized icons of facial expressions known as emoji are among the fastest-growing forms of visual telecommunication (Figure 4.1).[1] Equally obvious is the importance of being able to identify faces and infer emotions and character from them, the skill facilitated by a domain-specific and localized part of the human cerebral cortex dedicated to facial processing, the seat of the face recognition module in the brain.[2]

Charles Darwin was probably the first scientist to notice that humans, apes, and monkeys communicate certain emotions using similar facial expressions.[3] Among non-human and human primates the face is the most critical source of information about individual identity and emotional states. The human grimaces of fear, the smile, and even laughter have their parallels in the facial expressions of chimpanzees.[4] The ability to recognize one's kin is crucial for a baby's survival and future development, and very young infants are able to discriminate people from other objects by using faces to inform them whether or not something is a person. New-born infants (less

Figure 4.1 Iconic signs: schematized human faces on emoji toys. Courtesy of British Library/Open Culture.

than an hour old) show a significant preference (head and eye movement) for a schematized face over a scrambled or blank face.[5] This inborn disposition accounts for the almost automatic ease and speed with which we recognize a face. It is a function acquired very early during development, and it does not require any formal training or conscious thinking. There also seems to be no limit to the number of faces that we can recognize or remember. At the same time, perceiving and recognizing a face is a private experience, incommunicable to others and very difficult to verbalize, as police investigators know only too well.

As also mentioned in Chapter 1, certain facial expressions are symptoms of the basic set of emotions (sadness, anger, fear, surprise, disgust, contempt, and happiness) that are recognized everywhere, irrespective of socio-cultural background. The psychologists Paul Ekman and Wallace V. Friesen took photographs of Americans acting out these emotions, and they also photographed stone-age tribesmen from New Guinea as they told stories during which the same feelings were expressed. When members of one of the cultures were then shown the portraits from the other, they interpreted the meanings of the facial expressions with a better than 80 percent accuracy.[6] As our daily experience shows, facial emotions form an important non-verbal channel of social communication, capable of expressing universally a wide range of affective states: "the grimace of pain, the sneer of contempt, the glare of anger, the averted eyes of shame, the wide-eyed look of surprise, the intent stare of interest, the quizzical look of puzzlement, the frozen stare of horror, the radiant smile of joy, the sly grin of mischief."[7] Interestingly also, as psychological experiments have shown, women are generally more sensitive to facial expressions than men. According to Simon Baron-Cohen, women are better at decoding non-verbal communication, picking up subtle nuances in tone of voice or facial expression, and using them to judge a person's character. Baron-Cohen attributes this innate capacity in women to their greater, on average, than in men ability to empathize with other people and to understand their emotions and states of mind.[8]

One of the most common facial expressions is the smile, used universally to signal friendliness and approval, and to indicate a general sense of pleasure. According to Edward O. Wilson, the smile with its invariant communicative meaning is an inborn signal, identical among the hunter-gatherers' infants of South Africa's Kalahari desert and among American and European infants. Even blind and deaf-blind children develop the smile in the absence of any known psychological conditioning. What is more, from the time of birth girls smile more than boys: several independent studies have shown that new-born females respond more frequently than males with eyes-closed, reflexive smiling. Frequent smiling becomes one of the more persistent of female traits and endures through adolescence and maturity.[9]

Not only the face but also the hands and the entire body can partake in contiguous visual communication in the form of cues and signals. Neurophysiologists speak of specialized cells in the visual cortex of the brain processing data about the human body, both in whole and in part, especially faces and hands. Perhaps this is why artists such as Albrecht Dürer could spend most of their lives drawing just hands and faces.[10] Some body postures and hand gestures reveal identical cross-cultural emotive meanings, similarly to facial expressions, which would suggest a corresponding body-language module as part of genetically motivated predispositions. Appropriate reactions to certain body appearances and postures appear inborn and automatic, as in the recognition of cuteness in infants for example. As Nancy Etcoff suggests, features such as soft skin and hair, huge eyes, big pupils, chubby cheeks, small noses, big heads, and small limbs in all cultural contexts automatically trigger positive, tender emotions as well as caring and protective behavior in the viewers. Not surprisingly, these infantile cues are exploited by toy manufacturers and cartoonists, as witnessed by Mickey Mouse and Bambi with their exaggerated high foreheads and doe eyes, designed to elicit tender feelings and turn off aggression (Figure 4.2).[11]

All the great apes have well-developed gestural capacities and can read body language, which in humans accounts for about 65 percent of direct personal interaction. People exchange bodily signals in an unconscious manner most of the time and use a similar suite of spontaneous gestures across cultures and languages. For the greatest part of our waking lives the hand alone is constantly on the move, touching and feeling, holding and manipulating, or merely describing configurations in the air. Spontaneous manual movements accompany normal talk and are an integral part of communicative action.[12] Unlike the verbal language, which consists mainly of arbitrary signs, gesticulation tends to be iconic, by providing by manual action an image of something a person is talking about, including gestural imitations of actions and behaviors, of movements, shapes, and spatial relations between objects. Gestures

Figure 4.2 Cues of infantile cuteness in a Disney cartoon designed to turn off aggression and elicit tenderness. Courtesy of British Library/Open Culture.

can also be subject to cultural regulation and codes, acquiring more arbitrary meta-meanings, as in sign languages.[13]

As the neurologist William O. Dingwall demonstrates, humans share most of their gestures and body language with other primates, whose interpersonal communication involves a complex, partially redundant, multichannel system involving visual, auditory, tactile, and olfactory input modalities. For example, in the context of fear or apprehension chimpanzees touch or pat each other on the back, hold hands, or otherwise seek contact with one another. After separation, kissing, embracing, and patting have also been observed. A chimpanzee may bow in submission to a stronger rival, who then reaches out to touch him as a signal that this gesture has been accepted. Threat postures involve upraised arms, the brandishing of sticks, and the throwing of objects. Begging with outstretched palm, tickling, pinching, kicking, grooming, and scratching all resemble the same gestures in humans.[14] The psychologist Robert R. Provine also shows how tickle games and laughter among both chimpanzees and humans help establish and sustain in-group bonds: we only tickle and are tickled by those with whom we have close social relationships such as friends, relatives, and lovers. Such behavior belongs to the pre-linguistic, largely unconscious and affective form of communication, and its social nature is evident in the fact that it takes two to enjoy the tickling game: one cannot tickle oneself to produce laughter.[15]

Body Decorations

Non-phenotypic body decorations, largely absent in animals, represent a meta-cognitive, for the most part iconic, cultural extension of the innate body-language module which humans share with other primates. While paying instinctive attention to phenotypic signals such as facial expressions, gestures, and bodily postures is prompted by the corresponding innate cognitive modules, it would probably be difficult to argue in favor of an evolved module controlling our responses to body decorations and modifications such as makeup, tattoos, skin piercing, jewelry, head dress, and clothes. These artifacts, in contrast to cues such as body shape, facial traits, and the natural look of skin and hair, appeared too late in human history (most probably during the cultural "explosion" of the Late Paleolithic about 40,000 years ago), after the genome of the *Homo sapiens*, complete with its cognitive architecture, had become more or less fully formed. But as Ellen Dissanayake persuasively argues, certain types of body ornamentation might be selectively valuable for the same reasons that genetically programmed colors, markings, and exaggerated anatomical features are important in other animals: to attract mates, as in the peacock's colorful tail, to scare off rivals, as in the stag's broad antlers, to differentiate individuals, and to indicate status or gender in a herd.[16] People throughout history have inserted objects such as shells, bones, feathers, and so on through their ears and noses; they have pierced and bejeweled virtually every part of the face—the ears, noses, lips, eyebrows, and tongue—and all the erogenous zones of the body such as navels, nipples, penises, and labia.[17]

It could be argued therefore that human modifications of external appearance represent a meta-cognitive extension of the inborn body-language module, already present in animal behavior. Bodily adornments are by definition located *on* the body, and as a form of extended phenotype they represent a step toward displaced cultural communication. By contrast, phenotypic cues, symptoms, and signals still remain an integral part of the natural body. For example, the peacock's colorful tail belongs to first-order contiguous indexes signaling the bird's phenotypic quality to females. On the other hand, a feather head-dress of a native American chief is a second-order contiguous iconic sign, which announces the wearer's status and authority by enlarging his head. By the same token, smooth, unblemished facial skin and large eyes are phenotypic indexical cues of youth, health, and by extension fertility, which can be culturally enhanced by iconic signs of makeup: cream to smooth the skin, color to enlarge the eyes, and mascara to lengthen, thicken, and darken eyelashes to make the eyes look even bigger—all for a rejuvenating effect. Because of the importance of the attention-grabbing face in interpersonal communication, makeup as an iconic sign can be further enhanced in makeup art, modeling, acting and, in an even more exaggerated way, in drag makeup and circus clowning.[18]

As ethnographic studies also show, applying pigments and other ornaments to faces and bodies is part of universal contiguously iconic communication. In modern tribal Africa, for example, items of body decoration include feathers, cowrie shells, chains, beads, and body paint, as well as practices such as fashioning or mutilating parts of the body itself, as in hair styling, tooth filing, ear and nose piercing, tattooing, or other scarification.[19] Body ornamentation can also be a very social occupation, with participants spending hours decorating each other. The purposes of these iconic ornamentations are again similar cross-culturally: to increase personal attractiveness, to distinguish the noble and the rich from others, married from single, to suggest potency and physical prowess, and to protect parts of the body (Figure 4.3).[20]

In addition to serving as iconic enhancements of selected phenotypic traits, both the semi-permanent bodily adornments such as makeup and even more so the permanent ones such as piercings and scarifications are also indexes of individual and cultural memory and identity. The removable decorations testify to the changing elements of one's identity, like those relating to age or transient fashion, while permanent bodily modifications fix one's identity and status for life. Circumcision, clitoridectomy, tattoos, body piercing, branding, hair removal, cranial binding, feet binding, and so on are constant reminders of indelible ethnic affiliation, social status, and gender role.[21] The permanent markings on the surface of the body and alterations of body parts become indexes of one's life story—a visual, public, and portable curriculum vitae. Subsequent additions to these markings reflect changes in status and identity, such as transition from adolescence to maturity, from unmarried to married, or from child-bearing to past-child-bearing. In tribal cultures these social categories tend to be rigid and fixed, as reflected in the irremovable character of bodily modifications that mark them. The Marquesas Islanders, for example, used to add tattoos on their bodies gradually, usually as a result of an initiation rite marking the change of social status. Different patterns of tattoos and permanent scars would thus distinguish unmarried girls from married ones, and pubescent boys from adult warriors.[22]

In modern societies, with their social mobility, relative freedom of choice, and tolerance, social categories are more fluid, allowing for transitioning in and out of groups and status throughout life. Bodily adornments tend to be therefore more

Figure 4.3 Bodily adornments among Osage Indians, lithograph by Louis Leopold Boilly (1761–1845). Courtesy of Smithsonian American Art Museum.

a matter of personal lifestyle than of rigid social affiliation with its appertaining duties and privileges. Rebellious teenagers tattoo and pierce their bodies and dress "alternatively" to defy adult, conventional rules and values; some people indulge in plastic surgery more out of vanity than to indicate their celebrity status; and we attend to our odor-neutralizing hygiene to feel more comfortable rather than to emphasize our membership in "civilized" society. Body decorations in modern society tend therefore to be semi-permanent, like makeup or hair-style, lasting for a time until they are discarded without leaving a trace of former taste, role, or group affiliation. Indulging in permanent tattoos that reflect the attitude and lifestyle of the moment can therefore be a source of future nostalgia or embarrassment ("What was I thinking?"), whatever the case may be, as one's life circumstances and personality change (Figure 4.4).[23]

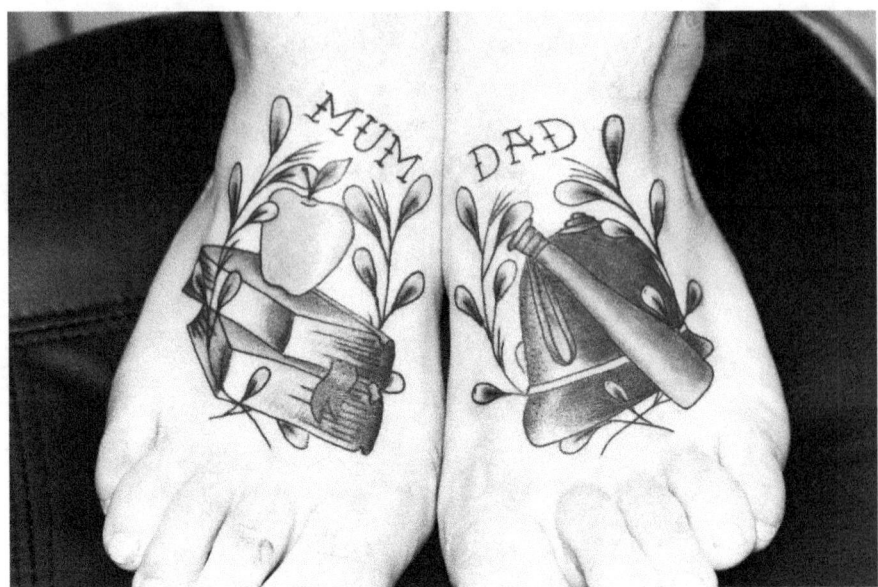

Figure 4.4 Modern tattoo as a lifestyle choice. Courtesy of British Library/Open Culture.

Clothes and fashion too help people, past and present, to negotiate their relations with the outside world, in addition to providing them with thermal comfort and protection. As visual iconic extensions of bodies and personalities, clothes mirror people's intentions and desires, related primarily to sexuality and status.[24] For Nancy Etcoff, the original purpose of clothing may have been to draw attention to the erogenous zones of the body rather than to hide them (Western puritanism notwithstanding). This is why tribal iconic art and body decorations tend to highlight the sources of fertility: clothing makes necks appear longer, breasts larger, shoulders wider, waists trimmer, hips curvier, feet smaller, and legs longer. Trends in (particularly female) fashion are continually changing, in turn revealing and concealing various erotic parts of the body, thus keeping sexual interest and social interactions alive and focused.[25] Bodily adornments belong to cultural universals; they are found in all documented tribal, farming, and urban societies. They are both iconic in enhancing certain natural features of the body, and indexical in signaling phenotypic quality of their wearers. Like today's fashion, these adornments build on the innate predispositions motivated by the body-language module, and form a meta-cognitive semiotic system to broadcast one's physical attractiveness, status, group affiliation, personality, and lifestyle.

Sham Menstruation and Performing Arts

The cultural practice of body painting can be viewed as a transition from animal bodily communication based on anatomical cues and behavioral signals to human conscious bodily signs, the latter in turn marking the first step toward fully displaced iconic signs of visual arts. The evolutionary logic of this transition has been persuasively demonstrated by the anthropologist Camilla Power in what she calls the "sham menstruation" strategy.[26]

Given the supreme evolutionary importance of survival and propagation, bodily cues, symptoms, and signals in animal females serve primarily the procreative need, by announcing fertility and readiness to mate. Among ape and primate females the period of fertility within the estrous cycle is loudly advertised by such symptoms as the swelling and reddening of the skin around the vagina, emission of menstrual blood and distinctive odors, and by signals such as inviting, provocative behavior. In human females ovulation has become concealed at some point in the evolution of archaic *Homo sapiens*, the fact that Power explains in terms of an evolved deception to confuse males about the precise period of the women's fertility, otherwise announced periodically only by menstruation—a clear symptom of imminent fertility and an index of not being pregnant that no mate seeking male could afford to ignore. At the same time, argues Power, by attracting male attention menstruating women pose a potential threat of "stealing" males from other pregnant, lactating, or menopausal women, causing jealousy and social tensions. To avoid this, archaic human females adopted a reciprocal coalitional strategy by inventing iconic signs mimicking menstruation to attract and sustain male support. Whenever a member of the female coalition menstruated, the non-menstruating members joined in to confuse and deceive males, either by borrowing a menstruating woman's blood or mimicking it with other blood or blood substitutes such as red ocher. The sham menstruation strategy practiced by fertile women alternating in their ovulation periods between phases of fertility and non-fertility was thus designed to generate extra male attention and mating effort distributed among the whole coalition, benefiting both non-ovulating and ovulating women.[27]

A cooperative dynamic within the coalition of menstruation faking females could further expand into more elaborate ways of broadcasting fertility signals in the form of visual and dramatic arts, with the use of cosmetics focused on red pigment as well as movement, dance, song, and costume to advertise phenotypic quality. Body-painting combined with dance and singing to attract male attention to the female body can thus be seen as a putative origin of performing arts, focused on contiguous indexical and iconic visual and auditory signs. This body-based art probably long predated the invention in the Late Paleolithic (*c.* 40,000 years ago) of permanent and fully displaced iconic signs of painting and sculpture that used surfaces other than the human body: cave walls, wood, stone, bone, or animal skin. We have no hard evidence of prehistoric performing arts because body painting is perishable, but large quantities of red ocher have been found in man-made deposits in Africa dating from at least 125,000 years, and it is generally accepted by archaeologists that ocher was used for body decoration rather than for painting cave walls or other artifacts.[28] The famous limestone figurine of the "Venus" of Willendorf, dated to about 25,000 BCE, still bears traces of red ocher (Figure 4.5).[29] Ethnographic studies also demonstrate that red pigment is used ubiquitously in modern tribal puberty and nubility rituals to advertise physical attractiveness and sexual maturity of young women and men. In modern societies the sham menstruation theory explains the perennial male erotic

Figure 4.5 Figurine of "Venus" of Willendorf (*c.* 25,000 BCE, 11 cm high) was probably originally covered with red ocher. Naturhistorisches Museum, Vienna, courtesy of Wellcome Collection CC BY 4.0.

interest in women's red lipstick, rouged cheeks, crimson dresses, and not least the "red-light" districts. The color red is attention-grabbing and emotionally stimulating in all cultures. Applied to the selected parts of the female body such as lips, buttocks, and breasts it produces a range of physiological reactions, including acceleration of heart rate and stimulation in certain parts of the brain, which is why it is also the color of stop signs, railway signals, fire engines, and flags and emblems of revolutionary political movements.[30]

Memory and Displaced Reference

The things that early humans did to and on their bodies are probably the first contiguously iconic signs, distinct from indexical cues and symptoms, and from instinctive behavioral signals. It is also possible to postulate a parallel evolution in vocal communication, to be discussed in the next chapter, from contiguously indexical emotive vocalizations, through imitative sounds, to syntactic speech based on symbolic signs and displaced reference. As argued earlier, these developments in visual and auditory communication are linked to advances in human meta-cognitive faculties such as memory and consciousness, and the resulting need to socialize knowledge in permanent signs. Both visual signs such as tools, weapons, clothing, works of art, architecture, and written documents, and auditory signs such as speech, oral storytelling, songs, and music—all culture in fact—became in turn indexes of collective memory cementing group identity built around its history and tradition.

The contiguously indexical body language and its extension in the form of iconic bodily adornments do not necessarily depend on long-term memory, because contiguous signals and signs are co-present with their meaning in the form of current physiological, emotional, and mental states. That is, a person's body and its adornments are practically self-referential. It is the external material artifacts as well as language that require memory to connect the contiguous sign with its absent referent. Animal artifacts such as ant hills, birds' nests, spiders' webs, and beavers' dams depend on specialized genetic memory, whereas human culture and technology are functions of conscious ontogenetic memory, cause-and-effect thinking, and long-term planning motivated by the teleological need. The second-order cultural environment superimposed upon the natural environment—the entire human presence on Earth—is itself an index of uniquely human meta-cognition. Every human artifact is a reminder of the initial reason for its design and the purposefulness of its execution, of ingenuity and skill, and of the social context of its production. This is what archaeologists and historians do in relation to the material records of human life in the past, and what social sciences do in relation to contemporary human activity.

Paradoxically, however, while human artifacts depend on conscious memory for their production, they also testify to the limitations of that memory. If human memory was like computer memory—capable of retaining all inputted data to be retrieved in original form at any time—we would not need external mnemonic devices of cultural artifacts to prompt the relevant content, because we would just consciously navigate the repository of remembered facts in our brains to access the knowledge we need. It would not be necessary to keep diaries, write documents, memos, or shopping lists, because everything once seen, heard, smelled, tasted, touched, or imagined would be recorded in the brain in perfect form forever. Nor would it be necessary to listen to familiar stories or favorite music, re-read literature, re-view works of art, attend regularly near identical religious ceremonies, or pore nostalgically over family photo albums. We would just close our eyes and relive the past events with the same accuracy, directness, and vividness that characterized the original experiences. Nor would we despair over the loss of sentimental objects that remind us of the past, because we would not need any reminding. Learning new things would also be easy: a single exposure to a stimulus in any sensory modality would automatically commit it fully to memory, like saving a computer file. Alas, as we know, human memory is imperfect. Unlike computers we forget many things, we suppress the memory of unpleasant or embarrassing events, and we have problems memorizing certain things to begin with, like learning a new language or people's names.

Like all cognitive faculties, human memory is a product of the brain's evolution, so why is it apparently not up to the job? Memory may either still be evolution's work in progress, or its imperfection is part of its design. The latter view is favored by the psychologist Daniel Schacter in his study of the "seven sins of memory," in which he argues that bad memory may be a blessing after all.[31] For example, human memory is *transient*, in the sense that it weakens over time, making it difficult for us to remember what we did or knew years ago. At the same time transience may be adaptive because not all experiences will have future benefit. Memory is also characterized by *absent-mindedness*, understood as a breakdown at the interface between attention and memory, as in forgetting to buy milk on the way from work. But absent-mindedness too can be adaptive, because we cannot realistically attend to everything at any given time. Next on Schacter's list of memory's sins comes what he calls *blocking*, that is, failing to retrieve information that we know we know, as in being unable to recall the name of a familiar person. This, argues Schacter, is also adaptive because the things we tend to forget are low in frequency and therefore not that important (indeed, what is the point of remembering the name of a person we may never see again). Another sin is *misattribution*, when we forget where the information comes from, as in claiming as our own an experience we read or heard about or saw in a movie. This too is apparently adaptive, because sometimes the information itself is more important than its source. When we distort what happened under the influence of leading questions or comments, our memory suffers from *suggestibility*, which can likewise be adaptive because exaggerating the events of the past under current pressure makes us look more confident and reliable. We are also susceptible to *bias*, when we unconsciously edit the past to present ourselves in a more positive light. Schacter's last memory sin is *persistence*, as in repeatedly recalling disturbing or unpleasant experiences in order to avoid making the same mistakes in the future. It is because our memory suffers, or benefits, from these "faults" that we need "exosomatic information storing devices," as Henry Plotkin calls them,[32] in the form of works of art, rituals, oral stories, written texts, photographic media, recorded sound, and computer data to support our memory and prompt specific cultural knowledge. The earliest historical signs relying on displaced reference, such as transient speech, durable tools and works of art, are indirect evidence of both the presence and deficiency of human memory.

The Beginnings of Iconic Culture

If bodily adornments do not necessarily depend on memory, exosomatic iconic signs testify to memory-based ability to associate similar but different things separated in time and space. The earliest evidence of displaced iconic thinking comes from about 2 million years ago in the form of a dark red, water-worn cobble found in the South African cave of Makapansgat in 1925. The cobble is 6 centimeters across and was brought by an *Australopithecine* (a fossil hominid) from at least twenty miles away, presumably because of the extraordinary resemblance to a human face on one side (Figure 4.6).[33] The cobble is not yet an artifact but most probably a natural formation that attracted the attention of a hominid by its iconic quality. The earliest to date iconic artifact comes from over a million years later in the form of a piece of "sculpture" found at the site of Berekhat Ram in Israel. It is a small, 35 mm-high shaped piece of volcanic rock dated to somewhere between 233,000 and 800,000 years ago, which bears a resemblance to a female figure, with grooves around its "neck" and along its "arms"

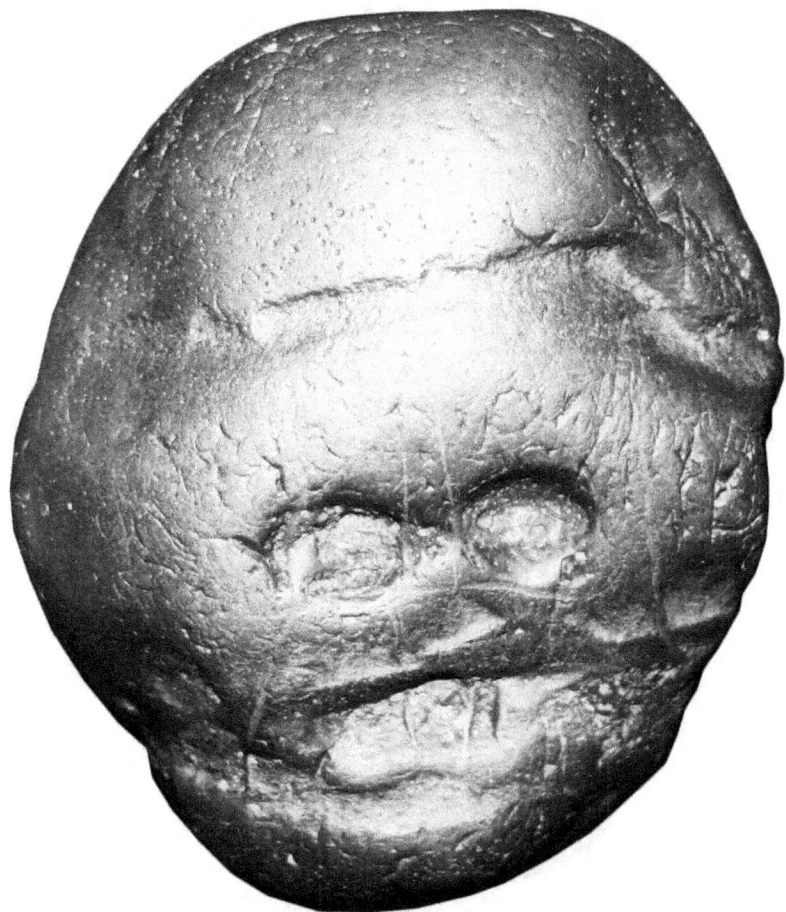

Figure 4.6 The cobble from Makapansgat cave, Africa (*c.* 2 million years old, 6 cm wide) as the earliest evidence to date of iconic meta-thinking. Courtesy of Smithsonian American Art Museum.

(Figure 4.7). Archaeologists have debated whether these grooves were natural or humanely made, and the microscopic analysis by Alexander Marshack has concluded that humans were responsible. In other words, the figurine is an intentionally enhanced, iconic artifact—the first sculpture on record.[34]

The Late Paleolithic period of 50,000 to 12,000 BCE, which belonged definitely to our species, the *Homo sapiens*, famously saw the explosion of iconic, figurative representations in the form of portable sculptures and paintings on rocks and cave walls. Impressive as the prehistoric paintings in the caves of Chauvet, Lascaux, and Altamira are, it is worth remembering that the surviving Late Paleolithic artifacts most probably represent only the tip of the iceberg. It is almost certain that a great deal of artistic activity at the time involved materials which are gone forever: work

Figure 4.7 Figurine of "Venus" of Berekhat Ram, Israel (*c.* 233,000 and 800,000 years old, 35 mm high) as the earliest to date permanent iconic artifact.

in wood, bark, or hides, also figures made in mud, sand, or snow, and, as discussed earlier, body-painting with the red ocher.[35] The surviving iconic signs of cave art are evidence of the mnemonic function of realistic images for prehistoric hunters, which reminded them of some of the things crucial to their survival: predators to be avoided and game animals to be pursued. The large (some about two meters long) paintings on cave walls can be interpreted as facilitating, not unlike modern textbooks of zoology, comparisons between the images of animals and their real-life equivalents. A high degree of naturalism of representation would also provide clues to identify the species and instruct the viewers about the animals' behavior.[36]

To date, the oldest cave with painted images of animals and human-like figures is Chauvet in the Ardèche region of France, discovered in 1994 and dated to about 32,000 years ago. It contains over 300 representations of animals such as rhinoceroses, lions, reindeer, horses, mammoths, bears, and bison, executed with a degree of realism that in some cases includes imitation of movement: one bison has seven or eight legs, as if it was running, while other animals give the impression of stalking. Some figures are rendered in what looks like perspective; others are shaded for relief and volume. Anatomical details include eyes, ears, nostrils, and mouth (Figure 4.8).[37] Paintings in the caves of Altamira and Lascaux, dated to 20,000 and 17,000 years ago respectively, also reveal preoccupation with hunting, often in scenes showing spears and arrows stuck in the bodies of the prey. Some scenes depict human figures in animal disguises standing with heads bowed in front of animals.

Predictably, the nutritional and protective needs reflected in cave paintings are complemented by the themes of fertility and procreation. Countless prehistoric drawings as well as small, portable sculptures show a female figure, like the "Venus" of Willendorf (Figure 4.5), usually with emphasis on the breasts, hips, and the reproductive organs. For the archaeologist André Leroi-Gourhan, not just the individual artifacts but the entire cave can be interpreted iconically as a spatial representation of the theme of fertility, centered on male-female dichotomy. The female images of a vulva, the breasts, the belly, the pelvic region, or the thighs with a pubic triangle are often situated in the central areas of compositions in the caves, either on their own or accompanied by large herbivores, the bison, or the mammoth, interpreted by Leroi-Gourhan as "female" animal species. The human male, on the other hand, is represented by ithyphallic figures, isolated phalluses, and faces in frontal or profile view. These "male" images are

Figure 4.8 Realistic profiles of horses' heads painted in Chauvet cave, France (*c*. 32,000 years BCE). Courtesy of British Library/Open Culture.

in nearly all cases situated at the back of the caves or around the central compositions, that is, in opposition to "female" signs, and are accompanied by such "male" animals as horses, ibexes, and stags. Among the more schematic but still iconic images are representations of the themes of death, sex, and procreation, as in the recurring signs showing a phallus-like spear embedded in a vulva-like wound.[38] The sexual meanings are also emphasized by red pigment applied to the caves' narrow passages, clefts, and smaller cavities. In Leroi-Gourhan's interpretation the entire cave becomes an iconic sign of the female body, as well as an index of human imitative capacity and the ability to manufacture durable vehicles of cultural knowledge, focused on the crucial needs of procreation, nourishment, and protection. For the anthropologist Terrence Deacon the prehistoric cave paintings offer the first irrefutable evidence of cognition involving the storage of culturally important information outside the human brain in the media of social communication.[39] For Steven Mithen too, the Late Paleolithic art and material culture testify to the expansion of social knowledge beyond the biological limits of individual brains, a process that probably coincided with the emergence of symbolic syntactic speech, which similarly allowed for ideas to migrate between minds, thus enabling a level of creativity that could never have emerged from a single mind alone.[40] When collective knowledge expanded beyond what an individual brain with its imperfect memory could store and utilize, socially shared material culture with its information storing devices became a form of non-biological memory to preserve ideas that could otherwise have only a transient existence in individual minds.

Indexical Magic

There is yet another important cognitive aspect of displaced signs, indexical, iconic, or symbolic, including the images of animals depicted in prehistoric caves. Because of a quirk of human cognition, displaced reference tends to be affected by a subjectively compelling if objectively false assumption of identity between the form of the sign and its meaning. For prehistoric painters and viewers of animal images, the difference between a real animal and its pictorial representation could be blurred, and painted images could be mistaken for their real-life equivalents, giving the Paleolithic hunters an illusion of control over the wild animals, which is what they probably wanted to achieve in real life. The so-called magical thinking, attributed by nineteenth-century Western anthropologists to "primitive" and "superstitious" tribesmen, is a result of a cognitive bias, which affects us all, of mistaking contiguous signs for displaced reference.

It seems that the bias originates from the experience of contiguity as the default condition of all communication. Contiguous communication is self-referential, with no meta-associations being necessarily involved, and is based on emotionally charged cognitive modules of the kind described in Chapter 1, which prompt reactions following the logic of adaptive self-regulation. Contiguous interactions thus understood are the ubiquitous norm, so much so that we just take them for granted: a tree in front of us is, well, just a tree, a thing in itself, a "Ding an sich" in Immanuel Kant's epistemology.[41] In the poem "Sacred Emily" from 1913 Gertrude Stein states that "Rose is a rose is a rose is a rose,"[42] as if to emphasize that things often are simply what they are, without any meta-meanings necessarily attached to them, at least not the ones intended by any sender—a sobering reminder that not everything always has a deeper meaning. But there would be no need for Kant or Stein to insist on things in themselves, if not for the persistent habit of overinterpretation on the part of meta-cognitive humans. A tree may be just a tree, but not when an artist or art critic looks at it. In the painting *Der einsame Baum* ("The Solitary Tree") from 1822 by Caspar David Friedrich, a lone battered oak in the foreground has been interpreted by William Vaughan as representing the "German soul in the landscape": "The oak tree was part of the primitive landscape. It had always been there and the Germans felt that it was part of them, that it defined them in a certain way." The tree in Friedrich's picture has also been interpreted as referring to the painter himself, "the lonely old oak"[43] (Figure 4.9). Just as physical states can subjectively become meaningful signs, so signs can in turn be overinterpreted as being one with what they refer to, as when prehistoric hunters looked in awe at the paintings of animals on cave walls, believing that they were looking at the animals themselves.

The assumption of identity between sign and meaning, obvious in the case of contiguous objects as "things in themselves," can thus be extended across the entire semiotic spectrum of displaced signs, from indexical through iconic to symbolic. However, the misapplication of the assumption of identity to displaced signs, simply

Figure 4.9 A tree as an iconic sign: *Der einsame Baum* (The Solitary Tree), oil painting by Caspar David Friedrich (1822). Reproduced with the permission of bpkbildagentur/ Staatliche Museen zu Berlin.

because they were once physically associated with certain objects (as in indexes), or resemble them perceptually (as in icons), or refer to them arbitrarily (as in symbols), should raise a few eye-brows among the so-called rational people. Whatever the reasons for this cognitive bias, however, it remains universal. The overinterpretation of indexes has been referred to by anthropologists as *contagious* (indexical) magic, reading too much into icons represents *homeopathic* (iconic) magic, and the assumption that by manipulating words one can somehow manipulate the things that the words refer to underlies *verbal* (symbolic) magic.

In his monumental study of religious beliefs James Frazer describes a wide-spread type of magical thinking based on the psychological law of contact or contagion, whereby things that once have been in contact with one another remain always in contact, even when physically separated.[44] In contagious magic a sympathetic link is believed to exist for example between a person and any separated part of that person, such as hair, nails, teeth, the navel-string, or the placenta. Whoever gets into possession of those once fully contiguous objects will be able, as the thinking goes, to exert an influence, from a distance, on the original owner of these displaced objects. Conversely, the object's original context is also believed to beneficially influence the current user: a saint's bone, a splinter from the "true" Cross, or a rosary blessed by the Pope.

A similar sympathetic link is believed to exist between an object and its indexical trace such as a footprint, a shadow, or a photograph. Frazer quotes it as a world-wide superstition that by injuring footprints one could also injure the feet that made them. The Australian natives from south-east of the country believed that a man could be harmed by having pieces of quartz, bone, or charcoal placed in his footprints. The aboriginals of Victoria would put hot ambers in the tracks of the animals they were pursuing.[45] The modern medium of photography presents a similar case: a photographic image can be instinctively identified with the object represented by it. Ever since their invention photographs were found fascinating because of their uncanny impression of truthfulness—a consequence of their indexical origin. Photographs were called "imprints of nature," and the new medium was praised for its "supreme realism."[46] Long before the concept of indexicality was devised by C. S. Pierce to account for the "existential relation" between sign and object,[47] Edgar Allan Poe found that "the closest scrutiny of the photographic drawing discloses only a more absolute truth, a more perfect identity of aspect with the thing represented."[48] Making a point of the fact that the lens, the basis of photography, is in French called the *objectif*, the film critic André Bazin stressed that the originality of photographic media, as distinct from the originality of painting, depends essentially on the "objective character of photography," whose images are "formed automatically, without the creative intervention of man."[49] Also for Susan Sontag a photographic index is "a trace, something directly stencilled off the real, like a footprint or a death mask."[50]

The physical connection at origin between an index and its referent partly at least validates contagious magic, even as the latter misapplies healthy attention to contiguous indexes such as shadows to displaced indexical signs such as photographs, which have left their referents behind. Still, displaced indexes would not exist without objects that caused them, which is why photographs and video footage constitute indisputable forensic evidence while painted representations or verbal reports do not. For sentimental viewers too things shown in photographs and films seem uncannily still to "be there," as the missing objects are subjectively "re-attached" to their indexical images. André Bazin went so far as to insist that "the photographic image is the object itself,"[51] as evidenced by some early cinema viewers who reportedly screamed and dodged when a train hurtled at them on the screen.[52] The indexical magic of mistaking contiguous images for displaced objects was common enough in the early days of cinema to inspire popular skits such as Edwin S. Porter's 1902 short comedy *Uncle Josh at the Moving Picture Show*, in which a naïve moviegoer, unmindful of the distinction between representation and reality, brings the cinema screen crashing down.[53]

Iconic Magic

Magical thinking can apply to iconic signs as well, which is even more interesting (and certainly more irrational) than indexical magic, because iconic signs lack any physical connection, contiguous or displaced, with their referents. Still, perceptual resemblance alone can create a compelling illusion of identity between an icon and its meaning. Mistaking icons of objects for objects themselves underlies the second universal type of magic identified by James Frazer, namely homeopathic magic, based on the principle of similarity, whereby things that resemble one another are believed to possess an invisible link, and that by manipulating an icon one can also manipulate the object depicted by the icon.[54] Like an angry crowd burning an effigy of a hated public figure, or a lover "punishing" a disloyal partner by tearing up his or her photograph, so iconic magic assumes control over the object by controlling its representation (Figure 4.10).

Around the world iconic magic has been used to produce both malevolent and benevolent alleged results. Some native American tribes believed that by drawing a figure of a person in sand, ashes, or clay, and then pricking it with a sharp stick they inflicted a corresponding injury on the person represented. Among the Bataks of Sumatra an infertile woman would make a wooden image of a child and hold it in her lap in the hope of becoming fertile. Some people today believe, despite occasional tragic consequences of the belief, that powdered rhinoceros horn is an aphrodisiac, apparently for no better reason than the superficial resemblance of the horn itself to an erect penis.[55] Among the natives of British Columbia, who used to live largely upon the fish caught in the rivers or the sea, in time of fish shortage a wizard would make an image of the swimming fish and put it in the water in the direction from which the fish normally appeared.[56] One could argue that the representations of game animals and predators in Chauvet and other prehistoric caves served a similar magical function of imposing imaginary control over these animals when encountered in real life.

Iconic magic is also an intrinsic part of the artistic process. A belief in the creative power of art, not just to portray but literally to create, has been the artists' ultimate dream and part of our experience of artistic illusion. In Ovid's *Metamorphoses* (about 8 CE), the sculptor Pygmalion famously creates "by wondrous art" an image of a beautiful woman, prays to Venus for a bride modeled after the image, and has his

Figure 4.10 Iconic magic: the burning of a wooden effigy of the demon Ravan, India. Photo by Tushar Dayal, courtesy of Courtesy of British Library/Open Culture.

prayer granted when the goddess obligingly turns the cold ivory into a living body (Figure 4.11).[57] Ovid's myth plays on the universal irrational disposition underlying iconic magic, found also in the worship of religious images. But however emotionally gratifying, mistaking icons for their referents remains an illusion, as artists more sober than Pygmalion can confirm. To a lady who once complained about Matisse's painting that "the arm of this woman is too long," the painter famously replied: "Madame, you are mistaken. This is not a woman, this is a picture."[58]

The confusion over relations between sign and meaning in iconic communication appears to arise again from a misapplication of the correct recognition of identity between sign and meaning in contiguous communication, and of a physical link actually existing at origin between sign and meaning in indexical communication. But while a person's shadow as a contiguous index is caused by and therefore physically inseparable from that person, Pygmalion's sculpture, Matisse's portrait of a lady, or painted animals in Chauvet cave only resemble the objects they are referring to. Apart from the similarity between the icon and its object, which is formed in the minds of those contemplating the icon, there exists no direct, physical connection between the two.

As also argued in Chapter 2, compared with indexicality, which is still bound to animal-like direct interactions with the environment, iconic communication represents an advance toward human-like meta-cognition, because it requires the ability to interpret perceptions on the basis of prior perceptions, and to hold in memory a comparison between similar but different things. Detached from direct experience iconic signs tend therefore to be comparatively less emotive and more "cerebral." If comparing like with like is still part of our instinctive first-order reactions to the world, the second-order representations of figurative arts are produced fully intentionally by

Figure 4.11 Iconic magic as a cognitive prerequisite of artistic illusion: *Pygmalion and Galatea*, oil painting by Jean-Léon Gérôme (*c.* 1890). Courtesy of the Metropolitan Museum of Art, New York.

the artist's imagination and skill rather than accidentally by nature, and the only link between the object and its representation exists in the artist's and the recipient's minds. Also, while indexes always point to things that objectively exist, iconic images often refer to non-existent, imagined things, as in fantastic representations, or to objects of unclear ontological status, as in religious art. Any alleged link between an iconic image and its referent remains therefore a matter of faith, as in homeopathic magic and religious worship of images, in which the viewer responds to images of objects as if they were objects themselves.[59] But as in all matters of faith, a belief that a painted figure or a carved statue is somehow con-substantial with something in the outside world, however compelling it may be, cannot but offer a factually false interpretation of reality.

The illusion that figurative arts reflect the empirical world, however indirectly, is captured in an ancient Roman love tale, found originally in *Natural History* by Pliny the Elder (23–79 BCE). In the story, Butades, a potter from Sicyon in Corinth, discovered with the help of his daughter how to model portraits in clay. The daughter was in love with a youth, and when he was leaving the country she traced the outline of the shadow which his profile cast on the wall by lamplight (Figure 4.12).[60] The father filled the outline with clay and made a model, thereby fixing a fleeting indexical shadow in a permanent iconic image of the young man's head, which is semiotically equivalent to photography invented nearly two thousand years later. Pliny's story became popular with Renaissance artists, keen to promote visual arts as a mirror up to nature. In his treatise *On Painting* (1435), the founding book of early modern art, Leon Battista Alberti states that "the earliest painters used to draw around shadows made by the sun, and the art [of portraiture] eventually grew by a process of additions."[61] By suggesting that sculpture and painting originated from cast shadows, the Renaissance artists expressed with uncanny intuition the evolution of visual communication from first-order, contiguous indexical representations to second-order, displaced iconic representations.

Fixing shadows of objects to preserve their appearance for posterity is of course the principle behind modern photography—another "magical" medium invented to gratify human desire to aid imperfect memory and to halt the destructive progress of time by

Figure 4.12 Indexical origin of iconic arts: *The Corinthian Maid*, oil painting by Joseph Wright (1785). Courtesy of the National Gallery of Art, Washington.

creating an illusion of the "eternal present," in which the perceived sign becomes one with its absent referent. As argued above, thus understood magical thinking springs from a misapplication of mental modules originally developed to cope with contiguous situations to signs that only refer to these situations. Attention to contiguous events is adaptive, because one cannot afford to ignore the here-and-now without either endangering oneself or missing some existentially important opportunity. The same disposition is subsequently applied by default to anything that reminds one of those existentially important situations. In the process the difference between present and past is subjectively obliterated, as when a person long dead seems to be still alive, smiling at us from a photograph (Figure 4.13), or when we nostalgically contemplate photographs of ourselves from a younger age, with more life ahead of us. The illusion

Figure 4.13 Remembering the dead: the iconic magic of photography (Holy Cross Cemetery, Yeadon, Pennsylvania). Courtesy of British Library/Open Culture.

of the eternal present implied in the merging of the sign with its past referent can only be overridden by accepting the cause-and-effect links in the real world, and by suppressing the psychologically compelling but objectively false connections between things. But even for the most rationally inclined persons the residues of indexical or iconic magic are often too irresistible, as evidenced by our sentimental attachment to mementoes, souvenirs, family photographs, and home videos.[62]

Iconic Indexicality

Despite its effectiveness in pointing reliably to causally connected referents, indexicality has its limits as a form of communication. On its own an index implies its object truthfully but often vaguely and imprecisely, leaving too much to conjecture and speculation. An imprint of a shoe sole in soft ground clearly indicates an earlier presence of a walker, but not much beyond that: the shoe size can roughly imply (iconically) the walker's age, but not his or her sex, physical appearance, personality, or life circumstances. On the other hand, a photograph, with its high degree of objective verisimilitude with the represented object, appears to combine fully both indexicality and iconicity, thus increasing its communicative effectiveness. Signs can be indexical and iconic at the same time.[63]

In fact, all signs are polysemiotic by embodying the characteristics of more than one type of sign in their origin and structure. A single speech act for example, consisting mainly of symbolic signs, also testifies indexically to the speaker's unique linguistic competence and often includes an expressive iconic dimension on the levels of phonology, morphology, and syntax.[64] In visual communication too, when an index resembles its object perceptually, which it does in photography, we are talking about an iconic quality of an indexical sign, or *iconic indexes*.[65] C. S. Peirce was probably the first to stress that index and icon can be combined in one sign, and that it is actually the indexicality of the sign that makes iconic quality possible:

> In so far as the Index is affected by the Object, it necessarily has some Quality in common with the Object, and it is in respect to these that it refers to the Object. It does, therefore, involve a sort of Icon, although an Icon of a peculiar kind; and it is not the mere resemblance of its Object, even in these respects which makes it a sign but it is the actual modification of it by the Object.[66]

In photography it is precisely the physical connection with the represented object that accounts for a high degree of verisimilitude. Accordingly, for Peirce a photograph is a classic instance of an iconic index: "A photograph, for example, not only excites an image, has an appearance, but, owing to its optical connection with the object, is evidence that that appearance corresponds to reality."[67]

The cognitive conditions for iconic-indexical communication were set as soon as the *Homo sapiens*, with their reflective consciousness and extended working memory, arrived on the scene about 170,000 year ago. The earliest purposefully executed permanent iconic indexes on archaeological record are imprints of human hands with outstretched fingers found among the paintings of animals in Chauvet cave (Figure 4.14).[68] The hands were placed flat on the cave's wall, and a red pigment was then applied around it and between the fingers. Such proto-photographic negatives of human hands have also been found in other Late Paleolithic caves in southern France and northern Spain, as have the positive impressions of hands coated with pigment and pressed against the wall. In one Spanish cave, the Gargas, there are nearly 150 red and black hands, some of them small, probably belonging to women or children.[69] These "signatures" are iconic in the sense that the impressions reflect the actual size and shape of hands, and indexical in the sense that the impressions were physically made by real people, who evidently wanted to preserve their presence for posterity, not unlike those modern tourists who cannot resist inscribing their names, with dates, on the walls of famous buildings they visit.

Iconic indexicality covers a fascinating area of visual culture, including some of the most perceptually and cognitively powerful media and art forms such as the shadow theater, magic lantern shows, silhouette portraits, the camera obscura, and of course the modern photographic media of film, television, and the internet. It is the combined effect of indexicality and iconicity that makes these media all the more efficacious in stimulating our eyes and emotions, than the purely iconic arts forms such as drawing, painting, and sculpting. The iconic indexicality of a silhouette portrait or a photograph implies not only iconic resemblance but also physical identity with the represented object in a way never attained by purely iconic media. In other words, iconic indexical

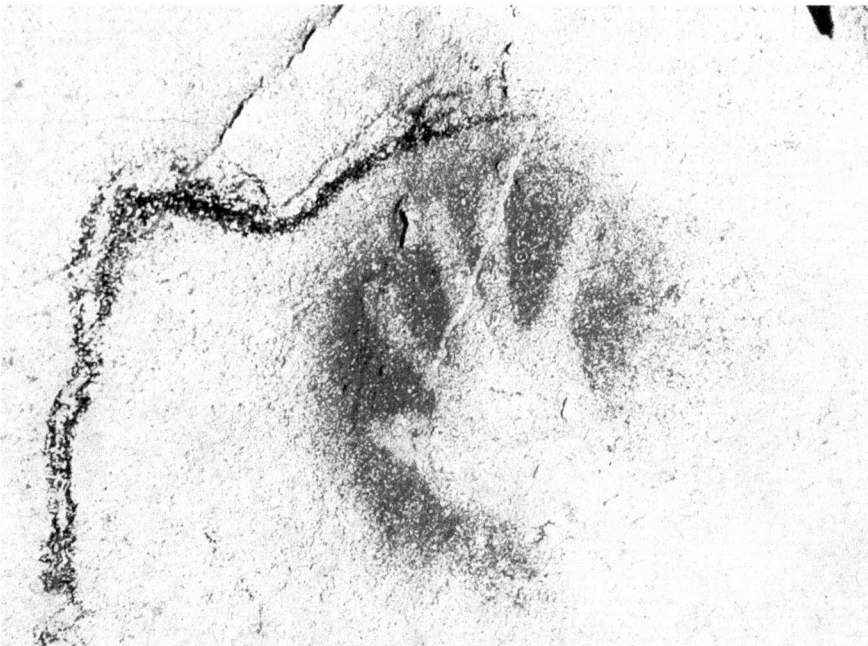

Figure 4.14 Iconically indexical negative imprint of a hand in Chauvet cave (*c.* 32,000 BCE). Courtesy of British Library/Open Culture.

media are truthful in depicting already existing realities, whereas iconic media are fictional in simulating often non-existent, imagined realities.

Considering the efficacy of photography, the most important visual medium for nearly two centuries now, it is curious that it should have taken humanity so long to produce this new form of permanent displaced iconic indexical signs, which is what photographs, silhouette portraits, death masks, and prehistoric imprints of hands are in semiotic terms. The reasons for this delay were practical rather than cognitive—photography is a highly technological medium—and the right conditions for it were only created as a consequence of the discoveries and inventions in mechanics, optics, and chemistry made during the Scientific Revolution. The direct precursor of the fixed light effects of photography were the fully contiguous iconic indexes produced by the camera obscura, an optical device and a drawing aid used by realistic painters of the seventeenth and eighteenth centuries. The camera obscura (literally, a "dark chamber") was a portable box fitted with a convex lens and an internal mirror, which righted the upside-down image created by the lens, so that it could be traced on a piece of paper placed on translucent glass plate installed at the top of the device. Drawings thus made helped artists like Canaletto (1697–1768) to trace the outlines of objects to be transferred onto canvas to achieve highly realistic and accurate, truly "photographic" paintings, mostly of cityscapes (Figure 4.15).[70] The camera obscura could capture a contiguous moving image, but it could not fix it for future contemplation—this part was accomplished by the painter who created a permanent icon out of a fleeting iconic index, losing the indexical character of the image in the process. This is why Canaletto's paintings of Venice, Rome, and London, colorful and realistic as they are, do not seem as viscerally truthful as early photographs, grainy and black-and-white (Figure 7.1), to say nothing of today's high-definition color images obtained with digital cameras.

Figure 4.15 From indexical camera obscura to iconic painting: *Piazza San Marco* by Canaletto (late 1720s). Courtesy of the Metropolitan Museum of Art, New York.

Iconic indexes are basically indexes that resemble their referents, with indexicality as guarantee of truthfulness of representation. Photographs and films of real events, as in photojournalism, documentary films, and TV news reports, are iconic indexes in this sense. But indexical media can also be used to record scripted and staged events, as in studio photography, fictional cinema, animation films, and television shows. In such cases the indexical record does not communicate independent facts but simulations of facts. It is the difference between non-fiction and fiction in literature, between the documentary and dramatic mode in film—generality, between reality and imagination. Semiotically, the iconic, simulated record captured on indexical media represents *indexical iconicity*. While iconic indexes, by virtue of their indexicality, have a causal, physical relationship with real-life objects and events, indexical icons, by virtue of their iconicity, are instead records of imaginative simulations or reconstructions of real-life events. A bio-documentary film using real-life footage is accordingly an iconic index, whereas a dramatized biopic, in which actors impersonate real-life characters in staged settings, is an indexical icon.

Nor is the distinction between iconic indexicality and indexical iconicity clear-cut but rather a matter of degree. In visual media, any feature of the image affected directly by the object is indexical, while a feature affected by the medium itself, including the human user, is iconic. Until the early 1960s most photographs were black-and-white due to then existing limitations of the photosensitive support, which reduced the indexical truthfulness of representation by eliminating natural colors in favor of inadvertent iconic stylization of monochrome tonality. Any technical or human intervention in the indexical media increases the iconicity (fictionality) and reduces the indexicality (truthfulness) of the resulting representation. For example, framing in photography and film limits the natural field of vision, creating relationships between objects that do not necessarily exist in reality. Such post-production manipulations as cropping, adjusting brightness and contrast, desaturating, color grading, or applying any of the numerous "effects" available in image editing software, all reduce indexicality and increase iconicity, thus bringing the photographic image closer to drawing or painting. Manipulating levels of indexicality and iconicity can also serve the purposes of deception and disinformation. A YouTube video of a real event constitutes an iconically indexical record, whereas a deepfake video is an indexically iconic fabrication of an event that never took place.

Idolatry and Iconoclasm—the Two Sides of Iconic Magic

The cognitive disposition underlying iconic magic is responsible not only for harmless nostalgia attached to photographs and home videos, but also for the millennia-old divisive ideologies and conflicts over idolatry and iconoclasm. The same cognitive bias that identifies iconic signs with their referents underlies both religious worship of images and the prejudice of those offended by this practice, as evidenced by attitudes to image-making in orthodox Judaism, Islam, and puritan Protestantism.

Iconoclasm may have its roots in religion, but the doctrinal prohibitions of the making of images apply to representations not just of the deity but in fact of everything. The biblical Second Commandment makes it clear: "Thou shalt not make unto thee any graven image, or any likeness of any thing that is in heaven above, or that is in the earth beneath, or that is in the water under the earth" (Ex. 20.4).[71] Iconoclasm appears inseparable from monotheistic religions with their insistence on the inscrutable, unfathomable central deity, whose spiritual essence is described as inaccessible to human mind and senses, so that any visual representation of it is deemed to be delimiting and therefore offensive, allegedly to the deity but primarily to the believers. At the same time, some religions, such as Catholicism, Eastern Orthodox Christianity, or Hinduism, allow and encourage the use of religious images as embodiments of the deity and aids in devotion. Notwithstanding their ideological differences, it seems that religious idolatry and iconoclasm represent two sides of the same cognitive disposition underlying iconic magic. Without the assumption that displaced iconic signs are somehow linked to their referents, neither would idolaters believe in the efficacy of their worship of religious images nor would iconoclasts feel indignant to see their deity "offended" by visual representation.

A possible reason for pitting one side of iconic magic against the other is divisive politics: a religion's struggle to assert itself in competition with other religions. The ancient Jewish prohibition against "graven images" can be seen in the context of opposition to other religious groups in the Middle East, many of which practiced some form of image worship, as in the biblical cult of the Golden Calf. With the rise of Christianity and its more tolerant attitude toward image-making, Jewish iconoclasm led to the cultural isolation of European Jewry, while at the same time strengthening the sense of Jewish identity.[72] The passages in the Hebrew Bible which forbid the making of images all appear in the context of prohibitions against the worship of other gods, which was often aided by sculpted images.[73] Also, nomadic peoples as a rule are not given to developing complex visual cultures, with statues and wall paintings, which require a settled way of life and stone buildings in which to display the images. Nor did the dispersal of the Jewish people from the Middle East following the destruction of the Temple in Jerusalem in 71 CE, and the exile continuing for nearly two millennia, contribute to the development of a rich visual culture.

Quite apart from a practical inconvenience of image-making in a nomadic culture, iconoclasm as a religious belief still had to be justified theologically. As the philosophers Moshe Halbertal and Avishoi Margalit explain, the Mosaic Law forbids representing God in sculpture and painting because since God's nature is not available to the senses, any similarity-based representation of the deity must necessarily be false and therefore blasphemous. Similar objections were raised in the iconoclastic literature of the Christian Reformation, when the early Protestants were asserting their identity by opposing the widespread use of religious images by Catholics. The iconoclastic reformers argued that the worship of statues and paintings cannot be a substitute for the worship of God, and that the statues were not capable of representing the deity, because the infinite and the spiritual cannot be given material, limiting representation, as this would lead to the conception of God himself as a material and limited being.[74]

For image worshipers on the other hand, images were not only permissible representations of the deity, but they also partook of its spiritual nature by allegedly possessing independent spiritual powers. In other words, in idolatry a displaced iconic sign with religious content is psychologically transformed into a fully contiguous sign present there and then—the essence of iconic magic. For idolaters, sacred anthropomorphic images are truly alive, like the weeping statues of the Virgin Mary in popular Catholic devotion, or the statues of saints believed to heal the sick, like medicine men. Sacred statues and paintings can also be addressed and prayed to, as if they were living persons, concerned about individual worshipers' well-being. At the same time, the efficacy of sacred images is not believed to lie in the identity between the deity and the material makeup of the image, but in the special relationship between the two, in that the image is assumed to share "indexically" some of the features of the thing it represents, as in relic worship. This implied connection ensures a reciprocal communication between the believer and the deity, whereby an act performed on the image becomes magically an act upon the deity itself, which can "repay" the worshiper by granting his prayers (Figure 4.16).[75]

Figure 4.16 Devotional painting as an aid to meditation: *Madonna and Child with Saints Francis and Jerome* by Francesco Francia (1500–10). Courtesy of the Metropolitan Museum of Art, New York.

While iconoclasts permit neither indexical nor iconic communication with the deity, as in the worship of relics and sacred images, respectively, there is evidence in the Jewish tradition of permissible limited symbolic representation of the deity in the form of linguistic description. The arbitrary signs of language, possessing neither physical nor imitative connection with their referents, are apparently less capable of "offending" the deity by circumscribing it in any way. In this view, only by using language is it possible to avoid the blasphemy of "debasing" the spiritual realm by reducing it to the physical constraints of the visible, sensual world. Hence the insistence in Judaism and Islam on the mediacy of the sacred book, the Torah and the Koran, in communicating the divine message. There is, however, a famous exception in Judaism to the permissible use of language to describe the divine attributes: the taboo prohibiting the very mention of God's name. Transcribed as YHVH and conventionally pronounced *Yahweh*, the name may never be spoken, except by high priests in the ancient temple on the holy day of Yom Kippur in the "holy of holies," the chamber housing the Ark of Covenant. In everyday conversation observant Jews resort to a meta-linguistic device of using a word to refer to the word, referring to God as *hashem*, "the name," to distance as much as possible the linguistic sign from its sacred referent to avoid offending the latter—an attitude again based on the magical assumption that a name is somehow con-substantial with its referent.[76]

The iconoclastic prohibition on visual representation, not just of the deity but of all things "in the earth beneath, or that is in the water under the earth" (Ex. 20:4), may also be viewed as a fundamentalist attempt to discredit contiguity—the world of every-day experience with its materialism and sensuality, in case it inspires a more empirical and secular type of thinking. For all their opposing views concerning images, painted or sculpted, both the superstitious idolaters and the indignant iconoclasts appear prone to treating visual representations in a magical way, as somehow directly connected with the things they depict. The only difference is that idolaters willingly succumb to the illusion of communication with the deity magically brought to the human level in the picture, whereas iconoclasts condemn this presumption and proscribe visual representations precisely on the assumption of their magical connection with the said deity.

The Enjoyment of the Arts

For idolators, iconoclasts, and seculars alike, the cognitive bias underlying iconic magic accounts for the universal fascination with figurative representations. The enjoyment of mimetic arts, visual, literary, and dramatic, is in fact so firmly embedded in our cognitive make-up that it can overshadow a more down-to-earth engagement with the contiguous, unmediated world. Notwithstanding Oscar Wilde's dictum that it is only the unimaginative who ever invent anything, we often prefer fictitious simulations of life to actual experience. Blaise Pascal found it puzzling that a painting should attract attention "by the resemblance of things the originals of which are not admired," and Henry James thought it "perverse" that people should innately prefer the represented object to the real one.[77] This is indeed paradoxical, because a painting or a photograph of something potentially dangerous, like a large cat or a crocodile, is of no immediate consequence to the observer's life and should therefore be treated with indifference. Admittedly, images of animal predators in prehistoric caves or nature films excite only limited interest, without comparison to the panicky, hair-raising urgency of a face-to-face encounter with a dangerous animal in the wild. But this is precisely why second-order, displaced representations stir our imagination: they give us a pleasure of muted excitement of a surrogate experience at no cost in terms of real-life consequences. "Art does not hurt us," wrote Oscar Wilde, "the tears we shed at a play are a type of the exquisite sterile emotions that it is the function of Art to awaken. We weep, but we are not wounded. We grieve, but our grief is not bitter," because "emotion for the sake of emotion is the aim of art, and emotion for the sake of action is the aim of life."[78]

Like other simulations of life such as literary narratives, theatrical plays, and cinema, permanent visual images, argues the philosopher Denis Dutton, have given our species an advantage of vital instruction, from a safe distance, about the problems, threats, and opportunities that life might have thrown before our ancestors.[79] Prehistoric hunters could learn to identify animal species, distinguish the dangerous from the harmless and edible ones, by safely contemplating the images painted on cave walls and hearing stories from experienced hunters, rather than by venturing unprepared into the wild to learn about the animals' appearance and behavior the hard way, by risking injury or death in direct confrontation. While contiguous events are potentially dangerous and prompt instant action, displaced images of art offer the luxury of quiet time to activate memory, encourage reflective thought, and stimulate the imagination. Also, unlike the "quick," that is, alive creatures, animals or humans in pictures and sculptures look unnaturally and eerily still, giving the viewer an opportunity, unavailable when confronting the real specimens, of examining and contemplating them closely at leisure.

Even iconic arts that do involve movement, like theatrical plays or films, are structured in ways that are both reassuringly similar to and teasingly different from real life. Drama transforms the spontaneous and chaotic flow of life into the artificiality of logically structured plots, while film editing disrupts the natural continuities of time and space in ways that can be disorienting but also perceptually challenging. For all their mimetic quality, the simulations of life in narrative arts are not straight mirrors up to nature, but they present human experience with a causal logic and emotional intensity far above what normally surrounds us in the spontaneous flux of life. Scripted stories are just that, scripted rather than unplanned, appealing also to our innate disposition to appreciate human creativity and search for order. Visual images are iconic in respect of the things they represent, but they are also indexical in respect of the people who make them. We are thrilled both by the image's content and by the artist's talent, skill, and imagination—all manifestations of the cognitive abilities we admire in other people. According to the psychologist Geoffrey Miller, art has evolved as a kind of human peacock's tail, ultimately to attract sexual partners by stimulating their senses with a display of fitness evidenced in artistic and intellectual creativity.[80] Compared with its artistic representation, a real animal, a plant, a human figure, or a landscape may appear esthetically unappealing and even banal, precisely by lacking human creative dimension. Natural objects seem unambiguous and obvious ("Rose is a rose"), until of course science reminds us of their mind-boggling complexity. But while nature is the domain of scientists, most people prefer man-made signs pregnant with intentional meanings. The writer André Gide may advise that the wise man be astonished by anything, but as social animals we tend to relate first of all to the fruits of other people' minds, we instinctively look for human-like agency in things, and so we are more thrilled by the mind-teasing suggestiveness of works of art rather than by the indifference, inertia, and unexciting predictability of natural objects.

5

The (Mostly) Symbolic Signs of Verbal Language

In contrast to indexical and iconic communication, symbolic signs are related neither physically nor perceptually to their meaning. The main advantage of signs unconstrained by their meaning is that their form can be reduced to a minimum difference between signs, allowing for their easier and quicker recombination to produce new meaningful configurations. In verbal language, elements meaningless in themselves, such as phonemes (discrete speech sounds), can be economically combined by means of phonological rules to form meaningful segments we call words. For example, just three English phonemes (out of forty four): [p], a voiceless labial plosive; [t], a voiceless alveolar plosive; and [æ], a near-low front unrounded vowel, can be combined in the following meaningful and semantically unrelated arrangements: [pæt] as in the word *pat*, [tæp] as in *tap*, [æpt] as in *apt*, [æt] as in *at*, and [æp] as in *app*. Other theoretically possible combinations include [ætp], [ptæ], [tpæ], and [pæ], but they are impermissible in English due to the language-specific phonological constraints, that is, due to constraints *within* the communication system itself rather than to relations between signs and their referents, as in indexical or iconic communication. Uniquely in the history of natural systems of communication, human verbal language represents a discrete combinatorial system, in which a finite number of elements such as phonemes, morphemes, and words can generate an infinite number of sentences, with meanings distinct from those of the constituent elements.[1]

The effectiveness of any communication system can be measured by the amount of information transmitted with least ambiguity in a unit of time. Indexical traces, for example, truthful as they are due to their dependence on physical reality, are nonetheless limited to objects that leave traces and are semantically vague. A smell of tobacco in a room clearly indicates a recent presence of a smoker, but not much beyond that: no further information about the identity, age, gender, appearance, personality, or life circumstances of the person is suggested by the smoke. Iconic communication too is comparatively inefficient by being slow and ambiguous, despite the advantage of holistically capturing the essence of a situation, as in pictorial instructions or face recognition. At the same time the requirement of formal resemblance to the referent limits both the speed of signal transmission and the freedom of signal recombination. Human speech limited to iconic signs would consist only of onomatopoeic sounds and variations in duration, volume, and pitch of vocal signals to imitate the properties of the corresponding referents. Only arbitrary signs—structurally simple and free from the physical and perceptual constraints—allow for concatenation and recursiveness that speed up the formation and transmission of signals and their meaning generating capacity.[2]

Interestingly, of all sensory channels available for communication, only audition allows for the highest rate of signal variation, for both physical and cognitive reasons. While vision permits the perception of up to sixteen discrete signals per second, a fast talker can pack over forty phonemes in as little time. It takes the brain about a quarter of a second to find a word to name something, and another quarter of a second to articulate the word. Understanding a spoken word takes about a fifth of a second, before the speaker even finishes pronouncing it. Also, unlike vision, which can be obstructed by opaque objects, vocal signals travel around physical obstacles and do not rely on light, which means that people can talk round the clock, not just during daylight. Nor does speech require face-to-face orientation: people can communicate just as effectively while engaged in other activities requiring visual attention, such as making tools, scanning the terrain, fighting, or tracking animals.[3]

Language as a Combinatorial System

Language based on arbitrary elements thus offers a more economical alternative to hypothetical indexical and iconic types of vocal communication, which would require a vast innate code for responding to innumerable natural stimuli and imitative sound-meaning correspondences. According to Steven Pinker and Paul Bloom, it was apparently neurophysiologically easier to evolve a cognitive device for learning arbitrary sound-meaning combinations specific to one's language, a process that also enhanced group cohesion by increasing cultural diversity along linguistic lines.[4] The liberation of language from the constraints of emotive and imitative communication not only triggered the multiplication and diversification of ethnic languages, but also enabled each language to acquire a structural complexity capable of practically unlimited creativity. As an open-ended system language would also have been enabled by, and would have encouraged in return, the human meta-cognitive mind, capable of generating ideas about ideas and expressing them in an unlimited number of topics through recursive, hierarchical structures of syntactic speech. By contrast, animal communication, chiefly indexical and in some measure iconic, reflects the contiguity-bound animal brains responding to a limited number of "topics" of animal communication. In Derek Bickerton's words, "all other creatures can communicate only about things that have evolutionary significance form them, but human beings can communicate about *anything*,"[5] which includes things relating to the past, present, and future, and things both factual, hypothetical, and unreal.

The advantages of a combinatorial language derive from the fact that the environment which language helps to negotiate is itself combinatorial in nature.[6] The human world consists of a large but ultimately finite number of autonomous systems such as humans and animals, engaged in a large but also finite number of actions such as walking, sleeping, eating, mating, fighting, and so on, taking place in any number of locations and times. Linguistic equivalents of objects and actors are nouns, with adjectives offering descriptions of objects' and actors' properties, and verbs as descriptions of actions. To account for all possible permutations between objects, actors, properties, actions, locations, and times—a potentially unlimited number—a non-combinatorial system of communication, with a one-for-one correspondence between signs and situations, would require a correspondingly unlimited and therefore unlearnable number of distinct signs. On the other hand, a combinatorial system like a syntactic language requires only the memorization of a large but finite number of words and an equally manageable number of grammatical rules—both within the capacity of an imperfect but fit-for-purpose human memory.[7] The *Oxford English Dictionary* contains over 600,000 lexical items from a thousand-year old history of the language, but an average English speaker today manages with between 20,000 and 50,000 words to talk about a potentially infinite number of topics.[8]

Language's combinatorial principle is applied all the way up its structure: phonemes combine to form morphemes (parts of words), morphemes combine to form words, words form phrases and clauses (parts of sentences), the latter in turn form sentences, and sentences compose speeches and texts. Even the language-specific grammatical rules that constrain the way elements of language can be combined on the levels of phonology, morphology, syntax, and narrative do not restrict language's semantic creativity. An individual speaker may not invent the phonemes of her language and rarely invents a word or phrase, but practically every sentence spoken by any person, unless it is a conventional expression or a quotation, is unique and original.

The Language Module

If language's power to facilitate the exchange of collective knowledge contributes to group cohesion and individual survival, one suspects the involvement of an innate cognitive disposition to learn one's native language the way it happens—quickly and effortlessly in infancy. For Steven Pinker language is primarily a distinct piece of the biological makeup of the brain rather than a cultural artifact that we learn the way we learn traffic rules or national history. The language module thus appears to have been acquired through the process of Darwinian selection because, argues Pinker, it produced communicative benefits that gave speaking humans adaptive edge in terms of procreation and survival. Far from being exclusively a product of culture, as has been claimed for centuries, the language faculty appears to be based on biological hardware, without which learning a particular ethnic language would not be possible.[9]

The acquisition of symbolic speech in infancy comes alongside other meta-cognitive developments such as consciousness and extended working memory. At the stage of pre-symbolic intentional communication (from nine to fifteen months) infants produce sounds and gestures tied first of all to specific current wants. Between a year and two years of age vocalizations become less tied to contiguous contexts and needs but more to external objects. A "naming explosion" takes place, in which a child learns the language-specific relations between sounds and objects as the foundation of displaced referential communication. At the age of about two grammatical inflections of vocabulary and syntax begin, as the child's innate language faculty meshes with the grammatical structures of the parent language to produce morphemes and word variations to mark plural number, past tense, co-ordination, ellipsis, and recursion. The combinatorial grammar now enables the child to produce a vast number of statements on subjects extending beyond the necessarily limited contiguous context. From the age of five onwards a post-syntactic phase begins, with such meta-linguistic skills as word-playing and fictionalizing, which completes the individual acquisition of language from emotive, animal-like vocalizations to fully referential syntactic, uniquely human speech.[10]

The indirect proof of the inborn, species-specific character of the language module is its universality across historical and contemporary human societies—none exists without symbolic, syntactic speech. We have no voice recordings from human prehistory, but the *Homo sapiens* (dating to about 170,000 year ago) had skulls like modern humans, and it can be conjectured that they possessed the meta-cognitive faculties of consciousness, memory, and symbolic speech long before the time of the spectacular cave art and other decorated artifacts produced by the Cro-Magnon humans during the Late Paleolithic period. Like contemporary hunter-gatherers, the Cro-Magnon people were accomplished tool makers and superb biologists with detailed knowledge of the life cycles, ecology, and behavior of plants and animals they depended on. Syntactic language would have been useful in such a lifestyle, by enabling its users to communicate precise information about time, place, and objects in the natural environment, as well as the intricacies of social relations, obligations, and alliances.[11]

Indeed, most likely it was the ever-growing complexity of social life within the hunting-gathering groups that put selective pressure on syntactic speech as an effective method of interpersonal communication, to facilitate negotiations and diffuse tensions. Language remains today the most important element of human interactions and culture, whether in face-to-face communication or via telephone, through voice recordings, public media, and written records. Language is used for commenting on the activities of others, keeping records of interpersonal relationships, for courtship, coordinating people, sharing practical knowledge, and making collective plans and decisions. Language is of course used for other purposes as well, including such lofty symbolic creations as religion, literature, philosophy, and science. However, as the psychologist Robin Dunbar has demonstrated, as much as two-thirds of conversations conducted daily by people of both sexes are devoted simply to gossip, that is, talking about social topics and the natural rhythms of communal life: what people are doing, is it a good or a bad thing, who is in and who is out, who is available and reliable and who is not, how to deal with a difficult situation, and so on. Only about a quarter of everyday conversations in today's populations is concerned with matters of such intellectual weight as the cultural, political, or philosophic issues of the day.[12] The anthropologist Jerome H. Barkow explains the universal human predilection for gossip by linking it with social intelligence, which evolved as a result of social competition. The things that people mostly gossip about contain important social knowledge that has most bearing on fitness: information about relatives, rivals, mates, offspring, social partners, and the high-ranking people. The gossip's informational content concerns invariably people's relative standing in society, control over resources, sexual activities, births and deaths, current alliances, friendships and political involvements, health, and reputation about reliability as a partner in social transactions.[13]

Linguistic Indexicality

While arbitrariness remains the defining characteristic of syntactic language, it seems neither likely nor indeed desirable that indexical emotiveness and imitative imaginativeness should be absent from language as a result: they are too much a part of our cognitive makeup. Like all other media and forms of communication, language is polysemiotic, with fine conceptualizations enabled by symbolic signs existing alongside emotive vocalizations and iconic mental images found in expressive and creative manifestations of language such as word-play, metaphor, and poetry.

Language is indexical by default in pointing to the presence of a speaker, with his or her unique personality, knowledge, and intentions. These personal characteristics also include the idiosyncrasies of voice such as timbre, intonation, pitch, and natural volume, as well as the individual "linguistic fingerprinting" found in the peculiarities of grammatical style and vocabulary, in speech as in writing, arising from a combination of personality and socio-cultural factors.[14] Like fingerprints and facial features, one's voice and idiolect are indexes of identity and individuality. Other, more universal indexical features of language, still ubiquitous in colloquial speech, also point to a pre-syntactic, primate state of symptomatic expressiveness as part of contiguous communication. The most archaic human auditory symptoms and signals include vocalizations of emotional and physiological states, such as interjections, grunts, moans, cries, whistles, clicks, coughing, hiccupping, laughing, expressive intonation, and so on.[15] These signals are usually a part of audio-visual displays involving bodily postures, gestures, and facial expressions, through which humans and other primates communicate such attitudes as submission, dominance, appeasement, friendliness, threat, or sexual arousal.[16] Largely involuntary, these behaviors are governed by phylogenetically old, subcortical neural structures in the brain stem and limbic system, heavily involved in emotion.[17] Emotive vocalizations are non-iconic, in the sense that they do not "imitate" anything, nor are they arbitrary, because the connection between vocal expression and the underlying emotive and physiological state is not learned but innate and more or less automatic. This is why emotive vocalizations, like emotions themselves, are recognized and interpreted identically across languages and cultures, like the onomatopoeic sounds and emotive exclamations conventionalized in cartoons, as in Homer Simpson's "doh!"[18]

Even phonemes, normally used only as "meaningless" units of morphological structures, can convey emotional coloring as part of a non-arbitrary expressiveness of verbal communication. After all, language's discrete combinatorial structure does not employ an abstract binary code of 0s and 1s such as that used by computer processors, but a range of speech sounds tied indexically to the anatomy of vocal organs and the physiology of articulation—the "natural sounds" that invite emotional and even esthetic response. The linguist Edward Stankiewicz argues in favor of expressive sound symbolism, in which some speech sounds, either for linguistic or extra-linguistic reasons, carry elusive but genuine pleasant or unpleasant connotations.[19] For example, the phoneme [f] is considered indecent in both Russian and English. Experiments with English speakers have also revealed consistent associations of the liquid phoneme [r] with "roughness," "strength," "heaviness," and "bitterness," and of the other liquid phoneme [l] with contrasting connotations of "peace," "smoothness," "lightness," "clarity," and "weakness."[20] In Yiddish, Basque, Russian, Polish, and some native American languages expressive palatalization appears frequently in affectionate speech, as in child-language and nursery songs—presumably due to the association of smallness and infantilism with high-frequency speech sounds such as [i] and [j].[21] The linguist Earl R. Anderson also draws attention to so-called paraverbals—emotive sounds of no grammatical function consisting of voiceless vowels and nasals, ingressives (sounds made by inhaling air), clicks, vowelless syllables, and word-initial consonant clusters such as [ts], [ps], [gl], or [gr]. Paraverbals are common and frequent enough to become eventually integrated in lexicon and grammar, as in *psst, shush, huh, ah, phew, phooey, ahem, aha, tut tut, oh-oh*, and so on.[22]

Linguistic Iconicity

Spontaneous emotive vocalizations as expressions of mental states of the moment are still part of primate contiguous social interactions. On the other hand, the iconic features of language offer opportunities of broader displaced auditory communication, in which the linguistic elements on the levels of phonology, morphology, syntax, and text can to an extent mimic their absent referents. Iconic speech may be less efficacious than visual media in imitating objects from the outside world, but it nonetheless remains a rich source of the plasticity, expressiveness, and stimulating imaginativeness of a medium relying otherwise on arbitrary, symbolic structures.

The most obvious, structurally simplest and probably the oldest type of linguistic iconicity are speech sounds mimicking non-linguistic sounds from the outside world—the familiar onomatopoeic expressions. Phonetic iconicity usually consists of individual phonemes in combination with morphological elements such as syllabicity and reduplication.[23] For example, quick and rapid external sounds and noises can be imitated by monosyllabic words using plosives, either voiced or voiceless, depending on the acoustic properties of imitated sounds. Thus *bang* (with a voiced [b] and [ŋ]) suggests a sudden loud noise, while *tap* (using a voiceless [t] and [p]) imitates a softer sound. In *cuckoo* the reduplicated syllable and a voiceless velar plosive [k] fairly closely mimics the repetitive call produced by the bird in question, just as *murmur*, with its syllable reduplication, low-frequency vowel, and the continuous bilabial nasal [m] convincingly replicates the low sound of flowing water. Equally suggestive of their respective referents are the familiar sound-imitating monosyllables such as *splash, whoop, whirr, scrape, crack, crash, crunch*, or *squeak*. These and many other onomatopoeic words found in all languages function as iconic "names" for objects and actions in the form of phonetic imitations of sounds produced by them.[24]

Ferdinand Saussure famously denied the onomatopoeic formations the status of organic elements of a linguistic system, arguing that they are "only approximate and more or less conventional imitations of certain sounds."[25] In other words, because they are usually integrated into the grammatical forms of language, onomatopoeic expressions are regarded by Saussure as conventional, arbitrary signs. For example, the sound made by a pair of scissors is reflected in English as *snip*, in Chinese it is *su-su*, in Italian *cri-cri*, *terre-terre* in Portuguese, *riqui-riqui* in Spanish, and *krits-krits* in modern Greek.[26] However, while inter-linguistic differences among onomatopoeic expressions certainly testify to their conventional nature, they do not preclude the simultaneous intra-linguistic iconic quality of these expressions. As noted earlier, signs tend to be polysemiotic to boost their communicative power. The above onomatopoeic expressions are all both different as reflections of language-specific features, and similar in their syllabic reduplications that mimic the repetitive movement and the sound made by a pair of scissors. Because of the anatomical constraints of human vocal apparatus, sound imitating words never offer a complete but only partial resemblance to the sounds they mimic, with language-specific phonological and morphological rules making up for the remaining inter-linguistic differences. In other words, iconicity is a matter of degree, in visual and auditory media alike, and so in language the iconic expressions consist of both arbitrary and non-arbitrary features.

In his comprehensive study of linguistic iconicity Earl. R. Anderson talks also of kinesthetic and synesthetic types of phonetic iconicity.[27] In kinesthetic iconicity it is the physical attributes of articulation that imitate the meaning, as in the case of some phonemes pronounced with bilabial rounding to refer to curvilinearity, as in *round, mouth, oral, pool*, or *world*. The English *here* and French *ici* are articulated with the mouth drawn back, as if toward oneself, while *there* and *là* are pronounced with the tongue brought forward, as if indicating a direction. There is a statistically significant cross-linguistic tendency to use high-front vowels, as in *here*, to indicate proximity, and to use lower or back vowels, as in *there* or the German *da* to indicate distance. In similarly kinesthetic phrases such as *namby-pamby* or *sneer* the mouth and nose are wrinkled in an expression of dislike. In synesthetic iconicity in turn certain phonological patterns are intuitively felt to represent visual or tactile properties of objects, such as size, shape, softness, temperature, movement, weight, even color.[28] Synesthesia covers an interesting area of cross-modal perception, when one sense is interpreted in terms of another, as in "seeing" musical notes as colors, "feeling" them as temperature sensations, or "hearing" different colors as musical notes.[29] Small size of objects and persons, as in diminutive noun forms, is in the majority of languages around the world conveyed by words and expressions using high or front vowels [i, i:, e], as in *tiny, teeny-weeny, a wee bit, baby, child*, etc.[30]

Physical movement and substance can also be suggested phonetically. The linguist Otto Jespersen observed a cross-cultural tendency of the liquid [l] to be associated with "light movement," as in the English words starting with *fl-, sl-*, and *gl-*: *flow, flutter, flicker, slide, slither, glide*, or *glance*.[31] David Reid has also noted a statistical prevalence of the [l] words to denote "light objects": *lance* (a light weapon), *latch* (a light fastening), *lather* (light foam), *lilt* (a light song), or *lunch* (a light meal).[32] A sub-type of synesthetic iconicity relates to perception of light or color evoked trans-modally through speech sounds, whereby brightness and light colors are suggested by high or front vowels, often with the consonantal cluster *gl-* in word-initial positions, as in *gleam, glitter*, or *glimmer*, and darkness is conveyed by lower back vowels, as in *gloom*.

In psycholinguistic experiments subjects were found to match bright colors with high pitch and dark colors with low or soft pitch.[33] Far from being rare or eccentric, transmodal perceptions are quite common, especially among artists, musicians, painters, and poets, who often talk about acoustic sensations of colors, about "warm" and "cold" color impressions, or about hearing "sweet" or "heavy" sounds. In colloquial speech tactile, gustatory, olfactory, or visual sensations are often transferred onto emotions and attitudes, as in meeting with "lukewarm" reception, suffering a "bitter" experience, being too "soft" on someone, having a "toxic" or "sweet" personality, "seeing the light" in the sense of understanding, and so on.

On the morphological, level linguistic iconicity includes such universal phenomena as forming a plural by adding (never subtracting) a morpheme, as in *house-houses*, where the extension of the word imitates the multiplication of referents. In Indo-European languages the positive, comparative, and superlative degrees of adjectives show a gradual increase in the number of phonemes: *big, bigger, biggest*; *altus, altior, altissimus*. The earlier-mentioned syllable reduplication (*ping-pong, zigzag*) imitates the impression of a repetitive sound or movement. Synesthetic reduplication includes colloquial expressions such as *fuzzy-wuzzy, hurly-burly, yo-yo, eentsy-weentsy*; onomatopoeic *dingdong, pitter-patter, ticktock*; or emotionally colored (phonesthetic) *claptrap, hugger-mugger, jeepers creepers, okeydokey, riffraff,* or *shilly-shally* to convey disesteem or comic effect.[34] On the syntactic level in turn word order can reflect chronology, hierarchy, preference, direction, or duration. Thus *age before beauty, friend and foe, good and bad* prioritize preference, while *pride comes before a fall* and *the calm before the storm* reflect chronology.[35]

In all languages the basic syntactic elements such as subject (S), verb (V), and object (O) reflect the fundamental types of functional relationships between interacting systems in the outside world. In a sample of over 400 languages 96 percent have been found to have SOV, SVO, or VSO word order, in which the syntactic chronology prioritizes subject (agent of action) over object (receiver of action), and none has OSV.[36] The regularities in basic word order appear to illustrate the natural, extralinguistic motivation that reflects the structure of the world, thus qualifying the sweeping claim about the arbitrariness of linguistic structures. Things that go together both objectively and mentally belong together in syntax as well, as when a building that happens to be tall is described as *a tall building,* or when a person with a decent character is referred to as *a decent man*. All languages are capable of expressing nonlinguistic phenomena and experience such as perception, social relationships, as well as physical and biological facts; and all languages conform to and are constrained by human anatomical, physiological, and cognitive structures, including our imperfect memory and the anatomy of our ears and mouths.

Language and Metaphors

Like visual communication, speech participates in negotiating the social environment both in direct, contiguous interactions and in indirect, displaced communication. *Pass me the salt, please* relies on clear parainformation linked to the immediate need, while *Last summer I went to Greece* evokes parainformation related to a displaced event stored in memory. Also, while direct meaning linked to a contiguous situation is what all animal communication appears to be about, meta-cognitive humans cannot resist adding layers of extra meaning to their messages to create subtexts, double entendre, allusions, irony, metaphors, and humor. Our cognitive fluidity allows us to make associations across different experiential domains: psychological, social, biological, and physical, often through analogies and similarities. Verbal metaphors are not just the domain of poets; compulsively comparing like with like is what human iconic thinking is about. Unlike the types of linguistic iconicity described earlier, verbal metaphors do not necessarily rely on iconic qualities of the signs themselves but rather on "icons in the mind"—mental comparisons that can also be evoked by arbitrary linguistic signs, as when Othello, after killing his wife, feels "Like the base Indian, [who] threw a pearl away/Richer than all his tribe."[37]

For the psychologist Pascal Boyer metaphors are created by perceived tensions between different but in some respects similar objects, as when a devious person is compared to a snake, or a showy person to a peacock. Humans and reptiles or birds are of course different things, but the imagined analogy between generically different objects captured in a metaphor attracts our attention and stimulates the imagination. Lack of identity between compared objects also accounts for the elusiveness of metaphors, found especially in religious imagery, verbal or visual, with their "superficial brilliance and hidden vagueness," which is "both persuasive and question-begging," by "suggesting a lot but demonstrating very little."[38] A particularly fruitful source of metaphoric, analogizing associations is numerology, found in religious and other occult systems of thought. The four ends of the Cross, the six tips of the Star of David, the seven lights of the ancient Hebrew menorah lampstand, the Holy Trinity, the Twelve Apostles, and so on—all use numerical analogies to iconize and systematize their respective doctrinal meanings. The seven-branch menorah, for example, is said to represent the six lamps of human knowledge guided by the seventh, central light of God, or else the seven days of Creation.[39] Iconic thinking can thus lead to spurious claims about alleged connections between non-existent things, based simply on the number of their constituent elements.

A typical example of the obsessive search for the metaphoric meanings of numbers and geometric figures is the obscure symbolism attached in the occult tradition to the regular five-pointed star, or the pentagram (Figure 5.1). Basically, anything can be associated with the pentagram as long it comes in sets of five. In the Cabbalistic tradition the pentagram was a sign of marriage, because five is the sum of three (a "masculine" number) and two (a "feminine" number), and also because the idea of generation and multiplication implied by marriage is related to the fifth day of Creation (Gen. 1:20–23).[40] In Christian symbolism some of the holiest names consist of five letters: Soter, Pater, Maria, Jesus, just as the Hebrew Bible, the Pentateuch, consists of five books. Number five has also been associated with the corporeal aspect of man, which incorporates the five senses, five extreme members (two legs, two arms, and the head), and five elements (fire, water, air, earth, and ether). For Pythagorean philosophers number five denoted man's spiritual powers: intelligence, wisdom, understanding, opinion, and self-perception. In the Hermetic tradition

Figure 5.1 Numerical and geometric iconicity: the pentagram man in Robert Fludd's *Utriusque cosmi… Historia* (1617–19). Courtesy of Wikimedia Commons.

the fifth element of the human mind, coming from ether, was bestowed by God on man alone; it also underlies the alchemical *quinta essentia*, the "fifth essence" or the Philosophers' Stone: the purest, incorruptible substance that holds the other spiritual elements together.[41] In the English fourteenth-century Arthurian poem *Sir Gawain and the Green Knight*, a pentagram displayed on the knight's shield has five symbolic pentads (sets of five) ascribed to each point, including the five wits (or senses), the five fingers, the five Wounds of Christ, the five Joys of Mary, and the five virtues (liberty, loving-kindness, continence, courtesy, and piety)—all interconnected through the intersecting lines of the pentagram.[42] Thus employed iconic thinking aided by numbers and geometric patterns can establish bogus classifications and connections between any domains: material, biological, psychological, moral, philosophic, and theological.

Medieval esoterica apart, analogizing thinking pervades verbal language, poetic and colloquial, as is only to be expected in a meta-cognitive species. Metaphors are also frequently employed in some types of intellectual discourse, as in psychoanalytic theory for example, where they often replace argument but still manage to create an illusion of depth, insight, and sophistication. Unsupported analogies between psychology, anatomy, physiology, and ancient mythology have produced such pseudo-scientific concepts as the "phallic stage," "oral stage," "mirror stage," "phallic women," "Oedipus complex," "Nirvana principle," "penis envy," "castration complex," "Electra complex," "cloacal theory," "anal-sadistic stage," "sadistic-oral stage," "father complex," "urinary eroticism," and so on.[43] Iconic thinking also underlies literary and art criticism, which depends mainly on identifying motifs, archetypes, tropes, images, allegories, metaphors, figures, similes, representations, and other formal patterns, and comparing them with similar elements found in other literary texts and works of art.

Idiomatic expressions too, abundant in any language, rely on a double-layer meaning including the original literal one, and the implied figurative one relevant to a current situation.[44] Thus the literal meaning of the pointless activity of "beating a dead horse" is applied to any situation of unnecessarily expending time and energy on a task that is already ended. The phrase "devil's advocate," in the sense of offering an alternative point of view in a debate, originated in the Roman Catholic Church during the canonization process, when a canon lawyer referred to as the Devil's advocate (*advocatus diaboli*) was appointed by the Church authorities to argue against the canonization of a candidate.[45] A literal DIY expression "to hit the nail on the head" can be metaphorically applied to any task performed with exactitude. The expression "keep your eyes on the ball," first used in baseball, has acquired a broader meaning of "being on the ball" in the sense of doing a good job, being prompt and responsible. To say that someone's promise is "empty" involves a mental transfer of a situation in which a container is free of any material objects to an abstract case of declarations not followed by actions. In all cases the original literal meaning is metaphorically transferred to any context similar enough to justify the comparison. As far as we know, non-human animals are incapable of creating or expressing metaphoric or any implied meanings, assuming even that impulses in their brains can accidentally jump between different cognitive modules. The absence of memory that would allow for comparisons between events taking place at different times, and of a fast combinatorial communication system effectively prevents animals from producing meta-cognitive messages such as metaphors, humor, or irony. From ancient fables to modern animated cartoons, attributing human cognitive faculties to animals has been a source of endearing surreal comedy. But as the actor Nathan Lane states skeptically in the comedy film *Mouse Hunt* (1997) about a particularly clever mouse causing trouble to humans: "Mice don't mock, they don't have a sense of humor or irony. He's not sitting in his hole in a smoking jacket, sipping cognac and giggling to himself."

Speech and Writing

Unlike speech, writing employs visual signs that fix elements of language in permanent forms for future reference. That is, unlike speech and sign languages, which are systems of contiguous linguistic communication, writing consists entirely of signs with displaced reference. Like pictorial arts, writing as a visual equivalent of speech was invented as an external memory device for storing and retrieving the ever-growing cultural knowledge that the individual brains, with their imperfect memories, were unable to hold. Similar *aides-mémoire* of pre-literate societies included tallying devices such as notched sticks, rows of pebbles, scratches on bones or rocks, or sticks with suspended knotted cords such as the Inca quipu.[46] Partly iconic but more abstract and schematized than figurative pictures, these mnemonic devices already marked a step toward visual symbolization: a notch, a pebble, or a knot does not resemble the thing it stands for, even if the number and order of these symbolic elements mimic the quantity and spatial or chronological arrangement of referents.[47] A script, however, is more than a memory aid: its signs, even when partly iconic in form, represent visually features of language rather than of physical objects.

The units of language reflected in writing include, predictably, phonemes, morphemes, syllables, words, as well as higher-level structures such as clauses and sentences.[48] Most writing systems in history were based on symbols designating the smaller units of language: the morpheme, the syllable, and the phoneme. Morphemic systems include the Mesopotamian cuneiform, Egyptian hieroglyphs, Chinese logograms, and Japanese kanji; syllabic systems are represented by Cherokee, Ancient Cypriot, and Japanese kana; and phonemic, or phonetic systems (comparatively rare) include Greek and Latin scripts.[49] The interesting thing is that while there is no human society without syntactic speech, fewer than one in ten of all the languages in the world have ever developed an indigenous written form. Of these, the number to have produced a significant body of literature barely exceeds one hundred.[50] Writing as a cultural achievement is thus a rarity, the overwhelming majority of societies on historical record having managed without it.

After the hypothetical emergence of syntactic speech in the Late Paleolithic period, the invention of cuneiform writing in Mesopotamia about 5,000 years ago was one of the great communication revolutions in history. The next one came several thousand years later, in the fifteenth century, with the advent of printing, followed after a much shorter interval by the development of telegraphy and telephony in the nineteenth century. Another revolution, which we are in the middle of, was brought about by the digital communication system of the internet in the late twentieth century. From the fourth millennium BCE in Mesopotamia down to the European Renaissance, handwriting had been the world's most advanced communication technology, which had liberated human communication from the limitations inherent in the impermanence and volatility of speech. By transcending the condition of the live presence of the speaker and her audience, writing created linguistic records which could survive transmission over time and distance, and which were divorced from the vagueness, redundancies, and the affective dimension implicit in face-to-face communication.[51]

If speech, with its reliance on memory-based displaced referents, distances human thinking from the contiguous situation, writing increases that distance by virtue of being, in the words of Roy Harris, "a symbol of a symbol, or symbolism twice removed."[52] Written names of objects are more disassociated from these objects than are the spoken ones, as written signs are interpreted first of all as referring to linguistic objects, that is, words, and only in the second instance as signs of non-linguistic objects. The relatively slow speed of writing—typically ten times slower than speech—further distances written signs from their objects, although the fact is not without its cognitive advantages. The slow and solitary process of writing improves concentration and textual analysis by eliminating redundancy omnipresent in speech, just as reading allows for "backward scanning" and closer scrutiny of the text through re-reading—a procedure impossible in fleeting speech. Unlike volatile sound waves carried by air, graphic traces on a stable surface are permanent, taking a life of their own. Revision, verification, correction, and comment allow for the systematic codification of ideas into the written texts of religion, law, literature, philosophy, and science.

The semantic double remove of writing, combined with combinatorial grammar and the arbitrary character of relations between signs and referents, also facilitate self-referential discourse, detached from empirical reality, driven solely by recursive grammar with its power to embed clauses within clauses and ideas within ideas *ad infinitum*. Writing is inherently creative but therein also lies a danger of its alienation from contiguous experience and real life. Abstract, textual domains of thought such as philosophy, theology, and law seem particularly susceptible to linguistic "magic," whereby words and grammatical structures can suggest meaning without extra-linguistic reference, simply because the combinatorial medium makes it technically possible. On balance, however, the benefits of unbridled intellectual speculation facilitated by written language appear to outweigh the dangers of empty verbiage and gobbledygook. The insights about the nature of the world offered by the best of philosophy, by literary classics, good journalism, and science writing manage to offset the confusion sown by impenetrable bureaucratese and falsehoods parading as truths peddled by intellectual charlatans, religious leaders, partisan journalists, and political demagogues. The intellectual benefits of literacy are still among the greatest achievements of civilization.

According to Walter J. Ong writing heightens consciousness, since isolation afforded by solitary writing reduces distractions, providing distance from life that is necessary for intellectual conceptualization.[53] For Florian Coulmas the invention of writing led to a positive cognitive reorientation and a restructuring of the intellectual faculties and symbolic behavior. In order to write down a thought it must first be lifted out of the realm of loose, vague, and amorphous constructions of speech, to be fixed in condensed, more precise patterns, whereby it becomes more accessible to quiet, conscious meditation during individual perusal. The detachment of written language from live, contiguous communication thus necessitates and encourages a more analytic, intellectual, "bookish" disposition (Figure 5.2). Learning to read and write becomes more than a technical skill; it means acquiring a new cognitive operating mode.[54] Only literate societies possess institutions that function as guardians and repositories of cultural memory: libraries, courts of law, archives, schools, learned societies and

Figure 5.2 Literacy and "bookish" disposition: *Erasmus of Rotterdam*, engraving by Albrecht Dürer (1526). Courtesy of the Metropolitan Museum of Art, New York.

research institutes, which code and preserve their vast cultural knowledge in a much more precise form than the illiterate societies, with their oral traditions and limited technology, could ever do.

Evolution of Writing: From Iconic to Symbolic Signs

It is generally accepted that writing did not develop out of pictures of early art but from the systems of counting, to record commercial transactions and make inventories of traded goods. Some method of permanent recording, still used in the paper trail of business and administration, became necessary once the level of trade reached the point when unaided memory was insufficient to keep track of who owed what to whom. Counting thus came before writing, and the human race had to become numerate in order to become literate.[55] The oldest records of commercial transactions come from Uruk in Mesopotamia (about 5,000 years ago) in the form of crude pictures scratched onto tablets of wet clay of whatever happened to be traded at the time: cattle, sheep, bushels of wheat, and so on. Once the tablets were baked they could be kept for many centuries without decaying. The pictures on clay tablets were iconic: either holistic, in the form of representations of tools, vessels, and plants, or metonymic, as when a horned head stood for the entire animal. These iconic images were also accompanied by symbolic number tokens such as circles, half-circles, triangles, rectangles, and cones, as well as by personal seals of identity. Notwithstanding the linguistic character of later writing, at its origin writing consisted for the most part of simple pictures of objects: hence the label "pictographic" applied by historians to the earliest script (Figure 5.3).[56]

With time the Sumerian scribes simplified the visual icons into more schematic pictograms, where drawn lines were replaced by stylus impressions resulting in the characteristic wedge shapes that gave the Sumerian script its modern name: cuneiform, from Latic *cuneus*, "wedge." As a result, the curved lines were replaced by a series of short, abstract strokes, and the iconic quality of the signs was either reduced or lost altogether. Their recognition no longer depended on similarity but on

Figure 5.3 Pre-cuneiform pictographic (iconic) writing: a limestone tablet (H: 4.5 cm, W: 4.3 cm, D: 2.4 cm) with a list of names of employees, Mesopotamia, late fourth millennium BCE. Louvres Museum, courtesy of Wikimedia Commons.

discrimination, as pictorial likeness was gradually replaced by the need to distinguish one sign from another. For example, that the sign of the bull resembled a bull became less important than that it differed from the sign of a cow. The number and direction of wedges became standardized and reduced to a few categories and directions: vertical, horizontal, and oblique. As in the phonemes of speech, the relationships between signs and their referents became superseded by multiple relationships between signs and other signs, as the graphic system became characterized by negative differentiation, typical for symbolic communication (Figure 5.4).[57]

As Florian Coulmas points out, a transition from iconic to arbitrary cuneiform writing occurred for linguistic reasons, as the graphic signs had the same referents as the spoken names of the depicted objects. It was only natural that a pictorial sign of, say, fish would prompt in the reader the word for "fish" together with the mental concept of a fish. In this way signs were inevitably given linguistic interpretations, including arranging the signs sequentially on a tablet, like words in an utterance. As the cuneiform signs were gradually losing their iconic character, writing moved closer to the spoken language by acquiring elements of syntax in the form of additional signs for grammatical forms.[58] The transition from iconic to symbolic (syllabic in the case of cuneiform) script took about a thousand years, until about 2800 BCE signs representing monosyllabic words could be combined to form other sign-words. Despite the complexity of the system (about 600 distinct signs in use), cuneiforms

Figure 5.4 Cuneiform (symbolic) writing on a clay tablet, Mesopotamia, 1500–539 BCE. British Museum, courtesy of Wikimedia Commons.

were eventually used to record legal and historical texts of considerable grammatical sophistication, such as the Code of Hammurabi (1800 BCE), and the first recorded work of fiction, the *Epic of Gilgamesh* (*c.* 2150 BCE).

Just as spoken words can be used metaphorically, so the corresponding written signs could acquire connotative meanings. For example, a Chinese pictograph showing a stylized picture of two trees does not literally represent two trees or the words "two trees," but metonymically the word and concept of "woods." In Egypt the iconic sign for the solar disc came to indicate not just the sun but metaphorically the ideas of "day," "light," "brightness," or a god associated with the sun, thus becoming what historians of writing call *ideographs*.[59] In ideographic writing pictographs represent not so much the things they depict as the underlying idea or concept associated with those things. In other words, ideographs employ metainformation as well as parainformation, whereby pictographs of concrete, physical objects convey abstract ideas that could not be represented visually. In Chinese script for example a stylized picture of a woman and child side-by-side represents metaphorically the word "good," while the image of a sword simplified to a brush stroke denotes the more abstract concept of "nobleman." Because Chinese ideographic writing operates at the level of concept rather than word, it is possible for speakers of different dialects or languages to share the same script. Spoken Mandarin and Cantonese are mutually unintelligible, but speakers have no difficulty communicating with one another across the linguistic barrier using ideographic script (Figure 5.5).[60]

Figure 5.5 The Dongba script from Southwest China, about a thousand years old, the only ideographic writing system in use today. Courtesy of British Library/Open Culture.

The Phonetic Alphabet

A single piece of convincing evidence of the evolution of writing from iconic to arbitrary forms is provided by the famous Rosetta Stone from Egypt, dated to 196 BCE and now kept in the British Museum, which helped Jean François Champollion (1790–1832) to decipher the ancient Egyptian hieroglyphs. The stone gives the same text in three scripts: hieroglyphic, demotic (a simplified, popular form of the hieroglyphic script), and classical Greek (the youngest of the three languages) (Figure 5.6). The three texts on the Rosetta stone illustrate a clear chronological progression from the pictorial to the non-pictorial in the evolution of script, in which the Greek alphabet represents the phonetic, purely symbolic writing system.[61]

Figure 5.6 From iconic to symbolic writing: the Rosetta Stone (H: 112 cm, W: 75.7 cm, D: 28 cm), 196 BCE. Photo by Hans Hillewaert, courtesy of Wikipedia Commons.

Interestingly, if writing as such is a historical rarity, the phonetic alphabet is even rarer; in fact, it was invented only once, by a Semitic people around 1700 BCE, 2,000 years after the cuneiform writing. (The word "alphabet" itself combines the names of the first two letters of the later Greek alphabet, *alpha* and *beta*.) The original Semitic alphabet consisted only of consonant symbols, although late in the history of the Hebrew script vowel "points" were added—little dots and dashes below and above the letters to indicate the proper vowel—mainly for the benefit of learners. The ancient Greeks, who adapted the alphabetic system of writing via the Phoenicians, added vowel letters to the Semitic consonantal alphabet, further separating script from the speech of its origin and from direct experience, as alphabet could now be used to write or read words even from languages one did not know. The small number of letters of the alphabet (about two dozen), compared with ideographic writing systems (often comprising tens of thousands of characters, as in Chinese), meant that writing could now be acquired relatively quickly, theoretically by almost everyone.[62]

In the pictographic or ideographic script there is no formal connection between the depicted sign and the spoken name for it, which means that the sign can be "read" in any language. In phonetic writing, however, graphic signs become the direct counterpart of speech. The signs no longer represent objects or ideas, but sounds or groups of pronounced sounds in a particular language. This means that the signs can assume any shape, and generally there is no connection between the external form of the sign and the sound it represents.[63] Similarly, despite the pictographic beginnings of the letters of the alphabet, their original iconic character becomes irrelevant to their later communicative function, although it may have helped in memorizing the early alphabet. For instance, the twenty-two letters of the Phoenician alphabet, inherited from prior Semitic tradition around 1000 BCE, had recognizable iconic quality (e.g. a circle stood for "eye," while a circle with a cross inside meant "wheel"). All the letters of the Roman alphabet, in which the present book is written, can be traced to some original pictograph. For example, the letter "A" (Semitic *aleph*, later Greek *alpha*) goes back to a vivid representation of an ox's head. The letter "O" started as an Egyptian painted image of a human eye (a long, horizontal oval with an interior circle), later simplified to a circle with a central dot, and then to a circle merely. The Semites called the sign *ayin*, meaning "eye," represented by a guttural sound with which the word *ayin* began. The Greeks then inherited the letter "O" but not the sound, and they assigned to it the vowel sound [o], probably because of the letter's shape, which suggests the shape of a speaker's mouth pronouncing [o].[64] With the change of language and the original association between the pictograph and the name of the represented object, the letters of the alphabet lost all visual connection with their referents and their names, becoming purely arbitrary.

It is remarkable, however, how persistent the idea of iconic "representativeness" of the visual sign can be even in relation to the alphabetic writing system which, unlike holistic pictographs and ideographs, cannot visually depict the objects it refers to. Like other instances of iconic magic discussed in Chapter 4, a desire to restore a "natural" connection between a visual sign and its meaning in writing has led on occasion to speculations about a hypothetical "ideal" original alphabet, which was supposed to have consisted of simple drawings of the appropriate lip and tongue positions for the different speech sounds. For example, in 1772 Charles Davy advanced a theory that the seven Greek letters—*gamma, delta, eta, kappa, lambda, rho,* and *tau*—served to point out sounds instead of things, a bit like today's phonetic transcription. For instance the vowel [a], represented by the letter *alpha*, was pronounced with a considerable aperture of the mouth which, according to Davy, was what the original shape of the letter was supposed to represent visually.[65] (As a matter of fact, the Hebrew *aleph* was phonetically a glottal stop with which the pronunciation of the word *aleph* began.[66]) Phonetic iconicity also lay behind the Korean script, now generally known as *Han'gŭl*, introduced in 1443. The script did not evolve gradually, like other writing systems, but was created by a group of scholars under the enlightened leadership of King Sejong (reigned 1418–50), because the Chinese script was ill-suited for the Korean language. King Sejong's purpose in devising a new writing system was to enable Koreans to pronounce correctly Chinese characters. To this end the basic letter shapes of the new script were designed to imitate tongue positions during articulation. Such writing was considered "natural to Heaven and Earth."[67]

The thing is that an entirely arbitrary visual linguistic sign, however useful it may be in a combinatorial system of alphabetic writing, is actually counterintuitive and "unnatural." The persistent expectation that the form of visual linguistic signs represents something lies for example behind a peripheral but psychologically appealing habit of forming words metaphorically from the graphic shapes of the letters, as in *A-beam, A-frame, C-clamp, O-ring, S-curve, T-bone, T-shirt, T-junction, U-turn,* and so on. The sharp angles of the letter Z are the basis of *zigzag*. The phrase *mind your p's and q's* alludes to the similarity of these two letters, which presented a special challenge to printers back in the old days of typesetting. Because of their alphabetical order, those letters were kept together in the tray, leading to possible confusion. What is more, because those letters were always arranged in mirror-image position in the tray, a *p* looked like a *q*, and a *q* looked like a *p*.[68]

Phonetic writing can be either syllabic or alphabetic, of which the former, such as the Assyrian cuneiform writing or the ancient Chinese script, can be regarded as a less advanced stage of the two, because it requires a much larger number of signs: theoretically, the number of consonants multiplied by the number of vowels.[69] By comparison, alphabetic writing consists of as few as about two dozen signs, each representing (ideally) one phoneme. In the original Semitic alphabet the letters corresponded with consonants, because it is relatively easy for phonetic reasons to attach a permanent value to consonantal sounds, while vowels are more prone to variation. For example, in today's English the same written word can be pronounced differently in different parts of the country, which is due mainly to the varied pronunciation of the vowels rather than of consonants. A consonant-based alphabet is therefore better hooked in the spoken language than a writing system based on vowels. In Hebrew for instance, the absence of vowel-letters is not a major obstacle because Hebrew, like other Semitic languages, is essentially consonantal and, unlike the Indo-European languages, the vowels serve principally to denote the terminations of inflection in nouns and of moods of verbs, or other grammatical variations.[70]

The phonemic character of alphabetic writing is, however, only an ideal, and the one letter-one sound correspondence is only an approximation. A spoken word is not a united compound of a definite number of independent sounds, of which each can be expressed by a separate alphabetical sign. Speech consists essentially of a continuous series of overlapping phonetic features, and alphabetic symbols do no more than bring out certain characteristic points of this series in a generalized, abstracted way. In writing, on the other hand, we see letters and words as independent entities, and we tend to think of them as discrete units that sound essentially the same every time we hear them. But if one looks at a spectrographic analysis or a picture of the vibrations of air molecules as a function of speech, it is clear that there is no neat separation of phonemes. For example, in the word *bat* it is impossible to isolate the consonants [b] and [t] without also hearing the vowels that either precede or follow these consonants. (It is impossible to produce a stop consonant without pronouncing a vowel.) The smallest segment of speech is therefore not a single phoneme but a syllable. Despite the fact that the sound pattern of speech is not discrete but composite, the human brain somehow manages to decode the acoustic signal in terms of the articulatory maneuvers that were put together to generate the syllable. As a result, psychologically if not physically the individual consonants [b] and [t] in the word *bat* are perceived as discrete entities.[71]

Equally problematic is the concept of the word. A "word" is a discrete thing only to the literate mind in a culture using the phonetic alphabet. Most languages have no word for "word." The concept of the word is the main unit of lexicology, which itself is part of linguistics as a Western science that uses the alphabetic language and neat word divisions in written communication. But "word" is in fact a highly ambiguous term and hard to define in a way valid for all languages. In Japanese, for instance, a single "word" can convey an idea expressed in English in a whole sentence with a subject, predicate, and object. Words are thus units at the boundary between morphology and syntax, carrying both semantic and syntactic information. For practical purposes, the word can be defined as the smallest unit that can stand alone as a complete utterance and that can be inserted, extracted, and moved around the sentence without destroying its grammaticality.[72] The physical reality of speech on the level of phonology and morphology is therefore one thing, and its mental interpretation another. When the phonetic and morphological properties of speech are analyzed mentally, they become separated into discrete units: phonemes and morphemes, however inaccurate such segmentation is from an acoustic point of view.[73] Alphabetic writing is therefore an expression of the mental interpretation of speech, not of objective phonetic features.

Put differently: speech is analog, while the mind and the alphabetic writing interpret speech as digital. Like music, speech relies on continuous, time-varying quantities, while the alphabet consists of discrete signals, like the zero-one binary code used in today's digital communication technology.[74] Human experience of the world is generally analog in the above sense: it consists of continuous, quantitative changes, as in vision, in which we perceive infinitely smooth gradations of shapes and colors. Representing continuous and overlapping speech sounds by means of discrete letters of the alphabet is a historically more famous and consequential way of digitally simulating an analog phenomenon of natural speech. The alphabet is therefore not a kind of phonetic notation, but a combinatorial system of independent characters employed to generate writing as an approximate visual representation of speech mentally interpreted in terms of digital signals (separate phonemes).

The digital format of the phonetic alphabet compared with the analog pictorial script is largely responsible for the relative precision with which messages can be communicated by means of the former. The ancient Chinese maxim that a single picture is more valuable than many words may be true in some sense, but pictures alone, despite their evocative, esthetic, and emotive power, are notoriously ambiguous and elusive. Also, as repositories of cultural knowledge both pictures and pictorial systems of writing—cuneiforms, hieroglyphs, and ideographs—impose tremendous burden on the memory, and their efficiency to communicate concrete information is therefore limited. That is to say, analog, holistic iconic signs convey analog, holistic messages but they cannot be broken down into constituent segments, each with its own separate meaning, to produce new meanings, the way syntactic speech and the phonetic alphabet can produce meaning. Pictures alone can at best "suggest" further meanings through iconic associations that bring together often objectively unconnected things, only because they happen to be similar in some respect. As we saw earlier in this chapter, association by analogy underlies metaphors and iconic magic—a psychologically appealing but factually false way of thinking.

The invention of the alphabet, with its arbitrary signs and digital code, thus provided a major boost to symbolic, as distinct from iconic, thinking for those using it. It also helped reduce the memory load imposed by reading skill, eventually allowing for a much wider diffusion of literacy. Instead of remembering 600 or 700 hieroglyphs or cuneiforms, or several thousand ideograms (as in Chinese or Japanese), a reader of a phonetic alphabet (as in early Greek writing) could achieve literacy using only about two dozen phonograms, or letters. The main advantage of the alphabet was thus the economy and precision with which it allowed the reader to map visual displays of symbols onto spoken language. Judging from the measurable success of writing systems—ease of use, speed, and popularity—the phonetic alphabet is by far the most successful method of writing ever invented. It is, as the historian David Diringer puts it, "the supreme achievement of man, which makes possible the very existence of the highest civilization,"[75] mainly by facilitating abstract, theoretical, and systematic thinking, without which mathematical logic and science in the present shape would not be possible.

Speech, Literacy, and Thinking

Reading and writing are systems of indirect linguistic communication and ways of augmenting the computational power of the mind already present in the spoken language. Both speech and literacy are responsible for what the philosopher Andy Clark calls "second-order cognitive dynamics," and what the cognitive linguist Keith Frankish calls "virtual belief formation": the ability to think about one's own thoughts, to engage in meta-cognitive operations, both as a way of generating new ideas and as an aid to introspection.[76] The combinatorial nature of language coupled with individual consciousness produces inner verbalizations and various meta-cognitive and meta-linguistic skills, including cognitive self-stimulation, when inner speech is channelled through a feedback loop from speech production to speech comprehension.[77] Reading and writing can further enhance this self-stimulating process by another feedback loop between the linguistic mind and the external visual text. The interaction between the cognitive and linguistic faculties also facilitates self-evaluation, self-criticism, and finely honed remedial responses, such as recognizing a flaw in our own plan or argument, and dictating further cognitive efforts to fixing it. The practice of putting thoughts into words, especially in writing, thus alters the nature of human experience. Our thoughts become apt for rational assessment and for all kinds of meta-cognitive scrutiny. In this way language and the combinatorial thinking it encourages become a powerful transformer of individual computational and experiential space (Figure 5.7).

Figure 5.7 Literacy as a transformer of thought: *Study in a Wood*, oil painting by Daniel Huntington (1861). Courtesy of the Metropolitan Museum of Art, New York.

The mutually reinforcing, positive feedback between language and mind that sets off the chain of syntactic and cognitive computations applies to both speech and writing. During a conversation, for example, interactions do not occur only between the interlocutors, but also within each interlocutor's head, between the language acquired from one's community and the mind, with its unique personality and highly individualized cognitive skills. It is largely due to these internal feedbacks rather than to external informational inputs that new thoughts and ideas are generated. When I am about to say or write something, at first I may have only a vague idea of what I want to express, and it may often be difficult to choose the first word, the first phrase or sentence. But once the first sentence is uttered or written down and its meaning is still fresh in memory, the structure and meaning of that sentence interact with the linguistic and cognitive faculties of the mind to produce the next sentence with greater ease. The new sentence links up with the first, establishing a narrative and semantic continuity, which begins to gather momentum, making the production of every next sentence easier, until the linguistic/cognitive interactive process takes care of itself to generate more and more sentences and new meanings with less difficulty. Unless this process is monitored for coherence, logic, and relevance, it may easily morph, especially in speech, into a "stream of consciousness"—incoherent rambling made easier by the fact that in transient speech we often forget how the verbal chain has started and what the topic of the conversation or monologue originally was. Indeed, constant shifts of topic, digressions, and unpredictable verbal meanderings are typical for relaxed, colloquial speech in informal social contexts.

This internal run-away linguistic-cognitive computational process can be checked to a large extent in writing, which is why this medium is so important in inducing mental discipline and systematic, logical thinking. As Andy Clark describes the writing process:

> By writing down our ideas we generate a trace in a format which opens up a range of new possibilities. We can then inspect and re-interpret the same ideas, coming at them from many different angles and in many different frames of mind. We can hold the original ideas steady so that we may judge them, and safely experiment with subtle alterations... In these ways... the real properties of physical text transform the space of possible thoughts.[78]

This is what happens during textual revision, a procedure impossible in speech in the absence of a permanent linguistic record to be scanned back and forth, and corrected where necessary through deletion, addition, or substitution of words, phrases, sentences, paragraphs, and sections of text. This is how redundancies, so frequent in spoken language, can be weeded out in writing to achieve economy, conciseness, and precision of thought. The process of textual revision is facilitated today by word processors, but even in the era of pen and paper, or quill and parchment, it was always possible to revise the text as it was being written, both in mind and directly on the page, as the annotations and corrections found in old manuscripts reveal.

The acquisition of literacy, understood as the ability to use script to record, store, and retrieve knowledge outside the individual minds, has had important and irreversible effects on the mind itself, and consequently on culture. The division between prehistory and history is largely based on whether or not there are written documents. However, despite the antiquity of writing it is only in the past few hundred years that reading and writing have become widespread, and today's global world has become so constructed that a non-literate person is culturally seriously handicapped. As said earlier, literacy leads to analytic, critical, reflective thinking, because things written down can be examined and classified into categories, hierarchies, and so on. The meaning of a written text can also be more precise than that of a spoken utterance, because permanent signs are more explicit than the implicit, ambiguous, emotively colored speech.[79] Reading and writing are also intimate, private, solitary activities compared with social speech, giving their users the opportunity for detached, mediated, and introspective experience, so important for personal intellectual development.

Speech has obvious chronological priority over writing, and while the former is a central and universal linguistic phenomenon, with roots going back a few million years to primate emotive vocalizations, the latter is a historically very recently acquired device for capturing speech in a less transient form. It is also evident that without speech there would be no writing: a literate but speechless culture is difficult to imagine. Moreover, while speech originates as a neurobiological function, like walking, writing is a technology, an "optional extra" that most cultures on historical record have managed without. The ontogeny of literacy is also different from the ontogeny of speech. In normal circumstances children acquire their native speech "naturally" and effortlessly, but they do not learn to read and write without adult encouragement, and sometimes not even then. Even in cultures that have invented ways of producing permanent linguistic records, literacy has for thousands of years been an elitist, specialized skill. Despite the fact that the written word now so dominates the world, from a linguistic point of view writing remains subservient to speech, or at least is predicated upon it: we are still primarily speakers and listeners and only secondarily readers and writers.

Part II

Applications

6

Oscar Wilde and Dynamism of Character

Premise 5 of systemic semiotics as summarized in the Introduction speaks of autonomous systems interacting with one another by exchanging information and energy. The theoretical part of the book has been concerned mainly with the cognitive side of communication, that is, with information, while the energy processes occurring in autonomous systems have been treated only marginally, as in the discussion of needs in Chapter 1. There remains, however, a vital and fascinating problem of the system's internal dynamism defined in terms of the exchange of energy between the system and its environment, and its impact on the system's internal properties and behavior. Applied to humans, the internal dynamism influences the cognitive processes that underpin the system's autonomy, including individual personality and needs as motivators of behavior—properties that remain relatively stable at any given time and only change gradually with age.

In this chapter I want to use the deductive model of the dynamic processes in autonomous systems to throw some light on the personality of Oscar Wilde (1854-1900), an Irish poet, playwright, and wit—one of the most colorful and influential artistic figures of the late Victorian age (Figure 6.1). The starting point is, again, the premise that humans as autonomous systems strive toward a functional equilibrium between the given properties of their personalities and the external circumstances. As pointed out in Chapter 1, to be autonomous systems must possess properties that do not depend on and do not change under the influence of environmental pressures—what I referred to as the system's internal reactivity (Figure 1.1). This autonomy begins with the unique genome meshing with unique circumstances of one's life and experience, combined with the equally unique nature of relations between the dynamic and cognitive processes occurring within the individual during his lifetime. These relations have a direct bearing on one's behavior and explain, for example, why some people follow social conventions while others bend or break them; why some strive for power and material wealth above all while others invest their time and energy to pursue creative, artistic ends; why certain people are idealistic and impractical while others are realistic and pragmatic; and so on. In the present case, it will be interesting to see what light the deductions from the systemic model can shed on the apparent incompatibility between Oscar Wilde's artistic personality and social expectations regarding moral and sexual behavior in late Victorian times—an incompatibility that exposed Wilde to public ignominy and cost him his freedom.

Figure 6.1 Oscar Wilde (1854–1900): a quintessential artist. Photo by Napoleon Sarony, New York, 1882 (courtesy of the Metropolitan Museum of Art, New York).

Dynamism of Character

For the cyberneticist Marian Mazur the stable properties in the autonomous system, that is, its reactivity, define the system's individual *character*.[1] Character, or given personality, includes such properties as intelligence, specialized talent, temperament, volition, and other psychological quirks and idiosyncrasies that uniquely "characterize" a person. As a quality which is by definition independent from the environment, one's character cannot be changed under social pressure or even by the person herself, even using all available introspection and will power. This would mean, for example, that obsessive broodings over one's character, Hamlet-like, lead only to mental exhaustion and frustration, but they cannot alter the stable parameters of one's character. Indeed, a tendency to compulsively self-analyze is itself a result of one's given character. Similarly, blaming others (parents, teachers, peer pressure, popular culture, religion, and so on) for one's character is groundless and unfair, just as promises to change one's character are simply impossible to keep. One's character is what it is at any given moment, dependent neither on one's resolutions nor on social influence. At best, one can try to bend one's character to the situation within the limits of one's tolerance, but tolerance too is a stable property of character and cannot be extended beyond a certain point, after which the personality breaks down. Nor is it possible to change someone else's character, whether through persuasion or coercion. A bullied person will suffer under intimidation, but his or her character will remain unchanged. The only sensible thing to do with one's own or somebody else's character is simply to accept it as it is. The above statements derive logically from the definition of character as a set of stable properties of the autonomous system, and as such require no additional proofs.

Character itself is defined by cognition powered by the energy processed by the system, that is, by the system's *dynamism*. Every system needs energy both to sustain its internal processes and to effect changes in the environment: the first type of energy will be referred to as *physiological*, and the second as *sociological*. A walking person is using physiological energy alone to move from place to place; a person covering the same distance on a bicycle is augmenting her physiological energy with sociological energy; a person driven around in a limousine depends only on sociological energy. Meditating with one's eyes closed means relying solely on the physiological energy of the brain, while cognition aided by external computational devices such as written texts, pictures, the internet, and computer software uses additional sociological energy. When people cooperate or exploit one another, someone's physiological energy can become someone else's sociological energy. In Edmond Rostand's play *Cyrano de Bergerac* (1897) the handsome but dull Christian has no gift of poetry to woo his beloved Roxana, and to win her heart he enlists the help of his ugly but poetic friend Cyrano to make love speeches on his behalf under the cover of darkness.

The system's internal dynamism depends on its ability to store and utilize physiological energy. This ability deteriorates over time, as physiological energy dissipates due to entropy, that is, the leveling of potential differences, which is what happens with the levels of liquids in connected vessels. Entropy is what causes the *aging* of a living system. The gradual loss of physiological energy can be compensated up to a point by the system's *growth* and the corresponding increase of physiological energy. However, all living organisms eventually reach the ceiling of their body size and mass as defined by their genome. The relations between growth and aging determine the system's dynamism, defined by Marian Mazur as "a logarithm of the ratio of the coefficient of growth to the coefficient of aging."[2] Basically this means that as the system's ability to process physiological energy diminishes over time, it can be compensated first by bodily growth, and then by an increasing use of sociological energy. This is why as people grow older they tend to rely more on material security, physical comfort, and health care.

As a natural variable, dynamism of character follows a bell-curved normal distribution during a system's lifetime (Figure 6.2), which Mazur describes in terms of three main phases:

1. *exodynamic* phase, in which the system enjoys a surplus of physiological energy, which means that its reactions are frequent, diverse in kind, and strong in intensity. The system's behavior in the exodynamic phase can be described as restless, vivacious, hyperactive, and extrovert. In the traditional "ages of life" trope the exodynamic phase corresponds with *childhood*;
2. *static* phase, in which the gradual loss of physiological energy is equally compensated by the acquisition of sociological energy. Consequently, the system's reactions at this stage are comparatively moderate in frequency and intensity, and are repetitive in character. The static phase corresponds temperamentally with the *middle age*;
3. *endodynamic* phase, in which further decline in physiological energy is for a time compensated by the increasing acquisition of sociological energy. The system's reactions are low in frequency, limited in kind, and weak in intensity, and the behavior can be described as withdrawn, subdued, and introvert. The endodynamic phase corresponds with the traditional notion of *old age*.

For physical reasons individual dynamism of character develops from exodynamic through static to endodynamic phase, not necessarily in terms of fixed calendar years as of individual development. That is, at what exact age a "child" becomes an "adult" or a "middle-aged" person grows "old" will vary to an extent from person to person. It is also possible to refine the dynamic scale by introducing intermediary stages, whereby we can talk about *exodynamic, exostatic, static, endostatic,* and *endodynamic* phases,

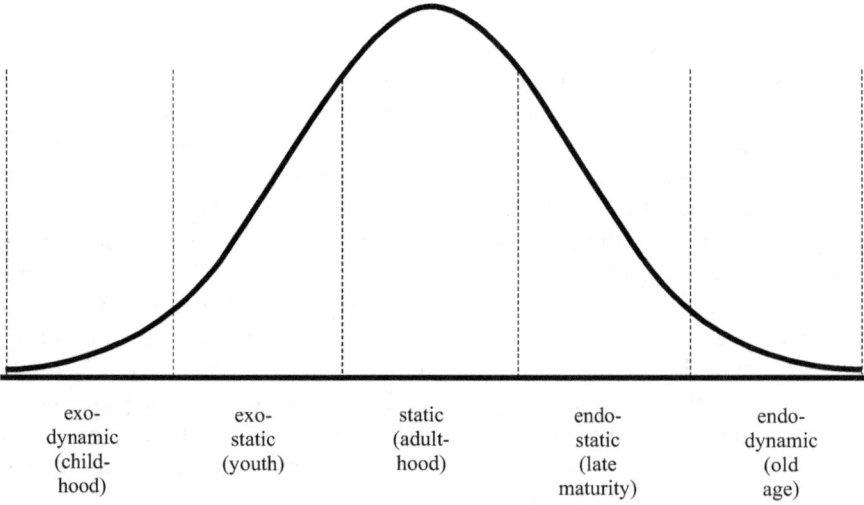

Figure 6.2 The dynamic spectrum of character.

corresponding with what in a loose psychological sense we call, respectively, childhood, youth, adulthood, late maturity, and old age (Figure 6.2). The normal distribution of the dynamic phases of character also means that any population will consist of a small minority of exodynamic people, a larger minority of exostatics, a majority of statics, a large minority of endostatics, and a small minority of endodynamics.

Dynamic Manifestations of Behavior

The inverted relations between physiological energy and sociological energy determine the specific manifestations of behavior in different dynamic types of character. As a general strategy of behavior it is possible to say the following:

— exodynamic people disperse everything (in terms of information and energy) and accumulate nothing;
— exostatic people disperse more than they accumulate;
— static people disperse as much as they accumulate;
— endostatic people accumulate more than they disperse;
— endodynamic people accumulate everything and disperse nothing.

In other words, dynamism of character determines a general, motivational strategy of behavior, the wants and needs at a particular stage of one's life. Thus exodynamic people desire first of all to express their personalities and gratify their hedonistic desires, forever searching for new sensations. Exostatics in turn like to show off to impress, amaze, or shock others by cultivating an individual eccentric style and manners. Static people desire order and respect for received norms, rules, and laws. Endostatics prefer logistical challenges to impress others with their efficiency and organizational skills. Finally, endodynamics desire above all material gains, privilege, and power over other people.

As a stable element of personality, a given dynamism of character effects all behaviors and attitudes at a particular stage of one's life. For example, in social interactions extrovert exodynamics dispense a lot of information, mainly about themselves, and often with little regard for factual reality. They gladly succumb to their imagination, preferring fantasy to facts. Typical exodynamic discourses include self-centered monologues, confessions, and poetic visions. Exostatics, on the other hand, do acknowledge external, factual reality, but they embellish their accounts with things that did not happen and do not exist. They tend to "lie" in Oscar Wilde's sense of confabulation and storytelling—a frank, superbly irresponsible "gift of exaggeration" with its "healthy, natural disdain of proof of any kind."[3] Creative fiction is the main type of exostatic discourse, where the purpose is not so much to inform as to entertain the audience with imaginative simulations of plausible or downright improbable scenarios. In debates, exostatic people do not argue their point by relying on logic and evidence, but use communication as a performance, as in TV talk shows, to impress and beguile their audiences with elusive witticisms, quips, and paradoxes, in which "one should always be a little improbable," and where "style, not sincerity, is the essential."[4]

Static people, on the other hand, are truthful and accurate, in that their accounts follow logic and are based in fact. Statics can, however, occasionally lie or conceal information in the name of some justified cause, to mislead the enemy for example. Typical static discourses include scientific and journalistic accounts, in which, for the exostatic Wilde, "if one tells the truth, one is sure sooner or later to be found out."[5] Endostatic people in turn tend to be reticent and evasive, saying less than they know, and can bend the truth if it suits their pragmatic interests. Finally, endodynamics keep all they know to themselves, but if they have to speak they routinely lie, deny facts, and hide their real goals and motives. Typical endodynamic discourses are political speeches and propaganda.

In decision-making exodynamics act on impulse and without forethought. When things do not turn out their way, they throw tantrums, at the same time feeling no responsibility for their actions. Exostatics in turn make rash decisions and improvise when things go wrong, and they often avoid responsibility for their actions, arguing in their defense that they meant well. Exostatic people consider only the immediate future and hope for the best. Statics make informed decisions based on facts and rules as defined by law, duty, instructions, and experience, and they are prepared to accept responsibility if things do not turn out as planned. Endostatics make their decisions cautiously, they try to foresee possible negative outcomes of their actions, and take necessary steps to avoid them. Finally, endodynamics make cunning and shrewd decisions, always sure to make no mistake. If they fail, they deny any wrongdoing and refuse to be held accountable, blaming everyone else instead.

As far as the attitude toward money and material possessions is concerned, exodynamics display total carelessness and extravagance, spending lavishly, mostly on pleasures. For them, "time is waste of money," in Wilde's phrase.[6] Exostatics are negligent about their possessions, spend more than they earn, and often borrow or live on credit, as Wilde did to float his bohemian lifestyle. Static people maintain their possessions, spend as much as they earn, and save if they can; their proud motto is "I paid my way." Endostatics increase their possessions whenever possible (for them indeed "time is money"), they spend less than they earn, and can be stingy. Finally, endodynamics expand their possessions, they are greedy and acquisitive, but would like to live without having to spend anything, like Ebenezer Scrooge.

With regard to personal appearance, exodynamics could not be bothered how they look and what they wear, and since they have no secrets before the world they would be happiest going naked. Exostatics consider their external appearance as an important extension of their personality: they like to dress up stylishly in an individual, unconventional way. According to Wilde, "one should either be a work of art, or wear a work of art."[7] Statics dress appropriately to the occasion and follow the general fashion. They can also be intolerant of people who dress extravagantly and eccentrically. For the exostatic stylish dresser like Wilde, the public (i.e., static) expectation that everyone dress alike was an unacceptable intrusion into one's privacy:

> A man is called affected, nowadays, if he dresses as he likes to dress. But in doing that he is acting in a perfectly natural manner. Affectation, in such matters, consists in dressing according to the views of one's neighbour, whose views, as they are the views of the majority, will probably be extremely stupid.[8]

Endostatic people in turn are more assertive in the way they dress; they want their clothes to emphasize their rank and status. Finally, endodynamics do not care how they look as long as they appear different from their subordinates to emphasize their power and authority.

In dangerous situations exodynamics display total recklessness and naiveté: they are afraid of nothing, not because they are brave but because of their inherent optimism and inability to appreciate the seriousness of the situation. Exostatics are showy and tend to underestimate danger, relying on wishful thinking and bravado to impress others. Statics generally avoid danger, but can take personal risks and act bravely in the performance of their duties or when fighting for a cause. Endostatics act cautiously, trying to foresee danger and to avoid it if possible; they are no fools to risk their lives for others. Finally, endodynamics are watchful and wary, take all steps to anticipate danger and to prevent it, and avoid taking any personal risks. Paranoid about personal safety, they smell poison in their food, fabricate rumors about plots and conspiracies against them, randomly change their whereabouts to evade real and imagined assassins, and live in fortresses and high-security mansions surrounded by bodyguards.

In their attitude toward the law exodynamics display total disregard for legal matters and regulations: they do not wish the law to interfere with their lives, seeing it as an intolerable infringement on their personal freedom. Exostatics obey the law superficially, dodging it when it interferes with their individual lifestyles. Statics in turn rigorously observe the law and expect consequences for those who break it. Endostatics respect the law as a general rule, but are prepared to cut corners when the law interferes with their profit-oriented, pragmatic goals. Finally, endodynamics place themselves above the law, and try to manipulate it to their advantage and to control other people.

In the sphere of creativity and vocational types the exodynamic character is responsible for spontaneous, original inventions in arts, music, literature, and philosophy. The creativity of exostatics in turn is limited to developing someone else's original ideas in an individual way. While exodynamics write plays and compose music, exostatics make good actors, theater and film directors, musical performers, art critics, and fashion designers. Statics, on the other hand, are most useful where persistence, patience, and discipline are required, as in scholarly research, the army, law, and civil service. They are the doers where goals are set and duties clearly defined. Endostatics are creative in improving pragmatic efficiency and in inventing new operational rules and procedures. They make good executive managers, diplomats, and senior civil servants. Finally, endodynamics create strategic plans for large organizations, popular movements, political parties, and whole nations, and feel best in positions of command and leadership at the highest level.

The Exostatic Personality of Oscar Wilde

The dynamic category that best describes the artistic personality of Oscar Wilde (of most artists in fact) is exostatism—an intermediary stage between the flamboyance, extravagance, and recklessness of the exodynamic character and the static propriety and decorum. Wilde's eccentric, extrovert, provocative bohemianism, his attention to dress, preference for art and fiction before hard facts of life, his poses and masks, hedonistic indulgences, constant desire to charm and beguile, spendthrift habits, scorn for authority and public opinion, his paradoxical wit and verbal playfulness, underestimation of danger—in a word, Wilde as a late Victorian dandy is an archetypal illustration of the exostatic character, as are his literary personae: Lord Henry Wotton from the novel *The Picture of Dorian Gray*, Lord Goring from the play *An Ideal Husband*, and the two dandies from Wilde's comic theatrical masterpiece *The Importance of Being Earnest*, Jack Worthing and Algernon Moncrieff.

Central to Oscar Wilde's life is his behavior before and during the infamous trials for his homosexuality, an offence legally labeled as "gross indecency" at the time, which in 1895 landed him in prison for two years. It is possible to argue that Wilde's conviction, by no means certain at the beginning of the trials, was due to two factors: the external, legal one, which criminalized homosexuality, and the internal, psychological one, related to Wilde's attitude during the trials. Given Wilde's postulated exostatism he could not—to put it tautologically—but act as dictated by his exostatic personality. Unable to resist his showy behavior in court, Wilde inevitably became the co-author of his downfall rather than a helpless victim of a sexual prejudice enshrined in law.

Early in 1895 Wilde carelessly allowed himself to be drawn into a legal battle with the Marquess of Queensberry, the father of Wilde's lover Lord Alfred "Bosie" Douglas, who wanted to save his son from Wilde's "immoral" influence. Unduly optimistic, Wilde had overlooked his legal vulnerability, displaying overconfidence in the devotion of his many friends in the political and literary world, who were in a position to shape public opinion in his favor. Also, while fully aware of the impropriety and danger of his relations with young men, Wilde unwisely chose not to regard his behavior as being of any legal consequence. He had also underestimated his opponent—a rich and influential man. For his part the Marquess of Queensberry appears to have had an endostatic character—calculating and pragmatic, "unruly though he loved rules," in the words of Richard Ellmann, Wilde's biographer, in reference to the Queensberry Rules of boxing, endorsed publicly by the athletic Marquess in 1867.[9] Queensberry was also a hypocrite: a brute and an adulterer in private presenting himself in public as a concerned father, a defender of family values, and a morally outraged citizen.

An endostatic, or even a static person in Wilde's place would have been more cautious, and would have suspected a booby trap set for him by Queensberry. The latter had provoked Wilde into legal action by insulting him in public with a visiting card left at Albermarle Club in London, with the words "To Oscar Wilde, posing Somdomite"—the offensive word misspelled aristocratically.[10] Several of Wilde's friends, more sober and circumspect than the flamboyant and careless artist, advised him to tear up the card and forget the whole thing. However, the exostatic Wilde, goaded also by his (exodynamic) lover, who hated his abusive father and wanted to see him as a defendant in court, formally accused Queensberry of slander and entered the legal case with full recklessness, in a histrionic, self-dramatizing pose, as if he was unconsciously acting a part of the fall from greatness. The theme, incidentally, runs prophetically through Wilde's literary work, from his Newdigate Prize poem on the fallen splendor of Ravenna of his Oxford years; through the tragic sacrifice of Vera in his first play, *Vera, or the Nihilists*; the sacrifice of Mrs. Erlynne for her daughter in the play *Lady Windermere's Fan*; and the sacrifice of Mrs. Arbuthnot for her son in *A Woman of No Importance*. For an artist who preferred literary themes to ordinary life, there was a strong attraction to cast himself in the tragic pose, to adopt the role of victim, like Saint Sebastian or Marsyas, just as earlier Wilde had adopted the role of the dandy and the apostle of joy.

The Trials of Oscar Wilde

Entirely in keeping with Wilde's exostatic character was also his liberality with truth during the trials. Colorful embellishments of facts may be of little consequence in private life, and of course perfectly justified in literary fiction, but entirely out of place in the court, whose purpose as a static institution is to establish facts as they actually happened. Wilde not only lied during the cross-examinations, but he entered the case denying cavalierly that there was any truth in Queensberry's libelous accusation. He then continued to lie to his lawyers, and as a result was unable to get proper advice on his actual situation. What also made a bad impression on the jury right from the start was Wilde's deliberate miscalculation of his age, when he admitted to being thirty-nine instead of forty-one. The inaccuracy was noted instantly by Queensberry's solicitor Edward Carson, Wilde's classmate from Trinity College Dublin, who conducted the hearing during the first trial. In the eyes of the static jury Wilde did of course lie about his age, but from his subjective point of view he probably felt that he did not. At the time a man over forty would certainly be classed as middle-age, but for an exostatic person like Wilde a willful miscalculation of real age probably reflected how old he actually felt: being young at heart Wilde simply did not want to appear in public as a (static) man of over forty.

Also in keeping with his exostatic disposition was Wilde's theatrical but in the context totally inappropriate behavior during the first trial. Wilde simply treated the hearing as a performance in which he would shine and impress everyone with his wit and artistic pose. Indeed, for much of the time he managed to play to the gallery and hold the audience in his hand. He arrived at the Old Bailey criminal court stylishly dressed in a long, dark-blue Chesterfield overcoat trimmed with velvet and sporting a white buttonhole, driven in a carriage complete with coachman and footman. In the fifteen counts brought against him by Queensberry's pleas of justification, thirteen accused Wilde of indecent acts with young men, and two spoke of the alleged immorality of *The Picture of Dorian Gray* and of Wilde's epigrams. Interestingly, Carson chose to begin with the last two counts, and initially the cross-examination dealt with literary matters where, predictably, Wilde easily held his ground. He retorted cavalierly to all questions, but instead of expounding his theory of art as an enhancement of life—a tactic that would have made a favorable impression on the jury—he presented himself as an immoral artist who scorned the moral mob. Wilde showed off and dominated the spectacle, at least for as long as literary matters were being discussed. When Carson read a passage from *Dorian Gray* and asked Wilde, "Did you write that?," Wilde answered that he had the honor of being the author. Next Carson read aloud a piece of verse by Wilde, and asked again: "And I suppose you wrote that also, Mr. Wilde?" Wilde waited till one could hear a pin drop and then said quietly, "Ah no, Mr. Carson, Shakespeare wrote that." Carson went scarlet, turned the pages again, read another piece of verse, and said, "And I suppose Shakespeare wrote that also, Mr. Wilde?" "Not as you read it, Mr. Carson, you read it very badly," Oscar said. There was uproar in the court, and Wilde deliberately turned his back, stood with his arms folded, looking away through the ceiling in rapt concentration. Carson thundered at him to conduct himself properly, while Wilde was staring deeper into the void for a full minute. Suddenly he swung round as if he heard Carson for the first time and said, assuming a most apologetic tone, "I beg your pardon, Mr. Carson; I do beg your pardon."[11] Carson for his part appears to have had a static character, and to give him his due he did not set out initially to destroy Wilde, at first refusing to accept the brief on the grounds that Wilde was a fellow-Irishman from the same University. Later, however, "college loyalty faded before Protestant morality," as Richard Ellmann puts it, and Carson became involved.[12]

Apart from the legal context, Wilde's courtroom exchanges with Carson are also interesting from a psychological point of view, as an illustration of a fundamental misunderstanding between exostatic concern for artistic effect alone and equally exclusive static insistence on morality and law. As the full transcript of the first trial demonstrates, Carson persisted in questioning Wilde about the alleged ethical implications of his literary work and ignoring their esthetic dimension, while the opposite was the case with Wilde: the two men simply did not understand one another, to their mutual irritation and exasperation. To Carson's crude accusation that *Dorian Gray* was a "sodomitical" novel, Wilde replied disdainfully: "Only to brutes and illiterates. The views of the Philistines on art are not to be counted: they are incalculably stupid."[13] Carson appears to be totally blind to the notion of esthetic beauty, while Wilde shows genuine incomprehension of the words "immoral," "perverted," "sodomitical," and "blasphemous" used in relation to literature. He would say, "Blasphemy is not a word of mine," or "I don't know what you mean by a sodomitical novel."[14] The protracted courtroom debate ultimately boils down to Carson's static preoccupation with literature being either moral or immoral, while for the exostatic Wilde the question is only whether literary works are well or badly written.

The turning point of the first trial came famously with Wilde's unfortunate, flippant answer to the question regarding the servant Walter Grainger, whom Wilde had found too ugly to kiss. Carson took full advantage of what was Wilde's de facto admission of improper relations with young men, and for the first time Wilde became flustered, dropped his nonchalant pose, and lost his nerve by calling Carson impertinent and insolent. Although he continued to deny any wrongdoing with young men, this was effectively the end of his show, and the end of Wilde as a dandy. As Merlin Holland, literary critic and Wilde's grandson, puts it, "One fatal witticism too many and Oscar had effectively talked himself into prison."[15] In later trials in May of 1895, now completely upstaged and outside of his role Wilde was, literally, not himself, tired of action and, like Hamlet, wishing to distance himself from his plight and be a spectator of his own tragedy, if he could no longer be its active protagonist. After listening to the Solicitor-General's final speech for the prosecution, which condemned him to two years of hard labor, Wilde commented, "How splendid it would be, if I was saying all this about myself!"[16] His need to "play a part," to be "in the role," so typical for exostatics, is also responsible for Wilde's instinctive refusal to leave England after the first lost trial, which probably would have spared him the final ignominy and incarceration. Richard Ellmann writes with great insight:

> A man so concerned with his image disdained to think of himself as a fugitive, skulking in dark corners instead of lording it in the limelight. He preferred to be a great figure, doomed by fate and the unjust laws of a foreign country. Suffering was more becoming than embarrassment.[17]

The tragic outcome of Wilde's trials poignantly illustrates that people do not always act optimally in their own interest, to say nothing of self-preservation, but rather act according to the given biases and limitations of their characters, which sometimes means acting against one's interests and self-preservation. When defending his literary works in court Wilde was obviously honest to his artistic ideals, but the elitism, scorn, carelessness, and megalomania of his answers and comments, and his showy behavior could not but prejudice the jury, consisting as it did of static citizens, honest to the letter of the law but less appreciative of histrionic and in the context inappropriate effects. If it makes sense to talk of Oscar Wilde as a victim, he was a victim of two sets of circumstances: of his own exostatic character, which made him act as he did (both in his life and during the trials), and of the external situation, involving not only the legal statutes against homosexuality but also the persistent malice and fury of Wilde's chief adversary Queensberry, the prosecutor, the jury, and the press, consisting for the most part of static people, on whose views and decisions Wilde's fate ultimately depended. It was difficult to expect understanding and compassion from people whom Wilde had openly criticized, patronized, and insulted, as when he called the public a monstrous mob without culture that will never stoop down to pick up a brush for a painter, but only to throw mud at him.[18]

Art and Morality

Wilde also became a victim of a fundamental misunderstanding regarding moral norms and the possible deviations from them. As the distribution of dynamic categories of character demonstrates (Figure 6.2), accepted rules and norms of conduct can be broken in two principal ways, depending on whether one's character lies on the exodynamic or the endodynamic side of the spectrum. Exodynamic, artistic persons often bend or break the rules in the name of individual freedom and self-expression. Any harmful consequences of such behavior are unintended and often negligible, and in any case they are usually suffered by the lovable exodynamic rogues themselves. On the other side of the spectrum, the unlovable endodynamic rogues tend to break or ignore rules in the name of calculated self-interest, advantage, and power—the behavior that often has serious adverse consequences for a large number of people. When exodynamics ignore the law they themselves often end up as victims, as Wilde did, whereas when endodynamics violate the law by committing large-scale frauds or political crimes, thousands or millions of others suffer. One might argue therefore that at the root of Wilde's tragic fall lies a misunderstanding on the part of the static, moral public, who confused the artist's *immoral*, relatively harmless conduct with *amoral*, often harmful actions. The inability to distinguish between exodynamic, artistic immorality and endodynamic, political amorality is a common enough mistake, as in finding "entertaining" and "funny" both a stand-up comedy act and a buffoonery of a narcissistic public figure. Or when puritanical philistines condemn "lying" both in the form of artistic fiction and in opportunistic deceptions. The two types of misdemeanor are often lumped together, both the immoral one, motivated by hedonistic gratifications and self-expression, and the amoral one, driven by selfishness, greed, and thirst for power. In consequence, the static moral majority often both misunderstands the immoral behavior of exodynamic eccentrics and underestimates the cynicism and unscrupulousness of amoral endodynamic power freaks.

The case of the exostatic Wilde was only a more tragic repeat of the trials for alleged obscenity and immorality involving the writers Gustave Flaubert and Charles Baudelaire forty years previously. In the event Flaubert was acquitted and Baudelaire fined 300 francs with some of his poems suppressed. Just as Wilde had to answer charges of immorality in relation to *The Picture of Dorian Gray* (1891), so thirty years later James Joyce had to endure the public hostility in relation to the alleged indecency of *Ulysses*. In a rare interview given to the German critic Alfred Kerr in 1939, Joyce said:

> The most natural thing for a writer to do is to call a spade a spade. The mistake which some moralists make, even today, is that they hate unpleasant phenomena less than they do those who record them. It's always the same. People go on judging an author immoral who refuses to be silent about what in any case exists. Immoral! Why, it's a mark of morality not only to say what one thinks is true, but to create a work of art with the utmost sacrifice; that's moral, too.[19]

Even today many (static) people are still shocked to see that (exostatic) celebrities like to be notorious as well as famous. Also, when artists sometimes express ethical views (a static disposition), as in publicly endorsing some political, humanitarian, or environmental project, it is probably safe to assume that their stance is an attention-seeking performance rather than an expression of a genuine commitment to a cause. Or, as Wilde would say: "An ethical sympathy in an artist is an unpardonable mannerism of style."[20]

The ineradicable misunderstanding between artists and their audience is thus a fact of life, a result of psychological diversity, ultimately based on physical laws, as reflected in a statistical distribution of dynamism of character in society (Figure 6.2). But diversity of character is Nature's blessing and a guarantee of life's richness and beauty. Artists will always belong to a misunderstood and, as in the case of Oscar Wilde, occasionally beleaguered minority. But it is also clear that both the visionary artistic individualists and the conservative public need one another: audiences need artists to provide them with entertainment, emotional release, and imaginative stimulation, while artists need their audiences to baffle, charm, beguile, and occasionally shock them. Even a proud individualist like Wilde would probably have been unhappy without the philistine public he so despised, because he needed it to define his individualism against. A society consisting entirely of individualists is a contradiction in terms: when everybody is somebody, nobody is anybody. For their part, all that the wider (static) public can humanely do with the minority of (exodynamic) artists and other harmless eccentrics and non-conformists is to accept their existence even without understanding them.

Dynamism of Character and Literary Fiction

Dynamism of character applies first of all to complex autonomous systems such as real people, but the concept can also be used to gauge the psychological consistency of fictitious personalities in literature and drama. Among the most important pleasures and educational benefits of fiction is the engagement with the psychological experience of virtual persons: the literary simulations of human-like characters and their relationships as stand-ins for real people in socially defined contexts.[21] Marian Mazur's systemic formulations regarding the dynamism of character can therefore be used to identify the imagined motivations of behavior in fictitious characters, especially those constructed with a degree of psychological realism, as in classic novels and plays.[22] For fictional characters to be dramatically effective and appealing, they must be psychologically convincing and sufficiently life-like. It is equally true, however, that novels and theatrical plays are not straight records of life, and they do not always have to follow strict psychological laws. Psychologically unrealistic, fantastic, or experimental works of fiction can still be good as fiction, but then it can also be argued that the best literary works are both esthetically satisfying and psychologically convincing. The systemic model of the dynamism of character can be a starting point in assessing the degree of psychological realism in literary personae, with its basic classification of characters into exodynamic (spontaneous, playful, childlike), exostatic (showy, histrionic, idealistic), static (dutiful, responsible, law-abiding), endostatic (pragmatic, opportunistic), and endodynamic (domineering, unscrupulous, power seeking).

Unlike the changing historical and cultural realities reflected in works of fiction, dynamism of character is based on universal physical and biological laws and as such reveals fundamental commonalities across historical time. One of the constants of human behavior is homeostatic self-regulation in interactions with other people and with the environment, and the related motivations and biases as defined by dynamism of character. Without the presence of unchanging psychological laws we would not be able to relate to characters and situations described in texts from culturally remote contexts, and we would not be able to understand and enjoy the adventures, predicaments, and emotions of characters from fairy tales, ancient myths, medieval romances, Shakespeare's plays, or early modern novels. If human experience was driven solely by the relative values of culture, without the constraints imposed on culture by human innate cognitive endowments, there is no reason why that experience should not be incomparably different in different cultural contexts. However, the fact that we can still relate to Odysseus's shrewdness and Penelope's faithfulness (endostatic and static traits, respectively), despite the millennia that separate us from Homer, is in itself an indirect proof of the existence of stable elements in human personality and behavior. Similarly, we are still both amused and worried about the capriciousness, emotional volatility, charm, and irresponsibility of Shakespeare's exodynamic Cleopatra opposite the static Antony; we have both sympathy and concern for the histrionic wit and impracticality of the exostatic Hamlet and Falstaff; we feel the inner dilemmas and existential crises of static protagonists such as Othello and Lear; and we watch with horror the utter depravity, ruthlessness, and destructive resourcefulness of the endodynamic villains such as Richard Gloucester, Iago, and Lady Macbeth.

A play with a sufficient number of characters can achieve psychological unity in a diversity of dynamic types. In *Hamlet*, for example, the main dramatic tension arises from the conflict between psychologically opposed characters of the idealistic, showy, exostatic Hamlet and the ruthless, scheming, power-thirsty endodynamic Claudius, with most of the remaining characters falling within the static range (Figure 6.3). To highlight Hamlet's exostatism—an unusual and therefore intriguing personality type for an avenger—Shakespeare placed his protagonist in the context of two other sons presented with the task of avenging their fathers' deaths, Fortinbras and Laertes: an opportunistic endostatic and an honor-bound static character, respectively. All three avengers carry out their similar tasks differently and achieve different results, not only due to their differing dramatic circumstances but also because of their different dynamisms of character and motivation. The endostatic Fortinbras is less concerned with the personal issue of avenging his father but more with its political implications: to regain for Norway the lands lost by his father to Denmark. The static Laertes in turn

Figure 6.3 Exostatic Hamlet (Kenneth Branagh) flanked by endodynamic king (Derek Jacobi) and static queen (Julie Christi) in the film version of the play, dir. by Kenneth Branagh © Castle Rock Entertainment (1996).

is concerned only with justice and family honor, which demand that he avenge his father's death no matter what, regardless of consequences. Finally the exostatic Hamlet, despite incessantly monologuing about revenge, appears to be less concerned with effective vengeful action or with gaining political power, but more with the emotional and theatrical effects of his behavior. Like another exostatic Oscar Wilde, the Danish prince compulsively turns all interactions with other characters into opportunities to baffle, emote, and play act, foregoing tactical advantages for the sake of pure histrionic effects, with disastrous consequences.[23]

7

The Esthetics of Light in Early Cinema

As discussed in Chapters 2 and 4, sight is the most efficacious sense and channel of communication in humans. Its only obvious disadvantage compared with hearing, our second most important sense, is that vision is by definition useless in the dark—an inconvenience reduced by human adaptation to sleep, and therefore to be inactive, at night. The two most powerful senses usually work together as a combined audio-visual channel in human communication, including the technological media, with hearing dominating in social interactions and vision remaining the most efficient sense for spatial orientation and exploration of the physical environment.

Drawing with Light

During daylight hours sight is always ON, while audition in social communication can be intentionally switched ON and OFF between speech and silence. Sight is also more suitable than hearing for creating permanent material records and artifacts to support individual and cultural memory. For tens of thousands of years, before the era of recorded sound launched a little over a century ago, visual artifacts were the only means of recording the ever-growing cultural knowledge about the social and natural environments. The communicative power of sculpture, painting, drawing, and writing was boosted in the early nineteenth century by the invention of the iconic-indexical medium of photography, able to record human immediate physical environment with unprecedented realism and accuracy. Famous not only for its appealing "indexical magic," photography (literally, "drawing with light") is the only visual medium to use light rather than sculpting material or pigments to produce its images. In other words, photographs result from impersonal physical forces rather than the artist's vision and skill, with human intervention limited to manufacturing the camera, pointing it at a chosen object, and allowing the light to "draw" the image on a photosensitive surface inside the camera. As discussed in Chapter 4, the resulting "drawing" is indexical insofar as it is physically caused by light, and iconic by virtue of its similarity to the photographed object. As always, iconicity is a matter of degree rather than identity: an image is not the object, just as a map is not the territory. Praised for their high verisimilitude, early photographs were nonetheless much smaller than the represented objects, they reduced natural colors to a monochrome tonality, and they were flat compared with the three-dimensionality of the photographed scene.

The first permanent iconic index achieved by the photographic process was obtained by the Frenchman Joseph Nicéphore Niépce, who in 1826 captured a view from his window of a courtyard in Chalon-sur-Saône (Figure 7.1).[1] The earliest photographs typically showed large and unmoving objects such as buildings, because of the time it took to expose the image: eight hours in the case of Niépce's picture. While this historic photograph was being taken, the sun had made much of its daily journey across the sky, leaving traces of changing patterns of light and shadows on the walls and roofs of the photographed buildings. In this way, due to its long exposure the first-ever photograph succeeded inadvertently in capturing indexical traces of the movement of the sun as well as the immobile buildings, nearly seventy years before the invention of the movie camera. Niépce's experimental photographs were subsequently improved by his business partner Louise-Jacques-Mandé Daguerre, who in 1829 produced commercially photographic images on silver-plated copper plates, which he called, after himself, daguerreotypes. The exposure time was gradually reduced to fifteen minutes in the late 1830s, and then to about thirty seconds in the early 1840s, allowing for photographs of people, if they agreed to remain still for a few moments. Indeed, as soon as the technical problem of the long exposure was solved, the human face and figure rather than buildings and city squares became the most popular—still are—objects to be photographed. This thematic preference is clearly due to the earlier-discussed innate face-recognition and body-language cognitive modules, so important

Figure 7.1 The first ever photograph: a view from Joseph Nicéphore Niépce's window in Chalon-sur-Saône (1826). Courtesy of British Library/Open Culture.

in negotiating our social life. In photography, human perennial fascination with faces received a truly miraculous aid, because for the first time in history it became possible to record people's appearance with accuracy and authenticity unmatched by the iconic media of painting, drawing, and sculpting.[2]

Animated Photography

Both still photography and film remain closely related as iconic-indexical media—the only difference being the added illusion of movement in the latter, which technically consists of the effect of intermittent flashing of still photographs supported by the phenomenon of the persistence of vision, in which the perception of an object continues for a split second after the rays of light proceeding from it have ceased to enter the eye.[3] In the late 1880s and early 1890s several inventors worked on the mechanics of animated photography: W. K. L. Dickson in the Thomas Edison Company; Louis Le Prince and the Lumière brothers in France; the Skladanowski brothers in Berlin; and Robert W. Paul and Birt Acres in Britain. The possibility of the film camera rested on the confluence of several inventions: high-sensitivity emulsion to allow multiple exposures per second (silent films were generally recorded at 14–16 frames per second); the invention of a transparent, flexible film base (developed by George Eastman in 1889); and the adaptation of the Maltese cross drive mechanism, previously used in machine guns and sewing machines, to advance the film and hold it still for a fraction of a second.[4] As in still photography invented earlier in the century, the immediate popularity of moving pictures was mainly due to their perceptual and cognitive appeal: for evolutionary reasons motion (quite apart from what is actually moving) automatically catches our agitated attention. As discussed in Chapter 1 in the context of human exploratory need, throughout our prehistory moving objects tended to be either animals or other humans, and it paid in survival terms to keep a watchful eye on what these moving objects were doing: did they behave like friends or enemies, did they look like potential sources of food or like potential predators? Our vision is instinctively alerted by movement, as evidenced by the greater effectiveness of flashing neon signs over still lights, by TV commercials over printed ads or billboards, and by the higher visual appeal of performances in motion such as theater, dance, and cinema over painting, photography, sculpture, or architecture.[5]

Light: From an Optical Phenomenon to a Semiotic Sign

Visual media are synonymous with light—the visible frequencies of electromagnetic waves which determine color perception, and the differences in illumination on the grayscale between whiteness and blackness which define tonality and contrast. Following the semiotic terminology introduced in Chapters 2 and 3, electromagnetic waves represent physical states; the portion of the electromagnetic spectrum available to human vision becomes information; a contiguous reaction to that information, as in saying "Look, it's dawning already," constitutes parainformation; while an assessment of the scientific or esthetic qualities of light belongs to the realm of metainformation. In Oscar Wilde's novel *The Picture of Dorian Gray*, a Victorian esthete Lord Henry Wotton, sitting in an artist's studio, looks at the window and observes meta-cognitively how

> now and then the fantastic shadows of birds in flight flitted across the long tussore-silk curtains that were stretched in front of the huge window, producing a kind of momentary Japanese effect, and making him think of those pallid jade-faced painters who, in an art that is necessarily immobile, seek to convey the sense of swiftness and motion.[6]

In artistic photography too the choice of light, natural or artificial, white or color-filtered, diffuse or directional, soft or bright can determine the tone, composition, and meaning of the resulting image, by guiding the viewer's attention to certain objects, their textures, colors, and brightness, and in the process determining their esthetic and dramatic impact. When light is not just a physical prerequisite of visual arts but becomes the object of attention and purposeful manipulation, it is subjectively transformed from a physical state to a semiotic sign. Similarly, colors become semiotic when the frequencies of electromagnetic wavelengths, which determine color perception, are endowed with iconic or symbolic meaning, or become objects of esthetic experimentation, as in Impressionist painting.

Nor was light always consciously incorporated as an independent element of composition in visual arts. The art historian Rudolf Arnheim demonstrates that in the early history of visual arts light as such is hardly represented. As in the pictures of young children, for most of art history light was used only for modeling, when brightness values marked differences within the object itself, as in giving a person dark hair to set it off against a light face. Similarly, on ancient Greek vases figures are visible by their contrast with the bright background rather than by scene illumination.[7] Also, largely absent in pre-modern art is the painted shadow—an explicit index of light and its source. Only occasionally do cast shadows appear in naturalistic wall paintings of the Hellenistic period (fourth to first century BCE), where the *chiaroscuro*, the play of light and shadow, was handled with a virtuosity not rediscovered until the Italian Baroque sixteen centuries later.[8] But even during the Renaissance, with its insistence on visual realism in the representation of geometric perspective and the anatomy of the human body, light itself rarely attracts the painters' attention, except in the use of shading to create volume and relief in solid objects (Figure 7.2).[9]

It was not until the *chiaroscuro* revolution launched by Caravaggio (1571–1610) in the Baroque period that light became an integral part of composition in painting. The best way to draw attention to light, and thereby to transform it into a semiotic sign, is to contrast it with its absence, namely shadows. With darkness as the foil, brightly illuminated patches on a canvas, photograph, or cinema screen assume meaning by highlighting key elements of the composition or dramatic action, just as a dark spot or a shadow becomes an intentional sign by concealing details that implicitly participate in the overall meaning of a scene. In Caravaggio's religious paintings scenes are usually illuminated by a single shaft of light from up left, or by a single lamp concealed within the

Figure 7.2 Light used for shading to create volume: *A Goldsmith in His Shop*, oil painting by Petrus Christus (1449). Courtesy of the Metropolitan Museum of Art, New York.

picture. The result are strong, deep shadows that offset bright, irregular patches of light which tear up the unity of bodies and objects, by dramatically tracing the borderlines of darkness across the surfaces. In this way *chiaroscuro*'s strong light and deep shadows unsettle the viewer, who finds familiar shapes disfigured by violent contrasts. Many artists of the seventeenth century were rapidly converted to Caravaggio's *tenebroso* (dark) style (Figure 7.3), which conquered not only parts of Italy but also whole regions of northern Europe, culminating in the art of Rembrandt.[10] Similar effects of light and shadows were reproduced centuries later in the low-key atmospheric lighting used in German Expressionist films of the 1920s, and in Hollywood *film noir* of the 1940s and '50s.

Figure 7.3 Caravaggesque *chiaroscuro*: *The Penitent Magdalen*, oil painting by Georges de La Tour (*c.* 1640). Courtesy of the Metropolitan Museum of Art, New York.

Natural Light in Early Cinema

Light and shadows as elements of visual composition tend to be enhanced in monochrome pictures, as in Renaissance *grisaille* paintings, modern etchings, woodcuts, drawings, and early photographs and films, with their heightened tonal contrasts to compensate for the absence of natural colors. Apart from occasional experiments with hand-painted films, such as Georges Méliès' trick films of fantasy and magic, or the more common monochrome dyeing and tinting of strips of film, early films were simply black and white and for the most part remained so throughout the first half of the twentieth century. Interestingly, however, absence of natural colors was little noticed until the color film eventually drew attention to the fact.[11] In other words, in the early decades of cinema the technical limitation of monochrome film was simply accepted as an integral part of the medium, and not as an esthetically meaningful choice. If, on the other hand, black-and-white cinematography is used at a time when color is standard on the screen, it acquires semiotic value, as in Steven Spielberg's *Schindler's List* (1993) shot in the visual style of European films made shortly after the Second World War. In the early days, however, cinema audiences hardly noticed the reduction of all colors to monochrome tonality, which in fact considerably modified the perception of the actual world. But with color film still absent for comparison, the monochrome world on the screen was accepted as being somehow true to nature. Nor were the objective constraints of black-and-white cinematography without their esthetic advantages. Color can often divert attention from light itself, its source, direction, distribution, and effects, including the modeling of surfaces and formation of shadows, which are all enhanced in monochrome photography.[12]

The autonomous focus on light effects in cinema did not become apparent until the medium matured esthetically, in America in D. W. Griffith's first feature films from the mid-1910s, and in Germany in the Expressionist films of Richard Oswald from the late 1910s.[13] For more than two decades following the invention of moving pictures in mid-1890s any independent light effects, including cast shadows, appeared on the screen purely by accident, simply because all filming used daylight for illumination, whether on open-air locations or in primitive studios with roofs open to the sky. The first purpose-built small studios were Thomas Edison's "Black Marias" from around 1893, named after the police paddy wagons that they resembled. The skewed part of the roof opened to admit sunlight for filming, while the whole structure moved on tracks to catch the best light. The short films shot in Edison's Black Marias were later displayed in so-called kinetoscopes, or peephole devices, situated in entertainment parlors in American cities.[14] The standard features of kinetoscope films included the black background, a patch of sunlight from the opening in the roof, with a natural shadow cast on the stage floor by a moving figure such as a dancer (Figure 7.4). Filming in studios open to sunlight, now fitted with glass roofs and walls, continued in America until the end of the 1910s when the first dark studios rigged entirely with electric lighting were built, making indoor filming independent from free but unpredictable natural light.[15]

In Europe the Lumière brothers' early films were shot on various outdoor locations exposed to available daylight, whether on clear or overcast days. The main thrill of the new medium was to see familiar objects, mainly human figures, photographed in realistic motion, and any occasional light effect such as shading or cast shadows were purely accidental. The main if inadvertent benefit of filming on sunny days was a clearer and more contrasty image, which enhanced surface sculpting and texture of objects, while cast shadows emphasized a sense of depth. The surviving Lumière films also show that when filming on sunny days the camera was placed with the sun behind, both to avail of the optimal "high-key" illumination and to avoid possible dazzling effects of back light. For example, in 1895 film *Sortie d'usine* the employees of the Lumière factory in Lyon walk through the wide factory gate in direct sunlight coming from behind the camera, as evidenced by the direction of shadows cast by the moving figures (Figure 7.5).

Figure 7.4 A natural shadow on the floor cast by sunlight coming through an open roof in Edison's "Black Maria" studio © Edison Manufacturing Co. (1894).

Figure 7.5 Filming in sunlight: *Sortie d'usine* by Lumière brothers (1895).

Figure 7.6 Filming on an overcast day: *Bataille de boules de neige* by Lumière brothers (1896).

The first-ever movie slapstick, *Le jardinière et le petit espiégle* (The Sprinkler Sprinkled), also from 1895, was likewise shot on a clear day with the sun to the right behind the camera, allowing both the gardener and his hose to cast visible shadows on the ground. Diffused natural light, on the other hand, could create occasional painterly effects in early films, as in the slapstick *Bataille de boules de neige* (Snowball Fight), shot by the Lumière brothers in 1896 on an overcast day (Figure 7.6). Here the soft contrast between the white-gray snow, the dark clothes of the fighters, the bare tree trunks, and the gray buildings in the background has an overall impressionist air to it, not unlike that found in Claude Monet's wintry scene in *The Magpie* (1869), or in Alfred Sisley's painting *Snow at Louveciennes* (1874).

Electricity: Imitating Daylight

Light defines cinema in a double sense: in production and exhibition. First of all, cinematic images are created by light, natural or artificial, reflected from objects and focused by the lens onto photosensitive support, chemical or electronic, inside the camera. Later the translucent images on the celluloid strip (today coded on a digital video file) are projected by electric light onto the screen. Given the medium's dependence on electricity for exhibition, it seems paradoxical that it took the emerging film industry several years to adopt electric lighting for shooting. But for a medium as commercialized as cinema, esthetic choices often depend on practical and economic considerations: lamps in the early twentieth century were cumbersome to use and electricity was initially prohibitively expensive.[16]

Interestingly, when studio photographers and early filmmakers invested in electric lamps, it was not so much to experiment with new esthetic possibilities and light effects as to replicate the soft, diffuse, shadowless look of natural light as found on an overcast day. The Cooper-Hewitt mercury lamps, invented in 1901, which produced high-key, dispersed light, were especially popular, while the older carbon arc lights, already used in the theater, which gave off hard, directional light and produced shadows, were generally avoided.[17] In using artificial light professional photographers and filmmakers seemed to draw their inspiration from nature rather than art: electric lamps, in combination with reflectors, screens, and awnings, were primarily used to imitate the dispersed and soft look of daylight.

Uniform lighting was indeed universal in the early days of cinema, where it was used mainly to illuminate the story rather than draw attention to itself. In the first decades of Japanese cinema, for example, the working rule was captured in the slogan *ichi nuke, ni suji* (clarity first, story second), where clarity (*nuke*) meant high-key lighting to reveal all details within the frame: human figures, faces, props, and settings. *Nuke* did not necessarily involve subtle tones, expressive contrasts, and the sculpting of surfaces, but rather the practical concern with overall brightness that would offer enough visibility even for worn-out prints projected with dim light bulbs. This meant illuminating the set with flat frontal lighting (as in today's flash photography), which would make everything clearly visible both to the audience and to the live narrator, who explained the film's plot and dialogue to the spectators. Motivated commercially rather than artistically, Japanese studio executives discouraged any experimentation with illumination, such as using back- or side-lighting to help model the figures and props. As late as mid-1920s, sets in Japanese films would still be lit flatly by a row of arc lights placed behind the camera, at a time when a more plastic combination of three-point lighting was already standard in Hollywood and Europe.[18]

The practice of using electric lamps iconically, to imitate dispersed natural light, was also standard in the first European and American studios. In Britain, Cecil Hepworth, who began making films in 1898, shot interior scenes on a temporary open-air stage, before building in 1903 a fully enclosed studio with muranese glass to diffuse daylight, with arc floodlights such as those used in the theater for subsidiary lighting. In a 1905 melodrama directed by Lewin Fitzhamon from Hepworth Company, about a middle-class baby kidnapped by gypsies and, as the film's title explains, *Rescued by Rover*, the family dog, arc lamps are used in the gypsy's attic to simulate natural light coming in through the window (Figure 7.7). Stagy as it looked, imitating daylight by electric lamps was more convincing than the more common practice of painting light effects on the set—an iconic device to "touch up" the filmed object to make it look, paradoxically, more realistic. For example, in *The 100-to-One Shot; or, A Run of Luck* (1906), made in America by the Vitagraph Company, in one interior scene the sunlight coming in through the window is painted on the wall, creating an awkwardly

Figure 7.7 Electric lamps simulate daylight: *Rescued by Rover*, short film by Lewin Fitzhamon © Hepworth Company (1905).

incongruous effect with hard shadows cast on the floor by the actual sunlight used to illuminate the scene.[19] Unavoidable shadows on the floor in interior scenes, an index of primitive open-roof studios unequipped with screens to disperse light, were common in early drama films. A typical example is *Histoire d'un crime* (Story of Crime) directed by Ferdinand Zecca for the Pathé Frères company in 1901, in which human figures in the courtroom, in a prison cell, and in the morgue cast inconsistent shadows produced by exterior daylight (Figure 7.8). Only later, in studios fully rigged with electric lights, did it become possible to eliminate undesirable cast shadows and other incongruous light effects in interior scenes.

In America during the nickelodeon era, between 1905 and 1915, successful companies could afford to build larger studios to replace the earlier open-air stages. The new studios were fitted with glass walls to admit sunlight, in addition to using electric lamps to provide uniform, high-key illumination on larger and deeper sets.[20] It also became possible to start experimenting with light. A scene from *Shamus O'Brien*, a film directed by Otis Turner in 1912 for Independent Moving Pictures, includes an arc lamp hidden in a fireplace to provide a cozy low-key light that casts the room in atmospheric semi-darkness.[21] Controlled studio lighting would become an important development in American film style of the late 1910s, when the first large dark studios were constructed, relying solely on artificial illumination.

Figure 7.8 Inconsistent shadows: *Histoire d'un crime,* short film by Ferdinand Zecca © Pathé Frères company (1901).

Intentional Cast Shadows on Cinema Screen

Semiotically speaking, natural cast shadows are physical states in the form of dark patches opposite the light source—contiguous indexes both of light and of opaque objects that obstruct directional light on a sunny day. Photographed shadows, on the other hand, are displaced indexical signs (Figure 2.3). Shadows can also be iconic, because they resemble the outline of the objects that cast them, as in dark silhouette portraits popular in the eighteenth century, which indicated a person's identity by capturing her unique profile. When a shadow is selected as an object of a photograph or painting, it becomes a fully semiotic, metainformational sign, as in Masaccio's fresco in the Brancacci Chapel in Florence (1425) about the healing power of St. Peter's shadow. In photography and film, cast shadows are either intentional and semiotic in the above sense, or else they are simply an accident of light which just happened to be recorded in a photograph. Sometimes, however, an unintentionally captured shadow can acquire semiotic significance. One of the most poignant visual indexes in history is a human shadow etched in stone—a dark patch on the bright steps of the Sumitomo Bank in Hiroshima, about 260 meters from the spot over which the atomic bomb went off on August 6, 1945 (Figure 7.9). The shadow is what has remained of a person who sat on the steps in the morning that fateful day waiting for the bank to open. The victim was exposed to the flash from the atomic explosion at 8:15 a.m. and must

Figure 7.9 Human shadow etched in stone by an atomic bomb in Hiroshima, August 6, 1945. Courtesy of British Library/Open Culture.

have vaporized on the spot. The surface of the surrounding stone steps was turned whitish by the intense heat rays, while the dark patch corresponds with the outline of the victim's body, which reduced the heat's exposure in that spot, making it darker.

In the early days of cinema, when low-sensitivity stock allowed for filming only in full daylight over which the filmmaker had no control, the camera often caught natural shadows as part of a scene. These accidental shadows probably mattered neither to the cameraman nor to the cinema audience, the whole attention being excitedly focused on animated images of people, trains, cars, or leaves moving in the trees. As discussed earlier in the context of indexical magic, photographed or filmed objects can invite the same emotional and behavioral responses as the objects in the real world. Similar to iconic media such as painting and the theater, cinema offers vicarious experience whose enjoyment is probably impossible without a partial suspension of disbelief, when one part of our mind knows that what we see on the screen are just immaterial light effects, while another part reacts to these indexical representations as if they were real, contiguous solid objects. An isolated human-like shadow in a crime or horror movie creates suspense because it indicates a near-presence of a concealed person with as yet unknown and therefore potentially threatening intentions. In Fritz Lang's 1931 psycho-thriller *M,* about a serial child murderer, a little girl innocently bounces a ball against a police poster bearing an inscription "Wer ist der Mörder?" (Who is the murderer?). Suddenly a shadow of a man wearing a hat moves ominously across the poster, the outline of his head projected accusingly on the word "Mörder" (Figure 7.10). The man's voice forms an additional auditory index of a suspected child murderer, his identity suspensefully still unknown.[22]

Figure 7.10 A threatening contiguous shadow of a child murderer in Fritz Lang's film *M* © Nero-Film AG (1931).

The indexically contiguous character of a cast human shadow makes it a potent motif in folklore and visual arts, especially in the photographic media, whose own inherent indexicality enhances the shadow effect. By their nature shadows, like other contiguous indexes such as mirror reflections, physically depend on their referents; that is, they cannot exist without the solid objects that produce them. But in physics defying folk beliefs ghostly creatures often appear without shadows, or else they exist only as shadows, without their bodily equivalents. It is precisely the counterfactual severing of an index from its physical source that makes the idea of a ghost "supernatural," as in Friedrich W. Murnau's 1922 classic horror film *Nosferatu* (Figure 7.11). In the physical world, however, the shadow testifies unmistakably to the solidity of an object, because what casts a shadow (or is reflected in the mirror) must be real. The indexical connection between a material object and its shadow also explains folk beliefs in the shared properties between the two, as in the legend of the healing power of the shadow cast by Saint Peter, illustrated by Masaccio's fresco in the Brancacci Chapel in Florence. At the same time the contrast between a solid object and its ethereal dark reflection is too captivating not to stimulate the imagination. A person's shadow will accordingly be considered metaphorically as a second, filmy self, an immaterial soul or spiritual double, a "dark" alter ego, a *Doppelgänger*. In Carl Gustav Jung's depth psychology,

Figure 7.11 A disembodied shadow of a vampire in Friedrich W. Murnau's film *Nosferatu* © Jofa-Atelier Berlin-Johannisthal (1922).

for example, the archetype of the shadow denotes the dark aspect of the personality formed by fears and other unpleasant emotions rejected by the conscious self.[23] Beliefs in the shadow as a person's inner self and indexical extension are indeed common: in some cultures to step on one's shadow is considered a serious offense, and a man can be "murdered" by having his shadow pierced with a knife. At a funeral, care must be taken to avoid having a living person's shadow caught by the lid of the coffin and thus buried with the corpse.[24]

Arthur Robison's *Warning Shadows* (1923)

A silent film with the largest amount of meaningful cast shadows is arguably Arthur Robison's melodramatic, sexually charged psycho-thriller *Schatten: Eine Nächtliche Halluzination* (Warning Shadows: A Nocturnal Hallucination), made in Germany in 1923 and set in the early nineteenth century. The idea and art design for the film came from Albin Grau (1884–1971), an occultist, a student of Eastern philosophy, and the author of pamphlets on the symbolic use of lighting in black-and-white films.[25] Whether for occult or esthetic reasons, Grau seems to have been virtually obsessed with shadows, as the film's title alone confirms. The story too is based entirely on cast shadows and their meta-significances, largely inspired by psychoanalysis, popular at the time.

The preoccupation with shadows already informs the film's Prologue, with its implicit reminder that cinematic images are always just shadows. The characters in *Warning Shadows*—the count, his wife, the youth, the three gentlemen, and the servants, all accompanied by their shadows—are introduced on an improvised theatrical stage. As each character enters, a gigantic shadow of an invisible hand moves across the white screen at the back of the stage and wipes out the flesh-and-blood figures (which in film are technically also shadows), leaving only their immaterial dark silhouettes behind (Figure 7.12). The shadows from the Prologue also iconically reveal the characters' respective passions. The count's shadow stands alone eaten by jealousy; his sensual wife makes inviting gestures toward her admirers; the youth draws his sword ready to fight for the woman he secretly loves; the three gentlemen make sleazy, lustful gestures about the count's wife; and the servants stand with their arms reaching forward, ready to grope the shadow of a coquettish maid. Last of all in the Prologue appears the shadow, accompanied by the real person, of a traveling puppeteer who puts on a shadow play in the count's house, ostensibly for entertainment but also with a therapeutic aim of curing the spectators of their uncontrollable sexual desires and murderous jealousy. In the Prologue the puppeteer is holding a candle—the source of light with which he "illuminates" his spectators' minds by extracting their hidden psychological "shadows," like a psychoanalyst uncovering the repressed contents of his patients' minds. The puppeteer's task is to use the shadow theater to allow the spectators to identify temporarily with their hidden selves personified in their shadows, and to give their repressed and destructive passions full rein, only to be cured of them in the end.

Figure 7.12 Characters as shadows in the Prologue of Arthur Robison's film *Warning Shadows* © Pan-Film (1923).

The shrewd puppeteer first steals into the count's house by amusing the servants with his improvised hand shadows, in which he ridicules the boorish footman by providing him with a succession of animal heads. He also wins the good will of the count by gently mocking his sullenness in a hand shadow impression of the count's head. The entertainer even mocks himself in a shadow that represents him as a fawning dog. In this way the traveling shadow-player establishes himself as a court jester licensed to expose and ridicule the weaknesses and follies of his superiors. The centerpiece of the film is the séance of the puppet shadow theater, before which the entertainer detaches the shadows of his hypnotized audience and cinematically projects them onto an improvised screen, to indicate that what his shadow theater is really about are the inner problems of the spectators.

Even before the séance, accidental shadows cast by the characters gathered at the mansion perform a double dramatic role: they betray to others their owners' hidden desires and cause embarrassing misunderstandings. For example, as the vain wife preens herself in front of the mirror, her shadow projected onto the curtained glass door attracts the attention and different reactions from the suitors and the husband. One by one the lustful suitors stroke, grope, and kiss the wife's shadow as a substitute for the real thing, while the count, standing on the other side of the glass door, is tormented with jealousy at what he interprets to be his wife's willing submission to the caresses of other men (Figure 7.13). During the dinner the exasperated count bursts upon what he takes to be two hands joining, his wife's and the guest's, when in fact they only touch as a result of the prolongation of their shadows. For a jealous husband even

Figure 7.13 A misinterpreted shadow in Arthur Robison's film *Warning Shadows* © Pan-Film (1923).

the flimsiest of evidence, or none at all, provokes an angry but in the context deeply embarrassing and self-demeaning reaction. As the evening progresses, the emotional tensions thicken. The suitors' shadows grow bigger as their lustful natures "come out" and their self-control diminishes under the wife's flirtatious behavior.

Next comes dancing, that "vertical expression of the horizontal desire legalized by music" in Bernard Shaw's phrase, which only makes matters worse by further enraging the count. With self-debasing masochism he frantically conducts the trio of musicians while his wife, Salome-like, swirls her body in front of the drooling and lip-licking male guests. The shrewd puppeteer increases the salacious effect by using a candelabrum to back light the dancer and reveal her sexy figure inside a gauzy dress. Having perceptively assessed the charged situation, the entertainer will organize a shadow theater to allow the spectators' sexual passions to play themselves out safely on the screen, rather than in real life with potentially disastrous consequences.

The shadow play begins innocently enough in the form of conventional *ombres chinoises* (Chinese shadows), popular in Europe in the eighteenth century (Figure 7.14). The silhouettes on the screen parallel the main plot with a story of female marital infidelity and the husband's jealousy, rage, and revenge. As the guests' minds tune in to the shadow play, the entertainer, as if by magic, directs their natural shadows toward the screen, then moves all the six spectators, now hypnotized, onto the other side of the table near the screen, allowing them to reconnect with their shadows. In this way both the spectators' bodies and their shadows become part of the entertainer's shadow play; or rather, the spectators become their own shadows, their dark inner

Figure 7.14 A shadow theater in Arthur Robison's film *Warning Shadows* © Pan-Film (1923).

selves. This is the beginning of the "nocturnal hallucination" from the film's subtitle, introduced as a film-within-a-film, in which the hypnotized characters experience the inner "shadow play" of their unrestrained passions with tragic, but thankfully only virtual, consequences. The transition from reality to hallucination is also marked by a change of tint: from day-time yellow to night-time purple (the usual tint for night-time scenes in silent cinema was blue, but here the red ingredient in color purple aptly captures the bloody course of hallucinatory events).

In the purple-tinted hallucination the hell of released sexual lust, adultery, jealousy, and murderous passion finally breaks loose. The suitors now grope and kiss the even more inviting wife openly and without any restraint. The wife seductively lowers one strap of her dress to make it more revealing and alluring, and invites the youngest of the admirers to her bedroom, while the remaining suitors gloat and openly mock the count's sexual humiliation. For his part the count, Othello like, gradually reaches the nadir of self-torment, jealousy, and madness, having confirmed his role of a cuckold and masochistic voyeur, as he contemplates the lovers' embraces reflected in the mirror. Too cowardly even to confront his wife or the rival directly, the count orders the servants to capture and tie the unfaithful woman with a rope. Mad with jealousy and a thirst for revenge, the count then compels the four suitors to stab the fettered wife with provided swords. This hallucinatory over-the-top melodrama culminates with the furious suitors throwing the count out of the window.

As the sordid tragedy of the film-within-a-film ends, the tint returns to day-time yellow, while the characters' shadows move from the screen back to their owners, who slowly awake from their collective nightmare to realize, not without embarrassment, their own folly. The puppeteer's experiment with the shadows in Robison's film has been compared by the critic Siegfried Kracauer to a psychoanalytic therapy, as a result of which the count changes from a puerile berserk into a composed adult, his coquettish wife becomes his loving and devoted partner, while the lover is put to shame and allowed to save his face by taking silent leave.[26] The dawn of a new day brings sobering natural light which banishes the night-time shadows and restores the light of reason. The count and his wife, now happily reconciled, open a window of their hitherto claustrophobic and shadow-haunted house to the bright, shadowless world outside, where the local folk cheerfully hustle and bustle on a market day.

8

Photography and the Limitations of Indexicality in Michelangelo Antonioni's *Blowup* (1966)

Set in London during the Swinging Sixties, Antonioni's existential film drama explores the modern dependence on photographic media to make sense of the world, while at the same time challenging photography's claim to veracity of representation. The film's misogynistic and obnoxious protagonist Thomas, played by David Hemmings, is a successful fashion photographer who also relies on his camera in social interactions, apparently unable to relate to other people except indirectly through the lens of the camera, his second "eye." Despite his professional success, however, Thomas' emotional life appears empty; his relationships, especially with women, are exploitative, shallow, and inconsequential. His briefly held belief that thanks to his camera he prevented a murder in a park—the only moment in the film when he seems concerned with someone other than himself—is, however, belied both by photography's technical limitations to represent the world accurately, and by the photographer's own doubts about his memory and senses. In the end, the alleged murder, its photographic record, a woman photographed in the park, the photographer's memory of the event, and even the photographer himself turn out to be an illusion: they all simply vanish, as if they had never existed.

Julio Cortázar's Short Story

Antonioni's screenplay, written with Tonino Guerra, is based on Julio Cortázar's 1959 short story "Las Babas del Diablo," literally "The Devil's Drooling," alluding metaphorically to the early morning fog that resembles gossamer filaments, also called "thread of the virgin."[1] The narrator-protagonist Roberto Michel, a French-Chilean translator with a passion for photography, recalls an event he has photographed in a Parisian park a month earlier. Observing from a distance an attitude of a mature woman toward a nervous teenage boy, Roberto concludes that an attempt at seduction on the woman's part is taking place. He decides to take a picture of the two, whereupon the boy runs away, "like a gossamer filament of angel-spit in the morning air,"[2] in which the "angel" replaces the "diablo" from the titular phrase. Soon Roberto discovers another actor of the drama he has just witnessed: a man resembling "a flour-powdered clown" watching from a parked car, apparently waiting for the woman to procure the boy for him. The woman's anger at the photographer's interference and the man's demand of the film roll confirm Roberto's suspicions and give him the satisfaction of having prevented sexual abuse, or possibly worse. Roberto later hangs the framed photograph of the scene in his study, and continues to contemplate it from above his typewriter.

Roberto's introspective narration reflects explicitly on the nature of photography as a medium of representation—what in Antonioni's film can only be inferred from Thomas' silent excitement as he snaps the pictures in a London park and later develops and prints them in his darkroom. An amateur photographer rather than a professional like Thomas, Roberto nonetheless regards photography as an important pastime which one should teach to children, "since it requires discipline, aesthetic education, a good eye and steady fingers." A devoted photographer, he argues, should have his camera with him all the time, because he has "a duty to be attentive, to not lose that abrupt and happy rebound of sun's rays off an old stone, or the pigtail's-flying run of a small girl going home with a loaf of bread or a bottle of milk." While in the park, Roberto's voyeuristic interest in the disquieting scene was similarly combined with an esthetic desire to capture an elusive moment in life:

> I raised the camera, pretended to study a focus which did not include them, and waited and watched closely, sure that I would finally catch the revealing expression, one that would sum it all up, life that is rhythmed by movement but which a stiff image destroys, taking time in cross section, if we do not choose the essential imperceptible fraction of it.[3]

Carried away by a speculation of what would happen to the boy once he was lured away by the woman (a tryst in "a basement apartment probably, which she would have filled with large cushions and cats"), Roberto carefully chooses his moment to take the picture:

> I decided not to lose a moment more, I got it all into the view-finder (with the tree, the railing, the eleven-o'clock sun) and took the shot. In time to realize that they both had noticed and stood there looking at me, the boy surprised and as though questioning, but she was irritated, her face and body flat-footedly hostile, feeling robbed, ignominiously recorded on a small chemical image.

As later in Antonioni's film, the woman reacts angrily at the violation of her privacy and demands the film roll. Following the logic of indexical and iconic magic, the universal objection to being photographed, even in the absence of any incriminating or embarrassing circumstances, springs from a strong if irrational sense of appropriation and control extended by the photographer over the photographed object. The anxiety of being photographed, especially against one's will, appears due to the combined effects of photographs as iconic indexes and of our instinctive recognition, underlying magical thinking, that both indexes and icons have a direct though hidden link with the objects they depict, in this case with the photographed humans. We may know that cameras do not "steal our souls" and take us into the photographer's possession, as tribesmen were reported to feel when first confronted with an explorer's camera, but the residual apprehension remains, making us feel awkward and uncomfortable, as if our privacy has been invaded, some trespass and disrespect have taken place, and some material part of ourselves has indeed been "stolen" by the photographer.[4]

In Cortázar's story the enlarged photograph "stolen" by Roberto keeps the memory of the event in the park vividly in his mind, and continues to stir his imagination:

> the first day he spent some time looking at it and remembering, that gloomy operation of comparing the memory with the gone reality; a frozen memory, like any photo, where nothing is missing, not even, and especially, nothingness, the true solidifier of the scene. There was the woman, there was the boy, the tree rigid above their heads, the sky as sharp as the stone of the parapet, clouds and stones melded into a single substance and inseparable.

Part of the reason for Roberto's continued fascination with the photograph is his moral satisfaction of giving the boy an opportunity to escape the trap. It was the pleasure of not only being a distant observer but also a decisive actor in the scene, if only for a moment, coupled with an advantage of not risking any consequences for his involvement. As an indexical medium photography is only connected with its object at origin and from a distance, afterward providing only a vicarious and safe retrospective experience of the original scene. The only real-life consequences suffered by Roberto for his photographic intrusion were angry words from the woman and the possibility of further, perhaps more serious, intervention from the man in the car. Roberto, however, ended the unfolding drama by quickly walking away, and now in the safety of his study he keeps reliving the scene prompted by the printed photograph, and speculating about what would have happened had the boy not been given an opportunity to escape the seduction:

> The rest of it would be so simple, the car, some house or another, drinks, stimulating engravings, tardy tears, the awakening in hell. And there was nothing I could do, this time I could do absolutely nothing. My strength had been a photograph, that, there, where they were taking their revenge on me, demonstrating clearly what was going to happen.

As in Antonioni's film, the "decisive moment" of real if limited influence on the contiguous event ended once the picture was taken, and the subsequent contemplation of the scene, now "fixed, rigid, incapable of intervention," reveals only the photographer's powerlessness and frustration. In the end, the longer Roberto contemplates the picture the less real the scene becomes, and the more illusory a sense of the original control of the situation. To compensate for the camera's limitation of capturing a single moment rather than recording the scene's full duration, in his imagination Roberto extends the momentary control of the event into a longer sequence, in which he is "filming" the scene and prolonging his interactions with the three people in the park beyond what actually happened. This fantasy, however, eventually evaporates, the memory of the encounter vanishes both from Roberto's mind and subjectively from the photograph on the wall, which now reveals only the clouds, the rain, until finally "little by little, the frame becomes clear, perhaps the sun comes out, and again the clouds begin to come, two at a time, three at a time. And the pigeons once in a while, and a sparrow or two."

Blowup and the Paradoxes of Indexicality

Antonioni's cinematic plot follows a similar trajectory of fascination with the camera; an irresistible urge to record voyeuristically an intimate event in a park; a post-factum imaginative reconstruction of the fuller context of the scene, unnoticed at the time, here involving a possible murder; creeping doubts about the veracity of the photographic record; and additionally, the final disappearance of both the record and any physical trace of the supposed crime. The photographic images, routinely used in forensic investigations as indexical evidence of past events, ultimately turn out to be just as elusive and unreliable as iconic images of art or verbal reports based on subjective memory. With the prints, the negative, and the dead body gone, and unable to verbally convince anyone of the supposed crime, Thomas finally loses trust not only in the veracity of photographic images but also in his own senses: not just the crime in the park but his whole life turns out to be an illusion.

Doubts about the truthfulness of representation are justified in iconic communication, as in painting, which reflects subjective imagination rather than objective reality. Antonioni, however, seems to extend the same skepticism both to the indexical images of photography and to sensory perception, which normally *are* referential by reflecting at least some of the physical properties of the outside world. Antonioni's preoccupation with illusion in this broader sense is highlighted in the opening scene by the arrival in central London of a group of mimes (the famous Rag Week troupe in real life) in a jeep. Clownishly costumed and with made-up faces, they shout and wave their hands to attract attention, otherwise playing no direct part in the story until the last scene. The photographer himself is introduced leaving a shelter for the homeless where he spent a night surreptitiously taking photos of the destitute men—in stark contrast to his own professional success and visible wealth (he drives a convertible Rolls-Royce with a built-in telephone radio transmitter—a luxury unavailable to most people at the time). As Thomas later explains to his agent Ron (played by Peter Bowles) over lunch in a yuppie restaurant in central London, he wants to bring out a photo book about the rough side of London. His attempt at honest photojournalism is belied, however, by his almost autistic self-alienation, lack of empathy and of social commitment. His sneaky photos from the doss house may reveal life at its most wretched and miserable but, as the critic Christopher Sharrett points out, Thomas' ambitions are too selfish and too involved in eye-catching spectacle and self-aggrandizement to suggest any sensitivity.[5] He deliberately drives his Rolls-Royce, honking, at a group of ethnic Africans crossing the street, and for a brief moment he feigns support for a protest march by allowing an anti-war placard to be placed on the back seat of his car. A moment later, however, the already forgotten placard, bearing an ironic slogan "Go away," is blown out onto the street, without Thomas even noticing.

As he tells Ron, London, with its urban decay, political ferment, and multi-culturalism simply "doesn't do anything" for him.

Thomas displays similar brusqueness to the staff in his spacious and impressive studio, where he treats the models during a photo shoot with undisguised contempt ("I'm fed up with those bloody bitches!"). The glitzy world of fashion staged in his studio contrasts sharply with the misery and indignity captured on his photographs from the doss house—the two extremes of modern London treated by Thomas with equal indifference and insensitivity. Incidentally, his two projects, fashion photography and photojournalism, also correspond with the two main kinds of photographic representation: the iconic indexicality of photography employed to document raw life, often referred to as vernacular photography, and the indexical iconic representations, which use an indexical medium to record staged fiction, often referred to as photographic pictorialism, here the glamorous and sexy artifice of women's fashion (Figure 8.1).[6]

Both for financial and personal reasons (implied sexual gratifications from the "birds"—the models and wannabe models), Thomas' opportunistic preference lies in the fictional, indexically iconic mode of photography. However, his immersion in the extravagant fiction of studio photography brings only disillusionment and disappointment. The "birds" and "bitches" he lives off are, in the words of the critic Peter Brunette, "grotesquely anorexic beings, horribly made up ... near-monsters," for whom "the screaming artificiality of their clothes, hairdos, and poses ... strip them of any residual humanity."[7] The flashy but disenchanting inauthenticity of Thomas' studio work is counterbalanced by his iconic-indexical documentary project designed to capture the ugly truth about the homeless in London—an urge to maintain some contact with the real world, which may explain his otherwise unplanned, playful snapping away with his camera in the park.

Figure 8.1 Thomas (David Hemmings) and the model Veruschka during a photo shoot: *Blowup*, dir. Michelangelo Antonioni © Premier Productions (1966).

The Maryon Park in Charlton, south-east London, where this haunting scene was shot, with the unnerving sound of the breeze rustling through the trees, is the center of the film's mystery, where things are not what they seem, and only the camera later reveals what has, or has not, really happened there.[8] As Thomas strolls into the park to kill some time, he takes random pictures with his single-lens reflex (SLR) Nikon F camera fitted with a 50 mm standard lens, which replicates the distance between the photographer and the photographed object as experienced by naked sight—a perspective also reflected in Carlo Di Palma's cinematography, which uses a standard lens to emphasize the distance between Thomas and the romantic tryst he happens upon. Had Thomas used a telephoto lens in this scene to take close-ups, like the disabled photographer in Alfred Hitchcock's *Rear Window* (1954),[9] he would not have had to blow up the frames later in his darkroom, thus depriving the film not only of its title and but also of the key element of enlarging the frames to get "closer" to the past event.

Also unlike *Rear Window*, Antonioni avoids point-of-view (POV) shots that would have replicated Thomas' voyeuristic perspective: we are just as detached from Thomas' subjective view as Thomas himself is from the love scene he observes from a distance. A classic rule of continuity editing, whereby a shot of a person's gaze is followed by a shot of the object of the gaze from the perspective of the observer, is dispensed with by Antonioni. Where we might expect a POV shot, we see either the lovers being watched from an angle that cannot possibly be that of Thomas, or the camera is panning, which is incompatible with the static quality of the snapshots that are being taken. What Thomas sees through the lens of his still camera and what we see through Carlo Di Palma's film camera are two different things. It is not until later in the studio, when Thomas develops, blows up, and prints the pictures, that our and the photographer's perspective merge in the joint search after the mystery captured by the camera in the park.

His own emotional life practically empty, limited to implied casual sex with the models and inconsequential interactions with other women (the girl in the antique shop, the woman in the park, the girlfriend of his painter friend from next door), Thomas takes instinctive opportunity to watch without being seen during the intimate scene in the park. He hides in a bush, behind a fence or a tree to take pictures of what looks like a secret rendezvous between an aging, prosperous-looking man and an attractive young woman (played by Vanessa Redgrave). As in Cortázar's story, the woman reacts angrily to the photographer's invasion of her privacy, and failing to retrieve the reel she retreats humiliated. Although they meet again later in Thomas' studio, her parting "we've never met, you've never seen me" foreshadows both her later disappearance together with the photographic evidence, and Thomas' own doubts about whether the whole thing happened at all.

The Photographic Investigation

The woman's extreme anxiety at being photographed (she even bites Thomas' hand in an attempt to snatch his camera) arouses his curiosity about what exactly happened in the park, and launches the "epistemological" theme of the film.[10] The long scenes in the darkroom where Thomas processes the film and prints the pictures display not only his professional competence but also a genuine passion for photography and its "alchemy," complete with developing tanks and trays, chemicals, sinks, enlarger, safelight, and print driers. The silent darkroom scenes also reveal some redeeming qualities of Thomas' misanthropic character, including his dedication to the photographic craft, determination, and creative restlessness. The developed negative reveals (by means of another optical device of the magnifying glass) the numerous frames which, like a film strip, reduce the continuous scene in the park to a series of still images (Figure 8.2).

However limited the photographic record compared with the original event, the post-factum selection of frames gives Thomas an opportunity to focus on elements of the scene which he originally seems to have missed. The experience is familiar to photographers: during a photo shoot it is never possible to notice and analyze all the multi-sensory information constituting the contiguous event. When taking a picture one's attention is focused on the camera and the photographed object, with all the background noise remaining below the threshold of consciousness. Only later in his studio, as he examines the prints of his wide shots, does Thomas manage to establish a connection between the woman's anxious sideway gaze and something hidden in the nearby shrubbery. After analyzing the enlarged prints of whole frames with a magnifying glass Thomas homes in on significant details, which he subsequently enlarges in his darkroom and prints again, blowing up the grain in the process and making the resulting images increasingly blurry. Still, as long as the enlarged details remain recognizable, the prints of spatially, chronologically, and causally related elements of the scene, now edited together like shots in a film, finally reveal what probably happened: while frolicking with her partner the woman was luring him toward a place where he could be shot by a third person, a hand with a gun visible in

Figure 8.2 Multiple still frames in a negative strip: *Blowup*, dir. Michelangelo Antonioni © Premier Productions (1966).

the bushes. The cropped and enlarged fragments also reveal the woman's agitated face at the photographer's intrusion which is about to spoil the murderous plan.

As the critic Walter Moser points out, the event reconstruction scene appears to blend the two photographic media, still photography and film (not only in the obvious sense of being part of Antonioni's film), thus bridging the time between then and now, contiguity and displacement. In this medium-transforming process, as Thomas pins his enlargements onto the wooden beams and walls in his studio, Antonioni uses both frontal and static shots to focus our attention on individual images. The film camera reproduces the frame-filling blowups in a series of fifteen clear cuts, accompanied by the spooky breeze rustling in the tress, as if editing a film made up of freeze-frames. In the process filmic angles and the photographic images match meta-cinematically—the effect that transforms this sequence in Antonioni's film into a "photo-film," like the documentaries using a montage of still photographs to recreate the sequence of events from the past.[11] Even the film's pace slows down, as if cinema was giving over to photography and its stillness, as Thomas composes his series of prints through a meticulous process of examination, selection, and trips to the darkroom. Through close-ups, zooms, and pans within and between the photographs, the film camera directs the viewer through the space and time of the original event, merging photography and film in the process, and reminding us again that cinema consists in essence of a series of still images blended together to simulate motion. As also noted by the critic Matilde Nardelli, Thomas' "photo-film" appears to be inspired by the popular post-war photo-novels and comic-strip cartoons, as well as by Antonioni's own early work in this format, explored for example in his script for Federico Fellini's *The White Sheik* (1952), with its comic tale of a young woman's fascination with the stories of oriental romance published in installments as a photo-novel in a newspaper.[12]

The numerous photographs pinned to the beams and walls of Thomas' studio to prompt his memory of the event in the park also reflect a new feature of photographic practice in the 1960s—its numerical abundance enabled by photography's ever-improving technical sophistication and automation. Thomas' Nikon F camera, introduced in 1959 and widely used by photojournalists, was one of the most advanced reflex-lens cameras of its day, equipped with a rapid rewind lever to enable taking pictures in quick succession. The rapid sequence of camera clicks during the fashion shoot and in the park allows Thomas to "cover" these scenes quickly, with a series of still images in principle not unlike the film camera with its twenty-four frames-per-second recording of movement. After the film roll is developed, the photographic abundance is displayed more directly by the sheer quantity of frames in the negative strip, as Thomas surveys them in detail with a magnifying glass (Figure 8.2). The cinematic effect of the photo negative is emphasized by Antonioni's camera, which identifies the frames first of all as frames while leaving their individual content indistinct. Out of the thirty-six frames in the roll Thomas selects fifteen for enlargement, printing, and further scrutiny, until the "montage" of spatially and chronologically related images reconstructs both what Thomas remembers from the park scene (the romantic tryst), and what he missed at the time (the possible murder). Short of making a hypothetical video of the entire scene in real time, Thomas pieces together the key moments, filling the gaps with cause-and-effect links, such as establishing an eye-line between the woman and an enlarged grainy close-up of a hand with a gun sticking from the shrub border.

However, given photography's technical limitations, including the restricted angle of vision and the reduction of image quality by grain, Thomas' attempt to expand his memory with the photographic record can only go so far. Frustratingly but unavoidably, the multi-stage cropping and enlarging intended to reveal the incriminating details also blow up the grain, making the resulting images more and more blurry and indistinct. Every time the motif is enlarged, part of the visual index it contains is lost to the eye by being buried deeper and deeper in the material texture of the support, until it becomes illegible, even though objectively speaking the information about the event is still there. As has been observed by critics, Antonioni radically challenges photography's claim to reflect the visible world, as he points out the medium's inherent opacity and indeterminacy in communicating contiguous objects and events. To an extent, just as the iconic map is not the territory, so the indexical photograph is not exactly the original scene: framing restricts the field of vision, the lens transforms the light, producing a distorted image of the scene on a grainy and (the then) monochromatic photosensitive support, while the specific format of the image's final display further alters and impoverishes the original information. In Antonioni's film the progressive croppings and enlargements only deepen the obscurity of the photographs' content by gradually exposing not the reality of the original scene but the reality *within* the medium.[13]

All the World's an Illusion

Photography's inherent paradox of both reflecting and distorting the world only increases the photographer's frustration: the more anxious Thomas gets to find out the truth about what happened in the park, the less reliable the obtained evidence becomes. Like in a physicist's lab, Thomas' tests seem only to destroy the tested object. The ultimate blowup of the crucial element of the scene, the alleged corpse, is obtained by taking a photograph of a photograph—a desperate and counterproductive attempt to enlarge a detail in the frame, which only compounds the grain effect and compromises the visual quality even more. The resulting image, blurred beyond all recognition, is unlikely to convince anyone, beginning with the photographer himself, of the supposed crime (Figure 8.3). The iconic indexical record, it turns out, has its limitations: it can be accepted as evidence only insofar as it perceptually, that is, subjectively, resembles its referent. Beyond a certain point defined by sensory perception, the indexical record refers back to its referent only hypothetically, but it can no longer be accepted as undeniable evidence in a forensic sense: the abstract pattern of black-and-white dots on the final blowup may or may not represent the corpse from the park. When a medium loses its referential function, what remains is the materiality of the medium itself, with no cues to point to anything outside the medium, real in the case of photography or imagined in the case of painting.

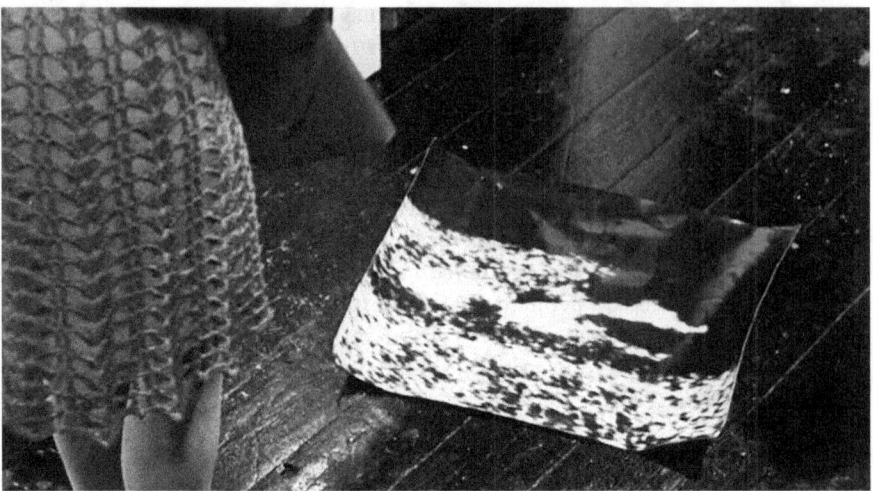

Figure 8.3 The final enlargement of a photographic detail as "abstract art": *Blowup*, dir. Michelangelo Antonioni © Premier Productions (1966).

One way to verify the truthfulness of questionable indexical evidence is to re-establish, if possible, the link with the "real thing" of the original contiguous event: here, the actual corpus delicti. This is what forensic experts do while investigating a crime scene: they identify, collect, and record (by taking photographs) indexical evidence such as fingerprints, footprints, tire tracks, bodily fluids, hairs, fibers, and other traces. Disappointed with his photographic evidence Thomas returns to the park at night to examine the crime scene directly, this time relying on his direct senses rather than on the indirect medium of photography. Interestingly, on this occasion the photographer, normally inseparable from his camera, arrives in the park without one, as if he wanted to depend entirely on his senses to verify his suspicions. Lo and behold, the dead body is actually there where his camera originally showed it to be, although the doubting Thomas still needs to touch it to make sure that neither his camera nor his eyes deceive him. However, the darkness and emptiness in the park (no one else seems to have discovered the body so far) only increase the sense of eeriness and unreality captured earlier in Thomas' photographs.

Meanwhile his studio has been raided and the prints and the negative removed. The only photograph missed by the raiders (it had slipped between two pieces of furniture) is, ironically, the titular, indistinct, and forensically useless ultimate blowup of the "dead body" (Figure 8.3). With the indexical evidence gone, the only trace of the supposed crime is Thomas' memory, both of his photographs and of the corpse he touched in the park, as well as his own verbal testimony—the least reliable type of evidence, of limited psychological and forensic value. "Are you sure?" asks the girl next door, played by Sarah Miles, when Thomas tells her of a man killed in the park. After examining the abstractionist photographic blowup of the dead body she is not convinced: "Looks like one of those paintings," as she refers to the experimental, non-figurative pictures painted by her boyfriend Bill. Antonioni anticipates this merger of photography and abstract painting in an earlier scene, in which Bill explains to Thomas that his pictures do not mean much to him while he is painting, and only later does he begin to see things in them. It is like finding a clue in a detective story, he says, which is of course exactly what Thomas is trying to do when he examines his enlargements. Once the iconic, representational quality of painting and photography is lost, the implied referents become either non-existent or illegible. An abstract image just teases the mind, which in the absence of identifiable referents overinterprets the sign by imputing to it meta-meanings neither suggested by the sign itself nor intended by the sender.

Increasingly anxious to find the truth behind his photographs and no longer trusting his memory and senses, Thomas tries to engage his friend Ron as a witness of the dead body in the park. As he drives to Ron's house through night-time London, he seems to spot the woman from the park standing in a queue. Amazingly, as she turns and walks away she literally disappears from view within the shot: Thomas is really chasing phantoms at this stage. As he runs after the vanished woman he ends up in a back-street music club (the Ricky-Tick), where a rock concert of The Yardbirds is interrupted when the guitarist (Jeff Beck), annoyed by a crackling speaker, tramples on his guitar, rips its neck off, and throws it into the crowd. In the mad scuffle after the rock fetish that follows, it is Thomas who grabs the torn guitar neck and runs away, pursued by the rock fans. Having evaded his pursuers, he pauses in the street, drops the guitar neck with hanging strings on the ground like a useless piece of junk, and walks away. A curious passer-by picks it up, and then quickly discards it. Scoring a momentary success in a rat race appears more important to Thomas than the actual nature of the success. Similarly, the search for the truth of what happened in the park may be real but short-lived, a momentary jolt, of no lasting consequence, in Thomas' emotionally empty and aimless life.

Thomas' attempt to involve Ron in his private investigation turns out to be just as futile. Having lost confidence in his senses, he needs an inter-subjective, external verification of whether the murder has occurred or not. Ron, however, is too stoned at a pot party in his large, strangely dark house on the Chelsea embankment, where everyone seems to be locked inside their own bubble of illusion anyway. One of the zombie-like guests is the real-life supermodel Veruschka von Lehndorff, who earlier that day has excused herself (as is implied) from after-work sex with Thomas, claiming that she was in a hurry to catch a plane to Paris. Now at Ron's party, to Thomas' remark "I thought you were supposed to be in Paris," Veruschka, stoned like everybody else, replies with an almost Beckettian "I *am* in Paris." Thomas may be the only sober person at the party (in fact, he refuses the offer of a pot cigarette), but he fails to involve Ron in his own illusions. "What did you see in that park?" Ron repeats uncomprehendingly, only to prompt Thomas' frustrated and resigned "nothing." Only Antonioni's camera, and with it the audience, *did* actually see the corpse in the park. In a 1966 interview for *Playboy* Antonioni explained rather metaphysically that both his camera and that of the photographer in the film were designed to communicate that what they record was real, although "reality has a quality of freedom about it that is hard to explain." In a similar ambiguous vein the director told the film critic Aldo Tassone: "I wouldn't say that the appearance of reality equals reality, because there can be more than one appearance. There can also be more than one reality, but I don't know it, and I don't believe it."[14]

The next morning Thomas finds himself back in the park in the final attempt to capture the photographic evidence, only to find that the dead body has disappeared, with only the swinging tree branches and the eerily sounding breeze as silent witnesses of what has or has not happened there. Thomas even looks up questioningly at the branch above the spot where the corpse was supposed to have lied, as if asking for help to settle the matter one way or the other. Both the contiguous hard evidence of the dead body, its indexical photographic record, the evidence of Thomas' senses, and his memory-based verbal reports all turn out to be illusory—the realization brought home by another sudden arrival in the park of shouting and hands waving mimes in a jeep. While their earlier appearance in central London was as yet dramatically unmotivated, now in the park the mimes focus their performance specifically on Thomas' predicament. Their silent pretend tennis game, on an actual court but without rackets or balls, appears to sum up both Thomas' empty, aimless life and his futile investigation of the supposed crime. At first only puzzled and amused by the mimes' pretend play, Thomas finally abandons his disbelief and allows himself to be fully drawn into their staged illusion, as he picks up the pretend ball and tosses it back into the court as if it was real.

The final merger of illusion and reality is also emphasized by a change in filming technique. While during the first scene in the park the film camera assumed an objective perspective by not allowing us to share the photographer's and his camera's viewpoint, now the film camera, without resorting to point-of-view shots however, converges with the protagonist's gaze, as it follows the trajectory of the tennis ball imagined by Thomas and the mimes. Unlike the mimes, however, who enjoy creating illusion in the knowledge that it is only illusion, the protagonist has finally accepted illusion as reality, just as earlier he chose the staged world of fashion glamor before actual human misery of the doss house, and mistook the photographic representation of a murder in the park for real crime. Having fully immersed himself in the mimes' pretend tennis game, Thomas watches the invisible ball exchanged between the players, and he even hears the ball being struck by the rackets. After succumbing to the illusion, the observing subject obliterates his own objective existence and becomes himself an illusion. In the bird's-eye wide shot that ends the film, Thomas' diminutive, solitary figure holding his camera simply fades into the grassy landscape a fraction of a second before the closing credits, leaving an empty green screen with which the film began.

The medium of film, with its direct appeal to vision, is perhaps better suited to represent the appearances and disappearances of material objects than literature with its reliance on imagination. In Cortázar's short story that inspired Antonioni's film, the "disappearance" of the original scene in the park is more subjective: as Roberto's memory fades with time, he no longer "sees" the human situation captured in his photograph, but only the accidental details of the surroundings such as clouds, rain, and pigeons, like the tree branches and the breeze in Maryon Park in Antonioni's film—silent witnesses of what has already faded from human memory.

9

The Iconicity of the Pictorial Frame

The enjoyment of painting, photography, cinema, television, and the internet depends on the visual information enclosed typically within the rectangular surface of a pictorial frame.[1] Except for three-dimensional media such as the human body, sculpture, theater, and architecture, visual signs communicate their messages either from flat walls in caves, houses, and churches, or from rectangular surfaces of books, panel painting, and screens. This chapter will argue that the pictorial frame, far from being just a technical accident in two-dimensional visual media, can be treated as an independent iconic sign with meta-meanings of its own, which partake in the meanings suggested by the images enclosed within the frame.

Natural Vision and the Pictorial Frame

The visual field covered by our naked eyes is of course wider than that of the pictorial frame but it is also limited, because our sight is strongest at the center of the retina and sharpness of vision deteriorates toward the edges. Foveal vision (fovea is a small central part of the retina exactly opposite the pupil, densely packed with cones responsible for color vision) encompasses a visual angle of only about 1 to 2 degrees. The less sharp parafoveal vision extends to about 10 degrees toward the peripheral vision, the latter being as wide as 180 degrees. Peripheral objects, however, appear fuzzy when the eye is focused on the foveal vision, but because our eyes, heads, and whole bodies are mobile, the difference in clarity between foveal and peripheral vision can be overcome. Without even lifting our feet from the ground but just by moving our eyes and heads and twisting out bodies to the right and left, we can detect some visual cues from a horizontal field of well over 180 degrees, and by raising and lowering our heads we can vertically cover a visual field of about 130 degrees (about 65 degrees up and 65 degrees down). The lack of symmetry between the horizontal and vertical visual fields is due to the occlusion by the nose.[2]

Our horizontal vision is wider for evolutionary reasons, to help us keep an eye on what is happening at some distance around us on the ground. As our eye movements also indicate, scanning from left to right and vice versa occurs more readily than scanning up and down.[3] This would explain the horizontal orientation of the cinematic frame, the dominance of panning shots over tilting shots in cinematography, as well as the fact that throughout its history the cinema screen has been expanding horizontally rather than vertically.[4] In this sense the shape of the cinematic frame and screen, and the typical camera movements reflect iconically the innate properties of our visual perception, the anatomy of bodily movements, and the features of the physical environment.

Our natural vision is also stereoscopic, able to perceive depth, while the pictorial frame is, by definition, two-dimensional. Many of the bodily organs are duplicated (e.g. hands, lungs, kidneys) but the eyes (as well as ears) are unusual in working in close cooperation. They share and compare information, and together they perform feats impossible for a single eye or ear—especially in signaling distance or depth for vision and direction for hearing. The images in the eyes lie on the curved surfaces of the retinas, but each eye, like a single-lens camera, produces only a two-dimensional representation of the visible world. Human eyes are horizontally separated by about 6.5 cm to receive somewhat different views for near objects, which are subsequently combined in the brain into a single perception of solid objects placed in three-dimensional space. The small difference between the images is known as disparity: this is what gives us a perception of depth as stereoscopic vision, albeit only for quite near objects, because with increasing distances differences between the images become too small, which means that we are effectively one-eyed for objects further than about 100 meters.[5]

Our stereoscopic vision (stereopsis), which evolved to negotiate proximate space in our ancestral environment, is, however, superfluous when contemplating the flat images of art such as paintings, drawings, photographs, or films. To create the illusion of depth on a flat surface artists must make use of perceptual cues available to a single eye, because the binocular distance cues of convergence and disparity work in fact against them. No matter how convincing an artist's rendition of shading and perspective is, stereopsis with its "depth sense" informs the viewer's brain that a painting, a photograph, or a cinematic shot of physical space is in fact flat. Both photographs and perspectival paintings are actually more compelling for depth when viewed with a single eye with the head kept still, because motion and the second eye reveal the flatness of the picture.[6] Renaissance artists keen to represent three-dimensional space in their two-dimensional paintings as seen with a single eye were aware of this proto-photographic principle, as illustrated by Leonardo Da Vinci's advice to young painters:

> Take a glass as large as your paper, fasten it well between your eye and the object you mean to draw, and fixing your head in a frame (in such a manner as not to be able to move it) at the distance of two feet from the glass; shut one eye, and draw with a pencil all that you see through it. After that, trace upon paper what you have drawn on the glass, which tracing you may paint at pleasure, observing the aerial perspective.[7]

The principle of linear perspective established with the use of one eye was first demonstrated in 1413 by the architect Filippo Brunelleschi in a "peepshow," in which one could look through the eyehole a view of the Florentine Baptistry as seen through the open doors of the Cathedral.[8] The recommendation that paintings should also be

Figure 9.1 *Draughtsman Making a Perspective Drawing of a Reclining Woman*, engraving by Albrecht Dürer (1538). Courtesy of the Metropolitan Museum of Art, New York.

viewed with only one eye gave rise to a brief fashion a few centuries ago to hang a dark curtain with a small viewing hole in front of a painting, so that viewers could appreciate the optimum illusion of depth without stereopsis working against the illusion.[9] Just as a one-eyed person is handicapped when negotiating physical space, so applying stereoscopic vision to perspectival pictures creates a handicap by diminishing the illusion of space within those pictures.

The single-eye viewpoint became the central element in perspective drawing and painting, widely used by Renaissance artists (Figure 9.1). The first written account of the one-eye perspective comes from Leon Battista Alberti's treatise *Della Pittura* (On Painting), published in 1435, with its mathematical construction of space as a prerequisite for realistic painting. For Alberti the geometric model of vision operates by means of a "triangle, whose base is the quantity seen and whose sides are those same rays which extend from the extreme points of that quantity."[10] Sets of such triangles in three dimensions comprise a visual pyramid, whose apex is the eye and its boundaries are formed by the outlines of each visible object. Inside the pyramid are bundles of "intrinsic rays," which are responsible for recording the surface quantities of color, light, and shade. At the very center is the "prince" of rays, the optical axis, which runs perpendicularly between the eye and the object, and by corresponding with the foveal vision it provides the strongest discrimination of detail and distance.[11] The visual pyramid discovered by Renaissance artists is a geometric, and therefore objective, method of imitating three-dimensional space on a two-dimensional surface.

A View from a Window

The frame as a principle of pictorial composition, first used in late-medieval panel painting, became the main vehicle for the perspectival painting of the Renaissance, when Leon Battista Alberti famously wrote in 1435 that the rectangular picture frame is like "an open window (*aperta finestra*) through which I see what I want to paint."[12] The analogy assumes that contemplating pictures and negotiating three-dimensional space are based on the same perceptual processes, but the comparison has its limitations. The main difference between a view from a window and viewing a painting or photograph is, of course, the involvement of the stereoscopic perception of real depth in the former and a mere illusion of depth created in the latter. A plain surface of the picture perpendicular to the line of sight is perceived simply as flat: it contains no perspective changes, no vanishing point or other cues of depth such as shading or occlusion (when objects in front block the view of objects behind them).[13] The flatness of the picture is also emphasized by the wall on which it is hung. We can also see the texture of the canvas or photographic paper (or the glassy transparent surface of the TV and computer screen), although the effect of flatness from texture can be reduced by viewing the picture from a sufficient distance, so that the textual surface is below acuity threshold, as in viewing a film in the cinema far in the auditorium, which minimizes the perception of grain or pixels on the screen.[14]

On the other hand, a rectangular aperture in the wall known as the window, invented to allow light and ventilation, engages full stereoscopic vision to offer contiguous three-dimensional experience of existing as opposed to imagined space, both when looking out the window and from the outside in. Or, as Dr Samuel Johnson put it, the window originated for "the sake of seeing and being seen."[15] The vain and pompous Doga Agnello of Pisa (1364) used to show himself to the adoring public from the window of his house, "as relics are shown," reclining on embroidered drapery and cushions.[16] In the film *Playtime* (1967) Jacques Tati parodies modern architecture by showing ground-floor apartments as a theatrical stage on full public display, with glass walls open to the front like shop windows (Figure 9.2).

Primarily, however, windows are designed for safe contemplation of three-dimensional space from inside out. As we approach a window we see more of the scene outside: as we move to one side, a portion of the scene on this side becomes hidden by

Figure 9.2 Ultra-modern apartments on display like shop windows: *Playtime*, dir. Jacques Tati © Specta Films (1967).

the window frame while more is revealed on the opposite side. More subtle changes, including shifts in projective relations, also occur when we move; for example, a church spire in the distance may have been directly in line with a tree in the foreground, but after we move it no longer is. Each different point of view results in a different picture with different informational content. On the other hand, a painting or a photograph has its information frozen on a two-dimensional surface, which no longer responds to the observer's movements or changes in the viewing angles.[17]

The necessarily limited window-effect of pictures can be enhanced by additional frames attached to the edges of the panel, which emphasize the separation of the pictorial illusion of depth from the flat surface of the wall. Picture frames can include architectural moldings or painted strips enclosing wall and ceiling paintings; the illuminated borders surrounding manuscript illustrations; the raised edges of early modern panel paintings; or the wooden, metal, and plastic strips enclosing modern photographs and other images, often with mountings to separate the picture itself from its frame. These independent, detachable frames first developed during the Renaissance with the commercial production of movable pictures to be hung on walls.[18] By meditating between the space of the room and that of the painting, frames also support the illusion of the fictional space within the painting. This effect can be enhanced by specific features such as the beveling of the frame toward the image, which guides the gaze into the picture and encourages the reading of the painting as a receding space.[19] Even in pictures that do not rely on perspectival vistas, as in portraits or abstract painting, the shape of the additional frame, argues Rudolf Arnheim, can enhance the function of the inner frame as a center of composition and indication of significance. For example, a heavy, bulging, gilded frame can add symbolic weight to the picture itself, or the frame may detach itself from the picture through its color, texture, and volume and thereby reduce interaction. On the other hand, a simple wooden strip, preferred by the modern taste, relieves the borders of some of their weight, while an unframed canvas, or even more so a cinema screen surrounded only by darkness, eliminates distraction altogether and focuses attention fully on the scene within the four edges of the inner frame.[20]

A geometric similarity between the pictorial frame and the horizontal and vertical features of the natural environment accounts for the iconic quality of the former, although historically both the window and the pictorial frame are relatively recent inventions. The Late Paleolithic painters used the rough surfaces of natural cave walls, without pictorial borders, for their vivid and realistic images of game and prey animals.[21] Cave images were not only painted but sometimes also carved on the walls to create bas-reliefs, or a natural rock crack or step could be used to provide the outline of an animal's body, with a few strokes of paint to supply the missing parts.[22] Whenever possible, the rough surface would be accommodated to enhance the effect of solidity and three-dimensionality. At the same time the natural shape of cave walls does not appear to be part of pictorial composition: the paintings consist of individual or grouped animals alone, without any boundaries or setting. In other words, pictures of animals in prehistoric caves are isolated, decontextualized portraits rather than scenes, with no cues of space beyond occasional occlusion, as when a series of horses' heads partly overlap one another (Figure 4.8).

Alberti's comparison between a framed picture and a view from a window also evokes architecture with its dependence on the gravitational stability of horizontality and verticality. Walls, floors, and ceilings provide the default points of reference for any ornamentation enclosed within their horizontal and vertical surfaces. In ancient Egyptian art, for example, figures painted on walls are often arranged in what the art historian Miriam Schild Bunim calls strip composition, where figures are supported on a series of base lines, one above the other, which divide the pictorial surface into horizontal zones.[23] In ancient Greek tombs the rectangular surfaces of walls were used for life-size paintings of human figures in rudimentary settings, a practice continued in Roman residential architecture. In Pompei (destroyed in 79 CE) perspectival architectural vistas painted on walls have been unearthed, with representations of cities, palaces, and sanctuaries, although without human figures. The illusion of depth suggested in these vistas included skillfully applied shadows within the wide tonal range of reds, yellows, whites, and blues, which helped convey a sense of depth. Subtle changes in color were used to enhance the illusion of distance, with the blurring of the farthest features. The receding lines of painted buildings also strongly implied imaginary space extending beyond the surface of the wall, even if the perspective was neither unified nor consistent judged by Renaissance standards. The painted vistas in Roman houses effectively turned interior walls into virtual windows, as in today's conservatories or floor-to-ceiling windows overlooking gardens and urban spaces.[24]

The framed picture independent from architecture first came into being in Renaissance Europe as part of the commodification of art. Earlier, during the Middle Ages, pictures were still integral components of architectural settings, commissioned for a particular wall in a church or palace. When in the fifteenth-century artists began to produce their biblical stories, landscapes, portraits, and genre scenes for the market, first for the aristocratic but increasingly also for bourgeois customers, panel paintings became smaller and more portable, to be hung on a wall of the customer's choosing. Changes in the format were reflected in experiments with the earlier-mentioned one-eye perspectival drawing, which included a rectangular glass pane, often supported by a wooden frame, and the sheet of paper onto which the Renaissance artists drew what they saw through the pane (Figure 9.1).[25] The restricted visual field meant that the horizontal and vertical edges of the frame separated the represented scene from the rest of the world, thus creating composition, in which selected elements assumed meaningful relationships, absent in the scene viewed with a naked eye.[26] For Rudolf Arnheim the frame around a picture, by virtue of its symmetry and visual focus, centralizes and stabilizes the objects within the picture, affording them significance that they may not otherwise possess.[27] In other words, framing transforms objects into signs, or pictorial motifs, even when this meaning-creating process is unplanned and accidental, as in today's casual snap-shot photography and spur-of-the-moment smartphone video capture. Any scene can reveal a practically unlimited number of esthetically and dramatically significant "framings," which is why professional cameramen often use viewfinders to scan the scene and set up optimal camera angles and positions. In visual arts, where framing is usually carefully planned and controlled, a setting is meta-cognitively transformed into a work of art, in which the frame, according to Arnheim,

> indicates that the viewer is asked to look at what he sees in the picture not as a part of the world in which he lives and acts, but as a statement about that world, at which he looks from the outside—a representation of the viewer's world.[28]

In other words, the informational content of iconic and indexical visual media is enhanced by intentional framing—itself an iconic feature that removes a painted or photographed scene from the world's inventory and turns it into a second-order sign pregnant with meta-meanings. Also, by separating the enclosed scene from the world outside, framing creates tensions between the explicit information within the frame and the invisible but implied information beyond it. The "cropping" of a wider setting in landscape painting or interior scenes suggests that the world extends beyond the edges of the pictorial frame, as in some paintings and drawings by Edgar Degas, where the edge of the frame "cuts through" a human figure (Figure 9.3). In cinema, when a character walks off the screen she is still present in the viewer's imagination, and the implied off-screen action, often supported by parallel editing, becomes a part of the extended plot.

Figure 9.3 Picture frame cutting through a body: *Dancer Onstage*, drawing by Edgar Degas (c. 1877). Courtesy of the Metropolitan Museum of Art, New York.

Horizontality and Verticality

Barring occasional cases of oval or round picture frames such as the ornately sculpted circular shape of Michelangelo's *Holy Family* (c. 1507, the Uffizi Gallery), from the late medieval period onward panel pictures (i.e., paintings other than frescoes) are typically rectangular in shape. Part of the reason is practical: it is easier to saw wooden boards into rectangular pieces than into round ones, or to make frames from straight pieces of timber joined at right angles, just as it is less wasteful to cut paper or canvas into rectangular sheets. But the height and width of a picture panel or frame are not the same as verticality and horizontality, as we are reminded to our annoyance every time we see a picture hanging crooked on the wall. Early modern picture frames, often weighty, artfully carved and gilded, resembled other pieces of furniture such as chairs, tables, beds, and cabinets, all of which were unified geometrically according to the vertical and horizontal surfaces of walls and floors as determined by the gravitational pull.[29] Our sense of balance, involving the cooperation between the visual feedback, the inner ear, and the skeletal system, makes us innately sensitive, mainly by inducing a dizzy feeling, to disturbances of verticality and horizontality, which upset gravitational balance and threaten potentially dangerous falls of ourselves and other large upright objects such as trees or rocks. This is also why to prevent walls and houses from collapsing builders apply spirit levels, plummets, and set squares to establish precisely the horizontal and vertical lines and surfaces. Ontogenetically, horizontal-vertical discriminations develop earlier in humans than the ability to differentiate left and right oblique lines. Babies as young as sixteen weeks spend longer looking at horizontal or vertical gratings than at oblique gratings. Children also have difficulty drawing oblique lines, being able to copy a square a year or two before a diamond, even though this may be the same shape rotated. And, very consistently, children begin by drawing houses with flat roofs.[30]

In Plato's cosmological geometry the cube (a three-dimensional square) is an iconic sign representing the element of earth, the most stable and solid of the four elements (the other being air, fire, and water): "Let us assign the cube to earth; for it is the most immobile of the four bodies and the most retentive of shape, and these are characteristics that must belong to the figure with the most stable faces."[31] Horizontality and verticality as functions of gravity and guarantees of physical stability and safety dominate in nature, while oblique lines and shapes are rarer, and are accordingly perceived as distortions of natural forms, instinctively interpreted as disturbing and threatening. A picture frame that hangs straight, that is, whose sides correspond with gravitational verticality and horizontality, is an iconic sign that replicates the two fundamental co-ordinates of natural space, and provides reference points for all horizontal, vertical, and oblique lines and shapes enclosed within it. The basic co-ordinates apply equally to two-dimensional pictures and three-dimensional spaces and objects: the dimension of depth in the latter results simply from adding another horizontal co-ordinate placed at the right angle to the first. Typical vertical objects found both in pictures and the real world include standing human figures, trees, pillars, walls, spires, and towers; horizontality is commonly represented by inert, resting objects, level ground, water

Figure 9.4 Diagonal lines and surfaces in architectural design: Bord Gáis Energy Theatre, Dublin.

surfaces, and of course the line of the horizon; while diagonals are formed by any straight lines intersecting the two main co-ordinates.

Because of our inner sense of balance diagonal lines and sharp angles are perceived as unsettling and threatening, or at least as attention-catching, in comparison with the stabilizing, "boring" effect of the main gravitational co-ordinates. Modern architectural design can on occasion upset our instinctive expectations of stability in buildings, with controversial results mitigated only by, for instance, artistic rather than residential purposes of eccentrically designed structures (Figure 9.4). In cinema the rectangular and "straight" screen provides a literal frame of reference for any departures from the reassuring stability of horizontality and verticality. For example, in a classic German Expressionist film, Robert Wiene's *The Cabinet of Dr. Caligari* (1920), the surreally stylized sets dispense almost entirely with right angles and naturalistic perspectives in favor of jagged shapes and diagonals to create a nightmarish vision of a small town gripped by terror—a visual allegory of the society after the First World War as traumatized and out of moral balance (Figure 9.5). Similarly, the camerawork in Carol Reed's *The Third Man* (1949) frequently employs the "Dutch angle": sideway tilted shots to create a visual metaphor of moral corruption and cynicism in post-war Vienna.

The dominance of horizontal over vertical natural vision is also reflected in the orientation of the pictorial frame, with "landscape" dominating over "portrait," to use the language of printer settings. This iconic principle is also in evidence in the evolution of the cinematic screen. From the beginning of cinema until the post-war period, the horizontally rectangular screen remained at the squarish Academy ratio of 1.37:1 (the width about one-third longer than the height). From the mid-1950s onward, mainly due to the competition with television, whose screen was also fixed

Figure 9.5 A small town as a nightmare: skewed perspective in *The Cabinet of Dr. Caligari*, dir. by Robert Wiene © Decla-Bioscop AG (1920).

at the Academy ratio until as late as the 1990s, the cinema screen was consistently widening. In 1955, for example, the musical *Oklahoma!* was shot at the staggeringly wide ratio of 2.55:1, and by mid-1960s the widescreen systems became standard in cinemas around the world.[32] The horizontally rectangular frame has also remained standard in photography, as reflected in the design of the first compact 35 mm cameras such as Leica since mid-1920s, and of the single-lens reflex (SLR) cameras popular after the Second World War. In these designs the camera box replicated the shape and orientation of the film frame inside. The camera's default orientation is nearly always horizontal (it always is in movie cameras), in imitation of natural vision, which means that taking pictures vertically, to frame a full human figure, a tree, or a church's spire for example, requires tilting the camera sideways by 90 degrees.

This practice has changed in recent years with the widespread use of smartphones with built-in digital cameras, whose shape is vertical, mainly because a vertical gadget is easier to handle and align with ear and mouth during a call, like the old telephone receiver. Because smartphones are primarily telephones rather than cameras, their vertical orientation has an unfortunate effect on the composition of most photographs and videos captured by them: their default orientation is now predominantly and counterintuitively vertical. No matter how horizontal the scene (most scenes are horizontal, unless it is a balcony scene from *Romeo and Juliet*), smartphone users insist on shooting it through a vertical frame, often wasting a precious opportunity to record optimally a situation of potential interest to the public. TV news bulletins and

Figure 9.6 Vertical smartphone video of a horizontally enfolding event as seen on a horizontal TV screen.

YouTube show countless of vertically shot smartphone videos of dramatic events such as floods, earthquakes, terrorist attacks, riots, demonstrations, car accidents, and so on—all unfolding horizontally in real life. The disappointing result of these video clips is that the upper third of the frame typically shows the sky, the bottom third shows the ground, with only the narrow (and horizontal!) band in the middle of the vertical frame devoted to the event in question. In other words, two-thirds of the frame is wasted on largely irrelevant elements of the scene. When subsequently shown on TV these video clips leave wide empty margins on both sides of the horizontal screen, which are either left black or filled with replicated, enlarged, and blurred parts of the video pretending to offer additional visual information (Figure 9.6).

Seeing without Being Seen

Natural verticality and horizontality as the prototypes of the pictorial frame also determine an advantageous point of view for humans, what the evolutionary psychologists Gordon H. Orians and Judith H. Heerwagen call "prospect and refuge"—an opportunity to see without being seen. Accordingly, people innately prefer edges rather than open spaces for better visual access to an area, and spaces that provide a covering over the head (a roof, a tree canopy, etc.) to ensure privacy and safety—protective needs more fully catered for by residential architecture with its walled and roofed spaces with windows.[33] The vertical edge of a bush and a horizontal covering of a tree branch from which our ancestors scanned the terrain for optimal habitat or to detect danger may well be the evolutionary prototypes of the window, the picture frame, and the cinema, television, and computer screens.

The information obtained from a safe viewpoint refers to the evolved responses to landscapes as part of human exploratory and esthetic needs discussed in Chapter 1. The geographer Jay Appleton presents a general account of an ideal landscape that human beings would find intrinsically congenial and pleasurable. It includes open horizontal spaces of low grasses and pools of water interspersed with vertical features such as thickets of bushes and groupings of trees, a window-like opening to an unimpeded vantage on the horizon, plus evidence of animal life and a diversity of greenery, including flowering and fruiting plants.[34] From the viewpoint of optimal habitation and safety humans avoid, if they can, expansive deserts and Arctic planes, and are attracted more toward a balanced mix of horizontality and verticality in moderate climatic zones, including hilly undulations with enticing vantage points for orientation and exploration—a preference reflected in landscape painting and calendar photographs, as well as in the design of gardens and parks (Figures 1.2, 1.4). A landscape ideal for exploration reveals moderate complexity compared with the undesirable extremes of thick, impenetrable jungles on the one hand, and monotonous, exposed flatlands on the other. A perfect "view from a window" obtained from a cave on the side of a mountain, a child's tree house, a house on a hill, the king's castle, and the penthouse apartment, includes also elements of mystery: a path as a cue for exploration leading into hills or down into a fertile valley, or a riverbank that disappears around the bend (Figure 1.2). Humans innately enjoy both a prospect from which to survey a landscape, and a sense of refuge—an advantage of safe observation and protection afforded by concealment.[35] The geometric perspective in Renaissance paintings, and the automatic capture of depth cues in photography and film can thus be interpreted as iconic signs inviting the viewer to explore the mystery of the virtual scene within the frame—a vicarious experience that imitates the exploration of the natural environment by our ancestors. For deep cognitive and evolutionary reasons therefore, the pictorial window-like frame, especially in the indexical photographic media, is probably the most appealing form of visual representation ever invented, or, given the stability of our innate cognitive dispositions, ever likely to be invented.

Frames within Frames

As always, meta-communication reveals the working of the communication process by drawing attention to the properties of the medium itself, even if the illusion created by indexical, iconic, or symbolic magic is broken in the process. In visual artifacts that expose their own artificiality, as in using a frame not only as a technical accident but as a pictorial element in its own right, artists display their awareness of the conventions underlying their art and invite the viewers to participate in this ironic play. In the process a semiotic sign becomes a meta-sign—a pictorial frame as both a vehicle and a subject of its own representation.

Just as the earlier-mentioned Doga Agnello of Pisa turned himself into a sign by vainly displaying his person in the window, so the two smiling women in Murillo's genre painting meta-semiotically look out the window-as-pictorial frame at the implied

Figure 9.7 *Two Women at a Window*, oil painting by Bartolomé Esteban Murillo (1655/60). Courtesy of the National Gallery of Art, Washington.

audience below (Figure 9.7). Windows tend to be oriented vertically, aligned in their design with the standing human body, as in Murillo's picture. The painted window frame practically blends with the picture frame, whose dimensions, 1.4 m by 1.25 m, match the size of an average window and make the realistically painted women real-life in size as well. If Murillo's picture is hung on the wall a little above the viewer's head, the spell of pleasing iconic magic may well involve the "eye contact" between the viewer and the women smiling down at him from the pictorial window. The border between the real space of the viewer and the virtual space of the painted women is further blurred by a realistic contrast between the dark interior of the room seen through the window and the light on the women's faces "coming from" the room where the picture is exhibited. The distinction between the viewer's contiguous experience and the picture's displaced fictional reference thus becomes subjectively obliterated—the essence of iconic magic. The viewer succumbing to the charm of Murillo's painting may also be forgiven for smiling back at the young woman in the window, as her

Figure 9.8 A "film" within a window: *Citizen Kane*, dir. by Orson Welles © RKO Radio Pictures (1941).

duenna, or governess, partly conceals her own half-amused half-embarrassed smile while chaperoning her charge from behind the window's shutter.

In Orson Welles' classic film *Citizen Kane* (1941), the turning point in the titular character's life happens when his mother signs a document authorizing the banker W. P. Thatcher to assume guardianship over her little son and provide for his education. In an interior shot (Figure 9.8) the stern mother dispassionately discusses the legal matters with the banker, while ignoring the helpless objections of the boy's alcoholic father. In the background, a small bright window shows the boy gliding on his sled in the snow. Welles' deep-space staging of dramatic action, supported by Greg Toland's cinematography, includes the large, powerful figures of the mother and the banker poring over the legal papers in the foreground; the largely irrelevant diminished figure of the father behind them in the middle ground; and the dramatic counterpoint in the background screen-like window, with the boy blissfully ignorant of the fact that his fate is just being decided, and that he is enjoying the last moment of childhood happiness. After the guardianship document is signed, the father moves toward the window and slides it down, marking the end of the "film" displayed in it: the boy's life with his parents is over. In the following exterior shot the mother opens the window again, as if to mark the beginning of a new chapter in her son's life, as she calls to him to break the news, which will leave him emotionally scarred for the rest of his life.

The title sequence of George Roy Hill's revisionist Western *Butch Cassidy and the Sundance Kid*, released in 1969 but looking like it was made yesterday, is in

Figure 9.9 Screen within a screen: opening titles of *Butch Cassidy and the Sundance Kid*, dir. George Roy Hill © Campanile Productions (1969).

part a sepia-tinted homage to the mythical times of the Wild West. The nostalgia is supported meta-cinematically by a reference to the silent Westerns of the type made popular by Edwin S. Porter's 1903 short film *The Great Train Robbery*, in which a gang of outlaws robs a train in the American West, flees across mountainous terrain, to be finally defeated by a posse of locals. In Hill's film the title sequence places today's viewers inside the darkness of an early twentieth-century cinema auditorium, with an inserted screen at an oblique angle, as the titles of the 1969 *Butch Cassidy* scroll on the side (Figure 9.9). The sepia tint, already introduced in the 20th Century Fox logo that starts the film, is carried through the title sequence in an anachronistic cinema newsreel about the Hole in the Wall gang of train robbers, with Burt Bacharach's nostalgic score as the link with the mythic past. As the critic Lola Landekic reminds us, the title sequence had been originally penned by the screenwriter William Goldman as part of a scene, eventually removed, to appear later in the movie, where Butch and Sundance, while watching the newsreel of their gang robbing the train and then being gunned down, shout at the indignity of their media portrayal.[36] By placing the newsreel at the start of the film, the implied early-twentieth-century cinema audience is replaced with late-twentieth-century viewers, while the prologue-like newsreel both nostalgically celebrates the mythic past of frontier outlaws and foreshadows the genre and plot of the main film.

When the film plot, characterization, and setting are sufficiently engaging, viewers may sometimes fail to recall later if, for example, the film was color or black-and-white, or in what aspect ratio it was shot. The latter, however, is difficult to miss in Wes Anderson's delightfully surreal *The Grand Budapest Hotel* (2014), which draws attention to framing by alternating between three different aspect ratios of the screen, depending on the time of the action and the corresponding period in cinema history (Figure 9.10). Most of the scenes, set in the 1930s, are presented in the Academy ratio

Figure 9.10 The three aspect ratios of *The Grand Budapest Hotel*, dir. Wes Anderson © Fox Searchlight Pictures (2014) in historical sequence: (from the top) 1.37:1, 2.35:1, and 1.85:1.

of 1.37:1, the standard screen format until the mid-1950s. The film's "present" is the year 1985, introduced by the framing device with a young woman holding a cherished copy of a work of fiction eponymically called *The Grand Budapest Hotel*, which introduces the main story narrated in flashbacks by its aged author. These scenes are shown in the widescreen 1.85:1 ratio used since the mid-1950s, to become for decades the most common cinema projection standard worldwide. Finally, the part of the story set in the 1960s is rendered correspondingly in the then popular panoramic 2.35:1 ratio.[37] The three screen formats thus provide meta-cinematic cues to help identify the time of action of the multiple narrative points of view, or "lenses": from a published book to its author to the person who told the story and back to the author.

10

The Iconic Magic of Cinema in Woody Allen's *The Purple Rose of Cairo* (1985)

If Antonioni's *Blowup* challenges the notion of photographic indexicality as a truthful representation of the visible world, Woody Allen's *The Purple Rose of Cairo* endorses the magic of cinematic fiction, in which the combined effects of indexical veracity and iconic verisimilitude enhance the viewer's psychological involvement with staged simulations of life. As discussed in Chapter 4, the universal phenomenon of iconic magic exploits the cognitive bias of mistaking displaced iconic signs (here, fictional screen characters in fictional settings) for contiguous objects such as real people in real-life situations. Also, if a fictional indexical-iconic medium offers a more satisfying version of the currently experienced life situation, choosing a pleasing illusion over harsh reality may be psychologically irresistible. Continuing stress and humiliation, boredom and frustration can diminish critical sense by making a person succumb to compensatory iconic magic with its gratifying fictional alternatives to life. Such is the premise of Woody Allen's *The Purple Rose of Cairo*, in which an unhappily married and still pretty Cecilia, played by Mia Farrow, finds emotional comfort in romantic comedies she watches every night in a local cinema during the Great Depression, until a dashing young hero "steps off" the screen to join her in the real world, later to invite her to pursue romantic adventures with him in his black-and-white virtual reality inside the cinema screen.

A Film within a Film

Cecilia's susceptibility to cinema magic is only indirectly caused by the 1930s economic recession, because she still has her waitering job in a New Jersey diner. More directly, her unhappiness is due to the abuse and emotional neglect by her unemployed, sponging husband, Monk, played by Danny Aiello. Cecilia takes extra laundry after work to pay the rent, while all Monk does all day is pitch pennies with other bums, play dice and cards, drink, and make passes at the girls. Cecilia makes several attempts to escape her loveless marriage by simply leaving her loutish husband, only to come back every time for more abuse because with no money, friends, or family she has nowhere else to go. Her husband knows that, and he is right when he shouts after her: "Go on, go on, you won't last. You see how it is out in the real world. Go on, you'll come back."[1] Cecilia's only emotional refuge are daily visits to the local cinema, the Jewel Theater, where she immerses herself in Hollywood fantasies by briefly exchanging her harsh real life for blissful "reel" life.[2] The parody of 1930s Hollywood made by Allen as a film-within-a-film which Cecilia enjoys every evening is based on what the director calls "champagne comedies" he watched as a child in New York, "with all those romantic people who wore tuxedos and went to big nightclubs and lived in penthouses and drank champagne all the time."[3] The inserted black-and-white movie even shares its title with Allen's main film shot in color, creating a multi-layer fantasy of real people as spectators-cum-actors, reminiscent of the ancient esthetic theory, handed down to us through Shakespeare, in which all the world is a stage and all men and women merely players—a view based on an analogy between theatrical acting and social role playing.[4]

A compensatory and therapeutic nature of meta-realities evoked by cinematic fiction is brought home by a series of contrasts between Cecilia's bleak life and the on-screen glamor. The "otherworldly magic" of cinema is impressed upon us right from the start by the production logo of the Orion Pictures, with its image of the starry sky, accompanied in Allen's film by the sound-track of Fred Astaire singing Irving Berlin's "Heaven, I'm in heaven." The song continues over the gaudy posters advertising the latest "cinema of distraction" at the Jewel Theater, the titular *Purple Rose of Cairo*, followed by a closeup of dreamy-eyed Cecilia. Ominously, her fantasy is interrupted by a harsh metallic sound of a letter falling on the pavement right next to her from the marquee overhead—the first reality check—followed by the theater owner's warning "Oh, Cecilia, be careful." Her daydreaming is finally broken by a cut to an angry woman demanding her oatmeal *before* her scrambled eggs in a diner where Cecilia works with her sister. Her mind constantly on movies and the stars, Cecilia is unable to concentrate on her work, and so she fumbles, forgets orders, and breaks crockery, eventually to lose her job. Fiction is only fiction, warns Allen, and meta-reality with its escapist vicarious experience cannot, on pain of serious life consequences, be confused with the real world.[5]

However, the black-and-white *Purple Rose*, Allen's brilliant parody of 1930s Hollywood romantic comedies, is too irresistible for Cecilia, what with its spacious and light Art Deco penthouses, tuneful soundtrack, and wealthy Manhattan socialites "bored with evenings at the opera and weekends at the races." We fully share Cecilia's cinema experience as the camera cuts between wide color shots framing a black-and-white screen inside the Jewel Theater, and full frames of the screened movie filling Cecilia's entire field of vision. Our experience of watching a parody of a 1930s "champagne comedy" merges with that of fictitious Cecilia watching a "real" Hollywood movie. As our and Cecilia's perspectives converge, we come to understand her surrender to the glamor of the black-and-white world inside the screen, with its white grand piano, the Copacabana nightclub, and exotic holiday destinations for the rich—all in painful contrast to the dismal colors and gloom of Cecilia's cramped apartment and the bleakness of a New Jersey town.

Breaking the Fourth Wall

As Cecilia's domestic misery deepens and her job situation worsens, so her dependence on romantic fiction increases and the line between fiction and reality becomes blurred. After her first cinema encounter among the Egyptian pyramids with dashing Tom Baxter, "poet, adventurer, explorer, of the Chicago Baxters," in a pith helmet and khaki suit (played by Jeff Daniels), Cecilia returns home only to find her gross husband flagrantly courting the sexual favors of an even grosser neighbor named Olga. The ever-widening gap between art and life brings about Cecilia's another failed attempt to leave her husband, while her sack from the diner following another dropped plate sends her back to the Jewel for desperate, repeated viewings of the *Purple Rose*. As her tear-stained face dissolves to the black-and-white movie, she becomes more and more engrossed in the virtual screen reality, where Tom, now in New York and still wearing his pith helmet and khaki, excitedly embraces a prospect of "a madcap Manhattan weekend," while his host hopes that Tom likes his martinis *very* dry. Cecilia sniffles and cries in her seat as the Black maid in the movie asks Rita, "a blonde-on-blonde in a slinky dress," whether she "be wanting" her bath in "the big bubbles, or the asses' milk." But it is not until Tom looks toward the off-screen Cecilia, starts talking to her, and steps off the screen into the auditorium of the Jewel Theater that the iconic magic begins in earnest.

When later an onscreen executive of the RKO Studio, which produced the black-and-white *Purple Rose*, reacts in disbelief "How can he come off the screen? It's impossible. It's never happened before in history," Woody Allen is sharing an in-joke with his audience. In Fritz Lang's 1922 thriller *Dr. Mabuse*, the titular criminal master mind appears in one of his disguises as a one-armed magician, casting a hypnotic spell over his audience in the form of a quasi-cinematic illusion, in which Bedouins from an Arabian desert step from the stage down the theater aisle. In the slapstick *Sherlock Jr.* (1924), Buster Keaton plays a cinema projectionist who falls asleep in his booth and dreams of entering the screen to resolve a criminal case, which will clear his falsely tarnished name and win him a girl he loves (Figure 10.1). Once inside the screen the Keaton character is just as maladapted to the ever-changing situations of a romantic crime thriller *Hearts and Pearls*, as is *Purple Rose*'s Tom Baxter in New Jersey.

With the breaking of the fourth wall the displaced indexical-iconic signs of fictional cinema are subjectively transformed for Cecilia (and for the rest of the audience at the Jewel, who gasp and scream in terror) into fully contiguous experience, in which the black-and-white onscreen two-dimensional shadow of Tom Baxter is metamorphosed into a three-dimensional flesh-and-blood person in living color. Cinema is thus magically transformed into a live theater, where actors break dramatic illusion by engaging directly with the audience—the sheer improbability of such an interaction in the cinema generates surreal comedy in Allen's film, as the upper-class onscreen characters make condescending remarks about the audience at the Jewel. Art and life begin now to mix fully, as Tom, instead of winding up with the onscreen Kitty Haynes (played by Karen Akers), a torch singer from the Copacabana club, decides to enjoy his freedom from the constraints of the script with the off-screen Cecilia. The other movie

Figure 10.1 A cinema projectionist steps inside the screen: *Sherlock Jr.* dir. by Buster Keaton © Buster Keaton Productions (1924).

characters too revert meta-cinematically to being actors playing their parts, as they complain about the inconveniences caused by the sudden disruption of the plot, and indulge their vanity by bickering about the relative importance of the characters they impersonate. With Tom crossing the magic line between fiction and life, displacement and contiguity, the black-and-white onscreen characters now freely interact in real time with the audience and the cinema manager, with everyone angry at the confusion unfolding on both sides of the screen. In the middle of the surreal mayhem Cecilia's dream of finding true love seems finally to come true, for Tom has been observing Cecilia in the audience for some time, found her "fetching," and now wants to shed his scripted character to make his own decisions (Figure 10.2).

The Love Triangle

Interestingly, Tom's rival is not Cecilia's bulling husband (although the two men do exchange punches), but the actor Gil Shepherd (also Jeff Daniels), who plays Tom Baxter in the black-and-white *Purple Rose* and whose career is now in danger as a result of the newly acquired freedom of his screen creation. Cecilia's romantic dream just gets more beautiful, for she is now facing a choice between two attractive men in love with her: the romantically perfect if fictitious Tom, and the gallant (and real!) matinee idol

Figure 10.2 Tom Baxter (Jeff Daniels) looks from the screen at Cecilia sitting in the cinema auditorium: *The Purple Rose of Cairo*, dir. by Woody Allen © Orion Pictures (1985).

much taken by Cecilia's appreciation of his talent. Tom is sweet but impractical in the real world, so while Cecilia is delighted with him, she can also see a problem: "I just met a wonderful new man. He's fictional, but you can't have everything."

Tom's naiveté and ignorance of real life are for a time disarming, and Cecilia enjoys teaching him the ways of this world, so different from the fairy tale of Hollywood fiction. "I wonder what it's like out there?" inquires the Countess left behind by Tom in the Manhattan penthouse, but after taking a good look at the cinema audience she remains skeptical: "They don't look like they're having too much fun to me." Tom is as maladapted to the real world as his pith helmet and khaki suit are out of place in New Jersey. He clearly misinterprets the name of the "Great War" by expressing regret to have missed it, and is surprised to learn that people do in fact get old and sick, and never find true love, rather than being "consistent" and "reliable" as in his world. After kissing Cecilia he is disappointed at the absence of the stock Hollywood fade-out. He is astonished to see a protruding belly of a woman passing by and holding another child by the hand; even when Cecilia, gesturing, explains what pregnancy is, Tom still reacts in disbelief. Inside a church Cecilia raises the subject of God, "the reason for everything," which Tom interprets in his own way: "Oh, I think I know what you mean—the two men who wrote *The Purple Rose of Cairo*." But Cecilia enjoys every minute of his company, getting all she has been missing in her life. She finds Tom's kissing "perfect" ("It's what I dreamed kissing would be like"), they dance at the supper club ("Monk never took me dancing") and drink champagne ("I never had champagne before"), even if later they have to run for it when Tom realizes that his fake movie money is of no use, and is surprised that their getaway car won't start without a key.

Meanwhile Gil Shepherd's acting career is about to take a new turn, away from "a kind of poetic, idealistic quality" of the Tom Baxter character, and the last thing he needs is his screen double on the loose, outside his control, perhaps "robbing banks" or "raping broads." Gil admits that he worked hard to make his screen character real, and now he realizes that maybe he overdid it, so he flies from Hollywood to New Jersey to find Tom before he ruins his reputation and career. In semiotic terms, the actor is an iconic sign, contiguous in live theater and displaced in film, who uses his body, movements, gestures, facial expressions, costume, makeup, and voice to simulate a virtual entity outside of himself—usually a human character but sometimes an animal and even an inanimate object or an abstract idea (as in medieval morality plays).[6] The actor and her physical attributes acquire, according to the critic Keir Elam, "mimetic and representational powers by becoming something other than itself,"[7] while for Konstantin Stanislavski "the actor creates a model in his imagination, then like a painter, captures every trait and transfers it not onto canvas but onto himself."[8] As in other iconic media, for acting to be effective some degree of suspension of audience's disbelief is necessary, whereby an actor as a sign is conflated with his impersonation as the sign's meaning, so that "watching acting may trigger all of our automatic person processing that happens in everyday interactions"[9]—the iconic magic without which no real enjoyment of dramatic fiction is possible. The actor and the impersonated character may thus be perceived as one by the audience, or at least the sign and its referent may be believed to be separate but somehow connected. For Raoul Hirsch, the producer of the black-and-white *Purple Rose*, it is the actor Gil Shepherd who created the character of Tom Baxter ("the facts are undeniable"), which makes him responsible for the behavior of his screen double. If something happened to Cecilia, the woman seen in Tom's company, Gil would have to bear the consequences, and "You know what they get for rape in a small town, especially by a man in a pith helmet."

Like a true fan immersed in cinema magic, Cecilia at first confuses Gil with Tom, the actor with his role. Even when told the difference, she is still too star-struck, gasping and almost swooning, to speak coherently, while Gil—a struggling, insecure actor—is pleased with her admiration. He is less pleased with his double, now enjoying freedom from his creator—art as an entity separate but not disconnected from life, or as meta-reality still tied to reality. As the fictitious Tom defends vehemently the autonomy of art ("it's because of the way I do it"), the actor counters with the factual "No, no, no, because of the way *I* do it. I'm doing it, not you." In other words, the meta-meanings of art cannot exist without the material basis of iconic signs (here, living actors) to produce the desired effects on the audiences' imagination: "I took you from the printed page and made you live. I fleshed you out," says Gil. As the altercation between the actor and his creation continues, each arguing his relative point, Cecilia is delighted, for whichever of the two gallants wins in competition over her, it will be a marked improvement over the boorish Monk: "Last week I was unloved. Now *two* people love me, and it's the same two people." Cecilia finds her fictional lover "perfect," but the actor deflates her unrealistic hopes with "What good is 'perfect' if the man's not real?!" Ultimately Gil wins the romantic argument and gets the last laugh by countering Tom's naïve claim "I can learn to be real" with the sobering "You can't learn to be real. It's like learning to be a midget. It's not a thing you can learn. Some of us are real, some are not."

Cecilia, however, remains undecided, for a time preferring Tom's wide-eyed boyishness to Gil's slick celebrity status. In one of the film's most imaginative segments

Cecilia joins Tom in his black-and-white world inside the screen for a night of her life. Her delirious happiness is conveyed through a montage of overlapping images of the glittering panorama of Times Square and the neon signs of New York night clubs: the Harlequin Club, the Hot Box, the Broadway Dance Palace, the Purple Grotto, the Club Harlem, Club Morocco, and the Latin Quarter—all overflowing with champagne and martini, and each with the appropriate dancing music (Figure 10.3). Back in the Manhattan penthouse suite Cecilia waxes lyrical over the white telephone, something she has always dreamed of having, just as her whole life she has wondered what it would be like to be on this side of the screen.

By comparison Gil's attempts to woo Cecilia offer her a possibility of a dream come true in the real world. For all his Hollywood charisma and ambition Gil, his career at cross-roads, remains inwardly insecure, hungry for compliments and reassurances offered sincerely by Cecilia, his admiring fan: "You'll always be a great movie star." Vulnerability seems to dominate over ego, as Gil honestly admits that he used to be a cab driver and technically he is not really a star yet, while Cecilia seems able to offer him the kind of emotional support he needs both as an actor and a human being. Of all the compliments she showers on him the one to really win him over is that he's got "a magical glow"—an honest praise all the more appreciated for coming from a real person with no agenda, rather than from "one of those movie colony bimbos." An addicted moviegoer, Cecilia is also an astute film critic when she suggests that Gil should play more heroic parts such as Lindbergh (an American aviator); by practically reading Gil's mind she finally wins his heart. He invites her to Hollywood, and the cheerful time they spend together singing in a music store, with Cecilia playing the ukulele, matches in mood the happy moments she enjoyed with Tom in black-and-white Manhattan.

Figure 10.3 Cecilia (Mia Farrow) and Tom (Jeff Daniels) inside the black-and-white screen world in *The Purple Rose of Cairo*, dir. by Woody Allen © Orion Pictures (1985).

Art, Artist, and Life

The short-lived bliss, fictional in itself, of attaining unity between life and art by being courted simultaneously by an artist and his creation, is inevitably bound to be shattered by harsh reality, confirming Monk's ominous taunts at Cecilia when she tries to leave him again: "Go, see what it is out there. It ain't the movies! ... It's real life, and you'll be back!" Monk is only right in his rejection of naïve idealism he attributes to Cecilia, and in his cynical prediction of her eventual return. What Monk does not realize, however, is that for all her dreaminess Cecilia does not have to choose between onscreen fantasy (what Monk calls "junk") and the unhappy life with him, but between a perfect onscreen lover and a charming actor. If Tom is a work of art: "honest, dependable, courageous, romantic, and a great kisser," Gil is an artist, one who combines life with art, while Monk just stands for raw, brutal life. Cecilia, "a real person" after all, has enough good sense ultimately to reject the sweet but ephemeral Tom, "some kind of phantom," because total abandon to meta-reality would be harmful and self-destructive, like succumbing to drugs, joining a fanatical sect, or losing oneself in romantic love, like Goethe's Werther. As Allen explains his story,

> Cecilia had to decide, and chose the real person, which was a step up for her. Unfortunately, we must choose reality, but in the end it crushes us and disappoints. My view of reality is that it has always been a grim place to be, but it's the only place you can get Chinese food.[10]

Choosing a matinee idol over his virtual counterpart is therefore a more sensible option, with two possible outcomes: a banal happy ending of a conventional romantic comedy, with Cinderella-like Cecilia finding her prince and moving to sunny California, or a sadder but more realistic ending, with Cecilia deserted by Gil and returning to the old misery with Monk (which is what happens). Allen cleverly keeps the more optimistic option of a "Hollywood finish" open until the very end, for Gil's declarations of love for Cecilia look and sound genuine enough. But he is an actor, whose habitual histrionic disposition can blur the difference, even for himself, between real feeling and pretend play.[11] He may well mean it when he says that he is jealous of Tom, that he cannot get Cecilia out of his mind, and that he loves her—self-deception, or method acting, that makes his declarations all the more convincing to emotionally vulnerable Cecilia. Her inevitable disappointment is foreshadowed during the cheerful scene in the music store, when she quotes from a fictitious movie *Dancing Doughboys*, in which Gil says to the heroine: "I won't, I won't, I won't be going south with you this winter." Cecilia emotionally recites the heroine's premonitory line: "When you leave, don't look back."

After leaving Monk again, this time to go with Gil to Hollywood, Cecilia's imminent disappointment is foretold by the sight of the *Purple Rose of Cairo* letters being taken down from the marquee at the Jewel Theater: the dream is over. At the beginning of the movie one of those big metal letters ominously crashed on the pavement dangerously close to Cecilia. Now she learns that Gil has in fact run out on her, after persuading her to reject Tom. The actor was only pretending to love her, but all he cared about all along was his professional future: "As soon as Tom Baxter went back up on the movie screen," explains the Jewel's manager to stunned Cecilia, "he couldn't wait to get outta here. He said this was a close call for his career." Contrary to expectations of a generic Hollywood happy ending, Woody Allen offers a sadder but wiser conclusion, for which the more critical part of the audience is already prepared. As the director explains:

> The whole reason for *Purple Rose* was for the ending. It would have been a trivial movie with the other ending. An executive from Orion called after the screening in Boston and asked very nicely, "Is that definitely the ending?" "Oh, yes," I said. "Okey," he said. But I'm sure the look on his face was a grimace.[12]

Allen allows the Depression and Monk to triumph over Tom Baxter and the Copacabana, because that is what happens in real life, if not in the movies. After puncturing her illusions, Allen closes his film with Cecilia seated once more at the Jewel, her pathetic suitcase and ukulele on the seat beside her, as she stares in rapture at Fred Astaire and Ginger Rogers dancing on the screen to the tune of "Heaven, I'm in heaven" with which Allen's film began. Again she becomes totally immersed in the movie, and a smile slowly returns to her face. The ukulele, a souvenir of the happy hour with Gil in the music store, marks for Cecilia the only difference between the end and the beginning of her surreal romantic adventure. Otherwise at the film's conclusion all the main characters land back to square one, with Gil, his career now safely back on track, as the nominal winner, perhaps slightly guilt-ridden, judging from his face expression on the airplane. Even the disappointed Tom should find his consolation in a love affair with Kitty Haynes, the singer for whom he falls in the original movie script, whose song now sounds like good advice: "Let's take it one day at a time/And who cares just how it turns out." As Cecilia's face changes from sadness to renewed happy absorption in screen fiction, Allen seems to imply that although escapist cinema offers no substantial alternative to the challenges of everyday life, it should be allowed at times to function as a therapeutic surrogate reality for the Cecilias of this world.[13]

In 1993, having made twenty-four films, Woody Allen regarded *Purple Rose*, his fourteenth creation, as a favorite among his films, "the closest I've come to a feeling of satisfaction... the best work that I have done as a film-maker."[14] The film certainly offers some of the director's most important reflections on the medium, including a synthesis of Allen's own farcical and parodic techniques and romantic themes. For the critic Richard Schieckel, *Purple Rose* is also "one of the best movies about movies ever made,"[15] not only in its satiric take on classic Hollywood but also, in a semiotic sense, in its meta-cinematic exploration of the cognitive appeal of an indexical-iconic medium, including its iconic magic—an instinctive and perverse tendency, which can be both beneficial and harmful, to mistake images of objects for the objects themselves.

Postscript

Academic Writing

There are arguably two types of academic writing: classic and postmodern. For the literary scholars Francis-Noël Thomas and Mark Turner, the classic style is like looking at the world: the writer sees something and through her writing guides the reader's imaginative gaze so that he can see it for himself.[1] The "seeing" metaphor indicates that the things the writer wants the reader to imagine exist in the outside world, and that the mental icons conjured up by the symbolic signs of language are like a window to that world. If the subject matter is more theoretical, classic writing appeals to the reader's reason and logical thinking, and aims at persuasiveness achieved by clarity and soundness of inference rather than by conformity with an intellectual community or faith in an argument from authority. The purpose of classic academic writing, as in all non-fiction, is informing and explaining, and the motive is to seek the truth about what is out there, not what the writer imagines or merely supposes. The style of presentation is defined by lucidity, simplicity, and accessibility. In this sense classic writing is cooperative and conversational; it appeals to the reader's curiosity and factors in her knowledge and intelligence, including the ability to read between the lines, to work out the implicit from the explicit, and so on.[2]

And then there is the postmodern type of academic writing. Where classic writers respect facts, logic, and clarity of exposition, for postmodern writers vague conceptualizations, word games, and obscure philosophizing dictate the writing style. The postmodern form of expression reflects its content: the assumption that knowledge has nothing to do with verifiable facts and falsifiable theories, and is not even a matter of individual imagination and experience, but is generated in the collective, self-reflective meta-sphere of language understood as a closed semantic system, with no reference to extra-linguistic reality.[3] Far from existing objectively and independently from the observer, the postmodern world is magically called into being by language, in which vocabulary and syntax are divorced from referential meaning, and discourse is reduced to a free play of the signifier in which nothing is discovered but everything is invented. The postmodern discourse "constructs" and "writes" social reality: individual and collective identity, emotions, body, gender, sexuality, beauty, childhood, and so on, rather than writing *about* these things. The frequent omission of the preposition "about" implies, against all evidence and common sense, that writing creates things *ab nihilo*, as in verbal magic where charms and incantations are believed to produce tangible results in the outside world.

Born in the heady days of the 1960s campus political radicalism and intellectual iconoclasm, initially in France, in the decades that followed postmodern discourse spread through arts departments in Western universities, where it inspired impenetrable language designed to bamboozle impressionable undergraduates and woo fellow academics. Driven by professional narcissism and dogmatism of its gurus and by gullibility and intellectual conformism of its followers, postmodern writing, instantly recognizable by its pretentious gobbledygook, drew on an eclectic mix of Marxism, Freudian and Lacanian psychoanalysis, structural linguistics, "constructionist" gender studies, Foucauldian historicism, and Derridean deconstruction, to mention just the main inspirations. In the last decades of the twentieth century postmodern discourse established itself in academia as a way of talking and writing about practically everything: literature, art, culture, media, science, history, politics, identity, gender, and society. With time, however, the postmodern dogmas, with their rejection of logic, clarity of exposition, and respect for evidence, have been systematically dismantled and comprehensively refuted, mainly by scientists and dissenting intellectuals.[4] In the new century this anti-scientific, anti-rational, and nihilistic chapter in modern intellectual history appears finally to be on the wane, mainly due to the natural decline of a fad but also thanks to the rise of neo-humanist theoretical approaches founded in cognitive and evolutionary sciences.[5]

The depressing nonsense of postmodern writing has been promoted, ironically, by some professors of English, deservedly ridiculed in the Bad Writing Contest run between 1995 and 1998 by the philosopher Denis Dutton in the journal *Philosophy and Literature*.[6] This publicity stunt celebrated the most stylistically lamentable passages found in contemporary scholarly literature, with first prize winners including such luminaries of postmodern thought as Judith Butler and Fredric Jameson. In 1998 the second prize went to Homi K. Bhabha, at the time a professor of English at the University of Chicago, for the following sentence from his book *The Location of Culture* (Routledge, 1994):

> If, for a while, the ruse of desire is calculable for the uses of discipline soon the repetition of guilt, justification, pseudo-scientific theories, superstition, spurious authorities, and classifications can be seen as the desperate effort to "normalize" *formally* the disturbance of a discourse of splitting that violates the rational, enlightened claims of its enunciatory modality.[7]

Two positive things that can be said about this sentence are that it is syntactically correct (if convoluted) and that it consists of otherwise familiar words. But it is the way these words are combined that is problematic. The verbal mix brings together, without any logical justification, several abstract and decontextualized concepts ("desire," "guilt," "justification," "pseudo-scientific theories," "superstition," "spurious authorities") that can mean anything. There are many types of desire: which one does Bhabha mean? Without this specification the "ruse of desire" makes no sense. And why should "'normalize'" be put in inverted commas and *"formally"* be italicized? What is "a discourse of splitting"? Splitting what? Or is "splitting" used in a psychiatric sense? The closing "enunciatory modality" is just as elusive. Postmodern discourse reminds one of Oscar Wilde's "Ah! That is clearly a metaphysical speculation, and like most metaphysical speculations has very little reference at all to the actual facts of real life, as we know them."[8] Far from explaining anything or advancing any recognizable argument, the semantic randomness of Bhabha's sentence appears designed instead to baffle the reader who, if he still trusts his critical judgment, begins to wonder whether someone may not actually be trying to pull his leg. In classic writing the reader feels invited to a conversation between equals; in postmodern writing the reader is humbled into a position of intellectual inferiority before the writer's inscrutable and superior authority.

I once asked a group of arts students and academic colleagues to do a "comprehension test" on a passage from Jacques Derrida, one of the gurus of postmodern philosophy. I presented them with two typed-up sheets: one containing a paragraph from Derrida's seminal 1966 essay "Structure, Sign, and Play in the Discourse of the Humanities" (the paragraph starting with "Nevertheless, the center also closes off the freeplay it opens up and makes possible."[9]), and the other sheet with the same sentences jumbled up. The readers were to decide which passage was the philosopher's original. The overall score was about fifty-fifty; in other words, readers were simply guessing because in neither text did they find any coherent progression of logical meaning from sentence to sentence. (Nor did they see much sense within the sentences for that matter.) Syntactic language may be the most efficient communication system ever invented, but only when its users aim in good faith at mutual understanding based, in non-fiction, on logic and external reference. Otherwise the symbolic signs of language can be easily manipulated through combinatorial grammar to generate meaningful-looking but in fact meaningless (illogical and non-referential) discourse.

The pretentiousness of postmodern writing has also been lampooned by the computer programmer Andrew Bulhak, who in 1996 designed a software called *Postmodernism Generator*, which automatically churns out, *ad infinitum*, random and meaningless scholarly-looking papers in High Theorese,[10] full of intimidating big names and profound-sounding stock postmodern phrases, complete with numbered footnotes.[11] In the same year the physicist Alan Sokal exposed the sham of postmodern scholarship by publishing in *Social Text*, a prestigious American academic journal, a hoax article "Transgressing the Boundaries: Towards a Transformative Hermeneutics of Quantum Gravity." The article consisted entirely of absurdities and non-sequiturs drawn from real publications by eminent postmodern thinkers, and argued in essence that physical reality is at bottom a social and linguistic construct. In a heated media debate that followed Sokal's disclaimer, the author invited "anyone who believes that the laws of physics are mere social conventions... to try transgressing those conventions from the windows of my apartment. I live on the 21st floor."[12]

The pseudo-intellectualism and deliberate obfuscations of postmodern writing have also affected semiotic theory. David Sless finds it ironic that semiotics, a discipline so profoundly concerned with communication, should produce so many incommunicative works, full of what he identifies as loose reasoning, absence of method, sweeping generalizations, tortured neologisms, and esoteric jargon.[13] Why should the semiotics of theater and drama, for example, not survive without "ostension," "proxemic codes," "vestimentary codes," "histrionic overcoding," "transcodification," "actantial model," "proairetic relationship," "commissives," "distal deictic orientation," "alethic necessity," "doxastic modality," "deontic modality," and so on.[14] Daniel Chandler, author of a blessedly readable survey of semiotic theory, also finds semiotic literature for the most part hard to understand, confusing, obscure, and simply dull.[15] It is difficult to disagree with these assessments when confronted for example with Floyd Merrell's *Sensing Semiosis: Toward the Possibility of Complementary Cultural "Logics"* (1998). The book sets out to integrate, in an incomprehensible mix, Peirce's theory of signs, "the non-Euclidean geometry of Bernhard Riemann," the Indian philosophy of Nagarjuna, the Buddhist "five skandhas" (which allegedly "substantiate Peirce's variation of classical logic"), the philosophy of William James, the physics of John Archibald Wheeler, information theory, and the philosophy of Jean Baudrillard—all reflecting "the vast, intractable, and ever transient rush of semiosis," in a world which "must include a sense of both-and and neither-nor, contradiction, inconsistency, and incompleteness," and in which "we are, ourselves, our arrogant, pompous, imperious selves, no more than signs among signs, signs incompletely knowing themselves."[16] Dubious poetic prose apart, nothing in Merrell's book justifies this exotic cocktail of inspirations, which makes one wonder why, for example, Neo-Platonism, the Cabbala, Celtic mythology, Christian mysticism, Taoism, astrology, quantum mechanics, chaos theory, or any other of the equally incompatible systems of thought have not been thrown into the semiotic witches' cauldron as well.

Even semiotic studies that largely steer clear of rhetorical excesses and conceptual chaos cannot escape the spell of postmodern discourse. For example, Mark Gottdiener's *Postmodern Semiotics* (1995)[17] insists, wrongly in my view, on applying linguistic poststructuralism to analyze modern visual culture—a form of communication that relies primarily on iconicity rather than on grammatical permutations of symbolic signs, as in verbal language. Linguistics-based semiotic approaches are ill suited to analyze visual culture, because language is a combinatorial system whereas visual communication (other than alphabetic writing) consists mainly of holistic iconic signs. For example, the phonemes and the letters in the word *dog* mean something completely different when spelled and pronounced backward. On the other hand, an iconic sign of a dog, as in a painting, photograph, or film, still denotes the same canine animal whether we start looking at it from its head or tail. Jumbling up the external anatomical parts of a dog—its head, legs, tail, and torso—will not produce another meaningful iconic sign but a meaningless, random set of butchered body parts. The spell of Saussure's linguistic semiotics is difficult to break, however, with loose concepts such as the "language" or "grammar" of film, theater, advertising, and so on frequently but misleadingly applied to essentially iconic media.[18] Even more misguided, it seems, is applying structural linguistics to animal communication,[19] which depends largely on contiguous indexical cues, symptoms, and signals—all beyond the ken of combinatorial grammar.

Going Forward

The main goal of systemic semiotics, as presented in this book, has been to apply deductive, set-by-step thinking to transform a set of premises, theoretical and empirical (see Introduction), into more detailed statements and definitions to account for the diversity and complexity of communicative situations found in animal and human behavior. Thus any case study, or application of systemic semiotics, should begin by acknowledging, even if only implicitly, the physical properties of the objectively existing natural world, with its evolved sentient organisms, including meta-cognitive humans and their culture as nature's latest achievement. Nature and the evolutionary process remain the bedrock of human psychology, culture, communication, and meaning formation. Interacting with the environment, natural and social, to explore and exploit its resources while avoiding its dangers is therefore what all living organisms as autonomous systems do to survive and flourish, which in practice means satisfying the manifold needs: procreative, nutritional, protective, social, exploratory, esthetic, and teleological (see Chapter 1).

The needs and the related innate cognitive modules are therefore the ultimate causes of communication. For example, the universal human practice of fictional storytelling can be defined as "socially organized self-regulation by means of meta-linguistic artefacts,"[20] where "self-regulation" refers to the behavior of autonomous systems leading toward the restoration of the functional equilibrium related to the needs. The "meta-linguistic," that is, implicit, connotative, and imaginative language of fictional narratives is here contrasted with para-linguistic, explicit, and literal verbal communication employed in the service of the various needs in non-literary, scientific or every-day, contexts (see Chapter 3). Thus the meta-linguistic artifacts linked to the procreative need and sexuality produce erotic poetry and romantic fiction, while the corresponding para-linguistic artifacts consist of the literal and empirical medical accounts of sexual behavior, with pornography and dirty jokes lying somewhere in between. Para-linguistic communication related to nutrition includes cookery books, recipes, and nutritional science, while food advertisements and religious food symbolism, with their metaphors and connotative associations, belong to metacommunication. Human protective need is regulated both by the explicit language of the law and public announcements, and by implicit, often emotive and manipulative meta-language of political speeches, propaganda, national epics, and "patriotic" art. The social need is catered for both by the para-language of social sciences, interactions between friends, family members, and fellow citizens, and by the meta-linguistic fiction of folk ballads, psychological novels, drama, and cinema. The esthetic sense is served both by the para-language of esthetic theory and criticism and by the inherently meta-cognitive phenomenon of art itself. The linguistic expressions of the exploratory need in turn include the para-communication found in scientific publications, journalism, instruction manuals, intelligence reports, and office memos, while the exploratory need's meta-linguistic expressions consist of travel literature, science fiction, and realistic and historical fiction. Finally, the specifically human preoccupation with goals, purposes, and the meaning of life is mediated both by the conceptual para-linguistic accounts of theology, philosophy, and scientific psychology, and by the evocative meta-language of religious and existential poetry, moral allegory, eschatological myths, and philosophical novels.

Critical applications of systemic semiotics should also acknowledge the essentially polysemiotic nature of all communication. Any discussion of cinema (see Chapters 4, 7, 8, and 10) should consider not just the medium's evident iconic character but also its indexicality, or causality, responsible for the medium's high degree of veracity of representation. The preponderance of indexicality or iconicity in photographic media also provides the reference points for the classification of the various photographic modes: the realistic, or documentary mode based on iconic indexicality, and the fictional mode, relying on indexical iconicity, with mixed modes and genres (e.g., the mockumentary or realistic, quasi-documentary fictional cinema) found in between. Also, while iconicity is what photography and painting have in common, indexicality is what separates the two media. In photography and film indexicality refers to the causal connection between image and object, whereas in painting indexicality refers to the connection between image and its maker—the painter. This is why we appreciate photographs more for their content than for their authors, whereas we value paintings more as expressions of the artists' talent and skill, quite regardless of the pictures' subject matter. This would explain why successful painters enjoy higher cultural prestige than successful photographers.

Verbal language too, a classic case of symbolic communication, is replete with expressive and stimulating iconicity on the level of speech sounds, word formation, syntax, and text structure (see Chapter 5), in addition to its indexical dimension manifest in the physiology of articulation and the idiosyncrasies of the speakers' idiolects, individual verbal styles and mannerisms. Literary studies, while dealing with arbitrary linguistic signs, is really about reconstructing the mental icons (metaphors, similes, motifs, themes, tropes, etc.) provoked by linguistic structures as determined indexically by the author's individual style, artistic temperament, and life experience embedded in a given socio-cultural context. In addition, the systemic formulations regarding the dynamism of character (see Chapter 6) offer a formal and systematic, rather than just intuitive and impressionistic, method of accounting for the motivations and behavior of real people as well as their fictitious equivalents. Finally, all media, linguistic and visual, depend for their communicative power and appeal on the universal cognitive bias of conflating the form of the sign with its distant or imagined referent (see Chapter 4), whereby a reader of a literary work or a viewer of a film, painting, or a play can become "magically" identified with the characters and events simulated in these media—an illusion without which no appreciation and pleasure of fiction are possible.

Taking classic writing style as its model, systemic semiotics aspires to offer a more reader-friendly, de-mystified, and hopefully useful account of communication and meaning, with limited jargon and clear reasoning as inspired by common sense and good science writing. The only arbitrary assumption that systemic semiotics asks the readers to accept is that the world includes autonomous systems, which strive to maintain their internal functional equilibrium by exchanging the needed information and energy with their environment. The rest of the story follows from this basic premise.

Notes

Introduction

1 John Tooby and Leda Cosmides, "The Psychological Foundations of Culture," in *The Adapted Mind: Evolutionary Psychology and the Generation of Culture*, ed. J. H. Barkow, L. Cosmides and J. Tooby (New York: Oxford University Press, 1992), 24, 88–9; Robin Dunbar, *The Human Story: A New History of Mankind's Evolution* (London: Faber and Faber, 2005), 138–45, 161–4; *The Evolution of Culture: An Interdisciplinary View*, ed. Robin Dunbar, Chris Knight and Camilla Power (Edinburgh: Edinburgh University Press, 1999); John Cartwright, *Evolution and Human Behaviour: Darwinian Perspectives on Human Nature* (Basingstoke: Macmillan, 2000), 307–17.
2 Karl Popper, *Objective Knowledge: An Evolutionary Approach* (Oxford: At the Clarendon Press, 1979), 59, 318.
3 Edward O. Wilson, *On Human Nature* (London: Penguin Books, 1978), 10; Elliot Sober, "Let's Razor Ockham's Razor," in *Philosophy of Science: An Anthology*, ed. Marc Lange (Malden, MA–Oxford: Blackwell Publishing, 2007), 126–38; Henry Plotkin, *The Nature of Knowledge: Concerning Adaptations, Instinct and the Evolution of Intelligence* (London: Penguin Books, 1994), 78–9.
4 Ervin Laszlo, *The Systems View of the World: The Natural Philosophy of the New Developments in the Sciences* (Oxford: Basil Blackwell, 1972), vi.
5 Popper, *Objective Knowledge*, 344, 346; Karl Popper, *The Logic of Scientific Discovery* (London: Routledge, 2002), 3–4.
6 Karl Friston, "Predictions, Perception, and a Sense of Self," *Neurology* 83 (2014): 1112–18.
7 Popper, *The Logic of Scientific Discovery*, 3, 7–9, 11–12; Plotkin, *The Nature of Knowledge*, 14–16, 19; Laszlo, *The Systems View*, 26; *Introduction to Systems Philosophy: Toward a New Paradigm of Contemporary Thought* (New York: Harper & Row, 1972), 16–18; Robin Dunbar, *The Trouble with Science* (London: Faber and Faber, 1995), 25, 97; Arturo Rosenbleuth, *Mind and Brain: A Philosophy of Science* (Cambridge, MA: The MIT Press, 1970), 80.
8 Jerry A. Fodor, *The Modularity of Mind: An Essay on Faculty Psychology* (Cambridge, MA: The MIT Press, 1983); Henry Plotkin, *Evolution in Mind: An Introduction to Evolutionary Psychology* (London: Allen Press, 1997), 173–4; Lance Workman and Will Reader, *Evolutionary Psychology: An Introduction* (Cambridge: Cambridge University Press, 2004), 1, 21; Christopher Badcock, *Evolutionary Psychology: A Critical Introduction* (Cambridge: Polity Press, 2000), 11–12; Steven Pinker, *How the Mind Works* (London: Allen Lane, 1998), 21–4, 31–2, 27, 45, 57, 210, 524; Donald E. Brown, *Human Universals* (New York: McGraw-Hill, 1991), 144; Cartwright, *Evolution and Human Behaviour*, 193–4; Joseph Carroll, *Literary Darwinism: Evolution, Human Nature, and Literature* (New York: Routledge, 2004), vii, 23, 191.
9 Wilson, *On Human Nature*, 20; Peter Carruthers and Andrew Chamberlain, "Introduction," in *Evolution and the Human Mind: Modularity, Language and Metacognition*, ed. P. Carruthers and A. Chamberlain (Cambridge: Cambridge University Press, 2000), 3; Workman and Reader, *Evolutionary Psychology*, 21.

10   Steven Pinker, *The Language Instinct: The New Science of Language and Mind* (London: Penguin Books, 1995); *The Stuff of Thought: Language as a Window into Human Nature* (London: Allen Lane, 2007).
11   Derek Bickerton, *Language and Species* (Chicago: The University of Chicago Press, 1990), 233; Plotkin, *The Nature of Knowledge*, 11–12.
12   Ludwig von Bertalanffy, *General Systems Theory: Foundations, Development, Applications* (Harmondsworth: Penguin Books, 1973); Laszlo, *Introduction to Systems Philosophy*, 16–19; Gerald M. Weinberg, *An Introduction to General Systems Thinking* (New York–London: John Wiley and Sons, 1975), 36–7; Piotr Sadowski, *From Interaction to Symbol: A Systems View of the Evolution of Signs and Communication* (Amsterdam: John Benjamins Publishing Company, 2009), 18.
13   The deductive classification of types of communication offered in this book validates in the main C. S. Peirce's semiotic triad of icon-index-symbol (Charles Sander Peirce, *Collected Papers of Charles Sanders Peirce*, ed. C. Hartshorne and P. Weiss [Bristol: Thoemmes Press, 1998], 143). However, as is elaborated further in Chapter 2, Peirce's sequence should be re-arranged as index-icon-symbol, with the addition of contiguity as the default of all communication, to reflect the evolution of animal and human cognition.
14   Sadowski, *From Interaction to Symbol*, 32–56.
15   Robert Trivers, *The Folly of Fools: The Logic of Deceit and Self-Deception in Human Life* (New York: Basic Books, 2011), chap. 8.
16   Richard Dawkins, *The God Delusion* (London: Bantam Press, 2006), 174–7, 187.
17   *The Oxford Companion to Philosophy*, ed. Ted Honderich (Oxford: Oxford University Press, 1995), 556.
18   Ferdinand Saussure, *Course in General Linguistics*, ed. C. Bally et al. (Glasgow: Fontana/Collins, 1974), 15–17, 65–78; Raymond Tallis, *Newton's Sleep: The Two Cultures and the Two Kingdoms* (London: Macmillan Press, 1995), 84.
19   Thomas A. Sebeok, *Contributions to the Doctrine of Signs* (Bloomington: Indiana University Press, 1976), 47–58; *An Introduction to Semiotics* (London: Pinter Publishers, 1994), 4.
20   Popper, *Objective Knowledge*, 309.
21   Bryan Magee, *Confessions of a Philosopher: A Journey through Western Philosophy* (London: Phoenix, 1998), 61.
22   Peirce, *Collected Papers*, 135.
23   Bronwen Martin and Felizitas Ringham, *Dictionary of Semiotics* (London: Cassell, 2000), 4.

Chapter 1

1   Bertalanffy, *General Systems Theory*, 2, 19.
2   Laszlo, *The Systems View*, 13, 23–4, 28, 40.
3   Philip Lieberman, *The Biology and Evolution of Language* (Cambridge, MA: Harvard University Press, 1984), 59; Bertalanffy, *General Systems Theory*, 42–5.
4   Laszlo, *Introduction to Systems*, 40, 75, 88–9; *The Systems View of the World*, 35–7, 42; Neil Campbell, *Biology* (Menlo Park, CA: Cummings Publishing, 1996), 136, 85–6.
5   Marc D. Hauser, *The Evolution of Communication* (Cambridge, MA: The MIT Press, 1998), 522.

6   Plotkin, *The Nature of Knowledge*, 51; Cartwright, *Evolution and Human Behaviour*, 40, 57, 344; Hauser, *The Evolution of Communication*, 3.
7   Pinker, *How the Mind Works*, 44–52.
8   Marian Mazur, *Cybernetyka i character* [Cybernetics and Character] (Warsaw: Państwowy Instytut Wydawniczy, 1976), chap. 4.
9   Tooby and Cosmides, "The Psychological Foundations," 45.
10 Cf. "For if the sun breed maggots in a dead dog," *Hamlet* 2.2.181.
11 Nancy L. Segal, *Twin Mythconceptions: False Beliefs, Fables, and Facts about Twins* (London: Academic Press, 2017), 260.
12 Steven Pinker, *The Blank Slate: The Modern Denial of Human Nature* (London: Penguin Books, 2002); Matt Ridley, *Nature via Nurture: Genes, Experience and What Makes Us Human* (London: Fourth Estate, 2003).
13 Theodore D. Wachs, "The Nature-Nurture Gap: What We Have Here Is a Failure to Collaborate," in *Nature, Nurture, and Psychology*, ed. Robert Plomin and Gerald E. McClearn (Washington, DC: American Psychological Association, 1993), 375.
14 According to the biologist Edward O. Wilson the inherited "epigenetic rules" are neural pathways and regularities in cognitive development by which the individual mind assembles itself (*Consilience: The Unity of Knowledge* [London: Abacus, 1998], 139). Elsewhere Wilson also states that "The genes hold culture on a leash. The leash is very long, but inevitably values will be constrained in accordance with their effects on the human gene pool. The brain is a product of evolution" (*On Human Nature*, 17, 20, 161).
15 Tooby and Cosmides, "The Psychological Foundations," 38–9, 83–4; Badcock, *Evolutionary Psychology*, 56–7, 228–9; Ridley, *Nature via Nurture*, 50, 127–30, 246; Cartwright, *Evolution and Human Behaviour*, 57.
16 Merlin Donald, *Origins of the Modern Mind: Three Stages in the Evolution of Culture and Cognition* (Cambridge, MA: Harvard University Press, 1991), 309.
17 Thomas J. Bouchard Jr., "Genes, Environment, and Personality," in *The Nature-Nurture Debate: The Essential Readings*, ed. Stephen J. Ceci and Wendy M. Williams (Oxford: Blackwell Publishing, 1999), 102; Joseph Carroll et al., "Imagining Human Nature," in *Evolution, Literature, and Film: A Reader*, ed. Brian Boyd, Joseph Carroll and Jonathan Gottschall (New York: Columbia University Press, 2010), 213.
18 Cartwright, *Evolution and Human Behaviour*, 57.
19 Jean Aitchison, *The Seeds of Speech: Language Origin and Evolution* (Cambridge: Cambridge University Press, 2000), 22, 32, 190.
20 John D. Barrow, *The Artful Universe* (Oxford: Oxford University Press, 1995), 245.
21 Joseph Carroll, *Evolution and Literary Theory* (Columbia: University of Missouri Press, 1995), 2–3; *Literary Darwinism*, 74–5; "Human Nature and Literary Meaning: A Theoretical Model Illustrated with a Critique of *Pride and Prejudice*," in *The Literary Animal: Evolution and the Nature of Narrative*, ed. J. Gottschall and D. S. Wilson (Evanston, IL: Northwestern University Press, 2005), 76–106.
22 Leda Cosmides and John Tooby, "Cognitive Adaptations for Social Exchange," in *The Adapted Mind: Evolutionary Psychology and the Generation of Culture*, ed. J. H. Barkow et al. (New York: Oxford University Press, 1992), 221.
23 Sadowski, *From Interaction to Symbol*, 73.
24 Richard Dawkins, *The Blind Watchmaker* (1986; London: Penguin Books, 2006), 50.
25 Bickerton, *Language and Species*, 89.
26 Plotkin, *The Nature of Knowledge*, 208.

27 Paul Ekman and Wallace V. Friesen, *Unmasking the Face* (Englewood Cliffs, NJ: Prentice Hall, 1975); Paul Ekman, *Emotions Revealed: Understanding Faces and Feeling* (London: Weidenfeld & Nicolson, 2003), 58; James A. Russel and José M. Fernández-Dols, "What Does a Facial Expression Mean?" in *The Psychology of Facial Expression*, ed. J. A. Russell and J. M. Fernández-Dols (Cambridge: Cambridge University Press, 1997), 10–13.
28 Carroll, *Literary Darwinism*, 114.
29 Brown, *Human Universals*, chap. 6.
30 Richard Samuels, "Massively Modular Minds: Evolutionary Psychology and Cognitive Architecture," in *Evolution and the Human Mind: Modularity, Language and Meta-Cognition*, ed. P. Carruthers and A. Chamberlain (Cambridge: Cambridge University Press, 2000), 13–16; Leda Cosmides and John Tooby, "Origins of Domain Specificity: The Evolution of Functional Organization," in *Mapping the Mind: Domain Specificity in Cognition and Culture*, ed. L. A. Hirschfeld and S. A. Gelman (Cambridge: Cambridge University Press, 1994), 91; Cartwright, *Evolution and Human Behaviour*, 193–4; Wilson, *On Human Nature*, 20; *The Social Conquest of Earth* (New York: Liveright Publishing Corporation, 2012), 255–86; Steven Mithen, *The Prehistory of the Mind: The Cognitive Origins of Art, Religion and Science* (London: Thames and Hudson, 1999), 67, 222–6.
31 Nick Lane, *The Vital Question: Energy, Evolution, and the Origins of Complex Life* (New York: Norton, 2015), 56–63, 80, 95, 293.
32 Richard Dawkins, *The Selfish Gene* (Oxford: Oxford University Press, 2006), esp. chap. 2.
33 Donald Symons, *The Evolution of Human Sexuality* (Oxford: Oxford University Press, 1979).
34 Symons, *The Evolution of Human Sexuality*, 22.
35 Piotr Sadowski, *Gender and Literature: A Systems Study* (Lanham–New York: University Press of America, 2001), 72–91.
36 Nancy Etcoff, *The Survival of the Prettiest: The Science of Beauty* (London: Abacus, 1999), 246.
37 Pinker, *How the Mind Works*, 484–5; Symons, *The Evolution of Human Sexuality*, 143.
38 Etcoff, *The Survival of the Prettiest*, 246.
39 Tammy T. Webb et al., "Perceptions of Body Figure Attractiveness among African American Male College Students," *Journal of African American Studies* 18, no. 1 (2014): 457–69.
40 R. D. Guthrie, "Evolution of Human Threat Display Organs," *Evolutionary Biology* 4 (1970): 259.
41 David Buss, *Evolutionary Psychology: The New Science of the Mind* (Boston, MA: Allyn and Bacon, 2004), 251.
42 Etcoff, *The Survival of the Prettiest*, 249.
43 James Joyce, *Ulysses* (London: Penguin Books, 1992), 613–14.
44 Sadowski, *Gender and Literature*, chap. 3; Geoffrey F. Miller, *The Mating Mind: How Sexual Choice Shaped the Evolution of Human Nature* (London: Vintage, 2001), chap. 7.
45 Susan Greenfield, *The Private Life of the Brain* (Harmondsworth: Penguin Books, 2001), 146; Arthur C. Guyton and John E. Hall, *Textbook of Medical Physiology* (Philadelphia: W. B. Saunders Company, 1996), 763; David Lewis-Williams, *The Mind in the Cave: Consciousness and the Origins of Art* (London: Thames and

Hudson, 2004), 190–1; Matthew Walker, *Why We Sleep: The New Science of Sleep and Dream* (London: Penguin Books, 2017), chap. 6.
46 Paul Rozin and A. Fallon, "A Perspective on Disgust," *Psychological Review* 94 (1987): 23–41.
47 Pinker, *How the Mind Works*, 378–83.
48 Elizabeth Cashdan, "A Sensitive Period for Learning about Food," *Human Nature* 5 (1994): 279–94.
49 Simona Stano, "Introduction: Semiotics of Food," *Semiotica* 211 (2016): 19–26.
50 William Shakespeare, *The Merchant of Venice*, ed. John Drakakis (London: Bloomsbury Publishing, 2010), 1.3.30–4.
51 Pascal Boyer, "Evolution of the Modern Mind and the Origins of Culture: Religious Concepts as a Limiting-Case," in *Evolution and the Human Mind: Modularity, Language and Meta-cognition*, ed. P. Carruthers and A. Chamberlain (Cambridge: Cambridge University Press, 2000), 108–9.
52 Mithen, *The Prehistory of the Mind*, 52–4.
53 Nobuyuki Kawai, *The Fear of Snakes: Evolutionary and Psychological Perspectives on Our Inner Fear* (Singapore: Springer Verlag, 2019), 59–71.
54 Brown, *Human Universals*, 115; Wilson, *On Human Nature*, 65; Pinker, *How the Mind Works*, 386–8.
55 Wilson, *The Social Conquest*, 57.
56 Dawkins, *The Selfish Gene*, 166–7.
57 Yuval Noah Harari, *21 Lessons for the 21st Century* (London: Vintage, 2018), 364.
58 C. Gilbert et al., "Energy Saving Process in Huddling Emperor Penguins: From Experiments to Theory," *Journal of Experimental Biology*, 211 (2008): 1–8.
59 Denise D. Cummins, "Social Norms and Other Minds: The Evolutionary Roots of Higher Cognition," in *The Evolution of Mind*, ed. D. D. Cummins and C. Allen (New York–Oxford: Oxford University Press, 1998), 33.
60 Cosmides and Tooby, "Cognitive Adaptations for Social Exchange," 206.
61 Mithen, *The Prehistory of the Mind*, 50–2; Kim Sterelny, "The Perverse Primate," in *Richard Dawkins: How a Scientist Changed the Way We Think*, ed. A. Grafen and M. Ridley (Oxford: Oxford University Press, 2006), 217; Wilson, *The Social Conquest*, 59.
62 Simon Baron-Cohen, *Mindblindness: An Essay on Autism and Theory of Mind* (Cambridge, MA: The MIT Press, 1997), chap. 1.
63 Cartwright, *Evolution of Human Behaviour: Darwinian Perspectives on Human Nature* (Basingstoke: Macmillan, 2000), 181–3.
64 Cartwright, *Evolution of Human Behaviour*, 154–5; Robert Trivers, *The Folly of Fools: The Logic of Deceit and Self-Deception in Human Life* (New York: Basic Books, 2013), chap. 1.
65 Dunbar, *The Human Story*, 43–6; Steven Mithen, *The Singing Neanderthals: The origins of Music, Language, Mind and Body* (London: Weidenfeld & Nicolson, 2005), 117.
66 Bickerton, *Language and Species*, 14.
67 Joyce, *Ulysses*, 797.
68 "Telemachus, Friend," in *100 Selected Stories*, ed. O. Henry (London: Wordsworth Classics, 1995), 99.
69 Richard Webster, *Why Was Freud Wrong: Sin, Science and Psychoanalysis* (London: HarperCollins Publishers, 1995), 480–1.

70 Pinker, *How the Mind Works*, 429–32; Cartwright, *Evolution of Human Behaviour*, 288.
71 The anthropologist Joseph Henrich sees the evolution of human societies from kin-based and tribal to individualistic and cosmopolitan as historically the main progressive trend in global civilization—the emergence of what he calls WEIRD people (Western, Educated, Industrialized, Rich, Democratic). See his *The Weirdest People in the World: How the West Became Psychologically Peculiar and Particularly Prosperous* (London: Penguin Books, 2021).
72 Steven Pinker, *The Better Angels of Our Nature: A History of Violence and Humanity* (London: Penguin Books, 2011), 38–48.
73 Martin Daly and Margo Wilson, *Homicide* (New York: Aldine De Gruyter, 1988), 275; Pinker, *The Blank Slate*, 315, 319; *The Better Angels*, 76–7.
74 Samuels, "Massively Modular Minds."
75 Plotkin, *The Nature of Knowledge*, 228–9, 235.
76 Roger N. Shepard, "The Genetic Basis of Human Scientific Knowledge," in *Characterizing Human Psychological Adaptations*, ed. G. R. Bock and G. Cardew (Chichester: John Wiley & Sons, 1997), 24.
77 Barrow, *The Artful Universe*, chaps. 2–4.
78 Barrow, *The Artful Universe*, vii, 117.
79 Stephen Kaplan, "Environmental Preference in a Knowledge-Seeking, Knowledge-Using Organism," in *The Adapted Mind*, ed. J. H. Barkow, L. Cosmides and J. Tooby (New York–Oxford: Oxford University Press, 1992), 588, 594; Wilson, *The Social Conquest*, 271–3.
80 Plotkin, *The Nature of Knowledge*, 103.
81 Eve V. Clark, *The Lexicon in Acquisition* (Cambridge: Cambridge University Press, 1993), 46.
82 Colin Allen and Eric Saidel, "The Evolution of Reference," in *The Evolution of Mind*, ed. D. D. Cummins and C. Allen (New York–Oxford: Oxford University Press, 1998), 195–6.
83 J-M. Chauvet and E. B. Deschamps, *Chauvet Cave: The Discovery of the World's Oldest Paintings* (London: Thames and Hudson, 1996).
84 Richard L. Gregory, *Eye and Brain: The Psychology of Seeing* (1966; Oxford: Oxford University Press, 1998), 244.
85 Oscar Wilde, *Complete Works* (Glasgow: HarperCollins Publishers, 2003), 1135.
86 Ralph Waldo Emerson, *Nature and Selected Essays* (New York: Penguin Books, 1982), 53.
87 Ellen Dissanayake, *What Is Art For?* (Seattle: University of Washington Press, 1991), 114.
88 Barrow, *The Artful Universe*, chap. 2.
89 Brown, *Human Universals*, 115–16; Wilson, *On Human Nature*, 2–3.
90 Barrow, *The Artful Universe*, 91–4.
91 Jay Appleton, *The Poetry of Habitat* (University of Hull, England: Department of Geography, 1978), 3–4; Kaplan, "Environmental Preference," 585–95.
92 Wilson, *The Social Conquest*.
93 Carroll, *Literary Darwinism*, 128, 164, 198.
94 Donald, *Origins of the Modern Mind*, 258.
95 Matthew Alper, *The "God" Part of the Brain: A Scientific Interpretation of Human Spirituality and God* (Naperville, IL: Sourcebooks, Inc., 2006).
96 Wilson, *On Human Nature*, 197; "The Meaning of Human Existence," in *Darwin's Bridge: Uniting the Humanities & Sciences*, ed. Joseph Carroll, Dan P. McAdams and Edward O. Wilson (Oxford: Oxford University Press, 2016), 3–10.

Chapter 2

1. Em Griffin et al., ed., *A First Look at Communication Theory* (New York: McGraw-Hill Education, 2019), 65–6.
2. Sebeok, *An Introduction to Semiotics*, 18.
3. Terrence W. Deacon, "Shannon–Boltzmann–Darwin: Redefining Information," Parts I and II, *Cognitive Semiotics* (September 2007).
4. Plotkin, *The Nature of Knowledge*, 103.
5. John Fiske, *Introduction to Communication Studies* (London: Routledge, 2001), 8, 18.
6. Judith Degen et al., "When Redundancy Is Useful: A Bayesian Approach to 'Over-Informative' Referring Expressions," *Psychological Review* 127, no. 4 (2020): 591–621.
7. James Frazer, *The Golden Bough: A Study in Magic and Religion* (New York: Simon & Schuster, 1996), III.3.
8. Joyce, *Ulysses*, 45.
9. Peter Buse, *The Camera Does the Rest: How Polaroid Changed Photography* (Chicago: The University of Chicago Press, 2016), esp. chaps. 1, 4.
10. Francis Wheen, *Television: A History* (London: Century Publishing, 1985), 12.
11. Peirce, *Collected Papers*, 143; Sebeok, *Contributions to the Doctrine of Signs*, 42; *An Introduction to Semiotics*, 24, 65, 72; Sadowski, *From Interaction to Symbol*, 34–6; Tony Jappy, *Introduction to Peircean Visual Semiotics* (London: Bloomsbury Academic, 2013), 84–90.
12. Wilson, *Consilience*, 55; Plotkin, *The Nature of Knowledge*, 20, 48.
13. Dunbar, *The Trouble with Science*, 121.
14. Peter Marler, "The Evolution of Communication," in *How Animals Communicate*, ed. T. A. Sebeok (Bloomington: Indiana University Press, 1977), 49, 51.
15. Gregory, *Eye and Brain*, 200.
16. R. H. Bremmer, ed., *The Fyve Wyttes: A Late Middle English Devotional Treatise* (Amsterdam: Rodopi, 1987), 16.
17. Edward T. Hall, *The Hidden Dimension: Man's Use of Space in Public and Private* (London: The Bodley Head, 1966), 40.
18. Wilson, *The Social Conquest*, 268; Workman and Reader, *Evolutionary Psychology*, 246.
19. Lauralee Sherwood, *Human Physiology: From Cells to Systems* (London: Wadsworth Publishing Company, 1997), 168; Gregory, *Eye and Brain*, 24–5, 84, 121–6.
20. Wilson, *Consilience*, 49; Gregory, *Eye and Brain*, 20–1.
21. Thomas A. Sebeok, "Discussion of Communication Process," in *Social Communication among Primates*, ed. S. A. Altmann (Chicago: The University of Chicago Press, 1967), 367.
22. Harvey R. Schiffman, *Sensation and Perception: An Integrated Approach* (New York: John Wiley & Sons, 1996), 195; Allen and Saidel, "The Evolution of Reference," 195–6.
23. Hauser, *The Evolution of Communication*, 153–4; Dawkins, *The Blind Watchmaker*, 23–37.
24. Workman and Reader, *Evolutionary Psychology*, 253.
25. Sebeok, "Discussion of Communication Process," 368.
26. Ekman, *Emotions Revealed*, 59–61; Schiffman, *Sensation and Perception*, 294; Wilson, *Consilience*, 166.
27. Wilson, *The Social Conquest*, 269.

28 Sherwood, *Human Physiology*, 194; Marler, "The Evolution of Communication," 45–6.
29 Wilson, *On Human Nature*, 62.
30 Hall, *The Hidden Dimension*, 46; Sebeok, "Discussion of Communication Process," 367.
31 Margret Schleidt, "Personal Odor and Nonverbal Communication," *Ethology and Sociobiology* 1, no. 3 (September 1980): 225–31.
32 Diane Ackerman, *A Natural History of the Senses* (London: Vintage, 1991), 9.
33 Schiffman, *Sensation and Perception*, 481, 484.
34 Etcoff, *The Survival of the Prettiest*, 252–3.
35 J.-K. Huysmans, *Against Nature*, trans. Robert Baldick (London: Penguin Books, 1959), 119.
36 Rachel S. Herz, "Influences of Odors on Mood and Affective Cognition," in *Olfaction, Taste, and Cognition*, ed. Catherine Rouby (Cambridge: Cambridge University Press, 2002), 160–77.
37 Marler, "The Evolution of Communication," 45.
38 Schiffman, *Sensation and Perception*, 449–51; Wilson, *Consilience*, 167.
39 Hall, *The Hidden Dimension*, 78.
40 Frank A. Geldard, "Tactile Communication," in *How Animals Communicate*, ed. T. A. Sebeok (Bloomington–London: Indiana University Press, 1977), 214; Sebeok, "Discussion of Communication Process," 368.
41 Gregory, *Eye and Brain*, 30; Schiffman, *Sensation and Perception*, 413.
42 Geldard, "Tactile Communication," 211–14; Donald, *Origins of the Modern Mind*, 188; William Orr Dingwall, "The Evolution of Human Communication," *Studies in Neurolinguistics* 4 (1979): 1–95; Etcoff, *The Survival of the Prettiest*, 96.
43 Derek Denton, *The Primordial Emotions: The Dawning of Consciousness* (Oxford: Oxford University Press, 2005), 102; Pascal Boyer, *The Naturalness of Religious Ideas: A Cognitive Theory of Religions* (Berkeley: University of California Press, 1994), 62.
44 Ernst H. Gombrich, *Art and Illusion: A Study in the Psychology of Pictorial Representation* (1960; London: Phaidon Press, 2003), 86.
45 Dawkins, *The Selfish Gene*, 64–5.
46 Dawkins, *The Selfish Gene*, 31; Trivers, *The Folly of Fools*, chap. 2.
47 Sebeok, *An Introduction to Semiotics*, 30, 84.
48 Hauser, *The Evolution of Communication*, 497.
49 Mithen, *The Prehistory of the Mind*, 77.
50 Desmond Morris, *The Biology of Art: A Study of the Picture-Making Behaviour of the Great Apes and Its Relationship to Human Art* (London: Methuen, 1962), 141.
51 Hauser, *The Evolution of Communication*, 651; Workman and Reader, *Evolutionary Psychology*, 358.
52 William Shakespeare, *Romeo and Juliet*, ed. René Weis (London: Bloomsbury, 2012), 2.2.43–4.
53 Saussure, *Course in General Linguistics*, 102.
54 Peirce, *Collected Papers*, 143.
55 Saussure, *Course in General Linguistics*, 69, 113.
56 Saussure, *Course in General Linguistics*, 111.
57 Raymond Tallis, *Theorrhoea and after* (London: Macmillan Press, 1999), 274; Saussure, *Course in General Linguistics*, 117.
58 Earl A. Anderson, *A Grammar of Iconism* (Madison: Fairleigh Dickinson University Press, 1998), 16, 67; Klass Willems and Ludovic De Cuypere, ed., *Naturalness and Iconicity in Language* (Amsterdam: John Benjamins Publishing, 2009); L. Hinton, et al., ed, *Sound Symbolism* (Cambridge: Cambridge University Press, 1994).

Chapter 3

1. Marian Mazur, *Jakościowa Teoria Informacji* [A Qualitative Theory of Information] (Warsaw: Wydawnictwa Naukowo-Techniczne, 1970), 35; Sadowski, *From Interaction to Symbol*, 41.
2. M. H. Abrams, "The Deconstructive Angel," *Critical Inquiry* 3 (1977): 425–38.
3. Wolfgang Iser, *The Act of Reading: A Theory of Aesthetic Response* (London: Routledge & Kegan Paul, 1978), 107, 115.
4. Ranulph Glanville, "Communication without Coding: Cybernetics, Meaning and Language (How Language, Becoming a System, Betrays Itself)," *Modern Language Notes* 111, no. 3 (April 1996), 444.
5. David Porush, *The Soft Machine: Cybernetic Fiction* (New York: Methuen, 1985), 64–5.
6. E. D. Hirsch Jr., *Validity in Interpretation* (New Haven: Yale University Press, 1967), 57, 62; *The Aims of Interpretation* (Chicago: The University of Chicago Press, 1976), 79.
7. Abrams, "The Deconstructive Angel," 429.
8. Qtd. in *Sokal Hoax: The Sham That Shook the Academy* (Lincoln: University of Nebraska Press, 2000), 91.
9. Trivers, *The Folly of Fools*, chap. 2; Hauser, *The Evolution of Communication*, 28.
10. Terrence Deacon, *The Symbolic Species: The Co-Evolution of Language and the Human Brain* (London: Allen Lane, 1997), 383.
11. Hauser, *The Evolution of Communication*, 586; Bickerton, *Language and Species*, 14.
12. Cartwright, *Evolution and Human Behaviour*, 180; Mithen, *The Prehistory of the Mind*, 83.
13. Piotr Sadowski, "Control, Information, and Literary Meaning: A Systems Model of Literature as Communication," *European Journal of English Studies* 5, no. 3 (2001): 293–5; *From Interaction to Symbol*, 57–9.
14. Walker, *Why We Sleep*, chap. 11; Wilson, *Consilience*, 81–2.
15. Peter D. Slade and Richard P. Bentall, *Sensory Deception: Scientific Analysis of Hallucinations* (London: Croom Helm, 1998), 14, 23, 32–3.
16. *Oxford Companion to Philosophy*, 666.
17. Wilde, *Complete Works*, 1244.
18. Steven Pinker, *Rationality: What It Is, Why It Seems Scarce, Why It Matters* (London: Allen Lane, 2021), 300–1.
19. Herman Hesse, *Steppenwolf* (London: Penguin Books, 1965), 134–5.
20. Bickerton, *Language and Species*, 58, 90.
21. Popper, *Objective Knowledge*, 74, 106, 119, 122, 155.
22. Sebeok, *Contributions to the Doctrine of Signs*, 42; *An Introduction to Semiotics*, 24.
23. Olivier Van Aken, "Plants Are 'in Touch' with the World around Them," https://www.news.uwa.edu.au/archive/201605258690/international/plants-are-touch-world-around-them
24. David F. Sherry and Dan L. Schacter, "The Evolution of Multiple Memory Systems," *Psychological Review* 94, no. 4 (1987): 439–54.
25. Pinker, *How the Mind Works*, 124; Schiffman, *Sensation and Perception*, 492; Merlin Donald, *A Mind so Rare: The Evolution of Human Consciousness* (New York: W. W. Norton & Company, 2001), 193, 196, 201.
26. Donald, *Origins of the Modern Mind*, 149, 160.

27 Howard Eichenbaum and Neal J. Cohen, *From Conditioning to Conscious Recollection: Memory Systems of the Brain* (Oxford: Oxford University Press, 2001), 471.
28 Mithen, *The Prehistory of the Mind*, 79; Eichenbaum and Cohen, *From Conditioning to Conscious Recollection*, 471.
29 Dunbar, *The Human Story*, 39; Mithen, *The Prehistory of the Mind*, 11.
30 Brown, *Human Universals*, 95.
31 Nicholas Humphrey, *The Mind Made Flesh: Essays from the Frontiers of Psychology and Evolution* (Oxford: Oxford University Press, 2002), 182.
32 Mithen, *The Prehistory of the Mind*, 74, 76; Dissanayake, *What Is Art for?* 113.
33 Wilson, *The Social Conquest*, 214, 223–4.
34 Dunbar, *The Human Story*, 65.
35 John C. Eccles, *Evolution of the Brain: Creation of the Self* (London: Routledge, 1989), 229.
36 Robert L. Solso, *The Psychology of Art and the Evolution of the Conscious Brain* (Cambridge, MA: The MIT Press, 2003), 27, 31; Richard F. Thompson and Stephen A. Madigen, *Memory: The Key to Consciousness* (Washington, DC: Joseph Henry Press, 2005), v.
37 Immanuel Kant, *Critique of Pure Reason*, trans. J. M. D. Meiklejohn (London: J. M. Dent, 1993), 54–8.
38 Magee, *Confessions of a Philosopher*, 315–16.
39 Richard Dawkins, *Unweaving the Rainbow: Science, Delusion and the Appetite for Wonder* (London: Penguin Books, 2006), 59, 278.
40 Peter Medawar and Jean Medawar, *The Life Science: Current Ideas of Biology* (London: Wildwood House, 1977), 171.
41 Christoph Hoerl and Teresa McCormack, "Perspectives on Time and Memory: An Introduction," in *Time and Memory: Issues in Philosophy and Psychology*, ed. C. Hoerl and T. McCormack (Oxford: Clarendon Press, 2001), 3; Steven Mithen, "Symbolism and the Supernatural," in *The Evolution of Culture*, ed. R. Dunbar, C. Knight, and C. Power (Edinburgh: Edinburgh University Press, 1999), 147–72.
42 Carl Gustav Jung, *Aspects of the Feminine* (London: Routledge & Kegan Paul, 1982).
43 Steven Pinker, *Enlightenment Now: The Case for Reason, Science, Humanism and Progress* (London: Allen Lane, 2018).
44 Trivers, *The Folly of Fools*, chaps. 1, 3.
45 Dunbar, *The Trouble with Science*, 132.
46 Dawkins, *The God Delusion*, 166.
47 Mithen, *The Prehistory of the Mind*, 148–9, 153, 174, 177.
48 Boyer, *The Naturalness of Religious Ideas*, 48, 59, 123; "Evolution of the Modern Mind," 95–8, 100–1.
49 Slade and Bentall, *Sensory Deception*, 23, 32–3.
50 Pinker, *Rationality*, chap. 10.
51 Barrow, *The Artful Universe*, 44–5.
52 Mithen, *The Prehistory of the Mind*, 160.
53 Dan Sperber, "Anthropology and Psychology: Towards an Epidemiology of Representations," *Man*, 20, no. 1 (March 1985): 73–6.
54 Dawkins, *The God Delusion*, 140–3, 166, 172–9; Joseph Lopreato, *Human Nature and Biocultural Evolution* (Boston: Allen & Unwin, 1984), 226–7.
55 Randolph M. Nesse and Alan T. Lloyd, "The Evolution of Psychodynamic Mechanisms," in *The Adapted Mind*, ed. J. H. Barkow et al. (New York–Oxford: Oxford University Press, 1992), 603–11.

56 Trivers, *The Folly of Fools*, chap. 7; Badcock, *Evolutionary Psychology*, 132–4.
57 Chris Knight, Robin Dunbar, and Camilla Power, "An Evolutionary Approach to Human Culture," in *The Evolution of Culture: An Interdisciplinary View*, ed. R. Dunbar et al. (Edinburgh: Edinburgh University Press, 1996), 6.
58 Raymond Tallis, *Enemies of Hope: A Critique of Contemporary Pessimism, Irrationalism, Anti-Humanism and Counter-Enlightenment* (London: Macmillan Press, 1999), 71.
59 Carl Sagan, *The Demon-Haunted World: Science as a Candle in the Dark* (London: Headline Book Publishing, 1997), 230.
60 Harari, *21 Lessons*, 281.
61 Wilson, *On Human Nature*, 176.
62 Trivers, *The Folly of Fools*, 134–7.
63 Dawkins, *The Selfish Gene*, 19, 24.
64 David P. Barash, "What the Whale Wondered: Evolution, Existentialism, and the Search for 'Meaning,'" in *Richard Dawkins: How a Scientist Changed the Way We Think*, ed. A. Grafen and M. Ridley (Oxford: Oxford University Press, 2006), 256.
65 Darrin McMahon, *The Pursuit of Happiness: A History from the Greeks to the Present* (London: Penguin Books, 2006), esp. chap 8; Wilson, "The Meaning of Human Existence."

Chapter 4

1 Marcel Danesi, *The Semiotics of Emoji: The Rise of Visual Language in the Age of the Internet* (London: Bloomsbury Academic, 2016).
2 Solso, *The Psychology of Art*, 136–8, 143; Hauser, *The Evolution of Communication*, 246, 265, 357, 361.
3 Charles Darwin, *The Expression of the Emotions in Man and Animals* (London: Penguin Books, 2009).
4 Wilson, *On Human Nature*, 23; Pinker, *How the Mind Works*, 198–9, 272–4.
5 Charles A. Nelson and Michelle de Haan, "A Neurobehavioral Approach to the Recognition of Facial Expressions in Infancy," in *The Psychology of Facial Expression*, ed. J. A. Russell and J. M. Fernández-Dols (Cambridge: Cambridge University Press, 1997), 183; Workman and Reader, *Evolutionary Psychology*, 122–3; Etcoff, *Survival of the Prettiest*, 34.
6 Ekman and Friesen, *Unmasking the Face*, 21–33; J. M. Fernández-Dols and M. A. Ruiz-Belda, "Spontaneous Facial Behavior during Intense Emotional Episodes: Artistic Truth and Optical Truth," in *The Psychology of Facial Expression*, ed. J. A. Russell and J. M. Fernández-Dols (Cambridge: Cambridge University Press, 1997), 257.
7 Craig A. Smith and Heather S. Scott, "A Componential Approach to the Meaning of Facial Expressions," in *The Psychology of Facial Expression*, ed. J. A. Russell and J. M. Fernández-Dols (Cambridge: Cambridge University Press, 1997), 229.
8 Simon Baron-Cohen, *The Essential Difference: Men, Women and the Extreme Male Brain* (London: Penguin Books, 2003), 34.
9 Wilson, *On Human Nature*, 59, 124; *Consilience*, 168.
10 Dale Purves and R. Beau Lotto, *Why We See What We Do: An Empirical Theory of Vision* (Oxford: Sinauer Associates, 2003), 85.
11 Etcoff, *Survival of the Prettiest*, 36–7.

12 Kathleen R. Gibson, "Overlapping Neural Control of Language, Gesture and Tool-Use," in *Tools, Language and Cognition in Human Evolution*, ed. K. R. Gibson and T. Ingold (Cambridge: Cambridge University Press, 1993), 187–92.
13 Adam Kendon, "Human Gesture," in *Tools, Language and Cognition in Human Evolution*, ed. K. R. Gibson and T. Ingold (Cambridge: Cambridge University Press, 1993), 48–53.
14 Dingwall, "The Evolution of Human Communication."
15 Robert R. Provine, "Yawns, Laughs, Smiles, Tickles, and Talking: Naturalistic and Laboratory Studies of Facial Action and Social Communication," in *The Psychology of Facial Expression*, ed. J. A. Russell and J. M. Fernández-Dols (Cambridge: Cambridge University Press, 1997), 170–3.
16 Dissanayake, *What Is Art For?*, 62.
17 Etcoff, *Survival of the Prettiest*, 104–5.
18 Paul Bouissac, *The Semiotics of Clowns and Clowning: Rituals of Transgression and the Theory of Laughter* (London: Bloomsbury Academic, 2015), chap. 1.
19 Hans Silvester, *Natural Fashion: Tribal Decoration from Africa* (London: Thames and Hudson, 2009).
20 Dissanayake, *What Is Art for?*, 55–6; Kendon, "Human Gesture," 48–53.
21 Victoria Ebin, *The Body Decorated* (London: Thames and Hudson, 1979), 25.
22 Ebin, *The Body Decorated*, 47, 53, 56.
23 Chris William Martin, *The Social Semiotics of Tattoos: Skin and Self* (London: Bloomsbury Academic, 2020), esp. chaps. 4–6.
24 Malcolm Barnard, *Fashion as Communication* (New York: Routledge, 2002), esp. chap. 4.
25 Etcoff, *Survival of the Prettiest*, 222.
26 Camilla Power, "'Beauty Magic': The Origins of Art," in *The Evolution of Culture*, ed. R. Dunbar, C. Knight and C. Power (Edinburgh: Edinburgh University Press, 1999), 93–109.
27 Camilla Power, "Sexual Selection Models for the Emergence of Symbolic Communication: Why They Should Be Reversed," in *The Cradle of Language*, ed. Rudolf Botha and Chris Knight (Oxford: Oxford University Press, 2009), 265.
28 Mithen, *The Prehistory of the Mind*, 27; Ian Davidson, "The Archaeological Evidence of Language Origins: States of Art," in *Language Evolution*, ed. M. H. Christiansen and S. Kirby (Oxford: Oxford University Press, 2003), 154.
29 Paul Bahn and Jean Vertut, *Journey through the Ice Age* (Berkeley: University of California Press, 1999), 99.
30 Mithen, *The Singing Neanderthals*, 251; Etcoff, *Survival of the Prettiest*, 113.
31 Daniel Schacter, *The Seven Sins of Memory: How the Mind Forgets and Remembers* (New York: Houghton Mifflin, 2001).
32 Plotkin, *The Nature of Knowledge*, 254.
33 Raymond A. Dart, "The Waterworn Australopithecine Pebble of Many Faces from Makapansgat," *South African Journal of Science* 70, no. 6 (June 1974): 167.
34 Alexander Marshack, "The Berekhat Ram Figurine: A Late Acheulian Carving from the Middle East," *Antiquity* 71 (1997): 327–37.
35 Bahn and Vertut, *Journey through the Ice Age*, 84.
36 Mithen, *The Prehistory of the Mind*, 170–2; Bahn and Vertut, *Journey through the Ice Age*, 135, 140–1.
37 Chauvet and Deschamps, *Chauvet Cave*, 104–10, 114.
38 André Leroi-Gourhan, *The Art of Prehistoric Man in Western Europe* (London: Thames and Hudson, 1968), 113; Lewis-Williams, *The Mind in the Cave*, 65.

39 Deacon, *The Symbolic Species*, 374.
40 Steven Mithen, "Mind, Brain and Material Culture," in *Evolution and the Human Mind: Modularity, Language and Meta-cognition*, ed. P. Carruthers and A. Chamberlain (Cambridge: Cambridge University Press, 2009), 217.
41 Kant, *Critique of Pure Reason*, 213 (A255/B311).
42 Gertrude Stein, *Geography and Plays* (Boston: The Four Seas Company, 1922), 187.
43 William Vaughan, *Friedrich* (New York: Phaidon Press, 2004), 43.
44 Frazer, *The Golden Bough*, 15–44 (III.2).
45 Frazer, *The Golden Bough*, 44.
46 Kendall L. Walton, "Film, Photography, and Transparency," in *The Philosophy of Film: Introductory Text and Readings*, ed. T. E. Wartenberg and A. Curran (Oxford: Blackwell, 2005), 70; Asa Briggs and Peter Burke, *A Social History of the Media: From Gutenberg to the Internet* (Cambridge: Polity Press, 2005), 133.
47 Peirce, *Collected Papers*, 159.
48 Alan Trachtenberg, ed., *Classic Essays on Photography* (New Haven, CT: Leete's Island Books, 1980), 38.
49 André Bazin, "Cinematic Realism," in *The Philosophy of Film: Introductory Text and Readings*, ed. T. E. Wartenberg and A. Curran (Oxford: Blackwell, 2005), 59.
50 Susan Sontag, *On Photography* (London: Allen Lane, 1978), 154; Rudolf Arnheim, "On the Nature of Photography," *Critical Inquiry* 1, no. 1 (September 1974): 156.
51 Bazin, "Cinematic Realism," 60.
52 Ian Jarvie, *Philosophy of the Film: Epistemology, Ontology, Aesthetics* (New York: Routledge & Kegan Paul, 1987), 50.
53 Wanda Strauven, "Early Cinema's Touch(able) Screens: From Uncle Josh to Ali Barbouyou," *European Journal of Media Studies* 1, no. 2 (Autumn 2012): 155–76.
54 Frazer, *The Golden Bough*, 12.
55 Dawkins, *Unweaving the Rainbow*, 181.
56 Frazer, *The Golden Bough*, 18.
57 Ovid, *Metamorphoses*, trans. Arthur Golding (London: Penguin, 2002), 303 (Bk. X, ll. 261–326).
58 Franklin R. Rogers and Mary Ann Rogers, *Painting and Poetry: Form, Metaphor, and the Language of Literature* (Lewisburg, Pa.: Bucknell University Press, 1986), 105.
59 Francis Steen, "A Cognitive Account of Aesthetics," in *The Artful Mind: Cognitive Science and the Riddle of Human Creativity*, ed. Mark Turner (Oxford: Oxford University Press, 2006), 66–7.
60 Pliny the Elder, *Natural History* (London: Penguin Books, 1991), 14, 187.
61 Leon Battista Alberti, *On Painting*, trans. John R. Spencer (New Haven: Yale University Press, 1966), 61, 64; Victor Ieronim Stoichita, *A Short History of the Shadow* (London: Reaktion, 1997), 38–41.
62 Piotr Sadowski, "In the Kingdom of Shadows: Towards a Cognitive Definition of Photographic Media," in *Operationalizing Iconicity*, ed. P. Perniss, O. Fischer, and C. Ljungberg (Amsterdam: John Benjamins Publishing Company, 2020), 237.
63 Perice, *Collected Papers*, 143; Sadowski, *From Interaction to Symbol*, 36–8; Jappy, *Introduction to Peircean Visual Semiotics*, 79–84.
64 Anderson, *A Grammar of Iconism*.
65 Piotr Sadowski, "The Iconic Indexicality of Photography," in *Semblance and Signification*, ed. P. Michelucci, O. Fischer and C. Ljungberg (Amsterdam: John Benjamins Publishing, 2011), 355–68.
66 Peirce, *Collected Papers*, 143.

67 Peirce, *Collected Papers*, 145; Noël Carroll, "Towards an Ontology of the Moving Image," in *Philosophy and Film*, ed. C. A. Freeland and T. E. Wartenberg (New York: Routledge, 1995), 69.
68 Chauvet & Deschamps, *Chauvet Cave*, 79.
69 Leroi-Gourhan, *The Art of Prehistoric Man*, 148.
70 J. G. Links, *Canaletto* (London: Phaidon Press, 2005), 118.
71 *The Bible. Authorized Version* (Swindon: Bible Society, ND).
72 Kalman P. Bland, *The Artless Jew: Medieval and Modern Affirmations and Denials of the Visual* (Princeton: Princeton University Press, 2000), 3, 7.
73 Ex. 20.3–6, 20; 34.17; Lev. 19.4; 26.1; and Deut. 4.15–18.
74 Moshe Halbertal and Avishoi Margalit, *Idolatry* (Cambridge, MA: Harvard University Press, 1992), 45, 260–1.
75 Halbertal and Margalit, *Idolatry*, 40.
76 Pinker, *The Stuff of Thought*, 19.
77 Blaise Pascal, *Pensées* (Harmondsworth: Penguin Books, 1985), 189; Henry James, *Short Stories* (New York: Random House, 1945), 194.
78 Wilde, *Complete Works*, 1135.
79 Denis Dutton, *The Art Instinct: Beauty, Pleasure, and Human Evolution* (Oxford: Oxford University Press, 2009), 105–6.
80 Miller, *The Mating Mind*, esp. chap. 3

Chapter 5

1 Pinker, *The Language Instinct*, 80–1.
2 Dingwall, "The Evolution of Human Communication," 21.
3 Lieberman, *The Biology and Evolution of Language*, 17; Steven Pinker, *Words and Rules: The Ingredients of Language* (London: Phoenix, 2001), 3; Hauser, *The Evolution of Communication*, 244; Pinker, *The Language Instinct*, 168; Sverker Johansson, *Origins of Language: Constraints on Hypotheses* (Amsterdam: John Benjamins Publishing Company, 2006), 77.
4 Steven Pinker and Paul Bloom, "Natural Language and Natural Selection," in *The Adapted Mind*, ed. J. H. Barkow, L. Cosmides and J. Tooby (New York–Oxford: Oxford University Press, 1992), 465–70; Daniel Nettle, "Language Variation and the Evolution of Societies," in *The Evolution of Culture*, ed. R. Dunbar, C. Knight, and C. Power (Edinburgh: Edinburgh University Press, 1999), 214, 219–24.
5 Bickerton, *Language and Species*, 8, 15.
6 Johansson, *Origins of Language*, 7.
7 Pinker, *The Language Instinct*, 365; "Language as an Adaptation to the Cognitive Niche," in *Language Evolution*, ed. M. H. Christiansen and S. Kirby (Oxford: Oxford University Press, 2003), 32; Robin Dunbar, "The Origin and Subsequent Evolution of Language," in *Language Evolution*, ed. M. H. Christiansen and S. Kirby, 226; Philip Lieberman, *Toward an Evolutionary Biology of Language* (Cambridge, MA: Harvard University Press, 2006), esp. chap 3.
8 Clark, *The Lexicon in Acquisition*, 13.
9 Pinker, *The Language Instinct*, 389; John Hurrell Crook, *The Evolution of Human Consciousness* (Oxford: Clarendon Press, 1980), 148.
10 Andrew Lock, "Human Language Development and Object Manipulation: Their Relation in Ontogeny and Its Possible Relevance for Phylogenetic Questions,"

in *Tools, Language and Cognition in Human Evolution*, ed. K. R. Gibson and T. Ingold (Cambridge: Cambridge University Press, 1993), 279–86.
11   Pinker, *The Language Instinct*, 388, 404.
12   Robin Dunbar, *Gossip, and Grooming and the Evolution of Language* (London: Faber and Faber, 1996), 4–5; *The Human Story*, 112.
13   Jerome H. Barkow, "Beneath New Culture Is Old Psychology: Gossip and Social Stratification," in *The Adapted Mind*, ed. J. H. Barkow et al. (New York–Oxford: Oxford University Press, 1992), 627–8.
14   Malcolm Coulthard, "Author Identification, Idiolect, and Linguistic Uniqueness," *Applied Linguistics* 25, no. 4 (2004): 431–47; Barbara Johnstone, "The Individual Voice in Language," *Annual Review of Anthropology* 29 (October 2000): 405–24.
15   Hinton et al., ed., *Sound Symbolism*, 2.
16   Chris Knight, "Sex and Language as Pretend-Play," in *The Evolution of Culture*, ed. R. Dunbar et al., 229.
17   Hauser, *The Evolution of Communication*, 196.
18   David Crystal, *The Cambridge Encyclopedia of the English Language* (Cambridge: Cambridge University Press, 1995), 250; Aitchison, *The Seeds of Speech*, 13.
19   Edward Stankiewicz, "Problems of Emotive Language," in *Approaches to Semiotics: Cultural Anthropology, Education, Linguistics, Psychiatry, Psychology*, ed. T. A. Sebeok, A. S. Hayes, and M. C. Bateson (The Hague: Mouton & Co, 1972), 244–5.
20   Roman Jakobson and Linda R. Waugh, *The Sound Shape of Language* (Berlin: Mouton de Gruyter, 1987), 187.
21   Stankiewicz, "Problems of Emotive Language," 249.
22   Anderson, *A Grammar of Iconism*, 124; Piotr Sadowski, "The Sound as an Echo to the Sense: The Iconicity of English gl- words," in *The Motivated Sign*, ed. O. Fischer and M. Nänny (Amsterdam: John Benjamins Publishing Company, 2001), 69–88.
23   Olga Fischer, "Cognitive Iconic Grounding of Reduplication in Language," in *Semblance and Signification*, ed. P. Michelucci, O. Fischer and C. Ljungberg (Amsterdam–Philadelphia: John Benjamins Publishing Company, 2011), 55–82.
24   Réka Benczes, *Rhyme over Reason: Phonological Motivation in English* (Cambridge: Cambridge University Press, 2019), esp. chaps 3, 4; Hinton et al., eds., *Sound Symbolism*, 3.
25   Saussure, *Course in General Linguistics*, 56.
26   Anderson, *A Grammar of Iconism*, 130.
27   Anderson, *A Grammar of Iconism*, 94, 167–90, 101, 191, 218.
28   Benczes, *Rhyme over Reason*, chap. 3.
29   Hinton et al., eds., *Sound Symbolism*, 4.
30   Anderson, *A Grammar of Iconism*, 203; Mithen, *The Singing Neanderthals*, 170.
31   Otto Jespersen, *Language: Its Nature, Development and Origin* (London: Allen & Unwin, 1922), 400.
32   David Raid, *Sound Symbolism* (Edinburgh: T. & A. Constable, 1967), 24; Crystal, *The Cambridge Encyclopedia*, 251.
33   Jakobson and Waugh, *The Sound Shape of Language*, 188–92; Anderson, *A Grammar of Iconism*, 101, 191, 218.
34   Anderson, *A Grammar of Iconism*, esp. chap. 8.
35   Anderson, *A Grammar of Iconism*, 267; Sadowski, *From Interaction to Symbol*, 221.
36   Russell S. Tomlin, *Basic Word Order: Functional Principles* (London: Croom Helm, 1986); Eve V. Clark and Herbert H. Clark, "Universals, Relativity, and Language Processing," in *Universals of Human Language*, ed. J. H. Greenberg (Stanford, CA: Stanford University Press, 1978), 247–54.

37 William Shakespeare, *Othello*, ed. E. A. J. Honigmann (Walton-on-Thames: Thomas Nelson & Sons, 1997), 5.2.345–6.
38 Boyer, *The Naturalness of Religious Ideas*, 53.
39 Steven Fine, *The Menorah: From the Bible to Modern Israel* (Cambridge, MA: Harvard University Press, 2016).
40 Gershom G. Scholem, *On the Kabbalah and Its Symbolism* (London: Routledge and Kegan Paul, 1965), 39.
41 Stanislas Klossowski de Rola, *Alchemy: The Secret Art* (London: Thames and Hudson, 2013), 10.
42 *Sir Gawain and the Green Knight*, trans. Bernard O'Donoghue (London: Penguin Classics, 2006), ll. 653–61.
43 Jean Laplanche and Jean-Bertrand Pontalis, *The Language of Psychoanalysis* (New York: W. W. Norton & Company, 1973).
44 Raymond W. Gibbs Jr., "What Do Idioms Really Mean?" *Journal of Memory and Language* 31, no. 4 (August 1992): 485–506.
45 "Promotor Fidei," in *The Catholic Encyclopedia*, ed. Charles G. Herbermann (New York: Robert Appleton Company, 1911).
46 Florian Coulmas, *Writing Systems: An Introduction to Their Linguistic Analysis* (Cambridge: Cambridge University Press, 2003), 19.
47 Roy Harris, *The Origin of Writing* (London: Duckworth, 1986), 136–7.
48 Coulmas, *Writing Systems*, 31, 33.
49 Harris, *The Origin of Writing*, 24; Walter J. Ong, *Orality and Literacy: The Technologizing of the Word* (London: Routledge, 2004), 81, 84.
50 Donald, *Origins of the Modern Mind*, 279; Harris, *The Origin of Writing*, 15.
51 Ong, *Orality and Literacy*, 40, 81.
52 Harris, *The Origin of Writing*, 27.
53 Ong, *Orality and Literacy*, 40, 81.
54 Coulmas, *Writing Systems*, 21, 210, 220.
55 Harris, *The Origin of Writing*, 135.
56 Coulmas, *Writing Systems*, 41, 43, 197; David Diringer, *The Alphabet: A Key to the History of Mankind* (London: Hutchinson's Scientific and Technical Publications, 1947), 10; Harris, *The Origin of Writing*, 37; Rosemary Sassoon and Albertine Gaur, *Signs, Symbols and Icons: Prehistory to the Computer Age* (Exeter: Intellect Books, 1997), 30.
57 Coulmas, *Writing Systems*, 43.
58 Coulmas, *Writing Systems*, 49.
59 Diringer, *The Alphabet*, 18; Donald, *Origins of the Modern Mind*, 288–9.
60 Andrew J. King, "On the Possibility and Impossibility of a Universal Iconic Communication System," in *Iconic Communication*, ed. M. Yazdani and P. Barker (Bristol: Intellect, 2000), 21; Ong, *Orality and Literacy*, 85–6.
61 Harris, *The Origin of Writing*, 78.
62 Harris, *The Origin of Writing*, 30; Diringer, *The Alphabet*, 358–60, 419; Ong, *Orality and Literacy*, 88–9.
63 Saussure, *Course in General Linguistics*, 117.
64 David Sacks, *Language Visible: Unraveling the Mystery of the Alphabet from A to Z* (New York: Broadway Books, 2003), 17, 251–5; Richard A. Firmage, *The Aphabet Abecedarium: Some Notes on Letters* (Boston: David R. Godline, 1993), 47–55, 168–76.
65 Qtd. in Harris, *The Origin of Writing*, 95.

66 Sacks, *Language Visible*, 51.
67 Coulmas, *Writing Systems*, 26, 156.
68 Anderson, *A Grammar of Iconism*, 175.
69 Diringer, *The Alphabet*, 12.
70 Diringer, *The Alphabet*, 166-7, 206.
71 Philip Lieberman, *The Biology and Evolution of Language* (Cambridge, MA: Harvard University Press, 1984), 17-19.
72 Coulmas, *Writing Systems*, 38-9.
73 Sue Savage-Rumbaugh, S. Shanker and T. J. Taylor, *Apes, Language, and the Human Mind* (Oxford: Oxford University Press, 1998), 66; Pinker, *The Language Instinct*, 166.
74 William Sinnema, *Digital, Analog, and Data Communication* (Englewood Cliffs, NJ: Prentice-Hall, Inc., 1986), 1; Fiske, *Introduction to Communication Studies*, 65; Pinker, *The Stuff of Thought*, 178-9.
75 Diringer, *The Alphabet*, 160.
76 Andy Clark, "Magic Words: How Language Augments Human Computation," in *Language and Thought: Interdisciplinary Themes*, ed. P. Carruthers and J. Boucher (Cambridge: Cambridge University Press, 1998), 164, 173-5; Keith Frankish, "Natural Language and Virtual Belief," in *Language and Thought*, ed. P. Carruthers and J. Boucher, 249; Pinker, *The Stuff of Thought* (Cambridge: Cambridge University Press, 1998), 436-7.
77 Keith Frankish, "Evolving the Linguistic Mind," in *Proceedings of the 3rd International Evolution of Language Conference*, ed. J-L. Dessalles and L. Ghadakpour (Paris: Ecole Nationale Supérieure des Télécommunications, 2000), 104.
78 Clark, "Magic Words," 173.
79 Dissanayake, *What Is Art For?*, 173, 176.

Chapter 6

1 Mazur, *Cybernetyka i Character*, 219; Piotr Sadowski, "Oscar Wilde, Morality, and Cybernetics," *Beyond Philology* 4 (2007): 173-91.
2 Mazur, *Cybernetyka i Character*, 237.
3 Wilde, *Complete Works*, 1073.
4 Wilde, *Complete Works*, 1244.
5 Wilde, *Complete Works*, 1244.
6 Wilde, *Complete Works*, 1244.
7 Wilde, *Complete Works*, 1245.
8 Wilde, *Complete Works*, 1194.
9 Richard Ellmann, *Oscar Wilde* (London: Penguin Books, 1987), 413.
10 Ellmann, *Oscar Wilde*, 412.
11 Ellmann, *Oscar Wilde*, 421-4.
12 Ellmann, *Oscar Wilde*, 417.
13 Merlin Holland, *Irish Peacock and Scarlet Marquess: The Real Trial of Oscar Wilde* (London: Fourth Estate, 2003), 80.
14 Holland, *Irish Peacock*, 79.
15 Holland, *Irish Peacock*, xxix.
16 Ellmann, *Oscar Wilde*, 448.

17 Ellmann, *Oscar Wilde*, 450.
18 Wilde, *Complete Works*, 1192.
19 Qtd in Richard Ellmann, *James Joyce* (Oxford: Oxford University Press, 1959), 688.
20 Wilde, *Complete Works*, 17.
21 Dutton, *The Art Instinct*, chap. 6.
22 Piotr Sadowski, *Dynamism of Character in Shakespeare's Mature Tragedies* (Newark: University of Delaware Press, 2003), chaps. 2, 3.
23 Sadowski, *Dynamism of Character*, chap. 4.

Chapter 7

1 Mary W. Marien, *Photography: A Cultural History* (London: Laurence King Publishing, 2006), 11.
2 Gisèle Freund, *Photography and Society* (London: The Gordon Fraser Gallery, 1980), 9–11.
3 Kristin Thompson and David Bordwell, *Film History: An Introduction* (Boston: McGraw-Hill Companies, 2003), 15.
4 Thompson and Bordwell, *Film History*, 17–20.
5 Rudolf Arnheim, *Art and Visual Perception: A Psychology of the Creative Eye* (Berkeley: University of California Press, 1974), 304.
6 Wilde, *Complete Works*, 17.
7 Arnheim, *Art and Visual Perception*, 253–4, 260–1.
8 Miriam Schild Bunim, *Space in Medieval Painting and the Forerunners of Perspective* (New York: Columbia University Press, 1940), 27–8.
9 Ernst H. Gombrich, *Shadows. The Depiction of Cast Shadows in Western Art* (London: National Gallery Publications, 1995), 19; Stoichita, *A Short History of the Shadow*.
10 Timothy Wilson-Smith, *Caravaggio* (London: Phaidon Press, 1998), 5–6.
11 Rudolf Arnheim, *Film as Art* (Berkeley: University of California Press, 1957), 15.
12 Piotr Sadowski, *The Semiotics of Light and Shadows: Modern Visual Arts and Weimar Cinema* (London: Bloomsbury Academic, 2018), chap. 4.
13 Norbert M. Schmitz, "Licht als Mittel und als Zweck: Zum Verhältnis des filmischen Lichts im Avant-gardefilm und in Kino," in *Ästhetik der Schatten. Filmisches Licht 1915-1950*, ed. C. Betz, J. Pattis and R. Rother (Marburg: Schüren Verlag, 2014), 119–23.
14 C. W. Ceram, *Archaeology of the Cinema* (London: Thames and Hudson, 1965), 84.
15 Thompson and Bordwell, *Film History*, 17, 42.
16 Frances Guerin, *A Culture of Light: Cinema and Technology in 1920s Germany* (Minneapolis: University of Minnesota Press, 2005), xiv; Richard Blank, *Film & Light: The History of Filmlighting Is the History of Film* (Berlin: Alexander Verlag, 2012), 20.
17 Patrick Keating, *Hollywood Lighting from the Silent Era to Film Noir* (New York: Columbia University Press, 2010), 33; Ralf Forster, "'Licht, Licht, auf alle Fälle!' Techniken der Filmbeleuchtung in Deutschland 1915 bis 1931," in *Ästhetik der Schatten*, ed. C. Betz, J. Pattis and R. Rother, 136.
18 Daisuke Miyao, *The Aesthetics of Shadows: Lighting and Japanese Cinema* (Durham: Duke University Press, 2013), 2, 47–9; Peter Baxter, "On the History and Ideology of Film Lighting," *Screen* 16, no. 3 (1975): 90; Blank, *Film & Light*, 9, 12.

19 Thompson and Bordwell, *Film History*, 46.
20 Charles Musser, *The Emergence of Cinema: The American Screen to 1907* (Berkeley: University of California Press, 1990), 337.
21 Thompson and Bordwell, *Film History*, 46.
22 Sadowski, *The Semiotics of Light and Shadows*, 14–16.
23 Carl Gustav Jung, *The Essential Jung*, ed. Anthony Storr (London: Fontana Press, 1998), 65; Stoichita, *A Short History of the Shadow*, chap. 4.
24 Arnheim, *Art and Visual Perception*, 258.
25 Thomas Elsaesser, "No End to Nosferatu (1922)," in *Weimar Cinema: An Essential Guide to Classic Films of the Era*, ed. Noah Isenberg (New York: Columbia University Press, 2009), 88–9.
26 Siegfried Kracauer, *From Caligari to Hitler: A Psychological History of the German Film* (Princeton: Princeton University Press, 1974), 114; Sadowski, *The Semiotics of Light and Shadows*, 63–9.

Chapter 8

1 Julio Cortázar, *Blow-Up and Other Stories*, trans. Paul Blackburn (New York: Collier Books, 1963), 100–15; Genaro J. Pérez, "Blow-Up (Las Babas del Diablo) by Julio Cortázar, 1959," *Reference Guide to Short Fiction. Encyclopedia.com* (July 14, 2020).
2 Cortázar, *Blow-Up*, 104.
3 Cortázar, *Blow-Up*, 108.
4 Sontag, *On Photography*, 54.
5 Christopher Sharrett, "*Blow-Up*," *Cineaste*, vol. 42, issue 4 (Fall 2017): 54.
6 Marien, *Photography: A Cultural History*, 171–81; Walter Moser, "Antonioni's Hypnotic Eye on a Frantic World," in *Blow-Up: Antonioni's Classic Film and Photography*, ed. W. Moser and K. A. Schröder (Vienna: Hatje Cantz Verlag, 2014), 7–8.
7 Peter Brunette, *The Films of Michelangelo Antonioni* (Cambridge: Cambridge University Press, 1998), 113.
8 Adam Scovell, "On Location: The London Park from Michelangelo Antonioni's *Blow-Up*," *Little White Lies: Truth and Movies*, online (September 2, 2019).
9 Thomas Harris, "*Rear Window* and *Blow-Up*: Hitchcock's Straightforwardness versus Antonioni's Ambiguity," *Literature/Film Quarterly* 15, no. 1 (1987): 60–3. The main characters in the two films are professional photographers, but the main difference is that while in *Rear Window* the telephoto lens, a substitute for binoculars, is part of the photographer's contiguous interactions with the courtyard he observes from his window, in *Blowup* the standard lens used to take pictures in the park is the starting point of the film's exploration of displaced, vicarious experience enabled by the photographic process of developing, enlarging, cropping, and printing of images—all absent in Hitchcock's film.
10 Brunette, *The Films of Michelangelo Antonioni*, 110.
11 Moser, "Antonioni's Hypnotic Eye," 15; Seymour Chatman, *Antonioni, or the Surface of the World* (Berkeley: University of California Press, 1985), 149; Brunette, *The Films of Michelangelo Antonioni*, 120.
12 Matilde Nardelli, "*Blow-Up* and the Plurality of Photography," in *Antonioni: Centenary Essays*, ed. J. D. Rhodes and L. Rascaroli (London: Palgrave Macmillan, 2011), 190–1.

13 Nardelli, "*Blow-Up* and the Plurality of Photography," 187; Jurij Lotman, *Semiotics of Cinema* (Ann Arbor: University of Michigan Press, 1981), 97–9.
14 Qtd. in Brunette, *The Films of Michelangelo Antonioni*, 121.

Chapter 9

1 Anne Friedberg, *The Virtual Window: From Alberti to Microsoft* (Cambridge, MA: The MIT Press, 2006), 5–18.
2 Solso, *The Psychology of Art*, 90–1.
3 Rudolf Arnheim, *The Power of the Center: A Study of Composition in the Visual Arts* (Berkeley: University of California Press, 1983), 37.
4 Thompson and Bordwell, *Film History*, 330–3.
5 Gregory, *Eye and Brain*, 60–1.
6 Gregory, *Eye and Brain*, 177.
7 Leonardo da Vinci, *A Treatise on Painting* (New York: Dover Publications, 2005), 44; *The Notebooks*, ed. Irma A. Richter (Oxford: Oxford University Press, 1998), 118–19.
8 Martin Kemp, *The Science of Art: Optical Themes in Western Art from Brunelleschi to Seurat* (New Haven: Yale University Press, 1990), 12; Ernst H. Gombrich, *The Image and the Eye: Further Studies in the Psychology of Pictorial Representation* (Oxford: Phaidon Press, 1982), 224; H. A. Sedgwick, "The Geometry of Spatial Layout in Pictorial Representation," in *The Perception of Pictures*, ed. Margaret A. Hagen, vol. 1 (New York: Academic Press, 1980), 38–9.
9 Margaret Livingstone, *Vision and Art: The Biology of Seeing* (New York: Harry N. Abrams, 2008), 140.
10 Alberti, *On Painting*, 45–6; Klaus Krüger, "Medium and Imagination: Aesthetic Aspects of Trecento Panel Painting," in *Italian Panel Panting of the Duecento and Trecento*, ed. Victor M. Schmidt (New Haven: Yale University Press, 2002), 57–82; Arnheim, *Art and Visual Perception*, 283–4; Erwin Panofsky, *Perspective as Symbolic Form* (New York: Zone Books, 1991), 65–72.
11 Kemp, *The Science of Art*, 21.
12 Alberti, *On Painting*, 56; Anthony Blunt, *Artistic Theory in Italy, 1450-1600* (Oxford: Oxford University Press, 1962), 13–14.
13 Livingstone, *Vision and Art*, 100–1.
14 Ralph Norman Haber, "Perceiving Space from Pictures: A Theoretical Analysis," in *The Perception of Pictures*, ed. M. A. Hagen (New York: Academic Press, 1980), 12.
15 Qtd. in Hentie Louw, "The Development of the Window," in *Windows: History, Repair and Conservation*, ed. M. Tutton et al. (Shaftsbury: Donhead Publishing, 2007), 18.
16 Jacob Burckhardt, *The Civilization of the Renaissance Italy* (London: Penguin Books, 1990), 24.
17 Sedgwick, "The Geometry of Spatial Layout," 40–1.
18 Henry Heydenryk Jr., *The Art and History of Frames: An Inquiry into the Enhancement of Paintings* (New York: Lyons & Burford, 1993).
19 Barbara E. Savedoff, "Frames," *Journal of Aesthetics & Art Criticism* 57, no. 3 (Summer 1999), 348, 350.
20 Arnheim, *The Power of the Center*, 55.
21 Chauvet and Deschamps, *Chauvet Cave*, 104–14.

22 Lewis-Williams, *The Mind in the Cave*, 28.
23 Bunim, *Space in Medieval Painting*, 17.
24 Susan Woodford, *The Art of Greece and Rome* (Cambridge: Cambridge University Press, 1982), 71–4; Bunim, *Space in Medieval Painting*, 175–9; Panofsky, *Perspective as Symbolic Form*, 49–53.
25 Kemp, *The Science of Art*, 80, 86–91, 102–3, 123–5, 130, 137, 149, 152–3, 169–91.
26 Christian Metz, *Film Language: A Semiotics of Cinema* (New York: Oxford University Press, 1974), 94; John Szarkowski, "Introduction to The Photographer's Eye," in *The Photography Reader*, ed. Liz Wells (London: Routledge, 2003), 100.
27 Arnheim, *The Power of the Center*, 42–3, 73; *Film as Art*, 17, 73–4.
28 Arnheim, *The Power of the Center*, 52.
29 Heydenryk, *The Art and History of Frames*, 31–2.
30 Richard Latto, "The Brain of the Beholder," in *The Artful Eye*, ed. R. Gregory, J. Harris, P. Heard and D. Rose (Oxford: Oxford University Press, 1995), 78.
31 Plato, *Timaeus* (Harmondsworth: Penguin Books, 1965), 76–7. In Plato's cosmology the remaining three elements are assigned the following "regular solids": air—octahedron (a regular solid figure with eight equal triangular faces), fire—pyramid, and water—icosahedron (a regular solid figure with twenty equal triangular faces). While the gravitational experience of verticality and horizontality defines the iconic nature of the cube as a sign for earth, it is difficult to see what physical properties of air, fire, and water are reflected in their respective geometric solids: these signs should therefore be classified as symbolic (arbitrary) rather than iconic.
32 Thompson and Bordwell, *Film History*, 330–1.
33 Gordon H. Orians and Judith H. Heerwagen, "Evolved Responses to Landscapes," in *The Adapted Mind*, ed. J. H. Barkow et al., (New York–Oxford: Oxford University Press, 1992), 571.
34 Appleton, *The Poetry of Habitat*.
35 Kaplan, "Environmental Preference," 588, 594.
36 Lola Landekic, *Art of the Title* (online February 18, 2014): https://www.artofthetitle.com/title/butch-cassidy-and-the-sundance-kid/ Accessed November 19, 2020.
37 Bordwell and Thompson, *Film Art*, 252–8.

Chapter 10

1 Woody Allen, *Three Films of Woody Allen: Zelig, Broadway Danny Rose, The Purple Rose of Cairo* (London: Faber and Faber, 1987), 326.
2 Arnold W. Preussner, "Woody Allen's *The Purple Rose of Cairo*," *Literature/Film Quarterly* 16, no. 1 (1988): 39–43.
3 Woody Allen, *Woody Allen on Woody Allen in Conversation with Stig Björkman* (New York: Grove Press, 2004), 149.
4 Michael Dunne, "*Stardust Memories*, *The Purple Rose of Cairo*, and the Tradition of Metafiction," *Film Criticism* 12, no. 1 (Fall 1987): 19–27.
5 Dunne, "*Stardust Memories*," 23; Vernon Young, "Movie within a Movie," *The Hudson Review* 38, no. 3 (Autumn 1985): 455–8.
6 Elizabeth Burns, *Theatricality: A Study of Convention in the Theatre and in Social Life* (New York: Harper & Row, 1972), 151.
7 Keir Elam, *The Semiotics of Theatre and Drama* (London: Routledge, 2002), 7.

8 Konstantin Stanislavski, *An Actor's Work: A Student's Diary* (London: Routledge, 2010), 25.
9 Thalia R. Goldstein and Aline Filipe, "The Interpreted Mind: Understanding Acting," *Review of General Psychology* 22, no. 2 (2018): 221.
10 Allen, *Woody Allen on Woody Allen*, 19, 99, 358.
11 Goldstein and Filipe. "The Interpreted Mind."
12 Eric Lax, *Conversations with Woody Allen: His Films, the Movies, and Moviemaking* (London: Aurum Press, 2007), 19.
13 Preussner, "Woody Allen's *The Purple Rose of Cairo*," 43.
14 Allen, *Woody Allen on Woody Allen*, 81, 116, 126.
15 Richard Schieckel, "Now Playing at the Jewel," *Time* 94 (March, 1985): 78.

Postscript

1 Francis-Noël Thomas and Mark Turner, *Clear and Simple as the Truth: Writing Classic Prose* (Princeton: Princeton University Press, 2017), 77, 81.
2 Steven Pinker, *The Sense of Style: The Thinking Person's Guide to Writing in the 21st Century* (London: Allen Lane, 2014), esp. Chap. 2.
3 Raymond Tallis, *Not Saussure: A Critique of Post-Saussurean Literary Theory* (Houndmills, Basingstoke: Macmillan Press, 1988); "The Linguistic Unconscious: Saussure and the Post-Saussureans," in *Theory's Empire: An Anthology of Dissent*, ed. Daphne Patai and Will. H. Corral (New York: Columbia University Press, 2005), 128–30.
4 Paul R. Gross and Norman Levitt, *Higher Superstition: The Academic Left and Its Quarrels with Science* (Baltimore: The Johns Hopkins University Press, 1994); Patai and Corral, ed. *Theory's Empire*; Alan Sokal and Jean Bricmont, *Intellectual Impostures: Postmodern Philosophers' Abuse of Science* (London: Profile Books, 1998); Tallis, *Newton's Sleep, Enemies of Hope; Theorrhoea and after*.
5 Carroll, *Evolution and Literary Theory*, 27; Jonathan Gottschall, *Literature, Science, and a New Humanities* (New York: Palgrave Macmillan, 2008); Brian Boyd, Joseph Carroll and Jonathan Gottschall, ed., *Evolution, Literature, and Film: A Reader* (New York: Columbia University Press, 2010).
6 Denis Dutton, "The Bad Writing Contest: Press Releases, 1996–1998," http://www.denisdutton.com/bad_writing.htm, 1; Denis Dutton, "Language Crimes: A Lesson in How Not to Write, Courtesy of Professoriate," *Wall Street Journal* (February 5, 1999, W11); D. G. Myers, "Bad Writing," in *Theory's Empire*, ed. Daphne Patai and Will H. Corral (New York: Columbia University Press, 2005), 354.
7 Dutton, "The Bad Writing Contest."
8 Wilde, *Complete Works*, 366.
9 Jacques Derrida, "Structure, Sign, and Play in the Discourse of the Human Sciences," in Jacques Derrida, *Writing and Difference*, trans. Alan Bass (London: Routledge & Kegan Paul, 1987), 351–70.
10 Jonathan Gottschall's phrase (*Literature, Science*, 83).
11 https://www.elsewhere.org/pomo/
12 *Sokal Hoax*, 200; Sokal and Bricmont, *Intellectual Impostures*.
13 David Sless, *In Search of Semiotics* (London: Croom Helm, 1986), 2; Marshall Blonsky, ed., *On Signs* (Baltimore: The Johns Hopkins University Press, 1985), ix.

14 Elam, *The Semiotics of Theatre and Drama*.
15 Daniel Chandler, *Semiotics: The Basics* (London: Routledge, 2002), xv.
16 Floyd Merrell, *Sensing Semiosis: Toward the Possibility of Complementary Cultural "Logics"* (Houndmills: Macmillan Press, 1998), ix–xiii.
17 Mark Gottdiener, *Postmodern Semiotics: Material Culture and the Forms of Postmodern Life* (Oxford: Wiley-Blackwell, 1995), chaps. 1–3.
18 E.g. Warren Buckland, *The Cognitive Semiotics of Film* (Cambridge: Cambridge University Press, 2004), 109–40.
19 E.g. Claus Emmeche and Kalevi Kull, ed., *Towards a Semiotic Biology: Life Is the Action of Signs* (London: Imperial College Press, 2011).
20 Piotr Sadowski, "What Is Literature?—A Systems Definition," *Semiotica* 123, no. 1/2 (1999): 46.

Bibliography

Abrams, M. H. "The Deconstructive Angel." *Critical Inquiry* 3 (1977): 425–38.
Ackerman, Diane. *A Natural History of the Senses.* London: Vintage, 1991.
Aitchison, Jean. *The Seeds of Speech: Language Origin and Evolution.* Cambridge: Cambridge University Press, 2000.
Aken, Olivier Van. "Plants Are 'in Touch' with the World around Them." May 25, 2016. https://www.news.uwa.edu.au/archive/201605258690/international/plants-are-touch-world-around-them
Alberti, Leon Battista. *On Painting*, translated by John R. Spencer. New Haven: Yale University Press, 1966.
Allen, Colin and Eric Saidel. "The Evolution of Reference." In *The Evolution of Mind*, edited by D. D. Cummins and C. Allen, 183–203. New York: Oxford University Press, 1998.
Allen, Woody. *Three Films of Woody Allen*: Zelig, Broadway Danny Rose, The Purple Rose of Cairo. London: Faber and Faber, 1987.
Allen, Woody. *Woody Allen on Woody Allen in Conversation with Stig Björkman.* New York: Grove Press, 2004.
Alper, Matthew. *The "God" Part of the Brain: A Scientific Interpretation of Human Spirituality and God.* Naperville, IL: Sourcebooks, Inc., 2006.
Anderson, Earl A. *A Grammar of Iconism.* Madison: Fairleigh Dickinson University Press, 1998.
Appleton, Jay. *The Poetry of Habitat.* University of Hull, England: Department of Geography, 1978.
Arnheim, Rudolf. *Film as Art.* Berkeley: University of California Press, 1957.
Arnheim, Rudolf. *Art and Visual Perception: A Psychology of the Creative Eye.* Berkeley: University of California Press, 1974.
Arnheim, Rudolf. "On the Nature of Photography." *Critical Inquiry* 1, no. 1 (September 1974): 149–61.
Arnheim, Rudolf. *The Power of the Center: A Study of Composition in the Visual Arts.* Berkeley: University of California Press, 1983.
Badcock, Christopher. *Evolutionary Psychology: A Critical Introduction.* Cambridge: Polity Press, 2000.
Bahn, Paul and Jean Vertut, *Journey through the Ice Age.* Berkeley: University of California Press, 1999.
Barash, David P. "What the Whale Wondered: Evolution, Existentialism, and the Search for 'Meaning.'" In *Richard Dawkins: How a Scientist Changed the Way We Think*, edited by A. Grafen and M. Ridley, 255–64. Oxford: Oxford University Press, 2006.
Barkow, Jerome H. "Beneath New Culture Is Old Psychology: Gossip and Social Stratification." In *The Adapted Mind: Evolutionary Psychology and the Generation of Culture*, edited by J. H. Barkow et al., 627–38. New York: Oxford University Press, 1992.
Barnard, Malcolm. *Fashion as Communication.* New York: Routledge, 2002.

Baron-Cohen, Simon. *Mindblindness: An Essay on Autism and Theory of Mind*. Cambridge, MA: The MIT Press, 1997.

Baron-Cohen, Simon. *The Essential Difference: Men, Women and the Extreme Male Brain*. London: Penguin Books, 2003.

Barrow, John D. *The Artful Universe*. Oxford: Oxford University Press, 1995.

Baxter, Peter. "On the History and Ideology of Film Lighting." *Screen* 16, no. 3 (1975): 83–106.

Bazin, André. "Cinematic Realism." In *The Philosophy of Film: Introductory Text and Readings*, edited by T. E. Wartenberg and A. Curran, 59–69. Oxford: Blackwell, 2005.

Benczes, Réka. *Rhyme over Reason: Phonological Motivation in English*. Cambridge: Cambridge University Press, 2019.

Bertalanffy, Ludwig von. *General Systems Theory: Foundations, Development, Applications*. Harmondsworth: Penguin Books, 1973.

Bible, The. Authorized Version. Swindon: Bible Society, ND.

Bickerton, Derek. *Language and Species*. Chicago: The University of Chicago Press, 1990.

Bland, Kalman P. *The Artless Jew: Medieval and Modern Affirmations and Denials of the Visual*. Princeton: Princeton University Press, 2000.

Blank, Richard. *Film & Light: The History of Filmlighting Is the History of Film*. Berlin: Alexander Verlag, 2012.

Blunt, Anthony. *Artistic Theory in Italy, 1450–1600*. Oxford: Oxford University Press, 1962.

Bouchard Jr., Thomas J. "Genes, Environment, and Personality." In *The Nature–Nurture Debate: The Essential Readings*, edited by Stephen J. Ceci and Wendy M. Williams, 98–104. Oxford: Blackwell Publishing, 1999.

Bouissac, Paul. *The Semiotics of Clowns and Clowning: Rituals of Transgression and the Theory of Laughter*. London: Bloomsbury Academic, 2015.

Boyer, Pascal. *The Naturalness of Religious Ideas: A Cognitive Theory of Religions*. Berkeley: University of California Press, 1994.

Boyer, Pascal. "Evolution of the Modern Mind and the Origins of Culture: Religious Concepts as a Limiting-Case." In *Evolution and the Human Mind: Modularity, Language and Meta-Cognition*, edited by P. Carruthers and A. Chamberlain, 93–112. Cambridge: Cambridge University Press, 2000.

Briggs, Asa and Peter Burke. *A Social History of the Media: From Gutenberg to the Internet*. Cambridge: Polity Press, 2005.

Brown, Donald E. *Human Universals*. New York: McGraw-Hill, 1991.

Brunette, Peter. *The Films of Michelangelo Antonioni*. Cambridge: Cambridge University Press, 1998.

Buckland, Warren. *The Cognitive Semiotics of Film*. Cambridge: Cambridge University Press, 2004.

Bulhak, Andrew. *Postmodernism Generator*. https://www.elsewhere.org/pomo/

Bunim, Miriam Schild. *Space in Medieval Painting and the Forerunners of Perspective*. New York: Columbia University Press, 1940.

Burckhardt, Jacob. *The Civilization of the Renaissance Italy*. 1860. London: Penguin Books, 1990.

Burns, Elizabeth. *Theatricality: A Study of Convention in the Theatre and in Social Life*. New York: Harper & Row, 1972.

Buse, Peter. *The Camera Does the Rest: How Polaroid Changed Photography*. Chicago: The University of Chicago Press, 2016.

Buss, David. *Evolutionary Psychology: The New Science of the Mind*. 1999. Boston, MA: Allyn and Bacon, 2004.
Campbell, Neil. *Biology*. Menlo Park, CA: Cummings Publishing, 1996.
Carroll, Joseph. *Evolution and Literary Theory*. Columbia: University of Missouri Press, 1995.
Carroll, Joseph. *Literary Darwinism: Evolution, Human Nature, and Literature*. New York: Routledge, 2004.
Carroll, Joseph. "Human Nature and Literary Meaning: A Theoretical Model Illustrated with a Critique of *Pride and Prejudice*." In *The Literary Animal: Evolution and the Nature of Narrative*, edited by E. O. Wilson and F. Crews, 76–106. Evanston, IL: Northwestern University Press, 2005.
Carroll, Joseph et al. "Imagining Human Nature." In *Evolution, Literature, and Film: A Reader*, edited by Brian Boyd, Joseph Carroll and Jonathan Gottschall, 211–18. New York: Columbia University Press, 2010.
Carroll, Noël. "Towards an Ontology of the Moving Image." In *Philosophy and Film*, edited by C. A. Freeland and T. E. Wartenberg, 68–88. New York: Routledge, 1995.
Carruthers, Peter and Andrew Chamberlain. "Introduction." In *Evolution and the Human Mind: Modularity, Language and Meta-cognition*, edited by P. Carruthers and A. Chamberlain, 1–12. Cambridge: Cambridge University Press, 2000.
Cartwright, John. *Evolution and Human Behaviour: Darwinian Perspectives on Human Nature*. Basingstoke: Macmillan, 2000.
Cashdan, Elizabeth. "A Sensitive Period for Learning about Food." *Human Nature*, 5 (1994): 279–94.
The Catholic Encyclopedia, edited by Charles G. Herbermann. New York: Robert Appleton Company, 1911.
Ceram, C. W. *Archaeology of the Cinema*. London: Thames and Hudson, 1965.
Chandler, Daniel. *Semiotics: The Basics*. London: Routledge, 2002.
Chatman, Seymour. *Antonioni, or the Surface of the World*. Berkeley: University of California Press, 1985.
Chauvet, Jean-Marie and Eliette Brunel Deschamps. *Chauvet Cave: The Discovery of the World's Oldest Paintings*. London: Thames and Hudson, 1996.
Clark, Andy. "Magic Words: How Language Augments Human Computation." In *Language and Thought: Interdisciplinary Themes*, edited by P. Carruthers and J. Boucher, 162–83. Cambridge: Cambridge University Press, 1998.
Clark, Eve V. *The Lexicon in Acquisition*. Cambridge: Cambridge University Press, 1993.
Clark, Eve V. and Herbert H. Clark, "Universals, Relativity, and Language Processing." In *Universals of Human Language*, edited by J. H. Greenberg et al., 247–54. Stanford, Calif.: Stanford University Press, 1978.
Classic Essays on Photography, edited by Alan Trachtenberg. New Haven, CT: Leete's Island Books, 1980.
Cortázar, Julio. *Blow-Up and Other Stories*, translated by Paul Blackburn. New York: Collier Books, 1963.
Cosmides, Leda and John Tooby. "Cognitive Adaptations for Social Exchange." In *The Adapted Mind: Evolutionary Psychology and the Generation of Culture*, edited by J. H. Barkow et al., 163–228. New York: Oxford University Press, 1992.
Cosmides, Leda and John Tooby. "Origins of Domain Specificity: The Evolution of Functional Organization." In *Mapping the Mind: Domain Specificity in Cognition and Culture*, edited by L. A. Hirschfeld and S. A. Gelman, 85–116. Cambridge: Cambridge University Press, 1994.

Coulmas, Florian. *Writing Systems: An Introduction to Their Linguistic Analysis.* Cambridge: Cambridge University Press, 2003.
Coulthard, Malcolm. "Author Identification, Idiolect, and Linguistic Uniqueness." *Applied Linguistics* 25, no. 4 (December 2004): 431–47.
Crook, John Hurrell. *The Evolution of Human Consciousness.* Oxford: Clarendon Press, 1980.
Crystal, David. *The Cambridge Encyclopedia of the English Language.* Cambridge: Cambridge University Press, 1995.
Cummins, Denise D. "Social Norms and Other Minds: The Evolutionary Roots of Higher Cognition." In *The Evolution of Mind*, edited by D. D. Cummins and C. Allen, 30–50. New York–Oxford: Oxford University Press, 1998.
Daly, Martin and Margo Wilson. *Homicide.* New York: Aldine De Gruyter, 1988.
Danesi, Marcel. *The Semiotics of Emoji: The Rise of Visual Language in the Age of the Internet.* London: Bloomsbury Academic, 2016.
Dart, Raymond A. "The Waterworn Australopithecine Pebble of Many Faces from Makapansgat." *South African Journal of Science* 70, no. 6 (June 1974): 167.
Darwin, Charles. *The Expression of the Emotions in Man and Animals.* 1872. London: Penguin Books, 2009.
Davidson, Ian. "The Archaeological Evidence of Language Origins: States of Art." In *Language Evolution*, edited by M. H. Christiansen and S. Kirby, 140–57. Oxford: Oxford University Press, 2003.
Dawkins, Richard. *The Selfish Gene.* 1976. Oxford: Oxford University Press, 2006.
Dawkins, Richard. *The Blind Watchmaker.* 1986. London: Penguin Books, 2006.
Dawkins, Richard. *The God Delusion.* London: Bantam Press, 2006.
Dawkins, Richard. *Unweaving the Rainbow: Science, Delusion and the Appetite for Wonder.* London: Penguin Books, 2006.
Deacon, Terrence W. *The Symbolic Species: The Co-Evolution of Language and the Human Brain.* London: Allen Lane, 1997.
Deacon, Terrence W. "Shannon–Boltzmann–Darwin: Redefining Information," Parts I and II, *Cognitive Semiotics* (September 2007).
Degen, Judith et al. "When Redundancy Is Useful: A Bayesian Approach to 'Over-Informative' Referring Expressions." *Psychological Review* 127, no. 4 (2020): 591–621.
Denton, Derek. *The Primordial Emotions: The Dawning of Consciousness.* Oxford: Oxford University Press, 2005.
Derrida, Jacques. "Structure, Sign, and Play in the Discourse of the Human Sciences." In *Writing and Difference*, translated by Alan Bass, chap. 10, 351–70. 1966. London: Routledge & Kegan Paul, 1987.
Dingwall, William Orr. "The Evolution of Human Communication." *Studies in Neurolinguistics* 4 (1979): 1–95.
Diringer, David. *The Alphabet: A Key to the History of Mankind.* London: Hutchinson's Scientific and Technical Publications, 1947.
Dissanayake, Ellen. *What Is Art for?* Seattle: University of Washington Press, 1991.
Donald, Merlin. *Origins of the Modern Mind: Three Stages in the Evolution of Culture and Cognition.* Cambridge, MA: Harvard University Press, 1991.
Donald, Merlin. *A Mind so Rare: The Evolution of Human Consciousness.* New York: W. W. Norton & Company, 2001.
Dunbar, Robin. *The Trouble with Science.* London: Faber and Faber, 1995.
Dunbar, Robin. *Gossip, and Grooming and the Evolution of Language.* London: Faber and Faber, 1996.

Dunbar, Robin. "The Origin and Subsequent Evolution of Language." In *Language Evolution*, edited by M. H. Christiansen and S. Kirby, 219–35. Oxford: Oxford University Press, 2003.

Dunbar, Robin. *The Human Story: A New History of Mankind's Evolution*. London: Faber and Faber, 2005.

Dunbar, Robin, Chris Knight and Camilla Power. eds. *The Evolution of Culture: An Interdisciplinary View*. Edinburgh: Edinburgh University Press, 1999.

Dunne, Michael. "*Stardust Memories, The Purple Rose of Cairo*, and the Tradition of Metafiction." *Film Criticism* 12, no. 1 (Fall 1987): 19–27.

Dutton, Denis. "The Bad Writing Contest: Press Releases, 1996–1998." http://www.denisdutton.com/bad_writing.htm

Dutton, Denis. "Language Crimes: A Lesson in How Not to Write, Courtesy of Professoriate." *Wall Street Journal* (February 5, 1999, W11).

Dutton, Denis. *The Art Instinct: Beauty, Pleasure, and Human Evolution*. Oxford: Oxford University Press, 2009.

Ebin, Victoria. *The Body Decorated*. London: Thames and Hudson, 1979.

Eccles, John C. *Evolution of the Brain: Creation of the Self*. London: Routledge, 1989.

Eichenbaum, Howard and Neal J. Cohen. *From Conditioning to Conscious Recollection: Memory Systems of the Brain*. Oxford: Oxford University Press, 2001.

Ekman, Paul. *Emotions Revealed: Understanding Faces and Feeling*. London: Weidenfeld & Nicolson, 2003.

Ekman, Paul and Wallace V. Friesen. *Unmasking the Face*. Englewood Cliffs, NJ: Prentice Hall, 1975.

Elam, Keir. *The Semiotics of Theatre and Drama*. 1980. London: Routledge, 2002.

Ellmann, Richard. *James Joyce*. Oxford: Oxford University Press, 1959.

Ellmann, Richard. *Oscar Wilde*. London: Penguin Books, 1987.

Elsaesser, Thomas. "No End to Nosferatu (1922)." In *Weimar Cinema: An Essential Guide to Classic Films of the Era*, edited by Noah Isenberg, 79–94. New York: Columbia University Press, 2009.

Emerson, Ralph Waldo. *Nature and Selected Essays*. 1836. New York: Penguin Books, 1982.

Etcoff, Nancy. *The Survival of the Prettiest: The Science of Beauty*. London: Abacus, 1999.

Evolution, Literature, and Film: A Reader, edited by Brian Boyd, Joseph Carroll and Jonathan Gottschall. New York: Columbia University Press, 2010.

Fernández-Dols, J. M. and M. A. Ruiz-Belda. "Spontaneous Facial Behavior during Intense Emotional Episodes: Artistic Truth and Optical Truth." In *The Psychology of Facial Expression*, edited by J. A. Russell and J. M. Fernández-Dols, 255–74. Cambridge: Cambridge University Press, 1997.

Fine, Steven. *The Menorah: From the Bible to Modern Israel*. Cambridge, MA: Harvard University Press, 2016.

Firmage, Richard A. *The Alphabet Abecedarium: Some Notes on Letters*. Boston: David R. Godline, 1993.

A First Look at Communication Theory, edited by Em Griffin et al. New York: McGraw-Hill Education, 2019.

Fischer, Olga. "Cognitive Iconic Grounding of Reduplication in Language." In *Semblance and Signification*, edited by P. Michelucci, O. Fischer and C. Ljungberg, 55–82. Amsterdam: John Benjamins Publishing Company, 2011.

Fiske, John. *Introduction to Communication Studies*. London: Routledge, 2001.

Fodor, Jerry A. *The Modularity of Mind: An Essay on Faculty Psychology*. Cambridge, MA: The MIT Press, 1983.

Forster, Ralf. "'Licht, Licht, auf alle Fälle!' Techniken der Filmbeleuchtung in Deutschland 1915 bis 1931." In *Ästhetik der Schatten*, edited by C. Betz, J. Pattis and R. Rother, 134–53. Marburg: Schüren Verlag, 2014.
Frankish, Keith. "Natural Language and Virtual Belief." In *Language and Thought: Interdisciplinary Themes*, edited by P. Carruthers and J. Boucher, 248–69. Cambridge: Cambridge University Press, 1998.
Frankish, Keith. "Evolving the Linguistic Mind." In *Proceedings of the 3rd International Evolution of Language Conference*, edited by J-L. Dessalles and L. Ghadakpour, 104–8. Paris: Ecole Nationale Supérieure des Télécommunications, 2000.
Frazer, James. *The Golden Bough: A Study in Magic and Religion*. New York: Simon & Schuster, 1996.
Freund, Gisèle. *Photography and Society*. London: The Gordon Fraser Gallery, 1980.
Friedberg, Anne. *The Virtual Window: From Alberti to Microsoft*. Cambridge, MA: The MIT Press, 2006.
Friston, Karl. "Predictions, Perception, and a Sense of Self." *Neurology* 83 (2014): 1112–18.
The Fyve Wyttes: A Late Middle English Devotional Treatise edited by R. H. Bremmer. Amsterdam: Rodopi, 1987.
Gawain and the Green Knight, Sir. Translated by Bernard O'Donoghue. London: Penguin Classics, 2006.
Geldard, Frank A. "Tactile Communication." In *How Animals Communicate*, edited by T. A. Sebeok, 211–32. Bloomington: Indiana University Press, 1977.
Gibbs Jr., Raymond W. "What Do Idioms Really Mean?" *Journal of Memory and Language* 31, no. 4 (August 1992): 485–506.
Gibson, Kathleen R. "Overlapping Neural Control of Language, Gesture and Tool-Use." In *Tools, Language and Cognition in Human Evolution*, edited by K. R. Gibson and T. Ingold, 187–92. Cambridge: Cambridge University Press, 1993.
Gilbert, C. et al. "Energy Saving Process in Huddling Emperor Penguins: From Experiments to Theory." *Journal of Experimental Biology* 211 (2008): 1–8.
Glanville, Ranulph. "Communication without Coding: Cybernetics, Meaning and Language (How Language, Becoming a System, Betrays Itself)." *Modern Language Notes* 111, no. 3 (April 1996): 441–62.
Goldstein, Thalia R. and Aline Filipe. "The Interpreted Mind: Understanding Acting." *Review of General Psychology* 22, no. 2 (2018): 220–9.
Gombrich, Ernst H. *The Image and the Eye: Further Studies in the Psychology of Pictorial Representation*. Oxford: Phaidon Press, 1982.
Gombrich, Ernst H. *Shadows. The Depiction of Cast Shadows in Western Art*. London: National Gallery Publications, 1995.
Gombrich, Ernst H. *Art and Illusion: A Study in the Psychology of Pictorial Representation*. 1960. London: Phaidon Press, 2003.
Gottdiener, Mark. *Postmodern Semiotics: Material Culture and the Forms of Postmodern Life*. Oxford: Wiley-Blackwell, 1995.
Gottschall, Jonathan. *Literature, Science, and a New Humanities*. New York: Palgrave Macmillan, 2008.
Greenfield, Susan. *The Private Life of the Brain*. Harmondsworth: Penguin Books, 2001.
Gregory, Richard L. *Eye and Brain: The Psychology of Seeing*. 1966. Oxford: Oxford University Press, 1998.
Gross, Paul R. and Norman Levitt. *Higher Superstition: The Academic Left and Its Quarrels with Science*. Baltimore: The Johns Hopkins University Press, 1994.

Guerin, Frances. *A Culture of Light: Cinema and Technology in 1920s Germany*. Minneapolis: University of Minnesota Press, 2005.
Guthrie, R. D. "Evolution of Human Threat Display Organs." *Evolutionary Biology* 4 (1970): 257–302.
Guyton, Arthur C. and John E. Hall. *Textbook of Medical Physiology*. Philadelphia: W. B. Saunders Company, 1996.
Haber, Ralph Norman. "Perceiving Space from Pictures: A Theoretical Analysis." In *Perception of Pictures*, edited by Margaret A. Hagen, 3–31. vol. 1. New York: Academic Press, 1980.
Halbertal, Moshe and Avishoi Margalit. *Idolatry*. Cambridge, MA: Harvard University Press, 1992.
Hall, Edward T. *The Hidden Dimension: Man's Use of Space in Public and Private*. London: The Bodley Head, 1966.
Harari, Yuval Noah. *21 Lessons for the 21st Century*. London: Vintage, 2018.
Harris, Roy. *The Origin of Writing*. London: Duckworth, 1986.
Harris, Thomas. "*Rear Window* and *Blow-Up*: Hitchcock's Straightforwardness versus Antonioni's Ambiguity." *Literature/Film Quarterly* 15, no. 1 (1987): 60–3.
Hauser, Marc D. *The Evolution of Communication*. Cambridge, MA: The MIT Press, 1998.
Henrich, Joseph. *The Weirdest People in the World: How the West Became Psychologically Peculiar and Particularly Prosperous*. London: Penguin Books, 2021.
Henry, O. "Telemachus, Friend." In *100 Selected Stories*, edited by Keith Carabine and Cedric Watts, 96–101. 1905. London: Wordsworth Classics, 1995.
Herz, Rachel S. "Influences of Odors on Mood and Affective Cognition." In *Olfaction, Taste, and Cognition*, edited by Catherine Rouby, 160–77. Cambridge: Cambridge University Press, 2002.
Hesse, Herman. *Steppenwolf*, translated by Basil Creighton. 1927. London: Penguin Books, 1965.
Heydenryk Jr., Henry. *The Art and History of Frames: An Inquiry into the Enhancement of Paintings*. New York: Lyons & Burford, 1993.
Hirsch Jr., E. D. *Validity in Interpretation*. New Haven: Yale University Press, 1967.
Hirsch Jr., E. D. *The Aims of Interpretation*. Chicago: The University of Chicago Press, 1976.
Hoerl, Christoph and Teresa McCormack. "Perspectives on Time and Memory: An Introduction." In *Time and Memory: Issues in Philosophy and Psychology*, edited by C. Hoerl and T. McCormack, 1–36. Oxford: Clarendon Press, 2001.
Holland, Merlin. *Irish Peacock and Scarlet Marquess: The Real Trial of Oscar Wilde*. London: Fourth Estate, 2003.
Humphrey, Nicholas. *The Mind Made Flesh: Essays from the Frontiers of Psychology and Evolution*. Oxford: Oxford University Press, 2002.
Huysmans, Joris-Karl. *Against Nature*, translated by Robert Baldick. 1884. London: Penguin Books, 1959.
Iser, Wolfgang. *The Act of Reading: A Theory of Aesthetic Response*. London: Routledge & Kegan Paul, 1978.
Jakobson, Roman and Linda R. Waugh. *The Sound Shape of Language*. Berlin: Mouton de Gruyter, 1987.
James, Henry. *Short Stories*. New York: Random House, 1945.
Jappy, Tony. *Introduction to Peircean Visual Semiotics*. London: Bloomsbury Academic, 2013.

Jarvie, Ian. *Philosophy of the Film: Epistemology, Ontology, Aesthetics*. New York: Routledge & Kegan Paul, 1987.

Jespersen, Otto. *Language: Its Nature, Development and Origin*. London: Allen & Unwin, 1922.

Johansson, Sverker. *Origins of Language: Constraints on Hypotheses*. Amsterdam: John Benjamins Publishing Company, 2006.

Johnstone, Barbara. "The Individual Voice in Language." *Annual Review of Anthropology* 29 (October 2000): 405–24.

Joyce, James. *Ulysses*. 1922. London: Penguin Books, 1992.

Jung, Carl Gustav. *Aspects of the Feminine*. London: Routledge & Kegan Paul, 1982.

Jung, Carl Gustav. *The Essential Jung*, edited by Anthony Storr. London: Fontana Press, 1998.

Kant, Immanuel. *Critique of Pure Reason*, translated by J. M. D. Meiklejohn. 1781. London: J. M. Dent, 1993.

Kaplan, Stephen. "Environmental Preference in a Knowledge-Seeking, Knowledge-Using Organism." In *The Adapted Mind*, edited by J. H. Barkow, L. Cosmides and J. Tooby, 581–98. New York: Oxford University Press, 1992.

Kawai, Nobuyuki. *The Fear of Snakes: Evolutionary and Psychological Perspectives on Our Inner Fear*. Singapore: Springer Verlag, 2019.

Keating, Patrick. *Hollywood Lighting from the Silent Era to Film Noir*. New York: Columbia University Press, 2010.

Kemp, Martin. *The Science of Art: Optical Themes in Western Art from Brunelleschi to Seurat*. New Haven: Yale University Press, 1990.

Kendon, Adam. "Human Gesture." In *Tools, Language and Cognition in Human Evolution*, edited by K. R. Gibson and T. Ingold, 48–53. Cambridge: Cambridge University Press, 1993.

King, Andrew J. "On the Possibility and Impossibility of a Universal Iconic Communication System." In *Iconic Communication*, edited by M. Yazdani and P. Barker, 17–41. Bristol: Intellect, 2000.

Klossowski de Rola, Stanislas. *Alchemy: The Secret Art*. London: Thames and Hudson, 2013.

Knight, Chris. "Sex and Language as Pretend-Play." In *The Evolution of Culture: An Interdisciplinary View*, edited by R. Dunbar et al., 228–47. Edinburgh: Edinburgh University Press, 1999.

Knight, Chris, Robin Dunbar and Camilla Power. "An Evolutionary Approach to Human Culture." In *The Evolution of Culture: An Interdisciplinary View*, edited by R. Dunbar et al., 1–14. Edinburgh: Edinburgh University Press, 1999.

Kracauer, Siegfried. *From Caligari to Hitler: A Psychological History of the German Film*. 1947. Princeton: Princeton University Press, 1974.

Krüger, Klaus. "Medium and Imagination: Aesthetic Aspects of Trecento Panel Painting." In *Italian Panel Panting of the Duecento and Trecento*, edited by Victor M. Schmidt, 57–82. New Haven: Yale University Press, 2002.

Landekic, Lola. *Art of the Title*. Online, February 18, 2014. https://www.artofthetitle.com/title/butch-cassidy-and-the-sundance-kid/

Lane, Nick. *The Vital Question: Energy, Evolution, and the Origins of Complex Life*. New York: Norton, 2015.

Laplanche, Jean and Jean-Bertrand Pontalis. *The Language of Psychoanalysis*. New York: W. W. Norton & Company, 1973.

Laszlo, Ervin. *Introduction to Systems Philosophy: Toward a New Paradigm of Contemporary Thought*. New York: Harper & Row, 1972.
Laszlo, Ervin. *The Systems View of the World: The Natural Philosophy of the New Developments in the Sciences*. Oxford: Basil Blackwell, 1972.
Latto, Richard. "The Brain of the Beholder." In *The Artful Eye*, edited by R. Gregory et al., 66–94. Oxford: Oxford University Press, 1995.
Lax, Eric. *Conversations with Woody Allen: His Films, the Movies, and Moviemaking*. London: Aurum Press, 2007.
Leroi-Gourhan, André. *The Art of Prehistoric Man in Western Europe*. London: Thames and Hudson, 1968.
Lewis-Williams, David. *The Mind in the Cave: Consciousness and the Origins of Art*. London: Thames and Hudson, 2004.
Lieberman, Philip. *The Biology and Evolution of Language*. Cambridge, MA: Harvard University Press, 1984.
Lieberman, Philip. *Toward an Evolutionary Biology of Language*. Cambridge, MA: Harvard University Press, 2006.
Links, J. G. *Canaletto*. London: Phaidon Press, 2005.
Livingstone, Margaret. *Vision and Art: The Biology of Seeing*. New York: Harry N. Abrams, 2008.
Lock, Andrew. "Human Language Development and Object Manipulation: Their Relation in Ontogeny and Its Possible Relevance for Phylogenetic Questions." In *Tools, Language and Cognition in Human Evolution*, edited by K. R. Gibson and T. Ingold, 279–99. Cambridge: Cambridge University Press, 1993.
Lopreato, Joseph. *Human Nature and Biocultural Evolution*. Boston: Allen & Unwin, 1984.
Lotman, Jurij. *Semiotics of Cinema*, translated by Mark. F. Suino. Ann Arbor: University of Michigan Press, 1981.
Louw, Hentie. "The Development of the Window." In *Windows: History, Repair and Conservation*, edited by M. Tutton et al., 7–96. Shaftsbury: Donhead Publishing, 2007.
Magee, Bryan. *Confessions of a Philosopher: A Journey through Western Philosophy*. London: Phoenix, 1998.
Marien, Mary W. *Photography: A Cultural History*. London: Laurence King Publishing, 2006.
Marler, Peter. "The Evolution of Communication." In *How Animals Communicate*, edited by T. A. Sebeok, 45–70. Bloomington: Indiana University Press, 1977.
Marshack, Alexander. "The Berekhat Ram Figurine: A Late Acheulian Carving from the Middle East." *Antiquity* 71 (1997): 327–37.
Martin, Bronwen and Felizitas Ringham. *Dictionary of Semiotics*. London–New York: Cassell, 2000.
Martin, Chris William. *The Social Semiotics of Tattoos: Skin and Self*. London: Bloomsbury Academic, 2020.
Mazur, Marian. *Jakościowa Teoria Informacji* [A Qualitative Theory of Information]. Warsaw: Wydawnictwa Naukowo-Techniczne, 1970.
Mazur, Marian. *Cybernetyka i Character* [Cybernetics and Character]. Warsaw: Państwowy Instytut Wydawniczy, 1976.
McMahon, Darrin. *The Pursuit of Happiness: A History from the Greeks to the Present*. London: Penguin Books, 2006.
Medawar, Peter and Jean Medawar. *The Life Science: Current Ideas of Biology*. London: Wildwood House, 1977.

Merrell, Floyd. *Sensing Semiosis: Toward the Possibility of Complementary Cultural "Logics."* Houndmills: Macmillan Press, 1998.
Metz, Christian. *Film Language: A Semiotics of Cinema.* New York: Oxford University Press, 1974.
Miller, Geoffrey F. *The Mating Mind: How Sexual Choice Shaped the Evolution of Human Nature.* London: Vintage, 2001.
Mithen, Steven. *The Prehistory of the Mind: The Cognitive Origins of Art, Religion and Science.* London: Thames and Hudson, 1999.
Mithen, Steven. "Symbolism and the Supernatural." In *The Evolution of Culture: An Interdisciplinary View*, edited by R. Dunbar, C. Knight and C. Power, 147–72. Edinburgh: Edinburgh University Press, 1999.
Mithen, Steven. *The Singing Neanderthals: The Origins of Music, Language, Mind and Body.* London: Weidenfeld & Nicolson, 2005.
Mithen, Steven. "Mind, Brain and Material Culture: An Archaeological Perspective." In *Evolution and the Human Mind: Modularity, Language and Meta-cognition*, edited by P. Carruthers and A. Chamberlain, 207–17. Cambridge: Cambridge University Press, 2009.
Miyao, Daisuke. *The Aesthetics of Shadows: Lighting and Japanese Cinema.* Durham: Duke University Press, 2013.
Morris, Desmond. *The Biology of Art: A Study of the Picture-Making Behaviour of the Great Apes and Its Relationship to Human Art.* London: Methuen, 1962.
Moser, Walter. "Antonioni's Hypnotic Eye on a Frantic World." In Blow-Up: *Antonioni's Classic Film and Photography*, edited by W. Moser and K. A. Schröder, 6–21. Vienna: Hatje Cantz Verlag, 2014.
Musser, Charles. *The Emergence of Cinema: The American Screen to 1907.* Berkeley: University of California Press, 1990.
Myers, D. G. "Bad Writing." In *Theory's Empire*, edited by Daphne Patai and Will. H. Corral, 354–9. New York: Columbia University Press, 2005.
Nardelli, Matilde. "*Blow-Up* and the Plurality of Photography." In *Antonioni: Centenary Essays*, edited by J. D. Rhodes and L. Rascaroli, 185–205. London: Palgrave Macmillan, 2011.
Naturalness and Iconicity in Language, edited by Klass Willems and Ludovic De Cuypere. Amsterdam: John Benjamins Publishing, 2009.
Nelson, Charles A. and Michelle de Haan. "A Neurobehavioral Approach to the Recognition of Facial Expressions in Infancy." In *The Psychology of Facial Expression*, edited by J. A. Russell and J. M. Fernández-Dols, 176–204. Cambridge: Cambridge University Press, 1997.
Nesse, Randolph M. and Alan T. Lloyd. "The Evolution of Psychodynamic Mechanisms." In *The Adapted Mind*, edited by J. H. Barkow et al., 601–26. New York: Oxford University Press, 1992.
Nettle, Daniel. "Language Variation and the Evolution of Societies." In *The Evolution of Culture: An Interdisciplinary View*, edited by R. Dunbar et al., 214–27. Edinburgh: Edinburgh University Press, 1999.
On Signs, edited by Marshall Blonsky. Baltimore: The Johns Hopkins University Press, 1985.
Ong, Walter J. *Orality and Literacy: The Technologizing of the Word.* London: Routledge, 2004.

Orians, Gordon H. and Judith H. Heerwagen. "Evolved Responses to Landscapes." In *The Adapted Mind*, edited by J. H. Barkow et al., 555–80. New York: Oxford University Press, 1992.

Ovid. *Metamorphoses*, translated by Arthur Golding. London: Penguin, 2002.

The Oxford Companion to Philosophy, edited by Ted Honderich. Oxford: Oxford University Press, 1995.

Panofsky, Erwin. *Perspective as Symbolic Form*. New York: Zone Books, 1991.

Pascal, Blaise. *Pensées*. 1670. Harmondsworth: Penguin Books, 1985.

Peirce, Charles Sander. *Collected Papers of Charles Sanders Peirce*, edited by C. Hartshorne and P. Weiss. Bristol: Thoemmes Press, 1998.

Pérez, Genaro J. "Blow-Up (Las Babas del Diablo) by Julio Cortázar, 1959." *Reference Guide to Short Fiction*. Encyclopedia.com (July 14, 2020).

Pinker, Steven. *The Language Instinct: The New Science of Language and Mind*. London: Penguin Books, 1995.

Pinker, Steven. *How the Mind Works*. London: Allen Lane, 1998.

Pinker, Steven. *Words and Rules: The Ingredients of Language*. London: Phoenix, 2001.

Pinker, Steven. *The Blank Slate: The Modern Denial of Human Nature*. London: Penguin Books, 2002.

Pinker, Steven. "Language as an Adaptation to the Cognitive Niche." In *Language Evolution*, edited by M. H. Christiansen and S. Kirby, 16–37. Oxford: Oxford University Press, 2003.

Pinker, Steven. *The Stuff of Thought: Language as a Window into Human Nature*. London: Allen Lane, 2007.

Pinker, Steven. *The Better Angels of Our Nature: A History of Violence and Humanity*. London: Penguin Books, 2011.

Pinker, Steven. *The Sense of Style: The Thinking Person's Guide to Writing in the 21st Century*. London: Allen Lane, 2014.

Pinker, Steven. *Enlightenment Now: The Case for Reason, Science, Humanism and Progress*. London: Allen Lane, 2018.

Pinker, Steven. *Rationality: What It Is, Why It Seems Scarce, Why It Matters*. London: Allen Lane, 2021.

Pinker, Steven and Paul Bloom. "Natural Language and Natural Selection." In *The Adapted Mind*, edited by J. H. Barkow et al., 451–94. New York: Oxford University Press, 1992.

Plato, *Timaeus*, translated by H. D. P. Lee. Harmondsworth: Penguin Books, 1965.

Pliny the Elder. *Natural History*. London: Penguin Books, 1991.

Plotkin, Henry. *The Nature of Knowledge: Concerning Adaptations, Instinct and the Evolution of Intelligence*. London: Penguin Books, 1994.

Plotkin, Henry. *Evolution in Mind: An Introduction to Evolutionary Psychology*. London: Allen Press, 1997.

Popper, Karl. *Objective Knowledge: An Evolutionary Approach*. Oxford: At the Clarendon Press, 1979.

Popper, Karl. *The Logic of Scientific Discovery*. London: Routledge, 2002.

Porush, David. *The Soft Machine: Cybernetic Fiction*. New York: Methuen, 1985.

Power, Camilla. "'Beauty Magic': The Origins of Art." In *The Evolution of Culture: An Interdisciplinary View*, edited by R. Dunbar, C. Knight and C. Power, 92–112. Edinburgh: Edinburgh University Press, 1999.

Power, Camilla. "Sexual Selection Models for the Emergence of Symbolic Communication: Why They Should Be Reversed." In *The Cradle of Language*, edited by Rudolf Botha and Chris Knight, 257–80. Oxford: Oxford University Press, 2009.

Preussner, Arnold W. "Woody Allen's *The Purple Rose of Cairo*." *Literature/Film Quarterly* 16, no. 1 (1988): 39–43.
Provine, Robert R. "Yawns, Laughs, Smiles, Tickles, and Talking: Naturalistic and Laboratory Studies of Facial Action and Social Communication." In *The Psychology of Facial Expression*, edited by J. A. Russell and J. M. Fernández-Dols, 158–75. Cambridge: Cambridge University Press, 1997.
Purves, Dale and R. Beau Lotto. *Why We See What We Do: An Empirical Theory of Vision*. Oxford: Sinauer Associates, 2003.
Raid, David. *Sound Symbolism*. Edinburgh: T. & A. Constable, 1967.
Ridley, Matt. *Nature via Nurture: Genes, Experience and What Makes Us Human*. London: Fourth Estate, 2003.
Rogers, Franklin R. and Mary Ann Rogers. *Painting and Poetry: Form, Metaphor, and the Language of Literature*. Lewisburg, PA: Bucknell University Press, 1986.
Rosenbleuth, Arturo. *Mind and Brain: A Philosophy of Science*. Cambridge, MA: The MIT Press, 1970.
Rozin, Paul and A. Fallon. "A Perspective on Disgust." *Psychological Review* 94 (1987): 23–41.
Russel, James A. and José M. Fernández-Dols. "What Does a Facial Expression Mean?" In *The Psychology of Facial Expression*, edited by J. A. Russell and J. M. Fernández-Dols, 3–30. Cambridge: Cambridge University Press, 1997.
Sacks, David. *Language Visible: Unraveling the Mystery of the Alphabet from A to Z*. New York: Broadway Books, 2003.
Sadowski, Piotr. "What Is Literature?—A Systems Definition." *Semiotica* 123, no. 1/2 (1999): 43–58.
Sadowski, Piotr. "Control, Information, and Literary Meaning: A Systems Model of Literature as Communication." *European Journal of English Studies* 5, no. 3 (2001): 293–95.
Sadowski, Piotr. *Gender and Literature: A Systems Study*. Lanham–New York: University Press of America, 2001.
Sadowski, Piotr. "The Sound as an Echo to the Sense: The Iconicity of English *gl*- words." In *The Motivated Sign*, edited by O. Fischer and M. Nänny, 69–88. Amsterdam: John Benjamins Publishing Company, 2001.
Sadowski, Piotr. *Dynamism of Character in Shakespeare's Mature Tragedies*. Newark: University of Delaware Press; London: Associated University Press, 2003.
Sadowski, Piotr. "Oscar Wilde, Morality, and Cybernetics." *Beyond Philology* 4 (2007): 173–91.
Sadowski, Piotr. *From Interaction to Symbol: A Systems View of the Evolution of Signs and Communication*. Amsterdam–Philadelphia: John Benjamins Publishing Company, 2009.
Sadowski, Piotr. "The Iconic Indexicality of Photography." In *Semblance and Signification*, edited by P. Michelucci, O. Fischer and C. Ljungberg, 355–68. Amsterdam: John Benjamins Publishing, 2011.
Sadowski, Piotr. *The Semiotics of Light and Shadows: Modern Visual Arts and Weimar Cinema*. London: Bloomsbury Academic, 2018.
Sadowski, Piotr. "In the Kingdom of Shadows: Towards a Cognitive Definition of Photographic Media." In *Operationalizing Iconicity*, edited by P. Perniss, O. Fischer and C. Ljungberg, 231–43. Amsterdam: John Benjamins Publishing Company, 2020.
Sagan, Carl. *The Demon-Haunted World: Science as a Candle in the Dark*. London: Headline Book Publishing, 1997.

Samuels, Richard. "Massively Modular Minds: Evolutionary Psychology and Cognitive Architecture." In *Evolution and the Human Mind: Modularity, Language and Meta-Cognition*, edited by P. Carruthers and A Chamberlain, 13–46. Cambridge: Cambridge University Press, 2000.

Sassoon, Rosemary and Albertine Gaur. *Signs, Symbols and Icons: Prehistory to the Computer Age*. Exeter: Intellect Books, 1997.

Saussure, Ferdinand. *Course in General Linguistics*, edited by C. Bally et al. 1916. Glasgow: Fontana/Collins, 1974.

Savage-Rumbaugh, Sue, Stuart G. Shanker and Talbot J. Taylor. *Apes, Language, and the Human Mind*. Oxford: Oxford University Press, 1998.

Savedoff, Barbara E. "Frames." *Journal of Aesthetics & Art Criticism* 57, no. 3 (Summer 1999): 345–56.

Schacter, Daniel. *The Seven Sins of Memory: How the Mind Forgets and Remembers*. New York: Houghton Mifflin, 2001.

Schieckel, Richard. "Now Playing at the Jewel." *Time* 94 (March 1985): 78.

Schiffman, Harvey R. *Sensation and Perception: An Integrated Approach*. New York: John Wiley & Sons, 1996.

Schleidt, Margret. "Personal Odor and Nonverbal Communication." *Ethology and Sociobiology* 1, no. 3 (September 1980): 225–31.

Schmitz, Norbert M. "Licht als Mittel und als Zweck: Zum Verhältnis des filmischen Lichts im Avant-gardefilm und in Kino." In *Ästhetik der Schatten. Filmisches Licht 1915–1950*, edited by C. Betz, J. Pattis and R. Rother, 119–23. Marburg: Schüren Verlag, 2014.

Scholem, Gershom G. *On the Kabbalah and Its Symbolism*. London: Routledge and Kegan Paul, 1965.

Scovell, Adam. "On Location: The London Park from Michelangelo Antonioni's *Blow-Up*." *Little White Lies: Truth and Movies*, online (September 2, 2019). Accessed September 14, 2020.

Sebeok, Thomas A. "Discussion of Communication Process." In *Social Communication among Primates*, edited by S. A. Altmann, 363–9. Chicago: The University of Chicago Press, 1967.

Sebeok, Thomas A. *Contributions to the Doctrine of Signs*. Bloomington: Indiana University Press, 1976.

Sebeok, Thomas A. *An Introduction to Semiotics*. London: Pinter Publishers, 1994.

Sedgwick, H. A. "The Geometry of Spatial Layout in Pictorial Representation." In *The Perception of Pictures*, edited by Margaret A. Hagen, 33–90. vol. 1. New York: Academic Press, 1980.

Segal, Nancy L. *Twin Mythconceptions: False Beliefs, Fables, and Facts about Twins*. London: Academic Press, 2017.

Shakespeare, William. *Othello*, edited by E. A. J. Honigmann. Walton-on-Thames: Thomas Nelson & Sons, 1997.

Shakespeare, William. *Hamlet*, edited by Ann Thompson and Neil Taylor. London: Thomson Learning, 2006.

Shakespeare, William. *The Merchant of Venice*, edited by John Drakakis. London: Bloomsbury Publishing, 2010.

Shakespeare, William. *Romeo and Juliet*, edited by René Weis. London: Bloomsbury, 2012.

Shakespeare, William. *Macbeth*, edited by Sandra Clark and Pamela Mason. London: Bloomsbury, 2015.

Sharrett, Christopher "*Blow-Up*." *Cineaste* 42, no. 4 (Fall 2017): 54–6.

Shepard, Roger N. "The Genetic Basis of Human Scientific Knowledge." In *Characterizing Human Psychological Adaptations*, edited by G. R. Bock and G. Cardew, 23–38. Chichester: John Wiley & Sons, 1997.
Sherry, David F. and Dan L. Schacter. "The Evolution of Multiple Memory Systems." *Psychological Review* 94, no. 4 (1987): 439–54.
Sherwood, Lauralee. *Human Physiology: From Cells to Systems*. London: Wadsworth Publishing Company, 1997.
Silvester, Hans. *Natural Fashion: Tribal Decoration from Africa*. London: Thames and Hudson, 2009.
Sinnema, William. *Digital, Analog, and Data Communication*. Englewood Cliffs, NJ: Prentice-Hall, Inc., 1986.
Slade, Peter D. and Richard P. Bentall, *Sensory Deception: Scientific Analysis of Hallucinations*. London: Croom Helm, 1998.
Sless, David. *In Search of Semiotics*. London: Croom Helm, 1986.
Smith, Craig A. and Heather S. Scott. "A Componential Approach to the Meaning of Facial Expressions." In *The Psychology of Facial Expression*, edited by J. A. Russell and J. M. Fernández-Dols, 229–54. Cambridge: Cambridge University Press, 1997.
Sober, Elliot. "Let's Razor Ockham's Razor." In *Philosophy of Science: An Anthology*, edited by Marc Lange, 126–38. Oxford: Blackwell Publishing, 2007.
Sokal Hoax: The Sham That Shook the Academy. Lincoln: University of Nebraska Press, 2000.
Sokal, Alan and Jean Bricmont. *Intellectual Impostures: Postmodern Philosophers' Abuse of Science*. London: Profile Books, 1998.
Solso, Robert L. *The Psychology of Art and the Evolution of the Conscious Brain*. Cambridge, MA: The MIT Press, 2003.
Sontag, Susan. *On Photography*. London: Allen Lane, 1978.
Sound Symbolism, edited by L. Hinton, et al. Cambridge: Cambridge University Press, 1994.
Sperber, Dan. "Anthropology and Psychology: Towards an Epidemiology of Representations." *Man* 20, no. 1 (March 1985): 73–6.
Stanislavski, Konstantin. *An Actor's Work: A Student's Diary*, translated by J. Benedetti. London: Routledge, 2010.
Stankiewicz, Edward. "Problems of Emotive Language." In *Approaches to Semiotics: Cultural Anthropology, Education, Linguistics, Psychiatry, Psychology*, edited by T. A. Sebeok, A. S. Hayes and M. C. Bateson, 239–64. The Hague: Mouton & Co, 1972.
Stano, Simona. "Introduction: Semiotics of Food." *Semiotica* 211 (2016): 19–26.
Steen, Francis. "A Cognitive Account of Aesthetics." In *The Artful Mind: Cognitive Science and the Riddle of Human Creativity*, edited by Mark Turner, 57–71. Oxford: Oxford University Press, 2006.
Stein, Gertrude. *Geography and Plays*. Boston: The Four Seas Company, 1922.
Sterelny, Kim. "The Perverse Primate." In *Richard Dawkins: How a Scientist Changed the Way We Think*, edited by A. Grafen and M. Ridley, 213–26. Oxford: Oxford University Press, 2006.
Stoichita, Victor Ieronim. *A Short History of the Shadow*. London: Reaktion, 1997.
Strauven, Wanda. "Early Cinema's Touch(able) Screens: From Uncle Josh to Ali Barbouyou." *European Journal of Media Studies* 1, no. 2 (Autumn 2012): 155–76.
Symons, Donald. *The Evolution of Human Sexuality*. Oxford: Oxford University Press, 1979.
Szarkowski, John. "Introduction to The Photographer's Eye." In *The Photography Reader*, edited by Liz Wells, 97–103. London: Routledge, 2003.

Tallis, Raymond. *Not Saussure: A Critique of Post-Saussurean Literary Theory*. Houndmills, Basingstoke: Macmillan Press, 1988.
Tallis, Raymond. *Newton's Sleep: The Two Cultures and the Two Kingdoms*. London: Macmillan Press, 1995.
Tallis, Raymond. *Enemies of Hope: A Critique of Contemporary Pessimism, Irrationalism, Anti-Humanism and Counter-Enlightenment*. London: Macmillan Press, 1999.
Tallis, Raymond. *Theorrhoea and after*. London: Macmillan Press, 1999.
Tallis, Raymond. "The Linguistic Unconscious: Saussure and the Post-Saussureans." In *Theory's Empire: An Anthology of Dissent*, edited by Daphne Patai and Will. H. Corral, 125–46. New York: Columbia University Press, 2005.
Theory's Empire: An Anthology of Dissent, edited by Daphne Patai and Will. H. Corral. New York: Columbia University Press, 2005.
Thomas, Francis-Noël and Mark Turner. *Clear and Simple as the Truth: Writing Classic Prose*. 1994. Princeton: Princeton University Press, 2017.
Thompson, Kristin and David Bordwell. *Film History: An Introduction*. Boston: McGraw-Hill Companies, 2003.
Thompson, Richard F. and Stephen A. Madigen. *Memory: The Key to Consciousness*. Washington, DC: Joseph Henry Press, 2005.
Tomlin, Russell S. *Basic Word Order: Functional Principles*. London: Croom Helm, 1986.
Tooby, John and Leda Cosmides. "The Psychological Foundations of Culture." In *The Adapted Mind: Evolutionary Psychology and the Generation of Culture*, edited by J. H. Barkow, L. Cosmides and J. Tooby, 19–136. New York: Oxford University Press, 1992.
Towards a Semiotic Biology: Life Is the Action of Signs, edited by Claus Emmeche and Kalevi Kull. London: Imperial College Press, 2011.
Trivers, Robert. *The Folly of Fools: The Logic of Deceit and Self-Deception in Human Life*. New York: Basic Books, 2011.
Vaughan, William. *Friedrich*. New York: Phaidon Press, 2004.
Vinci, Leonardo da. *The Notebooks*, edited by Irma A. Richter. Oxford: Oxford University Press, 1998.
Vinci, Leonardo da. *A Treatise on Painting*, translated by J. F. Rigaud. New York: Dover Publications, 2005.
Wachs, Theodore D. "The Nature-Nurture Gap: What We Have Here Is a Failure to Collaborate." In *Nature, Nurture, and Psychology*, edited by Robert Plomin and Gerald E. McClearn, 375–91. Washington, DC: American Psychological Association, 1993.
Walker, Matthew. *Why We Sleep: The New Science of Sleep and Dream*. London: Penguin Books, 2017.
Walton, Kendall L. "Film, Photography, and Transparency." In *The Philosophy of Film: Introductory Text and Readings*, edited by T. E. Wartenberg and A. Curran, 70–6. Oxford: Blackwell, 2005.
Webb, Tammy T. et al. "Perceptions of Body Figure Attractiveness among African American Male College Students." *Journal of African American Studies* 18, no. 1 (December 2014): 457–69.
Webster, Richard. *Why Was Freud Wrong: Sin, Science and Psychoanalysis*. London: HarperCollins Publishers, 1995.
Weinberg, Gerald M. *An Introduction to General Systems Thinking*. New York–London: John Wiley and Sons, 1975.
Wheen, Francis. *Television: A History*. London: Century Publishing, 1985.
Wilde, Oscar. *Complete Works*. Glasgow: HarperCollins Publishers, 2003.

Wilson, Edward O. *On Human Nature*. London: Penguin Books, 1978.
Wilson, Edward O. *Consilience: The Unity of Knowledge*. London: Abacus, 1998.
Wilson, Edward O. *The Social Conquest of Earth*. New York: Liveright Publishing Corporation, 2012.
Wilson, Edward O. "The Meaning of Human Existence." In *Darwin's Bridge: Uniting the Humanities & Sciences*, edited by Joseph Carroll, Dan P. McAdams and Edward O. Wilson, 3–10. Oxford: Oxford University Press, 2016.
Wilson-Smith, Timothy. *Caravaggio*. London: Phaidon Press, 1998.
Woodford, Susan. *The Art of Greece and Rome*. Cambridge: Cambridge University Press, 1982.
Workman, Lance and Will Reader. *Evolutionary Psychology: An Introduction*. Cambridge: Cambridge University Press, 2004.
Young, Vernon. "Movie Within a Movie." *The Hudson Review* 38, no. 3 (Autumn 1985): 455–8.

Index

adaptation 11
Aiello, Danny (actor) 199
Aitchison, Jean (linguist) 13
Akers, Karen (singer) 201
Alberti, Leon Battista (humanist) 96, 185, 188
Allen, Woody (film director) 199–200, 206–7
Anderson, Earl R. (linguist) 53, 113
animal communication 1
Antonioni, Michelangelo (film director) 171, 181
Appleton, Jay (geographer) 29, 194
Arnheim, Rudolf (art historian) 154, 187, 188–9
aspect ratio 191–2, 197–8
autonomous system (see also self-regulation) 3, 10–11, 135

Bad Writing Contest 210
Barkow, Jerome H. (anthropologist) 110
Baron-Cohen, Simon (psychologist) 77
Barrow, John D. (astronomer) 13–14, 25, 29, 71
Baudelaire, Charles (poet) 146
Bazin, André (film critic) 92, 93
Beck, Jeff (guitarist) 181
Bhabha, Homi K. (literary scholar) 210–11
Bickerton, Derek (linguist) 15, 108
blank slate (*tabula rasa*) 13
Blowup (dir. Michelangelo Antonioni) 171, 174–82
body decorations 79–82
Bonaparte, Napoleon 46
Bouchard, Thomas J. Jr. (psychologist) 13
Boyer, Pascal (philosopher) 70, 115
Brown, Donald E. (anthropologist) 29
Brunelleschi, Filippo (architect) 184
Brunette, Peter (film critic) 175
Bulhak, Andrew (computer programmer) 211
Bunim, Miriam Schild (art historian) 188

Butch Cassidy and the Sundance Kid (dir. George Roy Hill) 196–7

Cabinet of Dr Caligari, The (dir. Robert Wiene) 191
camera obscura 100
Canaletto (painter) 100
Caravaggio (painter) 154–5
Carroll, Joseph (literary theorist) 14, 15, 31
Carry on Spying (dir. Gerald Thomas) 59
Carson, Edward (solicitor) 143–4
Cartwright, John (biologist) 13, 21
Cashdan, Elizabeth (anthropologist) 19
Chandler, Daniel (semiotician) 212
character (see dynamism of character) 136–8, 147–8
Chauvet cave 87–90, 94, 99, 187
Citizen Kane (dir. Orson Welles) 196
Clark, Andy (linguist) 130
cognitive modules 3, 23
    animal-recognition 28
    body-language 79–82
    enemy-recognition 23
    face-recognition 75–9
    kin-recognition 23
communication (def) 3, 9
computers 10
consciousness (def) 66–7
contiguity (contiguous communication) 3, 36
Cortázar, Julio (writer) 171–4
Cosmides, Leda (psychologist) 13, 21
Coulmas, Florian (historian) 119, 122
cue (def) 63
Cummins, Denise D. (psychologist) 21
Cyrano de Bergerac (play by Edmond Rostand) 137

Daguerre, Louise-Jacques-Mandé (photographer) 152
Daniels, Jeff (actor) 201
Darwin, Charles (biologist) 76

Dawkins, Richard (biologist) 14, 66, 70, 72
Deacon, Terrence W. (neuroscientist) 36
deception 59–60
deconstruction 57, 58
deduction 1–2
Degas, Edgar (painter) 189
Derrida, Jacques (philosopher) 57, 211
Dingwall, William O. (neurologist) 79
Dissanayake, Ellen (psychologist) 29, 79
Donald, Merlin (psychologist) 31
Douglas, Lord Alfred 142
Duck Sup (dir. Leo McCarey) 72
Dürer, Albrecht (painter) 77
Dutton, Denis (philosopher) 105, 210
dynamism of character 135–40, 147–9

Ekman, Paul (psychologist) 15, 77
Elam, Keir (literary critic) 204
Ellmann, Richard (literary biographer) 142, 145
Emerson, Ralph Waldo (writer) 29
emotions 9, 15, 21
Etcoff, Nancy (psychologist) 17–18, 46–7, 78, 82
evolution 13

face 75–9
Farrow, Mia (actor) 199
feedback 35
femininity 17–18
film (invention of) 153
Flaubert, Gustav (writer) 146
frame 183, 185–9, 194–6
Frazer, James (anthropologist) 92, 93
Friedrich, Caspar David (painter) 91
Friston, Karl (neuroscientist) 2
functional equilibrium 10

Geldard, Frank A. (psychologist) 48
gender studies 13
genotype 13
Gide, André (writer) 106
Glanville, Ranulph (critic) 57
gossip 110–11
Gottdiener, Mark (semiotician) 212
Grand Budapest Hotel, The (dir. Wes Anderson) 197–8
Grau, Albin (occultist) 165
Greimas, Algirdas J. (semiotician) 6

Halbertal, Moshe (philosopher) 102
Hall, Edward T. (anthropologist) 43, 47, 48
Hamlet (dir. Kenneth Branagh) 148–9
Harris, Roy (linguist) 119
Heerwagen, H. (psychologist) 193
Hemmings, David (actor) 171
Henrich, Joseph (anthropologist) 220
Hesse, Herman (novelist) 61
Hirsch, E. D. Jr (literary theorist) 58
Holbein, Hans (painter) 56
Holland, Merlin (literary critic) 144
homeostasis (see also needs, self-regulation) 11, 14
horizontality (see also verticality) 190–3
Huysmans, Joris-Karl (writer) 47, 68

icon (iconic communication) 3, 49–52
iconic indexicality 98–101
iconoclasm 101–4
ideology 69–74
idolatry 101–4
index (indexical communication) 3, 40–2, 179
indexical iconicity 101
information (def) 3, 9
intentionality 63
interaction 9
Iser, Wolfgang (literary theorist) 57

James, Henry (writer) 104
Jespersen, Otto (linguist) 113
Johnson, Dr Samuel (writer) 186
Joyce, James (writer) 18, 146
    Ulysses 22, 38
Jung, Carl Gustav (psychoanalyst) 164–5

Kant, Immanuel (philosopher) 66, 90
Kaplan, Stephen (psychologist) 26
Keaton, Buster (actor) 201
Kerr, Alfred (literary critic) 146
Kubrick, Stanley (film director) 10

Lang, Fritz (film director) 163, 201
language 3, 4, 107–11, 214
Lehndorff, Veruschka von (supermodel) 181
Leroi-Gourhan, André (archaeologist) 89–90
light (in film) 156–61
linguistic iconicity 112–14
linguistic indexicality 111–12

literacy 128–31
Lloyd, Alan T. (psychologist) 72
Locke, John 13
Lumière brothers 157–9
lying (see also deception) 4

Magee, Bryan (philosopher) 5, 66
magic
    iconic 93–8, 101–4, 201–5
    indexical 90–3
Margalit, Avishoi (philosopher) 102
Martin, Bronwen (semiotician) 6
Marxism 13
masculinity 18
Matisse (painter) 94
Mazur, Marian (cyberneticist) 136–8, 147
meaning (def) 56–9
Medawar, Peter B. and Medawar, Jean S. (biologists) 66
memory 64–6, 84–6
Merrell, Floyd (semiotician) 212
metainformation 3, 49, 60–2
metaphor 114–17, 209
Michelangelo (artist) 190
Miles, Sarah (actor) 180
Miller, Geoffrey (psychologist) 105
Mithen, Steven (archaeologist) 20, 21, 51, 65, 71, 90
morality 145–7
Mouse Hunt (dir. Gore Verbinski) 117
movement (perception of) 36, 153
Murillo, Bartolomé Esteban (painter) 194–6
Murnau, Friedrich W. (film director) 164

Nardelli, Matilde (film critic) 178
natural selection 11
nature versus nurture 12–14
needs 3, 10, 14–16, 67–9, 213
    esthetic 29–30
    exploratory 23–4
    nutritional 18–19
    procreative 16–8
    protective 19–20
    social 20–3
    teleological 30–2, 67–9, 74
Nesse, Randolph M. (psychologist) 72
New Criticism 57

Niépce, Joseph Nicéphore (photographer) 152
noise 36

Oxford Companion to Philosophy, The 4, 61
O. Henry (writer) 22
Ong, Walter J. (historian) 119
Orians, Gordon H. (psychologist) 193
Ovid 93

Paleolithic period 28, 65, 70, 79, 83, 86–90, 99, 110
Palma, Carlo Di (cinematographer) 176
parainformation 3, 55–6
Pascal, Blaise (philosopher) 74, 104
Peirce, Charles Sanders (philosopher) 5, 40, 52, 92, 98, 216
pentagram 115–17
Percy, Walker (novelist) 58
perspective 184–5
phenotype 12
phonology 107
photography 98, 101, 151–3, 179
physical states 62
Pinker, Steven (cognitive scientist) 61, 109
Plato 190, 235
Playtime (dir. Jacques Tati) 186
Pliny the Elder (writer) 96
Plotkin, Henry (philosopher) 15, 24, 28
Poe, Edgar Allan (writer) 92
Polaroid camera 39
Pompei 188
Popper, Karl (philosopher) 2, 5, 62
Porter, Edwin S. (film director) 93
Porush, David (literary critic) 57
postmodernism 209–10
Postmodernism Generator 211
post-structuralism 5
Power, Camilla (anthropologist) 83
Provine, Robert R. (psychologist) 79
psychoanalysis 117
Purple Rose of Cairo, The (dir. Woody Allen) 199–200

Queensberry, Marquess 142, 143

reactivity 11–12, 35
Rear Window (dir. Alfred Hitchcock) 176, 233

Redgrave, Vanessa (actor) 176
Reid, David (linguist) 113
religion 70-4
Ringham, Felizitas (semiotician) 6
Rozin, Paul (psychologist) 19

Sagan, Carl (astronomer) 73
Saussure, Ferdinand (linguist) 5, 52, 112-13, 212
Schacter, Daniel (psychologist) 85-6
Schieckel, Richard (film critic) 207
Schindler's List (dir. Steven Spielberg) 157
scientific models 3
screen 186
Sebeok, Thomas A. (semiotician) 5, 36
self-deception 69-74
self-regulation (see also autonomous system) 10-11, 213
semiosis 1, 3
semiotics of food 19
senses
    audition 44-5
    olfaction 45-7
    taste 47-8
    touch 48-9
    vision 43-4, 183-4
shadow (see also *Warning Shadows*) 162-5
sham menstruation 82-4
Sharrett, Christopher (film critic) 174
sign (def) 63-4
Shakespeare, William
    Macbeth 19
    Merchant of Venice, The 19
    Romeo and Juliet 52
    sonnets 58
Shepard, Roger N. (psychologist) 24
Sless, David (semiotician) 211-12
Sokal, Alan (physicist) 211
Solso, Robert L. (psychologist) 66
Sontag, Susan (cultural critic) 92
Sperber, Dan (philosopher) 71

Stanislavski, Konstantin (theater director) 204
Stankiewicz, Edward (linguist) 111
Stein, Gertrude (poet) 90-1
symbol (symbolic communication) 3, 52-3, 107
symptom (def) 63
system (def) 3, 4, 9, 11-12
systemic semiotics (premises) 2-4

Tallis, Raymond (philosopher) 53, 73
Tassone, Aldo (film critic) 181
Thatcher, Margaret 18
television 39-40
theory of mind 21-2
Third Man, The (dir. Carol Reed) 191
Thomas, Francis-Noël (literary critic) 209
Toland, Greg (cinematographer) 196
Tooby, John (psychologist) 13, 21
Trivers, Robert (psychologist) 72, 73
Turner, Mark (literary critic) 209

Venus of Willendorf (figurine) 83-4
verticality (see also horizontality) 190-3
Vinci, Leonardo Da (artist) 184
Vivaldi, Antonio (composer) 49

Walker, Matthew (psychologist) 61
Warning Shadows (dir. Arthur Robison) 165-9
Webster, Richard (psychologist) 22
White Sheik, The (dir. Federico Fellini) 178
Wilde, Oscar (writer) 29, 61, 68, 104, 105, 135, 139, 140, 141-5, 146, 154, 211
Wilson, Edward O. (biologist) 2, 20, 31, 65-6, 77, 217
writing 118-20, 209
    alphabetic 124-8
    cuneiform 121-3
    ideographic 123
    pictographic 121

www.ingramcontent.com/pod-product-compliance
Lightning Source LLC
Chambersburg PA
CBHW062128300426
44115CB00012BA/1853